T3-BNW-802

Policy and Politics in
Canada

Policy and Politics in Industrial States

A series edited by Douglas E. Ashford, Peter J. Katzenstein, and T. J. Pempel

Carolyn J. Tuohy

Policy and Politics in
Canada

Institutionalized Ambivalence

 Temple University Press

Philadelphia

Temple University Press, Philadelphia 19122
Copyright © 1992 by Temple University. All rights reserved
Published 1992
Printed in the United States of America

∞ The paper used in this publication meets the minimum requirements of American
National Standard for Information Sciences—Permanence of Paper for Printed Library
Materials, ANSI Z39.48–1984

Library of Congress Cataloging-in-Publication Data
Tuohy, Carolyn J., 1945–
    Policy and politics in Canada : institutionalized ambivalence /
Carolyn J. Tuohy.
        p.   cm. — (Policy and politics in industrial states)
    Includes bibliographical references and index.
    ISBN 0-87722-870-1 (cloth : alk. paper)
    ISBN 0-87722-871-X (pbk. : alk. paper)
      1. Political planning—Canada.   2. Canada—Politics and
government—1945–   3. Canada—Economic policy.   4. Canada—Social
policy.   I. Title.   II. Series.
JL75.T86 1992   91–23006
320'.6'0971—dc20

For Marjorie and Carman Hughes, my parents

Contents

Editors' Preface

All industrial states face a tension between bureaucracy and democracy. Modern governments have found it increasingly difficult to formulate policies adequate to the complex tasks they undertake. At the same time the growing specialization and widening scope of government have led many to question whether it can still be controlled democratically. Policy and Politics in Industrial States explores how some of the major democracies have dealt with this dilemma.

Policy is a pattern of purposive action by which political institutions shape society. It typically involves a wide variety of efforts to address certain societal problems. Politics is also a much broader concept, involving the conflict and choices linking individuals and social forces to the political institutions that make policy. Comparative analysis of the interaction between policy and politics is an essential beginning in understanding how and why industrial states differ or converge in their responses to common problems.

The fact that the advanced industrial states are pursuing many similar aims such as increasing social well-being, reducing social conflict, and achieving higher levels of employment and economic productivity means neither that they will all do so in the same way nor that the relevance of politics to such behavior will always be the same. In looking at an array of problems common to all industrial states, the books in this series argue that policies are shaped primarily by the manner in which power is organized within each country. Thus, Britain, Japan, the United States, West Germany, Sweden, and France set distinctive priorities and follow distinctive policies designed to achieve them. In this respect, the series dissents from the view that the nature of the problem faced is the most important feature in determining the politics surrounding efforts at its resolution. Taken to its logical extreme, this view supports the expectation that all states will pursue broadly similar goals in politically similar ways. Though this series will illustrate some important similarities among the policies of different countries, one of the key conclusions to which it points is the distinctive approach that each state takes in managing the problems it confronts.

A second important feature of the series is its sensitivity to the difficulties involved in evaluating policy success or failure. Goals are ambiguous and often contradictory from one area of policy to another; past precedents often shape present options. Conversely, adhering to choices made at an earlier time is often impossible or undesirable at a later period. Hence evaluation must transcend the application of simple economic or managerial criteria of rationality, efficiency, or effectiveness. What appears from such perspectives as irrational, inefficient, or ineffective is often, from a political standpoint, quite intelligible.

To facilitate comparison, the books in the series follow a common format. In each book, the first chapter introduces the reader to the country's political institutions and social forces, spells out how these are linked to form that country's distinctive configuration of power, and explores how that configuration can be expected to influence policy. A concluding chapter seeks to integrate the country argument developed in the first chapter with the subsequent policy analysis and provides more general observations about the ways in which the specific country findings fit into current debates about policy and politics.

The intervening six chapters provide policy cases designed to illustrate, extend, and refine the country argument. Each of the six policy analyses follows a common format. The first section analyzes the *context* of the policy problem: its historical roots, competing perceptions of the problem by major political and social groups, and its interdependence with other problems facing the country. The second section deals with the *agenda* set out for the problem: the pressures generating action and the explicit and implicit motives of important political actors, including the government's objectives. The third section deals with *process:* the formulation of the issue, its attempted resolution, and the instruments involved in policy implementation. The fourth and final section of analysis traces the *consequences* of policy for official objectives, for the power distribution in the issue area, for other policies, and for the country's capacity to make policy choices in the future. The element of arbitrariness such a schema introduces into the discussion of policy and politics is a price the series gladly pays in the interest of facilitating comparative analysis of policy and politics.

An important feature of these cases is the inclusion, for each policy problem, of selected readings drawn primarily from official policy documents, interpretations, or critiques of policy by different actors, and politically informed analysis. We have become persuaded that the actual language used in policy debates within each country provides an important clue to the relationship between that country's policy and its politics. Since appropriate readings are more widely available for Britain and the United States than for the non-English-speaking countries in the series, we have included somewhat more policy materials for these countries. In all instances, the readings are selected as illustration, rather than confirmation, of each book's argument.

Also distinctive of the series, and essential to its comparative approach, is the selection of common policy cases. Each volume analyzes at least one case involving intergovernmental problems: reform of the national bureaucracy or the interaction among national, regional, and local governments. Each also includes two cases dealing with economic problems: economic policy and labor-management relations. Lastly, each book includes at least two cases focusing on the relationship of individual citizens to the state, among them social welfare. Our choice is designed to provide a basis for cross-national and cross-issue comparison while being sufficiently flexible to make allowance for the idiosyncracies of the countries (and the authors). By using such a framework, we hope that these books will convey the richness and diversity of each country's efforts to solve major problems, as well as the similarities of the interaction between policy and politics in industrial states.

D.E.A.
P.J.K.
T.J.P.

Preface

In the period during which this book was being written the Canadian political system was experiencing an unprecedented level of stress. Indeed, it has appeared at times that books such as this one might serve as the country's epitaph. Although the outcome of the current period of crisis will not be clear for some time after the publication of this book, I do not subscribe to such an apocalyptic view.

In this book I identify the distinctive competencies and incompetencies of the Canadian system by viewing it in comparative context. Like the other contributors to this series, I believe that it is only in comparative perspective that one can fully understand a national system. In particular, one can explain a nation's pattern of public policy responses only by comparing it with the policy responses of other nations and looking for similarities and differences in the processes that generate those patterns. Like the other contributors to this series, too, I look first to *institutions*—that is, structures exercising state authority in accordance with embedded values—as explanatory factors, and then to the *intersection* between those institutions and the structure of societal interests.

In this perspective what appears distinctive about Canadian institutions is their extraordinary capacity to embody conflicting principles within structures ambiguous enough to allow for ad hoc accommodations over time—what I have called Canada's "institutionalized ambivalence." It is this capacity that has generated the moderation and compromise that have become virtually a Canadian stereotype, and that have also made it possible for the Canadian system to tolerate profound underlying tensions. In this sense placing Canada in comparative context is important not only for students of Canada but for those who would draw lessons from the Canadian experience for other nations.

These lessons may be both positive and negative. Nations wrestling with issues of the appropriate balance of powers between regional and central governments may find elements of a model in the historical flexibility and adaptiveness of Canadian federalism, in its ability to generate ad hoc accommodations in response to policy challenges. That very flexibility, however, has ironically derived from a lack of consensus about the design of an overall framework. Nonetheless, Canadian political leaders have continued to attempt to define such a framework and, given the lack of consensus, a disproportionate amount of energy has been devoted to these attempts.

Similarly, Canada's ability to maintain social peace in a context of linguistic and ethnic diversity has resulted from a delicate, indeed fragile, balancing of principles. Many Canadians have dared to hope that this achievement could be built upon to provide what former Prime Minister Pierre Trudeau described as a "brilliant prototype for the molding of tomorrow's civilization." But again the lack of consensus about the appropriate design of that prototype (and in particular about whether linguistic rights regimes should be national or regional in scope) now threatens the very integrity of the country.

Finally, Canada's performance on a number of international "scorecards" suggests a model worthy of attention. In 1991 Canada ranked second among the 160 countries ranked on the United Nations Human Development Index (based on measures such as life expectancy, literacy, and wealth). It ranked fifth among the member nations of the Organization for Economic Cooperation and Development on the "competitiveness" index compiled by the International Management Development Institute and the World Economic Forum. Such scores reflect Canada's rich natural endowments, but they also suggest that those endowments have been marshalled toward the achievement of goals sought by most industrial states. It is a crucial question, however, whether the Canadian system can respond to the challenges presented by the global economic order of the twenty-first century as successfully as it has responded in the past. Such responses will require a renovation of Canadian institutions— not only the institutions of government, but also those linking the state and economic interests.

It is just such a set of renovations upon which Canada is currently embarked. It is the institutions of government that are now the focus of attention and the integrity of the national federation is at stake. The potential fissuring of one's country is an issue on which it is difficult to maintain a stance of scholarly detachment. My passionate hope, then, may colour my belief that the Canadian institutional legacy of flexibility, ambiguity, and often deft accommodation will carry through into a reformed framework and will enable the country to find in its ambivalences not a source of fission but a creative tension.

My thanks are due to various friends and colleagues for their contributions to this book. The series editors, Douglas Ashford, Peter Katzenstein, and T. J. Pempel, provided astute technical advice in the early stages of the project, and invaluable substantive criticism of a lengthy first draft. A number of colleagues at the University of Toronto played important roles at various stages of the book's preparation. To Marsha Chandler, with whom the idea for the book was originally conceived, I am grateful for the insights generated in our early discussions. Ronald Manzer, Louis Pauly, Peter Russell, and Robert Vipond provided commentary on early drafts, and I benefitted greatly from their rich understanding of Canadian politics and their comparative sweep. Careful, thoughtful, and cheerful research assistance was provided by Brian Donovan, Sharon Erlichman, Sian Evans, Patricia O'Reilly, and Laura Tuohy. Hyla Levy risked her eyesight in flawlessly transcribing some almost illegible documents. At Temple University Press, Michael Ames was patient and tolerant of delays as the preparation of the manuscript was paced to the evolution of certain key events (notably, the process leading to the failure of the Meech Lake Accord). Barbara Reitt, in her meticulous copy-editing of the manuscript, bore bemusedly with the mix of American and British spelling styles ("program" on the one hand, "labour" on the other), which she found to be "a corroboration from a rather minor area of the point of your book." Finally, Richard Gilbertie skillfully shepherded the manuscript through its final stages.

In the end, of course, my deepest thanks go to those who lived through the gestation of this book most closely with me—to Walter, Laura, and Kevin. To endure such a process was a fate they did not seek, but they bore my periodic distraction with love and good humour. They are the ground for this, as for all my endeavours.

Policy and Politics in
Canada

1 Introduction

Canada, like most other western industrial nations, faces major policy challenges in the late twentieth century. It must manage conflict among domestic interests over the distribution of wealth while responding to international economic pressures affecting the ability of the economy to generate wealth. It must maintain a sense of political community in a context of demographic diversity. And it must develop mechanisms of mediation between individual citizens and the state in the face of a rising "rights consciousness," out of which rights are asserted not only to demand protection from the state but also, and increasingly, to make claims upon the state.

National responses to these challenges are shaped by a number of factors: a nation's international economic position, its ideological and cultural complexion, the organization of domestic interests, and its state structures. Aggregate analyses of cross-national data have made significant contributions to our understanding of the impact of these factors in broad comparative perspective. Increasingly, however, attention has turned to the ways in which these factors *intersect* in particular national contexts to produce distinctive patterns of policy development.

This book, and the series of which it is part, fall within this latter line of analysis. Each contribution in the series examines a particular nation and identifies its characteristic policy pattern. But these analyses are not idiographic: They recognize that the distinctiveness of each nation becomes apparent only in comparison with and in contrast to others, and that the explanation of national distinctiveness lies in an appreciation of how similar categories of factors (economic relations, ideology, organization of interests, and institutional structures) intersect in different national contexts.

3

What distinguishes the Canadian policy process, seen in this context, is its quintessential *ambivalence*: ambivalence about the appropriate roles of the state and the market, about national and regional conceptions of political community, and about individualist and collectivist concepts of rights and responsibilities. This ambivalence arises from tensions that are endemic to three fundamental features of the Canadian context: the relationship with the United States, the relationship between anglophones and francophones within Canada, and the regionalized nature of the Canadian economy and political community. In each of these sets of relationships Canadians find themselves pulled in competing directions: between attraction to and repulsion from the United States, and between loyalty to the national and the regional or linguistic community.

The first of these phenomena, the relationship to the United States, underlies Canadian ambivalence about the appropriate roles of the public and the private sectors, and about "individualist" and "collectivist" ideological strains. Canadians find themselves both bound to and threatened by an international superpower, the largest western industrial economy and the primary exemplar of an ideology of individualism, limited government, and reliance on the market. The other two phenomena, cultural dualism and regionalism, compound ambivalence about the state with ambivalence about the political community itself. Particularly in francophone Quebec, but also in other regions of the country, the question of whether allegiance is owed primarily to one's region or to the nation as a whole, and of whether national and regional loyalties contradict or reinforce each other, continue to be at issue. The strength of individualist and collectivist ideological strains also varies across regions, with collectivist sentiment being strongest in Quebec.

Ambivalence is embedded in the very language of Canadian politics, a language replete with unique oxymorons. One of the two major political parties calls itself "Progressive Conservative." The term "red tory" is well recognized in Canadian political parlance. A major referendum was held on the question of whether Quebec should establish a form of "sovereignty-association" with the rest of Canada. The same province underwent what is commonly referred to as a "quiet revolution" of social and political change. This language reflects the Canadian aversion to either-or choices, the tendency to find distinctive ways of reconciling divergent concepts.

Canada is not, of course, the only western industrial nation whose policy processes are characterized by ambivalence. This theme is reflected in the subtitles of a number of the contributions to this series: "Creative Conservatism" (Japan); "Principled Pragmatism" (Sweden); "A Semisovereign State" (Germany). But more than is the case in any other of these nations, Canadian ambivalence extends to the very legitimacy of the state itself and to the identity of the political community. Swedish social democrats may find strength in division (Heclo and Madsen 1987); Japanese policymakers may find their capacity for selective innovation enhanced by the stability afforded by a conservative coalition (Pempel 1982); the German state may incorporate parapublic institutions that "tame" its power (Katzenstein 1987). But in different ways in each of these cases, as in Britain, France, the United States, Australia, and other nations with which Canada might be compared, the questions of the boundaries of the state, its relative degree of centralization or decentralization, and its role in the protection and advancement of individual or collective rights are matters either of consensus or of fairly consistent polarization. In Canada these questions are addressed virtually de novo with new policy issues.

More importantly, Canadian ambivalence is *institutionalized*: It is "built in" to the structures of the state. This institutionalization of ambivalence has three major aspects. First, the system legitimizes competing principles: It combines an unwritten with a written constitution, a Westminster model of centralized cabinet government with a decentralized federation, and, since 1982, parliamentary supremacy with a constitutional charter of rights. Second, it allows these principles to coexist in a context of constitutional and institutional ambiguity. Third, it favours elite accommodation: Canada's ambiguous constitutional and institutional structure allows considerable latitude for interpretation, and shifting interpretations over time have occurred for the most part through a process of accommodation among elites with fairly tenuous lines of accountability to the broader public. These features of the system have allowed it to operate in the face of conflicting conceptions of the political community and of the appropriate role of the state.

The institutionalization of ambivalence is apparent in the relationship between the legislatures and the courts. Canada inherited from Britain the Westminster model of parliamentary supremacy, but in 1982 it adopted a constitutional Charter of Rights and Freedoms setting forth rights and freedoms that no legislature may normally abridge. The adoption of the charter followed almost two decades of intense constitutional debate, as discussed in Chapter 2. And it was possible only with the inclusion of a distinctively Canadian clause: The charter provides that legislatures may expressly override certain rights, by declaring that legislation shall apply "notwithstanding" charter provisions. This "notwithstanding" clause represents not only an attempt to reconcile parliamentary supremacy with constitutionally entrenched rights but also the inclusion of a form of "collective right," to be exercised by legislatures on behalf of their respective communities, when the assertion of individual rights is perceived to threaten community values (Elkins 1989).

The institutional ambivalence of the Canadian state is most apparent, however, in its federal structures. The existence of federal and provincial governments, as in other federal states, provides footholds for different partisan views, for different "state traditions" and for different emphases on national and regional dimensions of political community. In Canada, moreover, the relationship between levels of government exhibits a remarkable degree of constitutional and institutional ambiguity. In each of the policy arenas discussed in this book, the federal-provincial balance has been at issue in the postwar period. And these contests over federal and provincial jurisdiction have inevitably entailed ongoing and unresolved debates over the views of state and market, individual and collectivity, and nation and region, which the various federal and provincial contestants have espoused.

Canada's written constitution provides for a division of jurisdiction between the federal and provincial levels that is, on its face, relatively centralized. Indeed, the existence of formal federal government powers such as the power to disallow provincial laws led K. C. Wheare, in his classic study of federalism, to classify Canada not as a true federation but as a "quasi-federal state" (Wheare 1964). A number of these federal powers with respect to provincial legislation have, however, atrophied through disuse. In practice, the Canadian federation shows a mix of centralist and decentralist elements. It is one of the most fiscally decentralized in the world: in 1985 tax revenues accruing to the federal level amounted to 54.6 percent of total government revenues in Canada, as compared with 68.1 percent in the Federal Republic of Germany,[1] 69.1 percent in the United States, and 76.1 percent in Australia (Heidenheimer, Heclo, and Adams 1990: 198). On the other hand, the principle of a federal "spending power" has developed over time, allowing the federal government to spend, and to attach conditions to its spending, in areas of exclusive provincial jurisdiction.

There is slight recognition of the federal principle in the formal structures of the federal government. The lower house, the House of Commons, is elected by district according to a rough "representation by population" principle. The upper house, the Senate, is appointed by the federal government, and the method of allocating Senate seats is an uneasy compromise between representation by population and representation by jurisdiction. The function of reconciling federal and provincial interests has hence fallen to informal mechanisms: the periodic conferences of ministers (especially the First Ministers' Conferences) and the associated staff machinery, which together constitute the structures of "executive federalism" (Smiley 1987).

The appropriate federal-provincial division of power and the structures of intrastate federalism continue to be matters of dispute. Since 1960, in particular, enormous energy has been devoted to wrestling without resolve with these constitutional issues. Any change, it seems, threatens the delicate ambiguity that allows the system to function. And given this constitutional ambiguity, the federal-provincial balance must be renegotiated on virtually every terrain as new issues arise.

Institutionalized ambivalence, as reflected primarily in federal structures but also in the legislative-judicial relationship, is of central importance for the understanding of the Canadian policy process. Its impact on policy outcomes in particular arenas depends upon the specific ways in which the institutional structures of the state intersect with the organization of interests in those arenas, a theme that is developed throughout this book. In general it has yielded outcomes that have been variously characterized by compromise, eclecticism, cautious experimentation and diffusion, inconsistency, and incompatibility.

This introductory chapter traces out the roots of Canadian ambivalence toward the dualities of state and market, centre and region, and individual and collectivity. It then describes the institutionalization of this ambivalence in the structures of the Canadian state and concludes with a description of the broad contours of the organization of interests in Canada. Subsequent chapters explore the intersection of these factors in particular policy arenas.

The Roots of Ambivalence

The Relationship with the United States

Canada occupies an "intermediate" position in the international economy. Canada's is the smallest of the seven largest Organization for

Economic Cooperation and Development (OECD) economies. It is, in broad comparative perspective, moderately open: imported and exported goods amounted to 46.1 percent of Canadian gross domestic product (GDP) in 1986, up from 40.5 percent in 1961.[2] This degree of openness places it among the more open of the large OECD economies— less open than Germany, about the same as Italy and Britain, and more open than France, Japan, and the United States. But it is considerably less open than the smaller economies of Scandinavia, the Low Countries, and Austria. If, as Cameron (1978) has argued, openness to the international economy creates pressure for state intervention, Canada's moderate levels of state activity are perhaps understandable.

In Canada's case, however, a focus upon size and openness alone misses a central feature of the Canadian economy: its interrelationship with an American economy more than ten times its size. As Lipsey and Smith have concisely put it: "Like it or not, Canada is a small country living next door to a giant. As a result, most Canadians hold ambivalent views about the United States. On the one hand, Canadians know that if we cut off all commercial, social, and political association with the United States, we would lose overwhelmingly. Thus, we realize that we must learn to live with, and actively co-operate with, a presence we cannot ignore. On the other hand, we wish to keep our distance. Most of us share a deep-seated fear of being swallowed up culturally, economically, and politically by the U.S. colossus" (1985: 89).

Canada's economic linkages and geographic proximity to the United States make for an enormous American influence on Canadian politics, policy, and performance. Even before the Free Trade Agreement, entered into in 1989, the two countries were each others' largest trading partners. In 1986, 77.8 percent of Canada's merchandise exports went to the United States, and 25.6 percent of U.S. exports went to Canada.[3] Canada's balance of payments with the United States on current account was in deficit for much of the postwar period. Until 1970 imports exceeded exports in the case of both merchandise and nonmerchandise trade. (The deficit in nonmerchandise trade was partly incurred in services, but for the most part it resulted from the outflow of payments of interest, dividends, and royalties to service the large stock of U.S. investment capital in Canada.) As of 1970 the merchandise trade balance has generally been in surplus, reflecting in part the implementation of the Auto Pact "managed trade" agreement for the automobile industry signed in 1965 (Chapter 5). Beginning in the late 1970s this merchandise trade surplus was also fueled by the decline in value of the Canadian dollar against the U.S. dollar, making Canadian exports correspondingly more competitive in U.S. markets. In the mid-1980s the merchandise trade surplus was sufficient to offset the deficit in services and investment income. By the end of the decade, however, the current account had once again dipped slightly into deficit—in part because of a narrower surplus in merchandise trade and a larger deficit in services as the Canadian dollar appreciated against the U.S. dollar, and in part because of an increased deficit in investment income, as Canadian interest rates were maintained well above those in the United States.

The stock of U.S. direct investment in Canada is substantial, although it has declined somewhat since the late 1960s. About 23 percent of the capital employed in Canadian industries in 1983 was owned in the United States, as compared with 29 percent in 1966. Until the late 1960s U.S. ownership was proportionately heaviest in resource extraction industries: In 1966 U.S. investors owned 51 percent of the capital employed in the Canadian petroleum and gas and mining industries, as compared with 44 percent in manufacturing.[4] Since then, and especially in the late 1970s and 1980s, the proportion of U.S. ownership in resource extraction industries has declined dramatically (to 29 percent in petroleum and gas and 22 percent in mining in 1983)—in part as a result of the public policies discussed in Chapter 5, but also as a result of the exodus of U.S. capital with the decline of international commodity prices. U.S. ownership in manufacturing declined less dramatically over the same period, to 36 percent in 1983. U.S. investment is also highly visible. Of the 200 largest nonfinancial private sector corporations (by sales) in 1983, 58 were owned 50 percent or more by a single U.S. corporation. (This excludes cases in which a U.S. investor was the largest single shareholder with less than 50 percent ownership [calculated from *Canadian Business* 1984]). Of the thirty largest private-sector employers in Canada in 1983, eight were more than 50 percent owned by a single U.S. corporate investor (calculated from *Canadian Business* 1984).

Attitudes toward U.S. investment in Canada and toward proposals for "free trade" between the two nations evince considerable ambivalence, varying over time and across regions, periodically yielding virtually even splits and providing support for policies both enhancing and inhibiting closer ties with the United States. Opposition to economic ties with the United States has waxed and waned throughout Canadian history, but it has been tracked in public opinion polls only since the mid-1950s. Those polls register a dramatic rise in such opposition until the mid-1970s, and then a gradual decline into the mid-1980s. The mid-1970s marked the extension of controls on foreign investment in Canada beyond the few sectors (such as banking) to which they had previously been applied (Chapter 5), and the shift in public attitudes reflects the mobilization of opinion around this issue. In the 1980s, however, perhaps as a result of disillusionment with such policies, fear of U.S. economic domination began to wane somewhat at the policy level and at the level of public opinion; and restrictions on foreign investment were loosened. The percentage of national Gallup samples opposed to more U.S. investment in Canada rose from 46 percent in 1964 to 71 percent in 1975 but had declined again to 53 percent by 1986 (Canadian Institute of Public Opinion June 7, 1980; August 7, 1986).

Also in the mid-1980s proposals for negotiating a "free trade" agreement with the United States emerged from a major commission, the Royal Commission on the Economic Union and Development Prospects for Canada, which reported in 1985, and from the Conservative government in Ottawa. Public support for the free trade initiative during the ensuing debate was volatile. In 1984 there was a substantial majority of support for free trade, virtually unchanged in the previous thirty years. Over the following four years, as a free trade agreement was negotiated, opinion shifted dramatically, becoming much more evenly split and showing an increase in indecision. In April 1984 polls showed 80 percent support for the concept of free trade with the United States, and less than 20 percent opposition. By June 1988 support and opposition were virtually even at about 40 percent, and indecision had risen to about 20 percent. By the time of the November 1988 election (which had become a virtual referendum on the free trade issue), a bare majority opposed the agreement (Adams 1988). The reported levels of "support" and "opposition," however, need to be somewhat qualified. Adams (1988) found that only 23 percent wished to cancel the agreement. Forty-four percent preferred a renegotiation of the agreement, and 26 percent preferred implementing the agreement as negotiated.

Canadian ambivalence about the economic size and power of the United States, and apprehensiveness about the possibilities of survival of a distinct Canadian identity and political system, need to be understood in historical context. The very founding of the nation can be traced in large part to a desire to resist the north-south economic, cultural, and political pull.

The debates surrounding Canadian Confederation in 1867 indicate that, in the minds of its founders, Canada was established to a large extent in defense against and in contradistinction to the United States. This oppositional and appositional stance arose from a peculiar and complex coincidence of interests among the British North American colonies. Survival in the face of the larger American republic was a major theme of the legislative debates surrounding confederation. For proconfederation anglophones in central Canada and the Maritimes, survival meant the establishment of a political link among the colonies strong enough to resist the American magnet and to preserve a "protective connexion with Britain" (McNaught 1982: 132). Survival in the face of the United States meant the fostering not only of political but also of economic ties among the colonies. The need to create and finance a transportation infrastructure, to expand westward, and to foster indigenous capital accumulation were further prods toward confederation and, as we see in Chapter 5, shaped the early relationship between the state and economic development.

Survival also dictated, in the argument that won the day, a federal structure, albeit with a strong central government. Survival of the "French fact" in the anglophone North American sea was an important motivation among francophone supporters of confederation. Only a federal structure with a strong central government, it was argued, could be loose enough to allow distinct regional minorities to survive and strong enough to hold them together. Again, in this context, the spectre of the United States shaped Canadian thinking. In particular, in attempting to establish a strong executive and strong central government, the founders of the Canadian federation were attempting to restrain the sort of localism of interest and ambition that, in their view, had led to the American Civil War (Smith 1987; McNaught 1982: 133). Ironically, the Canadian federation has become, despite these intentions, more decentralized than its American counterpart.

To suggest that Canada defined itself solely in defence against and in contradistinction to the United States would, however, be greatly to overstate the case, and to miss much of the complexity of ideologies and interests that shaped the birth and development of the nation. In Canada's early political culture, to be "British" or "French" implied more than just not being "American" (though it certainly implied that as well). These fundamental identities, as well as the ideas and interests of more recent immigrants, have resulted in a political culture that, although similar to that of the United States in many respects, is marked by strains that are more collectivist and more European in orientation.

One approach to explaining the differences between Canadian and American political cultures, which has gained wide currency in Canadian political science, characterizes each as a "fragment" culture. The argument runs roughly as follows. In the North American societies founded by European colonists, "fragments" thrown off from the full European ideological spectrum (from feudal or tory through liberal whig to liberal democrat to socialist) took root and developed independently in the new frontier (Hartz 1955; McRae 1964; Horowitz 1966).

The tension (or lack thereof) between collectivist and individualist strains in different political cultures can be understood in these terms. Both tories and socialists view society as community, an organic entity in which all parts function for the good of the whole. Toryism justifies an inequality of condition in the interest of the collective good: The positions of various "estates" are grounded in a comprehensive framework of social values prescribing their functional responsibilities, their social obligations, and to a large extent the just rewards attached to the fulfillment of these responsibilities and obligations. The liberal reaction to this inequality of condition is to attack ascribed privilege and to emphasize equality of individual opportunity, first in the ownership of property, then in access to the franchise and the largesse of the state. Socialism, in turn, extends this egalitarianism to embrace equality of condition, emphasizing common (at first class, then community) interests over individual interests. In a culture with no vestigial memory of the organic corporate concepts of toryism, such an appeal has less resonance.

Both English Canada and the United States are eighteenth-century "fragments" thrown off from England, and hence both cultures are dominated by liberal individualism. The debates surrounding the founding of both the United States and Canada can be understood to a large extent as debates between liberal "whigs" (emphasizing the role of the state in governing a complex market economy and promoting economic development) and liberal "Jeffersonian" democrats (emphasizing the role of the state in promoting political participation and the formation of citizens in local communities) (Smith 1987). In Canada, however, unlike the United States, "tory" elements were not renounced. "Loyalists" in English Canada, while basically eighteenth- and nineteenth-century liberals, retained and defiantly preserved what Hartz has called a tory "streak" or "touch." French Canada, moreover, dominated by the hierarchical

Roman Catholic church, preserved its "feudal fragment" faithfully into the mid-twentieth century. There is considerable debate among scholars as to whether the cultural motif thus inculcated in French Canada was feudal or absolutist, but in any event it was deferential toward authority and provided support for stronger concepts of the state than prevailed in the United States.

The "tory" or "feudal" touches can explain two Canadian phenomena: the greater vigour and electoral success of an indigenous socialist movement in Canada than in the United States, and the presence of "red toryism." The social democratic New Democratic Party (NDP) has formed the government in four provinces at various times and is a firm opposition party elsewhere in the country, including the federal level. A socialist strain has also characterized the Quebec separatist movement, and particularly the Parti québécois (PQ), which formed the government in Quebec from 1976 to 1985. Organized socialism was more successful in Canada than in the United States, it is argued, because its ideas and its vehicles were not alien. Socialist ideas "fit with a political culture which already contained some non-liberal components" (Horowitz 1966: 61). Furthermore, those ideas were borne by British immigrants who were not considered "foreigners." In the United States, in contrast, there were no tory echoes with which socialist ideas of community could resonate, and socialism was carried by immigrants from political cultures foreign to the dominant ethnic groups. "In Canada, socialism is British, non-Marxist, and worldly; in the United States it is German, Marxist, and other worldly" (Horowitz 1966: 61).

"Red toryism," within the Canadian political lexicon, refers to a variety of admixtures of tory conservative and socialist elements. It connotes the willingness of some conservatives to support programs (such as medicare) tending toward a greater equality of condition, or (less commonly) the willingness of social democrats to preserve traditional institutions (such as the monarchy) that express community values even though those institutions may contribute to the perpetuation of an inequality of condition. It is an ideology that emphasizes the social responsibilities and obligations of those who hold privileged positions in society, as part of the justification of those privileges; and it encourages a collaboration between the leadership of corporate groups and the state in the pursuit of redistributive policies.

The significance of such "organic" corporatist values in Canadian political life should not be exaggerated: They are part of a complex mix in which liberal democratic values are dominant.[5] The social democratic New Democratic Party has been a minor party at the federal level, with areas of regional strength as noted below. The two major parties, the Progressive Conservatives (PC) and the Liberals are essentially mass liberal democratic brokerage parties. The PCs stand to the right of the Liberals on most issues, but they embrace (at least at the leadership level) a "red tory" wing. The Liberals, for their part, harbour (among both leaders and supporters) a wing close to the NDP. Former Prime Minister Pierre Trudeau was a member of the NDP prior to joining the Liberals. Lambert and his colleagues (1986: 560), moreover, found in a 1984 survey that Liberal supporters showed a moderate but significant degree of identification with the NDP. They also found considerable ambivalence toward both the left and the right in Canada, particularly on the part of those who identify with the left or at least prefer it to the right. (Those identifying with or preferring the right were much less equivocal, tending to attribute only positive attributes to the right and negative attributes to the left.)[6]

Indeed, some recent scholarship has attributed both toryism and socialism in Canada more to anti-Americanism than to the persistence of organic values (Forbes 1987). On this argument, not the least of the attractions of these ideological strains for significant segments of the Canadian populace is the fact that they are recognizably "un-American" and hence serve to distinguish Canadian policy and politics.[7] Nonetheless, as we see when we come to discuss health policy (Chapter 3) and experiments with "liberal corporatism" (Chapters 4 and 5), an appreciation of the scope and limits of organic values is essential to an understanding of some dimensions of Canadian policy and politics.

English-French Relations

The motto on Quebec's automobile licence plates reads "je me souviens"—I remember. A sense of history (and of historical grievance) permeates English-French relations in Canada. The defeat of French by British forces on the Plains of Abraham in 1759 strategically and symbolically marked the British "Conquest" of New France, although British dominance was not sealed until the Treaty of Paris ended the Seven Years' War in 1763. But the French in Quebec, though defeated militarily, survived as a political and cultural "fact." "Through the operation of British imperial interest and political experience, as well as the firmly based French-Canadian sense of identity, the Laurentide homeland was to remain both unassimilated and uniquely influential. No Louisiana fate lay in store for the descendants of the fur traders and *habitants*. Nevertheless, the rankling presence of the Conquest in the imaginative and retentive mind of Quebec was itself to explain much of the vitality of latter-day Quebec nationalism" (McNaught 1982: 43).

After a brief and abortive policy of assimilation, early British governors of Quebec adopted a policy of tolerance and cooperation with French-Canadian elites and with the Roman Catholic church, a policy epitomized in the Quebec Act of 1774, which affirmed the seignorial landholding system, French civil law, and the tithing power of the church. A century later the constitution of the new Canadian Confederation provided for the use of both French and English in federal and Quebec government institutions, and provided guarantees for Protestant and Roman Catholic school systems. (Variations of these provisions were included in the constitutions of Manitoba, Saskatchewan, and Alberta as those provinces later entered confederation. But as discussed in Chapter 7, constitutional guarantees of linguistic rights were actually very limited, and even those that existed were eroded outside Quebec.)

The legacy of the Conquest is, in fact, one of deep ambivalence for Canadians, both francophone and anglophone, both inside and outside Quebec. On the one hand, the Conquest and subsequent British policies shaped Quebec's distinctiveness within Canada, and Canada's distinctiveness vis-à-vis the United States. On the other hand, it is a "rankling" source of conflict. For *québécois*, as Christian Dufour has perceptively put it, France's ceding of New France to Britain represented an abandonment as well as a conquest, a trauma seared into the collective unconscious. But subsequent British policies and Canadian federalism made it possible to resist assimilation into North American anglophone culture. As a result: "English is a deeply ambivalent and perturbing element of the Quebec identity: at the same time both friend and foe, a part of ourselves that makes us stronger and the conqueror that wants our blood. But there is no doubt. . . . the English is there" (Dufour 1990: 97). Similarly, for anglophones, the "French fact" clearly distinguished Canada from the United States: "English Canada has never existed alone, without its French counterpart. The Quebec identity, if it is able, because of its autonomous origins, to see itself outside Canada, has nonetheless benefitted from an English input at an important time in its historical genesis. The two identities have been related for more than two hundred years. They have penetrated each other's core" (ibid.: 57). On the other hand, English Canadians are well aware of the tensions that linguistic and cultural duality has generated within the political system. As Charles Taylor, a noted Canadian political theorist and a Quebec anglophone, has put it in a sympathetic review of Dufour's work, anglophones see "the French component of the Canadian identity [as] both cornerstone and potentially loose foundation, a source of fission and rupture" (1990: 48). Different political parties, movements, and leaders, both anglophone and francophone, have given different weight to the positive and negative attributes of this relationship of interdependence and conflict. In the late 1980s, as we shall see, discourse and opinion was apparently becoming increasingly polarized. But these manifestations of conflict should not obscure the ambivalence that has characterized anglophone-francophone relations throughout Canadian history, and that continues to condition policy responses.

In the more than two hundred years since the Conquest, Quebec has remained the "heartland" of French Canada. In 1986 francophones constituted 26 percent of the Canadian population, but 85 percent of francophones lived in Quebec. Put another way, the francophone proportion of the provincial population was 83 percent in Quebec, but only 34 percent in New Brunswick (the province with the second largest francophone proportion); it was just over 5 percent in Ontario and less than 5 percent all other provinces and territories (Chapter 7).

Until the 1960s Quebec francophone culture was based in the rural parish. A close accommodation between the church and the state governed the social and cultural aspects of Quebec life, and the economic system was dominated by "les anglais." Under the regime of Premier Maurice Duplessis from 1944 to 1959, Quebec was essentially run as the premier's personal fiefdom, and the political modernization of Quebec was forestalled. With Duplessis's death in 1959, however, the pent-up frustration of the urban liberal francophone intelligentsia, which had chafed under the repressiveness of the Duplessis regime, burst forth to fuel a dramatic transformation of the Quebec state. Under Duplessis, members of this intelligentsia had sought to have their impact through journalism, labour unions, and universities; now the state itself became not only their target but their vehicle. The entente between the state, the church, and the anglophone economic elite was shattered; and the provincial government under parties of varying partisan stripes became much more assertive of the role of the state itself in the promotion of francophone interests. This was Quebec's "quiet revolution."

The implications of this new role for the state were not at all universally agreed upon, however. There were profound differences of opinion regarding the relationship between the French-Canadian "nation" and the Quebec "state," as the two sides of *québécois* ambivalence toward Canada each found eloquent advocates. For a significant portion of the Quebec francophone political elite, epitomized in the "three wise men" (Jean Marchand, a labour leader; Gérard Pelletier, a journalist; and, especially, Pierre Trudeau, a law professor) who chose to enter federal politics in 1965, a focus on Quebec alone was, in the full sense, "provincial." French culture potentially enriched all of Canada; and once English Canada recognized that fact, not only the career prospects and life chances of francophones but also the cultural and political life of Canada would improve. Trudeau and others like him pressed for policies of "bilingualism and biculturalism": the use of French as well as English in federal government institutions, and guarantees of linguistic minority rights across Canada. Trudeau himself advocated such policies as a noble experiment that would demonstrate to the international community the possibility of national unity in the context of cultural division.

For others, however, *québécois* nationalism was seen as a much more positive force, and the building of the "national state" of Quebec had much higher priority than the defence of French Canadian minorities outside Quebec or the pursuit of dubious policies of bilingualism. Quebec nationalists such as René Lévesque, the first leader of the Parti québécois, held that the existence of francophone minorities outside Quebec "in no way lessens the fact that Quebec is our nation state and identifies itself politically with our nation. It is only as Quebec grows stronger in every way . . . that it can be of some assistance to the minorities" (Lévesque 1964: 132–33).

The very concept of "nation," so central to the debate sparked by French Canadian nationalism, is an ambiguous one in Canada, having different connotations in English and French. English Canadians have emphasized the conceptual dimension of sovereignty and have insisted that Canada is in that sense "one nation." In French the sociocultural connotations of the term predominate; hence the sovereign state of Canada can embrace "deux nations." French Canadians of both separatist and nonseparatist persuasions can use the language of "deux nations"; but English Canadians hear that phrase as a threat to Canadian sovereignty, as federal Conservative leader Robert Stanfield learned to his regret when he campaigned unsuccessfully on that slogan in the 1970s.

Quebec nationalism took a violent turn in the late 1960s, culminating in the kidnapping of a British diplomat and a Quebec cabinet minister, and the murder of the latter, by the Front de libération du Québec (FLQ) in 1970. For the most part, however, the primary vehicle for nationalist forces has been the separatist Parti québécois. The electoral fortunes of the PQ suggest the ambivalence within the Quebec electorate regarding the relationship between Quebec and the rest of Canada, but also the growing support for the separatist option. The PQ was elected to form the provincial government in 1976, and again in 1981. In both cases, however, its election campaigns downplayed the issue of separatism. Moreover, in 1980 a referendum in Quebec denied the PQ government a mandate to negotiate a form of dissociation of Quebec from the rest of Canada. The Parti québécois government's proposal of "sovereignty-association" itself arguably constituted an unsuccessful attempt to appeal to ambivalence—its ambiguous phrasing attracted support from those who favoured various degrees of "sovereignty" and "association" (Chapter 2).

The PQ was defeated in the provincial elections of 1985 and 1989. Over the four provincial elections from 1976 to 1989, however, the PQ vote had hovered in the range of 40 percent, the same percentage that approved "sovereignty-association" in the 1980 referendum. (The difference between victory and defeat for the Liberals and the PQ in Quebec was largely determined by competition from third parties and by electoral distribution.)

Like other provincial electorates, moreover, Quebeckers have often split their support at the federal and provincial levels. From the 1960s through the mid-1980s, the federal Liberals, notwithstanding their thoroughgoing "federalist" position, continued to win overwhelming support in Quebec even as the separatist debate raged. As one journalist has put it, "it is typical of the split personality of Quebeckers that they wanted a spell-binding nationalist [Lévesque] in charge of their province and a dynamic federalist [Trudeau] in Ottawa" (Goar 1988: D4). In the mid-1980s, however, the tension *between* federal and provincial Quebec incumbents was largely replaced by tension *within* the federal Quebec caucus and *within* the Quebec government. In 1984 Trudeau was replaced by another Quebec native son, the Conservative Brian Mulroney, a federalist with a decidedly more "decentralist" bent and with a Quebec caucus that included a number of (formerly) avowed separatists. And in 1985 the PQ government in Quebec was replaced by a Liberal government under

Robert Bourassa, a federalist (whose federal commitment was, however, much more pragmatic than principled). There appears, nonetheless, to have been a firming of support for Quebec independence in this period. Jacques Parizeau did as well, in terms of the popular vote, waging a strongly separatist PQ campaign in 1989, as René Lévesque had done on a much softer platform in 1976. And public opinion polls in Quebec charted a fairly steady secular rise in support for Quebec's becoming an "independent country." In 1968, only 11 percent of Quebec respondents approved such a concept; that proportion had risen to 18 percent by 1979 and to 39 percent by 1989 (Gallup Canada January 4, 1990). These levels were to rise further in the heated constitutional atmosphere of the early 1990s.

Support for various admixtures of federalism and nationalism in Quebec has emerged from a political culture in which the ambivalence about individual and collectivist values is deeper than it is elsewhere in Canada. To be sure, this ambivalence exists, and has existed historically, in English Canada as well, where it has infused the defence of provincial autonomy. In the latter part of the nineteenth century English Canadian advocates of "provincial rights" developed a complex blend of individual and collective perspectives in making their case. They defended the autonomy of provincial governments not only by appealing to concepts of provincial sovereignty but also by drawing analogies between individual and provincial rights (Vipond 1991). These advocates were essentially liberals; but theirs was a liberalism that entailed, at least in its metaphor, an organic view of provincial communities. This language, moreover, had modern echoes in the constitutional debates of the 1970s and 1980s.

In Quebec, however, the organic sense of community has considerably greater weight, and the tension between individual and collective values is more profound. As we see in Chapters 2 and 7, Quebec governments have used concepts of "collective personality" and collective rights in defending francophone interests, while confronting Quebec federalists in Ottawa who cleaved to a much more individualistic conception of rights. Francophone *québécois* have supported restrictions on individual linguistic rights in the interest of preserving the francophone community, while strongly supporting other forms of individual rights (Sniderman et al. 1989). On most policy issues, moreover, the Quebec populace emerges distinctively in public opinion surveys with the largest "statist" component among Canadian regions (Simeon and Blake 1980: 92–94).[8] Public support for governmental activism in Quebec is undoubtedly associated with the "quiet revolution" of the 1960s. To the extent that these "statist" attitudes reflect a sociocultural support for authoritative institutions, however, their roots arguably run deep into the history of the francophone culture and the Roman Catholic church in the province.

English-French relations have formed a dominant motif of Canadian political history, but they have been complicated by the growing phenomenon of multiculturalism. About one-eighth of Canadians have a mother tongue other than English or French, and this proportion varies considerably across provinces, from a high of more than one-fifth in Manitoba to less than 1 percent in Newfoundland. Furthermore, with shifting patterns of immigration, Canada's three major cities—Toronto, Montreal, and Vancouver—have become increasingly multiracial in the postwar period. The experience of living in a multicultural society hence varies considerably across Canada. The "Anglo-Celtic" tradition still exerts a certain cultural hegemony, but it is less and less possible to refer to "English Canada" as a cultural and political entity.

The increasing political mobilization of Canada's aboriginal people, moreover, has given urgency to issues of aboriginal rights, land claims, and self-government. Native people constitute less than 2 percent of the Canadian population. But the moral status of their claims to historic rights and their assertion of traditional values have called into question, among other things, the privileging of English and French as the languages of the "founding races" of Canada.

Regionalism

Canadian regionalism, as a political force, arises from superimposed economic, linguistic, cultural, and governmental cleavages within defined geographic areas. Regional economic disparity, measured in terms of inequalities in the distribution of average personal after-tax income across regions, is substantial relative to most other western industrial nations (Jenkin 1983). Furthermore, the structure of regional economies differs significantly. Ontario forms the core of an industrialized central region; regional economies to the west, north, and east are variously based upon the extraction or harvesting of the natural resources of timber, petroleum, minerals, and fish. This diversity gives rise to different sets of economic interests in different regions of the country. To generalize broadly, the resource producers of the Atlantic provinces, the prairies, and British Columbia have been export oriented, have sought to maintain and expand markets abroad, and have been highly vulnerable to swings in world commodity prices. Secondary manufacturing, concentrated in Ontario and Quebec, has been oriented primarily toward the domestic market, has sought protection from import competition, and has looked to the hinterland as producers of inputs and consumers of final products. The differential effects of shifts in international prices for commodities have made for uneven patterns of growth and development across regions. Boom and bust cycles have been out of phase across regions and have been more sharply felt in the regions with resource-based economies. Unemployment has been chronically high in parts of the Atlantic provinces and Quebec: between 1973 and 1983, when the average annual unemployment rate was 7.9 percent in Canada as a whole and 6.9 percent in Ontario, it was 14.5 percent in Newfoundland (calculated from Mansell and Copithorne 1986: 7). Differences in average personal income continue to exist, although they have narrowed somewhat over time. In 1986 average personal income before tax was 67 percent of the Canadian average in Newfoundland and 114 percent in Ontario.[9]

A second major source of regional tension is the fact that the country's largest and most historically significant linguistic and cultural minority—francophone Canadians—is concentrated in one region: Quebec. To a lesser extent, patterns of immigration have produced other regional communities with distinctive cultural traditions—Celtic in the Atlantic provinces, for example, and eastern European on the prairies—but for the most part it is true that, as one study has found, "Quebec constitute[s] a more distinctive political community than any other Canadian region or population in all . . . dimensions of political culture" (Ornstein, Stevenson, and Williams 1980).

These economic and cultural differences give rise to regional identities and loyalties that compete with attachments to the nation as a whole. Canadian politics is also characterized, however, by "centralism" or, as Breton (1981) has put it, by "anti-regionalism." To some extent, this force can be interpreted as a "regionalism of the centre." Ontarians, who constitute the most "federally oriented" segment of the population (apart from anglophone Quebeckers), are most likely to believe that their own region has benefitted most from confederation. (Quebec and Atlantic residents are likely to share the view that Ontario has benefitted most, whereas the western provinces are more likely to identify Quebec in this role [Canadian Institute of Public Opinion December 18, 1986]).

The structures of Canadian government, as discussed below, reinforce both regionalist and centralist (or "antiregionalist") sentiments. The existence of provincial governments creates vehicles for the expression of regional interests and provides political elites with incentives to foster those interests as a source of political support. The existence of the federal government, similarly, creates vehicles and incentives for federal elites. As Breton has put it, conflicts between regionalism and antiregionalism can be seen "in part, [as] attempts on the part of social, political and economic groups to mobilize support for the institutional level to which their careers and well-being are mostly tied" (Breton 1981; see also Cairns 1977).

Definitions of Political Community   Regional identities and interests are strong in Canada, competing with the nation as a whole as a focus of direct political attachment. Paradoxically, however, Canadians may be bound to the national political community by the strength of those regional ties. As one student of Canadian political culture has put it: "Without a 'sense of place,' without 'the imaginative sense of locality,' without the pride of one's region, there would be much less support for and affect toward Canada. I do not know which is correct: 'I am a British Columbian, and therefore I am a Canadian,' or 'I am a Canadian, and this makes me part of British Columbia.' But either way it works, there can be for most Canadians no pleasure in being forced to choose between one identity and another. Multiple loyalties can have, therefore, a civilizing result, since they encourage us to reject absolute choices and teach us to give assent and express dissent in graduated and qualified terms" (Elkins 1980: 26).

Elkins supports his argument with an analysis of 1974 postelection survey data. Another analysis, using the same data base but different measures, produced more ambiguous results (Clarke et al. 1979: 77). Whether or not they reinforce national attachments, however, provincial orientations in Canada are undeniably strong, especially in comparison with its continental neighbour. Canada and the United States are both geographically large and diverse federal nations sharing the same continent, yet in Canada regional attachments are much stronger. Indeed, as Gibbins (1982: 170) has noted, "The dominance of national identification [in the United States] is so widely accepted that empirical documentation is difficult to obtain"; in Canada there is a plethora of documentation of national-regional differences.

Public opinion data have consistently demonstrated cross-provincial differences in orientations to federal and provincial governments, and a

general "provincialization" of identities over time. Ontario and anglophone Quebec respondents are, as noted, the most "federally" oriented,
and Atlantic, francophone Quebec, and western respondents the most
"provincially" oriented (Elkins 1980: 18–19; Canadian Institute of Public
Opinion September 24, 1980).

Electoral Politics   Voting patterns are also regionalized. As noted above,
the two major parties, the Liberals and the Progressive Conservatives,
are essentially mass brokerage parties. For most of the postwar period
these two parties were distinguished at least as much by differences in
their regional bases as by ideological differences per se.

At the national level party support has also been highly regionalized.
Both Liberals and Conservatives have been competitive in Ontario and
the Atlantic provinces. Until 1984 the Progressive Conservatives were
strong in the west but (with the exception of the 1958 federal election [10])
won fewer than 20 percent of Quebec's parliamentary seats. The Liberals, obversely, regularly won more than 70 percent of Quebec's seats
(again with the exception of 1958) but fewer than 20 percent of seats
west of Ontario. The base of the federal New Democratic Party has been
in Ontario and the west. The landslide Conservative victory in 1984,
however, included fifty-eight of Quebec's seventy-five seats, as well as
sixty-two of the eighty seats allocated to the western provinces and the
northern territories. Unlike the previous Conservative landslide in 1958,
moreover, the 1984 Conservative win was followed by another Conservative majority in 1988. The Conservatives added to their representation in
Quebec while continuing to win a majority of seats in the west. The 1984
and 1988 elections appeared to have established the Conservatives as a
national party and to have eroded the Liberals' traditional base in Quebec. It has been suggested, however, that the Canadian electorate in the
1980s was characterized, to a greater degree indeed than the British and
American electorates, by "volatility" rather than realignment (LeDuc
1985). The plummeting of the popularity of the federal PCs and the rise
of new parties such as the Reform Party and the Bloc québécois give
further credence to this interpretation.

It should also be noted that interregional differences in the popular
vote are not as great as these differences in seats won would suggest.
Canada's single-member district plurality electoral system exacerbates
regional electoral cleavages. Liberal voters in the west have generally
been underrepresented in the postwar period, as were Conservatives in
Quebec until 1984. The percentage of popular votes won by the Liberals

in the west regularly exceeded the percentage of western seats won by the party by 10 to 20 percentage points; and a similar gulf existed between Conservative popular support and seats won in Quebec. The popular vote for the NDP has also regularly exceeded the proportion of seats that it has won in all regions except the west, where the pattern has been inconsistent across time. A number of Canadian political scientists have drawn attention to these phenomena (Cairns 1968; Gibbins 1982: 116–19), and both academics and governmental advisory bodies have advocated some form of proportional representation to overcome such distortions (Irvine 1979; Task Force on Canadian Unity 1979).

The parties themselves draw on different electoral coalitions in the different regions. The demographic and socioeconomic complexion of the Alberta PC, Liberal, or NDP parties, for example, like that of the province itself, differs from that of their counterparts in Nova Scotia, and both again differ from Ontario. The brokerage problems faced by the parties are exacerbated by these differences in regional electoral coalitions. Furthermore, a number of provincial party organizations (notably, the Liberals and the NDP in Quebec) are formally autonomous from the national organization; and in general, as Gibbins (1982: 137, 139) notes, "Relations in Canada between national and provincial parties of the same name have been cool and frequently combative. . . . The evolutionary pattern . . . has been toward increased autonomy for both national and provincial parties." Even given this trend, however, what is notable is the *tension* between national and provincial party organizations: The Canadian party system exhibits neither the centralist tendencies of the German system (Katzenstein 1987: 377–80)[11] nor the decentralization of the United States (Gibbins 1982: 122–23, 134–37).

The regionalization of electoral politics in Canada is also apparent in provincial elections. Parties relegated to the role of "third" or "minor" parties at the national level (the NDP and the Social Credit party) have enjoyed extended periods in office at the provincial level. Both the NDP and Social Credit had their genesis as agrarian protest parties of the left and the right respectively.[12] In the forty-five years from 1945 to 1990, the NDP was in power in Saskatchewan for a total of thirty years, in Manitoba for a total of fourteen years, and in British Columbia for three years. In the same period, Social Credit formed the government in British Columbia for a total of thirty-five years, and in Alberta for a total of twenty-seven years. In 1990 the NDP for the first time formed the government in Ontario; and in 1991 NDP governments took office again in

Saskatchewan and British Columbia. Parties exclusive to Quebec have gained office in that province (the Union nationale from 1936 to 1960 and 1966 to 1970; the Parti québécois from 1976 to 1985).

These provincial results constitute special cases of a more general tendency: the propensity of Canadians to "split their votes" (and their party identifications) federally and provincially, to support different parties at different levels of government (Gibbins 1982: 133–34). One British Columbia political scientist, indeed, has described federal and provincial electoral politics in that province as constituting "two political worlds" (Blake 1985). This phenomenon, it has been argued, "appears to be of much greater importance in understanding the nature of partisanship in Canada than is the case in other federal systems such as the United States and Australia" (LeDuc 1985: 391).

This regionalization of electoral politics has important implications for the policy process. The diversity of parties that have been brought to power at the provincial level has been an important source of policy innovation. On the other hand, federal-provincial negotiations have been complicated by the likelihood that parties that are out of office at the federal level will gain provincial footholds. Finally, political parties in the Canadian system have been ill-suited to play the role of interregional mediator. Each of the national parties has, at least until the mid-1980s, been consistently weak in certain regions of the country; and in any event the autonomy and distinctiveness of provincial parties from their federal counterparts attenuates the partisan bonds that might be drawn upon in a mediation process.

Multiple loyalties, to Canada, to a cultural group, to a region, may "civilize" Canadian political life, but they also complicate it. Together with Canadian ambivalence about relationships with the United States and the political and economic principles that it represents, these multiple loyalties have shaped the political institutions through which public policy is developed and implemented. The following section traces out this institutionalization of ambivalence.

The Institutionalization of Ambivalence

The Nature of the Constitution

The history of constitutional and institutional development in Canada is marked by the competing influences of the British (and to a lesser extent the French Catholic) heritage, and the economic and cultural environment of North America. From Britain, Canada inherited the Westminster model of parliamentary government and the concept of an "unwritten" as well as written constitution. Much of Canada's constitution is written in the form of a series of constitution acts dating from 1867 to 1982. The first of these, formerly titled the British North America Act, 1867, provides in a preamble for a "constitution similar in principle to that of the United Kingdom." That act established the basic framework of parliamentary government, the federal-provincial division of powers, and guarantees of certain French and English language rights and Catholic and Protestant education rights. Through its incorporation by reference of British constitutional principles, however, it adopted guarantees of natural justice and the concept of *unwritten* constitutional "conventions" that constrain political action as effectively as codified prescriptions.

Constitutional development since 1867 has been marked by evolving changes in the federal-provincial division of powers and by a long and at times rancorous struggle to "patriate" the constitution, discussed more fully in Chapter 2. From 1867 until 1982 Canada's written constitution was in the form of acts of the British Parliament (the "British North America" acts). Any amendment to the written constitution hence formally required action by the British Parliament. This ignominious state of affairs was the result, not of any jealous hoarding of imperial power on the part of Britain, but rather of the failure of successive Canadian federal and provincial governments to agree upon the content of an indigenous Canadian constitution—most particularly, an appropriate amending formula. Attempts in 1965 and 1971 came tantalizingly close to fruition but ultimately foundered on the opposition of Quebec. Although federal Liberal politicians from Quebec played leading roles in designing each set of proposals, successive Quebec Liberal provincial governments judged that neither sufficiently took account of Quebec's distinctiveness and would not accept what they believed to be a constitutional straitjacket (Cheffins and Johnson 1986: 60–61).

Finally, in April 1982, and only after a passionately contested referendum in Quebec defeated a PQ proposal to reorganize the relationship between Quebec and the rest of Canada in a form of "sovereignty-association," the Canadian constitution was patriated despite the opposition of the Quebec government. But much of the constitutional agenda—and particularly the issue of the place of Quebec within Confederation—remained unresolved.

The Place of Quebec

Issues that touch upon the status of the two "founding races" constitute, as we see in the next sections of this chapter and again in Chapters 2 and 7, the major unresolved tension in Canadian policy and politics—sometimes repressed, sometimes papered over with ambiguity, but inevitably resurfacing in conflict. One dimension of this conflict is the contest between a strategy of constitutional parallelism—in which all provinces have equal status, and the rights of francophone and (in Quebec) anglophone linguistic minorities are equally guaranteed across Canada—and a strategy of granting "special status" to Quebec as the guarantor of francophone culture. The constitutional framework adopted in 1867 combined these strategies. Constitutional parallelism was apparent in the provisions that entrusted matters on which anglophones and francophones were likely to differ (notably, education, property and civil law, and social services) to provincial governments, and that guaranteed denominational education rights across provinces. A form of special status was also incorporated, however, in that Quebec was the only province in which constitutional provision for both English and French in the provincial legislature and the courts was made. (As discussed in Chapter 7, a similar provision was later incorporated explicitly in the constitution of Manitoba and implicitly in the constitutions of Alberta and Saskatchewan, but these provisions were effectively ignored.) In the period since 1960 a policy of constitutional parallelism was vigorously pursued by Pierre Trudeau as prime minister, and various forms of "special status" have been advocated by successive Quebec governments.

The 1982 constitutional changes were informed by constitutional parallelism: They extended minority language rights and added New Brunswick to the list of provinces with provisions for bilingual government institutions.[13] In 1985 the desire to "bring Quebec in" to the Constitution—that is, to secure the willing assent of the Quebec provincial government to the Canadian constitution to which it was, in 1982, unwillingly bound—catalyzed yet another round of constitutional negotiations. (The defeat of the Parti québécois government and the election of a Liberal government in Quebec in December 1985 made the prospect of negotiating such assent more likely.) In August 1986 the eleven first ministers agreed to give priority to Quebec's concerns, and in April and June 1987 they agreed to a list of proposed amendments to the Constitution.

The so-called Meech Lake Accord, named after the locale of the April meeting, met all of the conditions of the Quebec Liberal government. The accord and its subsequent demise are discussed more fully in Chapter 2. Among its several important provisions, the most controversial were those recognizing Quebec's status as a "distinct society" within Canada, and also the role of the legislature and government of Quebec to "preserve and promote" this distinct identity. But with characteristic qualification, the amendments also stated, "Nothing in [the distinct-society] section derogates from the powers, rights or privileges of Parliament or the Government of Canada or of the legislatures or governments of the provinces, including any powers, rights or privileges relating to language." They also shielded existing constitutional provisions for aboriginal rights and for "the preservation and enhancement of the multicultural heritage of Canadians" from the effects of the distinct-society section.

The Institutions of Executive Federalism

Canada's governmental system has been characterized as one of "executive federalism" (Smiley 1987). The intersection of the Westminster parliamentary model with a federal division of jurisdiction has meant that power is centralized at each level of government but dispersed between levels.

Unlike most federations, the formal institutions of Canada's federal government do not provide mechanisms of regional influence irrespective of population. At the central level the 295-seat House of Commons is elected on a single-member district plurality basis. Representation in the Senate, whose members are appointed to "life" terms (retirement is compulsory at age seventy-five) by the governor general (effectively by the prime minister), is roughly regional: 30 members are appointed from the Atlantic provinces, 24 from Quebec, 24 from Ontario, 24 from the western provinces, and 1 from each of the northern territories, for a total of 104.[14] In practice, however, the Senate has provided a mechanism of patronage for the governing party, not a forum for the expression of regional interests. Senate approval is required for all legislation, but in practice the Senate lacks the legitimacy to withhold consent, although some senators have occasionally threatened to do so.[15] The Senate may delay approval, however, and this power took on considerable significance in the passage of free trade legislation in 1988 (Chapter 5). Amendments at the Senate stage (requiring repassage by the House) are rare, although the House has often taken account of the recommendations of Senate committees in the original passage of legislation. All provincial legislatures are unicameral.

Periodic calls for reform or abolition of the federal Senate have so far borne no fruit, although western provincial governments pressed the issue throughout the 1980s. In the "spirit" of the Meech Lake Accord, Prime Minister Brian Mulroney agreed in 1987 to draw senatorial appointees from lists submitted by provincial governments. To press its case for an elected Senate, the government of Alberta held a province-wide election (coincident with its municipal elections) in the fall of 1989 to elect its nominee for a vacant Senate slot.

Representation on the Supreme Court of Canada also reflects a balancing of regionalism and population weight. By federal statue, three of the nine members of the Supreme Court of Canada must be from Quebec, and the practice has been in addition to appoint three from Ontario, two from the west, and one from the Atlantic provinces.

The most important mechanism of "intrastate" federalism (that is, the representation of regional interests within the institutions of the central government) is one on which the constitution is silent: the federal cabinet. It has been argued that the framers of the Constitution Act of 1867 paid such little attention to formal mechanisms of intrastate federalism because they took for granted that the nucleus of power, the federal cabinet (nowhere explicitly mentioned in this written version of a British-style constitution), would be regionally representative (Mallory 1977: 18; Sabetti 1984: 15). Normal practice has been for the prime minister to select as regionally representative a cabinet as possible, given his caucus. (*In extremis*, prime ministers whose parties were electorally shut out of certain regions have drawn cabinet members from the Senate, or have even appointed individuals to the Senate so that they might serve in cabinet.)

The absence of effective formal mechanisms for the representation of regions qua regions (or provinces qua provinces) at the central level has had a number of effects, all of which have tended to further centralize power in the political executive at both levels of government. At the central level the fact that the cabinet bears "the main burden of territorial legitimation" of national institutions (Sutherland and Doern 1985: 26–27) tends to strengthen its authority at the same time as it complicates the process of cabinet building. Furthermore, the lack of a legislative forum comprising representatives of provincial governments (on the model of, for instance, the German Bundesrat) or a directly elected second chamber based on regional representation (on the model of the U.S. Senate) has by default elevated the importance of meetings of first ministers (the federal prime minister and provincial premiers) as the major forum for the resolution of national-regional issues. The elaboration of these coordinating mechanisms of intergovernmental relations (comprising not only first ministers' conferences, but conferences of finance ministers, health ministers, and so forth, together with their supporting secretariats) is a predominant feature of Canadian policy and politics. It is one with limited constitutional grounding, however,[16] and with only tenuous lines of accountability to the electorate.

The legitimacy of such closed executive processes was considerably eroded in the late 1980s, particularly in the constitutional arena (Chapter 2). The Meech Lake Accord fell squarely within the traditions of Canadian constitutional politics: Its phrasing was a masterpiece of careful ambiguity, and it was drawn up through a closed process of negotiation between federal and provincial political executives. In presenting these proposals to their respective legislatures for ratification, the first ministers announced that they would accept no changes other than those necessary to correct "egregious errors" in drafting.

It may be that concepts of the Canadian political community are indeed matters of such ambivalence and dispute that only such focused executive action can bring about constitutional change. The process leading up to the 1982 constitutional reforms had been, until the eleventh hour, characterized by closed interexecutive negotiations. But the subsequent history of the Meech Lake Accord suggests that such action is increasingly contentious. Immediately upon the conclusion of the accord, opponents began to mobilize to protest the Meech Lake process as well as the content of the agreement. The federal government's strategic response to this opposition, which was to exploit the tradition of executive federalism even while criticizing it, further depreciated the value of that tradition.

Federal and Provincial Bureaucracies

The operation of executive federalism in Canada has been influenced not only by general centralist and decentralist tendencies, but by changes in the organization of federal and provincial bureaucracies. As was the case in most other western industrial nations, governmental bureaucracies grew more rapidly at the subnational than at the national level in the postwar period. Total civilian government employment (excluding those working on a contractual basis) at the federal level rose from 336,478 to 493,684 between 1960 and 1982, but in proportional terms this change represented a *decrease* from 5.2 percent to 4.2 percent of the labour force. Total provincial government employment rose from 225,565 to 568,562 during the same period, or from 3.5 percent to 4.8 percent of the labour force (Sutherland and Doern 1985: 93, 96, 116–17). If one takes into account employees of local governments, as well as employees in the education and hospital sectors (which are largely funded through the public treasury), total civilian government employment stood at 2,105,124, or 17.9 percent of the Canadian labour force in 1982 (ibid.: 134–35). In these terms, as in many others, Canada stands between the United States, where public-sector employment (excluding defence) accounted for about 15 percent of the labour force in the early 1980s, and Britain, where the comparable figure was about 25 percent (Rose 1989: 61).

More important than these quantitative trends, however, were changes in organization. The organization of Canadian bureaucracies shows the imprint of the British heritage and the influence of the North American environment. These factors are evident in what has been described as the tension between "departmentalized" and "institutionalized" models of cabinet government in Canada (Dupré 1988). Canada inherited an essentially "departmentalized" bureaucratic model from Britain. This model persisted until the 1970s: Policy was developed and administered largely within line departments, and the groundwork of federal-provincial negotiations was laid in discussions between program specialists within corresponding departments at federal and provincial levels. In the late 1960s the increased scope and complexity of government programs led, in Canada as in most other western industrial nations, to increased pressures for the central coordination of policies. In the United States these pressures have led to the strengthening of staff units advisory to the president as chief executive; in Britain they led to brief experimentation with mega-departments and policy review units in the cabinet secretariat, but more significantly they led to even greater influence for the major horizontal department, the Treasury.

In Canada pressures for policy coordination led to the development and strengthening of both staff units and horizontal departments. Under the style of "rational management" that characterized the governments of Pierre Trudeau, the Privy Council Office (the cabinet staff agency) was expanded and reorganized to serve a network of cabinet committees.

Horizontal departments proliferated: The Treasury Board had been split off from the Department of Finance in 1965 and made responsible for budgetary and much personnel policy; and under Trudeau a number of "ministries of state" were created, with responsibility for policy coordination but not for program delivery. In the early 1980s the Ministry of State for Economic and Regional Development and the Ministry of State for Social Development, each headed by a senior cabinet minister, were responsible not only for policy coordination but for administering the allocation of budgetary "envelopes." The hegemony of the traditional horizontal department, the Department of Finance, was hence compromised. By 1982 the budgets and staffs of coordinating machinery within the Canadian federal government (the "central agencies") were proportionately much greater than those that existed in either Britain or the United States (Campbell 1983: 18–20). Such was the "institutionalized" cabinet.

Similar pressures for policy coordination were being felt at the provincial level. And given the necessity of federal-provincial negotiation in virtually all policy areas, the development of coordinative machinery at one level of government catalyzed and was in turn reinforced by the development of corresponding machinery at the other. Management boards and policy secretariats became the order of the day.

These developments had important implications for the processes of executive federalism. Until the 1960s these processes were characterized by policy networks based on "trust relationships" between federal and provincial program officials in line departments who "share[d] common values and [spoke] a similar vocabulary as a result of common training in a particular profession or discipline" (Dupré 1988: 236) and between officials in federal and provincial finance departments with shared expertise in fiscal relations. These networks were quasi-formalized in an elaborate structure of federal-provincial committees. The development of "institutionalized" cabinets introduced new players—the central agency bureaucrats—into these processes, and disrupted and attenuated the existing trust relationships. The central agency players included not only the secretariats and horizontal ministries devoted to the coordination of economic and social policies but also those with a specific mandate to manage federal-provincial relations. By the mid-1980s the federal government and all provinces except Nova Scotia had established either a horizontal ministry or a policy secretariat with a sole mandate for federal-provincial relations (Adie and Thomas 1987: 450–55).

The increasing centralization of decision making at each level of government meant that virtually all federal-provincial issues came to be seen in the light of their implications for the overall balance of federal and provincial power. And this in turn meant a change in the federal-provincial template that shaped the political activity of organized interests. The established relationships between line departments and their clientele groups were increasingly countervailed by "central agents"; and organized interests were increasingly required to take general federal-provincial concerns into account in their lobbying efforts.

In the last half of the 1980s the degree of cabinet centralization was somewhat tempered, both at the federal level and in provinces such as Saskatchewan and Ontario. Trudeau's successors as prime minister (briefly, the Liberal John Turner and then the Conservative Brian Mulroney) brought with them different styles of management and a desire to distance themselves from Trudeau's approach. Turner abruptly disbanded the ministries of state for economic and social policy; and under Mulroney and his finance minister, Michael Wilson, the Department of Finance regained much of its former power. An experiment with new horizontal ministries was also abandoned in Ontario. Cabinet secretariats, however, remain strong at the federal level and in most provinces. Indeed, the pressures that led to centralization have not abated; and, as Dupré notes, "in one form or another institutionalized cabinets are here to stay" (1988: 249).

The close involvement of bureaucrats in policymaking, in Canada as elsewhere, raises the issue of their "politicization." Canada has inherited the British tradition of a politically neutral civil service, in contrast to the American system of political appointments to the senior levels of the bureaucracy, or of the common movement of French or German bureaucrats into political roles. Canada does diverge somewhat from the British model: Bureaucrats at the most senior level, the deputy ministers, hold their appointments "at pleasure" and are not protected by civil service rules; and restrictions on the political activity of civil servants are not as tight as those in Britain and may be loosened further under the impact of the Canadian Charter of Rights and Freedoms, adopted in 1982. Canadian civil servants are not, however, generally politicized in a partisan sense. Deputy ministers are normally appointed from the career civil service, and although lateral entry into the senior ranks of the civil service is not uncommon, such appointments are not usually made on a partisan basis. There have been cases at the provincial level in which the replacement of one government by another of very different partisan stripe (notably, the replacement of NDP by non-NDP governments, or vice versa, in Saskatchewan) has led to the resignation of significant numbers of senior bureaucrats, but this is not the norm. The election of Prime Minister Brian Mulroney in September 1984 raised concerns within the civil service, given Mulroney's criticism during the election campaign of the "commingling that has gone on with the Liberal Party and the upper reaches of the civil service . . . the clique that has developed" (quoted in Zussman 1987: 256). This was, indeed, a concern often expressed by Conservatives, given the Liberals' long tenure in government at the federal level. In office, however, Mulroney drew the great majority of his senior appointees, including the critical position of clerk of the Privy Council (secretary to the cabinet), from within the civil service. He did, however, upgrade the salary and the bureaucratic profile of ministers' executive assistants,[17] who are exempt from civil service rules and are typically appointed on a partisan basis.

The Federal-Provincial Balance of Power

Canada's written constitution sets out a division of powers between the two levels of government. On its face the Constitution Act of 1867 provides for a fairly centralized federation. The provincial governments are granted a number of exclusive powers by enumeration—including responsibility for "property and civil rights" and for "hospitals, asylums, charities and eleemosynary institutions," the head of provincial authority over health and welfare programs. The federal government, however, in addition to its enumerated powers such as the regulation of trade and commerce, defence, and the criminal law, has authority to make laws for the "peace, order and good government" of Canada in all matters not exclusively assigned to the provinces. (The now atrophied federal power to disallow provincial legislation has been noted above.) The federal government also has unlimited taxing authority, whereas the provinces are limited to direct taxation.[18] In addition there are a number of areas of concurrent authority, such as agriculture, immigration, and (as just noted) direct taxation. Subsequent constitutional amendments have added to federal powers (over unemployment insurance, in 1940), to provincial powers (over natural resources, in 1982), and to concurrent powers (over old age and disability pensions, in 1951 and 1964).

In practice, the balance of power between the two levels of government has varied considerably over time, and it continues to be a matter of conflict and compromise. Most observers agree that the constitution allows for considerable latitude in the interpretation of the division of powers. In this context at least two opposing developments in the postwar period need to be noted. The first was the sheer administrative necessity of finding pragmatic solutions when the constitutional division of powers fit poorly with the nature of the policy challenges. In Canada these problems largely concern regional economic disparities, the imbalance between the relatively limited taxing powers and the extensive functional responsibilities of the provincial governments, and the emergence of issues (such as the regulation of telecommunications and broadcasting) unforeseen at the time of confederation in the mid-1800s. Dealing with such problems has required the negotiation of innumerable agreements regarding conditional and unconditional grants, equalization payments, shared-cost programs, jointly administered programs, and the like. These agreements are struck, as noted above, through networks of administrative and political intergovernmental committees and conferences, and there is considerable disagreement among both participants in and observers of this process as to whether it constitutes federal-provincial "diplomacy" among relatively sovereign units or bargaining within an administrative system.[19]

There is at least one sense in which the search for pragmatic solutions has tended to have a centralizing effect: It has legitimated the liberal use of the federal government's so-called spending power. The term refers to the federal government's ability to adopt programs of transfer payments—payments to provincial governments, institutions, and individuals—in areas of exclusive provincial jurisdiction. Although this power is nowhere mentioned in the written constitution, it has been recognized by both federal and provincial governments and affirmed in court decisions. One eminent constitutional authority has interpreted the power as follows: "The federal Parliament may spend or lend its funds to any government, or institution, or individual it chooses, for any purpose it chooses; and . . . it may attach to any grant or loan any condition it chooses, *including conditions it could not directly legislate*" (Hogg 1985: 126; emphasis added).

The use of the federal spending power is largely a postwar phenomenon. The major social programs adopted in the areas of postsecondary education, health, and welfare from the late 1940s through the 1960s would not have been possible without the liberal use of the federal spending power, given the disparity between provincial responsibilities in these areas and limited provincial revenue sources. The price of federal-provincial agreement on certain of these programs, however, was to provide that provinces might "opt out" of the programs without financial penalty. Only Quebec, which was most adamant in insisting upon this option, chose to exercise it (Chapter 2).

The second postwar development affecting the distribution of federal and provincial powers was what Cameron and Dupré (1983) have called "the provincialization of regionalism and dualism"—the tendency for provincial governments to assume the mantle of authority for the promotion of regional and, in the case of Quebec, French Canadian interests. The period of the 1960s and 1970s was, as we have seen, an era of growing "provincialization" of the political culture. It was also a period of "province-building" as provincial governments built up their institutional structures and administrative capacity.[20] The concomitant assertion of provincial jurisdiction brought the provinces into conflict with a federal Liberal administration of a decidedly centralist bent. Much of the period 1968 to 1984 (the years in which Prime Minister Pierre Trudeau headed a Liberal government in Ottawa, with the exception of a nine-month period in 1979–80 when the Progressive Conservatives were in office) was marked by an increasingly sour climate of federal-provincial relations. Nonetheless, constitutional reform was achieved in this period, and the resulting package contains a number of provisions that affect the balance of federal and provincial powers. Provisions of the Charter of Rights and Freedoms (to be discussed in the following section) constrain the discretion of provincial as well as federal governments and establish a set of national standards for legislative action. The provinces, however, gained significant authority over natural resources (Chapter 6).

An ethos of decentralization was much clearer in the ill-fated Meech Lake Accord. There were a number of reasons for this decentralist thrust, including a general desire to "bring Quebec in" to the constitutional fold and a PC federal administration elected in 1984 that was much more sympathetic to provincial demands than its Liberal predecessor had been. The result would have been to concede to all of the provinces virtually all of Quebec's "minimum demands" (with the exception of distinct-society status).

In summary, recent constitutional revisions (and proposed revisions) have marked a new era in Canadian politics. The desire for patriation and the necessity of recognizing the demands of Quebec leaders (both PQ and Liberal) for a restructuring of the federation forced changes in the written constitution and threatened the ambiguities and the unwritten understandings that have been important mechanisms for dealing with ambivalence about the Canadian political community. The resulting written documents are still, to be sure, ambiguous—rife with equivocation and qualifying sections. But the price of equivocation has been a concomitant increase in the significance of the courts as constitutional interpreters. And Canadians are only beginning to recognize the fundamental implications of this change—a change that arguably moves Canada considerably closer to the American pole of its European-American axis.

The Courts, the Charter, and the Federal-Provincial Balance

As Peter Russell has noted, written constitutional provisions regarding the judiciary in Canada are "rather scant": "Actually it is not surprising that the authors of Canada's Constitution had so little to say about the judicial power. Unlike the revolutionary constitutions of the United States and France, the Canadian Constitution did not purport to be a comprehensive plan for a new and ideal system of government. . . . The principal objective of the confederation project was to combine the legacy of British institutions with a federal system of government. Thus the judicial branch did not have to be created in 1867; its main components already existed" (1987: 47). The main components of Canada's legal and judicial system are based on British common law, despite the fact that a French civil-law system was preserved in Quebec after the British conquest through the Quebec Act of 1774 and in the 1867 constitution.[21] The French civil-law tradition in Quebec has been heavily "anglicized" through both state and societal influences. Foremost among the influences of the state upon the anglicization of Quebec civil law is the fact that the highest appeal courts in Canada since confederation have been composed entirely or primarily of judges trained in the British common-law tradition of respect for precedent rather than codification.

Until 1949 appeals from decisions of Canadian courts ultimately lay to the Judicial Committee of the British Privy Council (JCPC). In 1949 appeals to the JCPC were abolished, and the Supreme Court of Canada emerged from what Russell (1987: 335) has called its "long adolescence" to become the highest appeal court in Canada. According to the federal legislation establishing the Supreme Court, three of its nine members must be from the bar of Quebec, and in appeals involving Quebec civil law these Quebec judges have usually exercised the dominant influence (ibid: 36).

The courts of the Canadian system (including, until 1949, the JCPC), though historically more deferential to legislative authority than those of the United States, have nonetheless had a significant effect on the constitutional interpretation of federalism, of rights, and of the intersection between federalism and rights in Canada. And in so doing, they have shaped policy processes.

The Courts and the Federal System   Since 1950, the courts have been increasingly active arbiters of the Canadian federal system. Prior decisions by the JCPC had had a decentralizing thrust, but decisions of the Supreme Court as ultimate arbiter have shown an "uncanny" balance (Russell 1985: 162) in interpreting federal and provincial powers (see also L'Écuyer 1978). The Court has generally avoided expansive interpretations of either federal or provincial heads of power. Regarding policy over economic management, for example, the Court upheld federal wage and price control legislation under the general federal power to ensure "peace, order and good government" without establishing an expansive definition of that clause. Provincial powers over natural resources were interpreted as extending to certain policy instruments but not to others (Chapter 6).

The increasing activity of the courts in the arena of federal-provincial relations could be seen as a shift in mechanisms of conflict resolution, from informal to formal and from accommodative to adversarial types. This perception would be only partly accurate. In the federal-provincial arena, litigation is only one of the tools that governments use in their interactions, and constitutional capacity only one of their resources. The process of deploying these resources often involves complex trade-offs and strategic considerations. For example, as discussed in Chapter 6, the federal government's exclusive constitutional capacity to impose indirect taxes on nonrenewable resources, clarified by court interpretations in the mid-1970s, became an important "bargaining chip" for the federal government in subsequent negotiations over the revision and patriation of the constitution (Russell 1985).

Rights   With regard to contests involving rights, the impact of the courts on the policy process has been even greater than it has been with respect to those involving jurisdictional issues. Contests involving rights tend to be not between levels of government but between governments and members of various "rights-bearing" groups. During the postwar period in

Canada as elsewhere, such groups have become increasingly mobilized, and the judiciary more involved in adjudicating rights issues.

The watershed event in this respect in the Canadian context was the adoption of the Canadian Charter of Rights and Freedoms in 1982. The process of adopting the charter is discussed in chapter 2; here it is necessary only to summarize its provisions and its implications for the policy process. The charter entrenches "fundamental freedoms" (including religion, expression, and association), "democratic rights" (including certain voting rights), "legal rights" (notably, the right not to be deprived of "life, liberty and security of the person . . . except in accordance with the principles of fundamental justice"), and "equality rights" (notably, rights to "the equal protection and equal benefit of the law without discrimination, and in particular without discrimination based on race, national or ethnic origin, colour, religion, sex, age or mental or physical disability"). In addition, the charter entrenches "mobility" rights (essentially the rights of citizens to enter and leave Canada and to move freely across provincial borders to take up residence and work) and language rights (essentially guarantees of the use of English and French in governmental institutions, including educational institutions, as discussed more fully in Chapter 7).

The scope of the charter is, then, extensive—more extensive, for example, than the scope of the U.S. Bill of Rights. Furthermore, the potential scope of the remedies provided for infringements of rights is extraordinarily broad—whatever a court of competent jurisdiction considers to be "appropriate and just in the circumstances." But the rights granted therein are qualified in a number of ways. In the first place, there are a number of interpretation sections, which essentially throw to the courts the task of balancing charter rights against other considerations. For example, nothing in the charter is to derogate from treaty or other rights of aboriginal peoples, or from other existing rights in Canada; and the charter is to be interpreted "in a manner consistent with the preservation and enhancement of the multicultural heritage of Canada." Specific rights are also qualified: Equality rights may be infringed to allow for affirmative-action programs, and mobility rights may be curtailed in provinces experiencing unemployment rates higher than the national average.

Rights are also qualified in a general sense by section 1 of the charter, which provides that charter rights are subject to "such reasonable limits prescribed by law as can be demonstrably justified in a free and democratic society." And they may also be abrogated entirely, by legislatures that choose to exercise their option under section 33 of the charter to declare, for renewable periods of five years, that legislative provisions shall prevail "notwithstanding" the charter. (Democratic, linguistic, and mobility rights may not be so overridden.) Sections 1 and 33 constitute a uniquely Canadian compromise between the principle of parliamentary supremacy and the constitutional entrenchment of rights.

The temperate language of the charter has been the subject of controversy among Canadian legal scholars. McWhinney, for example, invidiously contrasts the language of the Canadian charter with the more dramatic exhortatory tone of the U.S. Bill of Rights and the French Declaration of the Rights of Man. He also criticizes the charter's use of "weasel-words" in attempting to "reconcile the politically irreconcilable according to Preuss' celebrated strategy in the drafting of the Constitution of the Weimar Republic: when faced . . . with two mutually opposing philosophical or ideological principles, put them both in your constitutional text and leave it to history to resolve the antithesis" (McWhinney 1983: 62–63). Russell, however, argues that the tendency to qualify rights is characteristic of a number of "modern" bills of rights, such as the European Convention of Human Rights and the International Convention of Civil and Political Rights (both of which served as models for the Canadian charter). He sees the explicit qualification of rights in these documents as reflecting "the greater sophistication of peoples who have learned through historical experience that no rights and freedoms are so 'fundamental' that they can be enjoyed in an absolute sense. We may well be past that point in history where popular belief in the merits of a regime can be sustained or fortified by grandiloquent constitutional language" (Russell 1983: 38).

Indeed, the significance of the charter was not so much to establish rights as it was to change the policy process for dealing with rights claims. The charter added another basis for securing rights to the variety of bases that existed prior to 1982. Fundamentally, democratic and civil rights rested (and continue to rest) on the basis of the traditions of democracy and the rule of law, which constitute the parameters of the Canadian political system (Cheffins and Johnson 1986: 132; Russell 1983: 45–46). Some legal scholarship and a number judicial *obiter dicta* have pushed this understanding of the democratic tradition to recognize an "implied bill of rights" established in Canada through the constitutional provision that Canada's constitution was to be "similar in principle to that of the

United Kingdom." This theory has never been accepted as a basis for court decisions, but it has been used through allusion to bolster decisions made on other grounds (Cheffins and Johnson 1986: 133).

Civil liberties and "equality rights" have also been afforded protection in statutory bills of rights and human rights codes (the latter usually administered not by courts but by administrative commissions). Bills of rights were adopted at the federal level [22] and by the provinces of Saskatchewan, Alberta, and Quebec; human rights codes have been adopted by the federal government and all provinces. As ordinary legislation, these instruments are formally much easier to change than is the Canadian charter; Quebec, for example, strengthened certain provisions of its Charter of Human Rights and Freedoms in 1983, as discussed in Chapter 7. Unlike the Canadian charter, which applies to both federal and provincial levels of government, the federal Bill of Rights applies only to the federal government, and the provincial bills of rights apply only within their respective jurisdictions.

The adoption of the Canadian charter, then, added another basis for resisting potential governmental assaults on democratic, civil, and equality rights to those that already existed. In addition, it created "mobility rights" and provided a basis for the extension of language rights beyond those already conferred by constitutional and ordinary federal and provincial legislation. It established a hierarchy of rights by distinguishing between rights that may be overridden and those that may not. And most significantly, it enhanced the role of the courts in balancing rights against other rights and against other considerations of social welfare. This enhanced role of the courts has a number of implications for the policy process. As Russell has pointed out, it promotes a more systematic review of public policies from a "rights" perspective. It provides another set of points of access to the decision-making system, and it means that the agenda of law reform can be influenced through judicial as well as executive and legislative channels (Russell 1983: 46–49). In so doing, as discussed in the next section, it may have a "nationalizing" effect on the policy process.

Federalism and Rights   Prior to the adoption of the charter, the Canadian constitution was concerned primarily with the institutional enterprise of wedding the Westminster model of parliamentary government to a federal system. Express limitations on governmental action were almost entirely jurisdictional, having to do with the intergovernmental division of powers. The charter added another constitutional perspective, a set of limitations on governmental actions based on citizens' rights. To a considerable extent, these two perspectives are in tension.

One of the most important reasons for the championing of the concept of a charter of rights by the federal Liberal government in the 1970s was its perceived "nationalizing" effect. It would, in this view, establish a set of national standards to which all governments would be held and provide a unifying national symbol (Russell 1983: 34–37). The charter is also likely to have a nationalizing effect on the policy process itself, by encouraging the mobilization of groups defined by "rights" rather than by region; by raising constitutional issues in which the principal protagonists are interest groups and not governments;[23] and by extending the mandate of a judicial system that culminates in a national institution, the Supreme Court (Russell 1983: 41; Swinton 1988). It is possible that the "reasonable limits" test under section 1 of the charter may allow for some judicial flexibility in enforcing rights across regions (Swinton 1988); and, of course, the legislative override provision also allows provinces to "opt out" of a national rights regime. In general, however, court decisions under the charter have had a greater impact on provincial than on federal legislation: provincial legislation nullified as a result of charter challenges has been of more recent vintage and of more substantive content than the federal legislation struck down under the charter (Morton et al. 1989).

The resistance of some provincial governments to the charter also drew upon the ongoing tension between individualistic and collective conceptions of rights. In insisting upon the legislative override, western premiers argued that judicial arbitrage of individual rights claims would undermine not only the principle of parliamentary supremacy but also a "sense of community" and the ability of governments to adapt social policy to "community values" (Vipond 1991).

Much of the controversy over the Meech Lake Accord reflected similar tensions, although in that case the focus was entirely on Quebec. The distinct-society clause of the accord would have required that the charter (and the rest of the constitution) be interpreted "in a manner consistent with the recognition that Quebec constitutes within Canada a distinct society." Fears were raised, by women's groups and others, that this clause would allow Quebec to infringe charter rights in the interest of preserving its "distinctiveness." Others argued that the preservation of distinctiveness could be used to justify only such limits as would be judged "reasonable" under section 1 of the charter—that "Quebec's limitations on rights must be demonstrably justified in a free and democratic society, albeit one that is distinct culturally and linguistically" (Swinton 1988: 286). In contemplating some differential treatment of rights in Quebec, the Meech Lake Accord would have further tempered the nationalizing and individualistic thrust of the charter.

The Organization of Interests

The effects of Canada's ambivalent institutions on policy outcomes have varied across policy arenas, depending upon the intersection of those institutions with the particular structure of organized interests in each arena. These effects are traced out in later chapters; what follows here is an introductory outline of the organization of the two major protagonists: business and labour.

There is a basic irony to the Canadian pattern of interest organization. Despite the pattern of elite accommodation that has prevailed in the state and to a considerable extent in state-society relations, "peak associations" of business and labour have not developed, at least at the national level: Business and labour are fragmented along national-international, regional, sectoral, and ideological lines. In this respect, a contrast with the Federal Republic of Germany is instructive. The German federation is marked, like its Canadian counterpart, by fiscal decentralization and administrative pragmatism. But the development of national policies in the German "decentralized state" (at least from what we know of West German experience) is facilitated by its "centralized society" (Katzenstein 1987). Cohesively organized business, finance, and labour interests, linked through networks of "parapublic institutions" and through structures of codetermination, provide a fabric of support for policy development (Katzenstein 1987: 58–76; Esser, Fach, and Dyson 1984).

In Canada such a fabric of support is lacking. The fragmentation of interests means, in general, that it is the federal-provincial template, often complicated by bureaucratic intricacies, that dominates policymaking. In the inevitable negotiations over the balance of federal and provincial power, interests seek to exert influence through one or other level of government (or both), depending on their strategic advantage.

Business

A number of cleavages cross-cut business interests in Canada: sector, size, export or domestic market orientation, foreign or domestic ownership. In 1985 the primary resource-extraction sector accounted for less than 7 percent of employment in Canada, the secondary manufacturing sector for less than 24 percent, and the tertiary service sector (including transportation) for almost 70 percent. Nonetheless, the primary sector remains of key importance: Not only is it directly linked to the more than 25 percent of employment in the secondary sector that is engaged in resource processing and fabrication, but it also continues to represent Canada's international comparative advantage. Canada is on balance an exporter of raw and semiprocessed goods, and an importer of manufactured end products. Crude and fabricated materials comprised 45 percent of Canada's exports, and 24 percent of imports in 1986 (Statistics Canada 1987). Canada has, however, improved its position in manufactured goods in the 1970s and 1980s, due in part to the Auto Pact agreement with the United States (Chapter 5). End products comprised 46.6 percent of Canadian exports in 1986, up from 35.6 percent in 1971 (Statistics Canada 1973, 1987).

Canadian industrial organization is markedly more concentrated than is the case in the United States, both in aggregate and by industry (Green 1980: 46ff.). There is no clear relationship between foreign ownership and concentration at the level of particular industries—that is, no evidence that foreign firms seek out concentrated industries or increase concentration levels once they enter (ibid.: 49–51). It is nonetheless true that a significant number of large firms are foreign owned, a phenomenon that has political as well as economic implications. The problems of achieving intersectoral agreement on industrial strategy are exacerbated by the fact that much ultimate decision making occurs offshore. Furthermore, governments seeking to maintain employment levels are more vulnerable to demands from large employers when those employers are perceived to be able to withdraw relatively easily to domiciles elsewhere.

As for financial institutions, Canada has, like the United States and Britain, enforced until recently a strict distinction between industrial and financial capital, through limitations on the ownership (including foreign ownership) and the investment powers of banks. The banking industry in Canada has been highly concentrated, as a matter of deliberate federal government policy in the granting of banking charters. In 1983, the year before substantial deregulation of financial institutions began in Canada, the "Big Five" chartered banks accounted for just under 80 percent of banking assets. Despite this concentration and largely because of their enforced distinction from industry, the banks have not provided a vehicle for intersectoral concertation as they have done, for example, in Germany—their role has been limited largely to the provision of short-term financing, and their orientation has been heavily toward the resource sectors (Chapter 5). The liberalization of financial regulations begun in the mid-1980s is eroding the barriers between the four traditional "pillars" of the financial community (banks, trust companies, investment dealers, and insurance companies) and is making the financial community as a whole much more permeable to foreign investment (Pauly 1988). The associational structure of the financial community has not immediately responded to these developments; as Coleman (1988: 174) notes, that structure "continues to mirror the long-standing four-pillar arrangements." Over the longer term, however, it is likely that the political organization of financial interests, and their relationship to organizations in the "real" (industrial and commercial) sector, will change in ways as yet unpredictable.

Despite these divisions, it is possible to identify a traditionally dominant coalition of business interests, and a newer insurgent minority coalition (Atkinson and Coleman 1989: 48–52). The dominant coalition comprises resource-staple industries and related processing industries (such as steel, petrochemicals, and pulp and paper), financial institutions primarily oriented to these sectors, and secondary manufacturing for the domestic market. As noted above, the resource and processing industries (except steel) have had relatively high levels of foreign ownership, and secondary manufacturing for the domestic market (especially in autos) has been heavily populated with branch plants of foreign firms. As we discuss further in Chapter 6, public policies in the first half of the twentieth century favoured the interests of this coalition: The development of a transportation infrastructure favoured the extraction and export of resources, and the maintenance of tariffs provided a protective barrier not only for domestically owned and oriented firms but also for those foreign firms that had leapt the tariff wall to establish branch plants with access to the Canadian market.

Challenging this dominant coalition is an insurgent set of interests that Atkinson and Coleman have termed the "nationalist" coalition. It comprises firms that are heavily dependent upon state support: Canadian-owned firms oriented to export markets, for whom government procurement provides a secure base from which to pursue those markets; cultural industries; and new French Canadian firms that were fostered by the Quebec government as part of the "quiet revolution."

These two coalitions are imperfectly reflected in the political organization of business interests. Each of the two major brokerage parties, the Liberals and the PCs, has appealed over time to the dominant coalition. The nationalist coalition has found support within a wing of the Liberal party and to some extent within the NDP. No "peak association" (that is, no encompassing federation of business groups) can claim to speak for business at the national level; rather, a plethora of sectoral and intersectoral associations exist.

The closest structural approximation of a peak association is the Canadian Chamber of Commerce (CCC), whose complex structure comprises local chambers and boards of trade (which are also affiliated with independent provincial chambers) as well as trade association affiliates and individual corporation members. The decentralized structure of the CCC reflects its greater orientation to (and success rate at) local and provincial government levels.

The CCC, however, in no sense possesses a representational monopoly; other national business associations represent different crosssections of business interests. The Canadian Manufacturers Association (CMA) draws its membership of some 3,800 firms broadly from across manufacturing sectors. It maintains a staff of about one hundred, 70 percent of which is located in its head office in Toronto. Its structure is federal, with seven regional divisions, although its membership is heavily concentrated in Ontario (61.8 percent) and Quebec (18.1 percent) (Coleman 1988: 195–96). It is consulted by governments often, but on an ad hoc basis and largely by default—there being no other manufacturing group with as wide a range of membership. Its function is more one of external advocacy than of ongoing participation in the policy process; and, like the Chamber of Commerce, its policy influence is largely achieved in serving as a conduit for the specialized technical input of particular member firms on relevant issues, and not in forging a policy consensus across fragmented business interests (Coleman and Jacek 1983).

Arguably the most powerful business association at the national level is the Business Council on National Issues (BCNI), founded in 1976 and representing primarily the interests of large businesses in the dominant resource-financial-domestic manufacturing coalition discussed above. Its membership comprises chief executive officers of 150 large corporations, plus the chairs of the CCC, the CMA, and the Conseil du patronat du Québec (discussed below) as associate members. But the BCNI, with a policy staff of about ten, must also fall back on the resources of its member firms on most policy issues (Coleman 1988: 86). It is less reactive and more anticipatory in its approach than are the CCC and the CMA, and it operates through a task-force structure to forge carefully articulated and supported consensus positions.

The interests of small business are represented by a number of associations, most notably by the Canadian Federation of Independent Business (CFIB). The CFIB was founded in 1970 and by the mid-1980s represented some 70,000 small firms through direct membership. It makes considerable use of polling in determining its members' views on a variety of policy issues, which it communicates to government.

In addition to these intersectoral national associations, independent intersectoral business organizations exist in two provinces: Quebec and British Columbia. In both cases the development of these associations was prompted by a particularly adversarial climate of labour relations in the late 1960s (Coleman 1988: 92–95). The Conseil du patronat du Québec (CPQ) comprises associational as well as individual firm members. Associational members include the Quebec division of the CMA, the Montreal Board of Trade, and a small-business organization, the Centre des dirigeants d'entreprise (CDE). The Quebec and Montreal Chambers of Commerce are not members but meet informally with the CPQ in strategy sessions. The ability of the CPQ to maintain formal and informal coalitions with other business organizations, however, has varied over time, especially as different partisan factions are advantaged by changes in the partisan complexion of the provincial government.

The other independent intersectoral provincial association, the Business Council (formerly the Employers' Council) of British Columbia, bases its membership on firms (primarily larger firms), not associations, and plays a significant role in forging and articulating a policy consensus among its members. In other provinces the major intersectoral business associations are the provincial chambers of commerce. Although the provincial chambers are generally more influential vis-à-vis provincial governments than is the Canadian Chamber at the federal level (Van Loon and Whittington 1976: 296), they do not approximate the strength of the CPQ and the British Columbia Business Council.

By far the largest proportion of business organizations is composed of sectoral associations, some of which (like the Canadian Chemical Producers' Association) are organized at the national level with direct membership by firms, whereas others (like the Canadian Construction Association) are more or less loose federations organized primarily at the provincial level, and still others (like the Council of Forest Industries of British Columbia) are specific to the provincial level. The resources, strategies, and policy stances of these numerous sectoral organizations vary widely, depending on industry structure, organizational culture, and the distribution of governmental authority in the relevant policy arenas.

Labour

Labour in Canada is also fragmented, in this case along unionized-non-unionized, national-international, and sectoral lines. In 1985, 37 percent of wage and salary earners in Canada were unionized, as compared, for example, with 51 percent in Britain and 18 percent in the United States (Kumar, Coates, and Arrowsmith 1987: 364).

These proportions, however, vary considerably across industries and regions. Quebec and British Columbia, for example, provinces in which the formal organization of business interests is strongest, also have relatively high levels of unionization. (In 1984 about 43 percent of employed paid workers in Quebec and British Columbia were union members.) Also of note is the high degree of unionization in the public sector. (Two-thirds of employees classified in "public administration" are union members.) Employees in public administration account for about 15 percent of union membership in Canada (indeed, this figure rises to 45 percent if teachers and health workers are included). Of the membership of the thirty largest unions, 33 percent is in public-sector unions and another 11 percent in unions of teachers and nurses. In comparison, in Britain, where divisions over strategy between public- and private-sector unions have contributed to the fragmentation of the labour movement (Gourevitch et al. 1984: 60), public-sector unions comprise 19 percent of the membership of the twenty-one principal unions affiliated with the Trades Union Congress (and 24 percent if teachers and health care workers are included).[24]

Another line of division is between national and international unions. Membership in international (that is, U.S.-based) unions declined from 70 to 39 percent of total union membership between 1951 and 1986, while membership in national unions rose from 20 percent to 57 percent (Kumar, Coates, and Arrowsmith 1987: 363). In part, the increase in the national union share reflects the growth of public-sector unions since the 1960s, but it also reflects the breakaway of some unions from their U.S. parents—most notably, the split of the Canadian Auto Workers (CAW)

from the United Auto Workers (UAW) and the split of the International
Woodworkers of America into Canadian and U.S. unions in 1986.
Membership has become, over time, somewhat more concentrated in
large unions. The ten largest unions comprised 33 percent of the total
membership in 1951, and more than 40 percent in 1985 (Kumar, Coates,
and Arrowsmith 1986: 301). Unions with more than 30,000 members
comprised 21 percent of union membership in 1951 and 66 percent in
1985 (ibid.: 296). But the organizational structure remains relatively
fragmented and decentralized: "The 'movement' consists of 74 international unions, 146 national unions, 366 directly chartered local unions
of central federations, and 240 independent local organizations. The 220
international and national unions charter nearly 14,000 self-governing
'locals,' the basic organizational unit of trade union organization and the
legal entity for purposes of collective bargaining. Membership of locals
varies from under 10 to more than 25,000. In 1981, . . . while over one-
half of the locals had fewer than 100 members, only one-half of one per
cent had a membership of 5000 and more; the average size of a local was
235" (ibid.: 97–98). The major national federation, the Canadian Labour
Congress (CLC), has represented a declining proportion of the total membership over time and by 1985 comprised less than 60 percent. Forty-five
international unions (most of which are also affiliated with the AFL/CIO
in the United States), twenty-six national unions, and seventy-four directly chartered locals are affiliated with the CLC. National unions have
accounted for an increasing proportion of CLC membership over time
and in 1986 represented more than 60 percent. The organizational structure of the CLC itself is decentralized. Its affiliated unions and directly
chartered locals pay dues to the CLC and are entitled to representation at
the biennial CLC convention, according to the size of their membership.
The CLC also charters provincial federations of labour, whose membership comprises the locals of CLC-affiliated unions located in each
province, and whose financial support is in the form of dues from those
locals, again on the basis of the size of their membership. Some locals
of CLC-affiliated unions, however, choose not to affiliate with provincial
federations.
    In the second rank in terms of size are two other national federations.
The Confederation of National Trade Unions (CNTU), with 6 percent
of total Canadian membership, is based in Quebec. It has a somewhat
more centralized structure than does the CLC, but CNTU affiliates have

**TABLE 1-1   Union Membership by Affiliation in Canada, 1956–1986
(percentage distribution)**

Affiliation*	1956	1961	1971	1981	1986
CLC	76.2	74.0	74.8	68.0	58.0
CLC only	15.0	13.6	22.9	31.0	34.8
AFL–CIO/CLC	61.3	60.4	51.9	37.0	23.2
AFL-CIO only	0.1	2.4	**	0.1	3.6
CNTU	7.5	6.8	9.6	7.3	5.9
Unaffiliated internationals	9.3	8.1	4.6	2.9	2.8
Unaffiliated nationals	6.1	5.1	8.5	18.4	16.6
Independent local organizations	0.9	3.6	2.5	2.5	3.1
CCU				0.9	1.0
CSD				1.9	1.0
CFL					5.6
CEQ					2.4
Total	100.0	100.0	100.0	100.0	100.0

Source: Kumar, Coates, and Arrowsmith 1987:369.
*For full names of organizations, see text.
**Less than 1.0 percent.

on occasion pursued political strategies in contradiction to the policies of the CNTU central. The Canadian Federation of Labour is primarily composed of ten of the thirteen international unions in the building trades that split from the CLC in 1982; it represents about 6 percent of total Canadian union membership. (The other three construction unions remained affiliated with the AFL/CIO only.) Smaller federations include two in Quebec—the Confédération des syndicats démocratiques (CSD), a group composed primarily of textile unions that split from the CNTU in 1972, and a teacher's federation, the Centrale de l'enseignment du Québec (CEQ)—and the Confederation of Canadian Unions (CCU), an avowedly nationalist central founded in 1968. Unaffiliated unions, such as the Teamsters and unions of teachers and nurses, account for about 20 percent of total membership. Membership figures are summarized in Table 1-1.

Given the large number of unions and federations and their organizational decentralization, Canada ranks relatively low among OECD nations on measures of the "organizational unity" of the labour movement—similar to the United States and Britain, but well below the levels of Germany, Scandinavia, and Austria (Cameron 1984: 164–65). Furthermore, Canada has one of the most decentralized systems of collective bargaining among western industrialized nations (Chapter 4).

Although there are some region- and sector-specific exceptions, single union–single plant bargaining is the rule. As Banting has noted, this places the "real economic power" in the hands of union locals and severely limits the ability of the CLC executive, or even the executives of affiliated unions, to commit locals to "movement-wide courses of action" (1986: 20).

To focus on the fragmentation of labour's economic power at the national level is, however, to miss some measure of its political power. Responsibility for labour policy (industrial relations, employment standards, occupational health and safety) rests constitutionally with the provinces in Canada (Chapter 4). The political organization of labour has therefore evolved most strongly at the provincial level—and the provincial federations play a substantially stronger role in their respective provincial policy arenas than does the CLC at the national level. The strength of provincial federations varies considerably, however, depending upon such factors as the extent of unionization of the provincial labour force, the comprehensiveness of the provincial federation, and the partisan complexion of provincial governments.

The effect of partisan control of government upon labour power deserves some brief comment in this context. (We return to the issue in Chapter 4.) The CLC is formally affiliated with the New Democratic Party, both at the federal and at the provincial levels (except in Quebec, where the CLC-chartered Quebec Federation of Labour has refused to endorse the NDP because of the latter's federalist position and has instead allied itself informally with the social democratic and Quebec nationalist Parti québécois). This alliance with social democratic parties has reinforced the fact that labour has tended to be stronger at the provincial than at the national level. The power of social democratic parties, either in office or in opposition, in key provinces has been an important factor in the survival and the political significance of organized labour—and labour, in turn, has contributed to the provincial strength of these parties.

Conclusions

Of Canada's ambivalent institutions, the most significant is its particular version of federalism. The existence of federal and provincial governments creates institutional niches for different views about the appropriate melding of state and market, individual and community, and region and country—depending upon the political complexion of incumbent governments and the particular state traditions and political cultures

of the various provinces. The fact that the division of federal and provincial jurisdiction is never *settled* means that these competing views are
always in play and are addressed anew with new policy issues.

The positive implications of the Canadian policymaking context are
not negligible. The ongoing search for balance generates a moderation
and civility, a lack of dogmatism that is a matter both of self-deprecation
and of pride for Canadians. Furthermore, in a situation in which different
regions may be characterized by quite different configurations of interest and political cultures, and in which the distribution of power across
regions is ambiguous, there has been considerable experimentation with
and diffusion of policy options. This capacity to innovate and to diffuse
is well suited to the development of responses to complex and changing
policy issues.

But there are negative dimensions to the Canadian policy context as
well. The failure to resolve fundamental anglophone-francophone tensions postponed and attenuated the process of constitutional development
in Canada—much political energy and capital in the economically critical period of the 1970s and 1980s was devoted to constitutional issues
that might have been long since resolved. Attempts to resolve these
issues through written constitutional amendments (however ambiguously
phrased) and consequent litigation ran against the grain of the pattern of
informal accommodations that have characterized Canadian policy and
politics in the past. In the key arena of constitutional politics, that traditional pattern appears to be losing a good deal of its legitimacy. In other
arenas as well, there are indications that traditional patterns of elite accommodation are under pressure. The Canadian political system is faced
with the challenge of developing new mechanisms of state-society relations that will represent a wider range of interests while still coping with
fundamental ambivalence toward the state and the political community.

In the following chapters it is shown that the balance of positive and
negative implications of the Canadian policy context varies considerably across policy arenas. In each of these arenas, Canadian ambivalence
about the state and the political community is manifested somewhat differently. And in each case the structure of interests has tended either to
frustrate or to facilitate the ability of Canada's ambivalent institutions to
resolve conflict and to respond to policy challenges. Chapter 2 deals with
constitutional politics, the arena in which the fundamental ambivalences
about the political community, and about individual and collective rights,
are most starkly apparent. Although some constitutional issues have been

dealt with through ingenious Canadian compromises, the presence of francophones as a minority within Canada but a majority within Quebec has placed strains on the federation that have never, despite periodic obsessive episodes of constitutional debate, been resolved.

Chapter 3, on the other hand, deals with an arena—health care—in which institutionalized ambivalence has allowed Canada to respond successfully to policy challenges. "Red toryism," prodded by social democracy, has provided the ideological foundation for a system of "private practice and public payment" for medical and hospital services—a system that provides universal and comprehensive coverage while keeping health costs as a proportion of GDP at relatively moderate levels. The key to success in this arena has been the possibility of provincial-level accommodations between health care providers and the state within a national framework.

Chapter 4, dealing with labour relations, also indicates the importance of provincial-level accommodations. Organized labour has attempted, with considerable internal conflict, to reconcile the preservation of adversarial collective bargaining at the workplace level with experimental participation in collaborative mechanisms of policymaking at the sectoral, provincial, and federal levels, and to reconcile suspicion of the state with the necessity of relying on the state. The extraordinary decentralization of legislative authority over labour relations to the provincial level in Canada has allowed for considerable experimentation along these lines. Because social democratic parties have had important influence in key provincial jurisdictions, this decentralization has resulted in the development and preservation of labour relations regimes that have allowed organized labour to maintain its membership base. This "survival" of organized labour, which stands in contrast to the precipitous decline in union membership in the United States, has led to increased pressure for institutional change to better accommodate labour interests.

Chapters 5 and 6, dealing with economic adjustment and oil and gas policy, demonstrate the difficulties of dealing with national issues pitting regions against each other, for which provincial-level accommodations are not possible. The question of the role of the state has been immensely complicated by tensions between national and regional development objectives. These tensions have never been reconciled but have led to piecemeal and sometimes contradictory policies. In the case of oil and gas policy, the atmosphere of crisis of the early 1980s led to one of the few examples of an unequivocal option by a Canadian federal government to favour one side in an interregional and ideological dispute—the unabashedly statist and nationalist National Energy Program. The NEP failed in both political and technical terms: It did not resolve conflict, nor, because of unforeseen developments in the international market, did it establish a feasible oil and gas pricing regime. Later interregional accommodations were possible once the oil price crisis abated, but the likelihood of conflict in another such crisis remained.

Finally, Chapter 7 brings us full circle to deal with a fundamental constitutional debate—the greatest interregional dispute and the single most intractable issue in Canadian politics: the rights of linguistic minorities. Canadians have never resolved the issue of whether francophone minorities outside Quebec and the anglophone minority inside Quebec are to be treated in parallel fashion, or whether Quebec, with its inversion of the majority-minority relationship that prevails elsewhere, constitutes a special case. The possibility of provincial-level accommodations, which works to resolve conflict and generate policy options in other areas, is itself at issue in this arena: The legitimacy of cross-provincial differences in the treatment of linguistic minorities is exactly what is being contested.

Notes

1. This proportion somewhat overstates the fiscal capacity of the federal level in the Federal Republic of Germany, since it includes social security contributions to funds administered by social insurance funds under federal legislation.

2. The 1961 figure is calculated from Statistics Canada 1986a table II, and Dominion Bureau of Statistics 1967, table 2.2. The 1986 figure is from OECD 1988.

3. Calculated from OECD 1988 and Statistics Canada 1988, tables 1 and 2.

4. It should be noted that the proportion of capital *controlled* in the United States shows a somewhat different pattern across industries. In general, U.S. investors have been more likely to hold controlling interest in resource industries than in other sectors, and less likely to hold controlling interest in railways and other utilities. Measured as proportions of capital employed, then, American control has been greater than

American ownership in resource industries, while the degree of control and ownership has been roughly the same in manufacturing, and the degree of ownership has been less than the degree of control in railways and other utilities.

5. Some Canadian political scientists, e.g., Russell (1987: 33), would argue that liberal values are increasing in significance.

6. "Left and right" were identified by respondents largely with reference to concepts of socialism, communism, conservatism, and free enterprise. Direct references to the role of government or the welfare state were much less common. Laponce (1978: 148–49) also found that the degree of ambivalence of party supporters toward their preferred party differed considerably across parties, but he did not report *which* parties were most likely to elicit such ambivalent support.

7. The fact that Canadians attach "un-American" labels to these ideological strains should not blind us to the existence of similar belief systems (albeit not as strong in the overall mix) in the United States as well. David Elkins (1985: 73), for example, has described similarities between Canadian political subcultures and the "individualistic," "moralistic," and "traditionalistic" subcultures identified by Daniel Elazar (1972) in the United States.

8. Over time, according to various Gallup surveys, *québécois* have been least likely of all regional populations to favour an increase in private control of the economy, least likely to favour "privatization" initiatives, and least likely to fear the threat of "big government." Gallup has periodically asked Canadians, "Speaking of our future, which do you think will be the greatest threat to Canada in the years to come—big business, big labour or big government?" In 1985, for example, when a 47 percent plurality of the national sample cited "big government," only a 29 percent minority of the Quebec sample did so (Canadian Institute of Public Opinion, January 30, 1986).

9. Comparable figures for 1957 were 51 and 122 percent, respectively. Differences in personal income have been further narrowed by the growth of social security programs, notably unemployment insurance. Average personal income after tax and transfers was 80 percent of the Canadian average in Newfoundland in 1986, compared with 111 percent in Ontario (Lithwick 1986: 146; Statistics Canada, 1986b: table VI).

10. The 1957 election brought a minority Conservative government to power. The election that soon followed in 1958 was won in a landslide by the Conservatives, riding a wave of popular dissatisfaction with the Lib-

erals, who were deemed to have become arrogant and patronage-ridden after an extended period in office.

11. In part, as we shall see, this is due to the lack of a mechanism of "intrastate federalism" at the national level, such as the German Bundesrat, in which provincial party members per se are present.

12. In Canada, as elsewhere, the ability of the political left to garner agrarian support has been a crucial determinant of its success or failure. And this ability has varied significantly across regions. In Saskatchewan the experience of the Depression catalyzed the emergence of a democratic socialist party, the Cooperative Commonwealth Federation (CCF), from the cooperative movement (Lipset 1968). In the 1960s a Canadian "red-green" coalition brought the CCF together with organized labour (especially in Ontario) to form the New Democratic Party. In Alberta, however, agrarian protest merged with regional resentment of the financial power of eastern interests to produce a populist revolt, in the form of Social Credit, not against capitalism but against eastern "colonialism" (Macpherson 1953).

13. Indeed, these constitutional provisions for New Brunswick go well beyond the earlier provisions for Quebec and the prairie provinces.

14. See note 15.

15. In the late 1980s there was considerable conflict between the Liberal-dominated Senate and the House of Commons under a majority Conservative government. The Senate delayed passage of a number of controversial pieces of legislation, including changes to the unemployment insurance program, tax-back provisions for universal benefits such as old age security pensions and family allowances, and, most significantly, the institution of a goods and services tax (a form of value-added tax). This conflict came to a head in the fall of 1990, when Prime Minister Brian Mulroney, under a never-before-used section of the Constitution Act, 1867, added 8 additional senators to the Senate, bringing the number of members temporarily to 112 and giving the Conservatives sufficient strength to pass the legislation. The constitution further provides that the Senate is to return to its normal size of 104 members through attrition.

16. Only constitutional conferences of first ministers on a few specific and time-limited issues are explicitly mentioned in the Constitution Act, 1982; previously there was no constitutional mention of intergovernmental conferences.

17. These positions were termed "chief of staff" positions—a change

in English, but not in French. Executive assistants had been called *chefs du cabinet* in French during the Trudeau years (Zussman 1987: 266).

18. The distinction between direct and indirect taxation is not straightforward and has been the matter of considerable constitutional litigation. Furthermore, the assignment of tax powers in the natural resources arena was modified in 1982 (Chapter 6).

19. The "diplomacy" thesis is most clearly stated in Simeon 1972; the "bureaucratic politics" thesis, most clearly in Schultz 1980.

20. The concept of province building was first advanced by Black and Cairns (1966) and applied to the experience of the 1960s. It has since received wide acceptance among Canadian political scientists. Young, Faucher, and Blais (1984), however, remind us that the 1960s and 1970s were not the only period of rapid institutional development and activist public policy at the provincial level in Canadian history, and that the early years of the twentieth century can also be considered a period of province building. Furthermore, they argue, the concept tends to mask cross-provincial variations in institutional development, policy activism, and orientation toward the federal government.

21. The granting of the power over "property and civil rights" to the provinces (section 93[12] of the British North America Act, 1867) allowed Quebec to retain jurisdiction over most of the subjects in its Civil Code.

22. The Canadian Bill of Rights, as Cheffins and Johnson note, "is still in effect and will undoubtedly be cited from time to time, but it has certainly been overshadowed by the enactment of the Charter of Rights and Freedoms" (1986: 134; see also Hogg 1985: 640).

23. Charter provisions on language rights, as discussed in Chapter 7, constitute an important exception to this general tendency.

24. Calculated from Gourevitch et al. 1984: 75.

2 Constitutional Change

Until 1982 Canada presented, in cross-national perspective, a constitutional anomaly. If it is true that "legal 'sovereignty' resides in that combination of bodies with power to effect changes in the fundamental law" (Dellinger 1984: 284), then for the first 115 years of its existence Canada was not, in formal terms, a sovereign nation. Because Canadian federal and provincial governments could not agree how the "power to effect changes in the fundamental law" should be allocated among themselves, they lived by default under a regime in which the written components of the Canadian constitution could formally be amended only by the British Parliament.

The root of the problem was that any codified Canadian amendment procedure would threaten the ambiguity that made it possible for the system to function in the face of a fundamental lack of consensus about the nature of the political community and hence about the relationship of federal and provincial governments. In most federal systems agreement on the procedure to change the allocation of power between levels of government generally flows from consensus on the initial allocation. But "where there is no agreement on the proper allocation of authority, or (more fundamentally) no agreement on the desired level of unity within society, as has been the case in Canada, agreement on a wholly satisfactory amendment process becomes impossible" (ibid.).

Periodic ad hoc agreement about the division of power over particular programs, or even about specific constitutional amendments, was possible. But the level of centralization of the federation remained ambiguously defined, and in practice varied over time and across policy arenas. This ambiguity had the advantage of allowing for the flexible adaptation of the federal-provincial division of powers to changing circumstances.

But it also reflected a fundamental lack of consensus, and setting amending procedures into the firmer form of constitutional provisions proved much more difficult than achieving occasional ad hoc agreements. Since 1960 constitutional change has occupied the political agenda more than any other set of policy issues.

Throughout Canadian history periodic attempts to reach agreement on a formal amending procedure wrestled with recurring questions. Was any province to have a veto over constitutional change? Was *each* province to have a veto? Over what categories of issues could provincial vetoes be exercised? What level of agreement was necessary to adopt the amending procedure itself? In the 1960s and 1970s these questions were compounded with others: Was agreement on the amending procedure to be tied to agreement on a redefinition of the federal-provincial division of powers? In such a redefinition what was to be the place of Quebec—was it to be a province like the others, or was it to have special status?

Finally, in 1982 an amending procedure acceptable to the federal government and nine of the ten provincial governments was enacted into law, and the Canadian constitution was "patriated." The amendment procedure was part of an agreement package that included the adoption of a constitutional Charter of Rights and Freedoms, and revisions to the federal-provincial division of power over natural resources. The Constitution Act, 1982, resolved some ambiguities while creating others. Most importantly, however, it left unresolved one of the major ambiguities of Canadian Confederation: the place of Quebec within the Canadian federation.

Context

The original terms of Canadian Confederation constituted an "ambiguous bargain" (Mallory 1977). As discussed in Chapter 1, the framers of the British North America Act of 1867 thought that they were establishing a relatively centralized federation, but in fact the result of their negotiations was to lay the foundation for strong provincial governments. The major mechanism of intrastate federalism—a regionally representative federal cabinet—was not specified but rather, was, assumed. The relationship of the anglophone and francophone communities per se was not directly addressed: Strategies of constitutional parallelism in the treatment of linguistic groups, on the one hand, and "special status" for Quebec as the guarantor of francophone culture, on the other, coexisted uneasily in the 1867 constitution.

Most ambiguous of all, however, was the power to amend the constitution, which formally rested in British hands. In practice, the British Parliament simply acted upon formal requests from the government of Canada. But there remained considerable ambiguity in Canada about what degree of federal-provincial consensus, if any, was necessary in order for a request to proceed to Britain. In 1931, by the Statute of Westminster, the British Parliament renounced its authority to legislate for its former "dominions" and empowered the legislatures of each dominion to revise or repeal any imperial statutes applying to that dominion. The Canadian provincial governments, however, insisted that the British North America Acts be exempted from these provisions, lest the Canadian federal government acquire the formal authority to amend the Canadian constitution unilaterally. In the absence of federal-provincial agreement on a domestic amending formula, the constitutional fiction of the British power to amend the Canadian constitution was preferable to provincial subordination to the federal government.

Failure to agree on an amending formula did not prevent constitutional change, or even formal constitutional amendment. As discussed in Chapter 1, the Canadian constitution has evolved over time as a result of judicial decisions and governmental practices (such as those that led to a recognition of the federal government's "spending power"). It has also been formally amended on a number of occasions. Over the course of these formal amendments certain traditions began to develop. By the 1960s constitutional provisions fell into several categories for purposes of amendment. Matters relating to a provincial constitution only could be amended by the respective provincial legislature. Matters relating to federal institutions only could be amended by the federal Parliament. (The demarcation of these two categories, however, remained undefined.)[1] With regard to matters relating to the balance of federal and provincial power, a tradition had arisen whereby the federal government would seek the consent of all provinces affected before proceeding with a request to Britain to amend the constitution.

Between 1927 and 1960 five federal-provincial conferences attempted to agree on an formula that would be both more formal and less demanding in terms of the level of consensus required to amend the constitution. Each of these conferences considered some method of categorizing constitutional matters so that only a limited set would require unanimity. None of these attempts was successful.

Nonetheless, the constitution did prove relatively flexible in adapting to changing circumstances without formal change; and when formal change was necessary (as in the case of amendments allowing the federal government to act in areas of unemployment insurance and old age pensions), unanimous consent was obtained. In the 1960s, however, political changes were occurring that would both fuel the issue of constitutional patriation and amendment, and make unanimity more difficult to achieve.

Foremost among these changes was the "quiet revolution" in Quebec. The Liberal provincial government under Premier Jean Lesage, elected in 1960, was very much concerned with building up the powers and the institutional capacity of the Quebec state. One of the first emphases was on constraining the use of the federal spending power in Quebec, while still securing access to federal funds. The Duplessis government had refused to participate in a number of major federal shared-cost programs in areas of provincial jurisdiction. Duplessis's immediate successor, Paul Sauvé, had negotiated an arrangement under which Quebec received unconditional "tax points" in lieu of federal grants to universities. At the Lesage government's insistence, the federal government incorporated "opting-out" provisions into a number of its new and established shared-cost programs in the 1960s, notably hospital and medical care insurance and the Canada Assistance Plan. These provisions allowed provinces to opt out of federal programs and yet receive federal transfer payments equivalent to what they would have received under the federal programs, provided that the provinces administered similar programs and ensured that benefits were portable across provinces. The federal transfers were to be for an "interim period," during which provincial programs were to be subject to federal audit, and after which the arrangements would be renegotiated.

Only Quebec exercised its option to develop its own programs under these opting-out provisions. In fact, it developed or continued programs very similar to the federal programs from which it had opted out. And the arrangements, rather than applying only for an "interim period," were continued through periodic renegotiations. But opting out enhanced the institutional capacity and the political legitimacy of the Quebec government as the source to which *québécois* should look to meet their needs (McRoberts 1988: 141–42).

Of even greater significance was the establishment of the Quebec Pension Plan as a completely independent program paralleling the Canada Pension Plan. Both contributory public pension programs were established in 1964, and there was an exact correspondence between them in terms of contribution and benefit rates and portability provisions. By administering its own program, however, the Quebec government secured *québécois* control over a pool of capital that became an important instrument of industrial policy (Chapter 5).

In the 1960s, then, Quebec acquired a de facto special status, outside the arena of constitutional politics, in important areas of social and industrial policy. (When Ontario attempted to avail itself of the same opting-out provisions for shared-cost programs in 1971, Ottawa maintained that those provisions were no longer open.) In the eyes of the Quebec government, however, Quebec had gained no new powers: It had merely "repossess[ed] some of its own territory" or, in the case of the Quebec Pension Plan, had "simply occupied a field of its own that Ottawa had been preparing to mine" (Morin 1976: 16, 9).

Agenda

The Quebec government desired not only to defend but also to extend its powers. By the mid-1960s, as Russell puts it, Quebec had become "constitutionally radical." Whereas earlier Quebec governments had sought "to avoid a constitutional amendment system which would enable English-speaking Canada to reduce Quebec's powers," the architects and the inheritors of the "quiet revolution" sought "to increase Quebec's powers so that the 'State of Quebec' could assume a comprehensive responsibility for the functions of the modern positive state" (1988: 14–15).

This shift in Quebec's position was apparent in the discussions around the so-called Fulton-Favreau amendment formula proposed at a federal-provincial conference in 1964. This formula would have required unanimous consent of the federal and provincial legislatures in order to amend certain key sections of the constitution, notably those relating to provincial powers and the use of the English and French languages. Various other categories of constitutional provisions were specified for amendment purposes, including those that could be amended unilaterally by provincial and federal legislatures. The general amendment formula offered by Fulton-Favreau, however, was approval by the federal Parliament and the legislatures of two-thirds of the provinces (that is, seven provinces, as long as there continued to be ten provinces) representing at least 50 percent of the Canadian population—a so-called 7/50 rule. These provisions effectively meant that no province, acting alone, could veto a constitutional amendment falling within the general category, although *any* province could veto an amendment directly affecting provincial powers or linguistic rights.

Premier Lesage at first endorsed this formula, but opposition in Quebec soon led him to withdraw Quebec's approval. Essentially, this shift in position confirmed a shift from a "conservative" to a "radical" constitutional posture for Quebec. The rigidity of the unanimity provisions of the Fulton-Favreau formula would have made amendments to the existing division of powers difficult; and, on second thought, the Quebec government rejected it as reducing the likelihood of the "radical restructuring of Confederation" that Quebec now sought (Russell 1988: 15).

The Union nationale (UN) government under Premier Daniel Johnson, which replaced the Quebec Liberal government in 1966, continued the constitutional crusade. The Johnson government pressed for a redefinition of the constitutional division of powers and was even less concerned than its predecessor to make common cause with other provinces. It presented a view of Canada as a "binational country" and maintained that, although on some issues such as environmental and transportation policy the various provinces might "meet on common ground," on sociocultural issues "Quebec's position is altogether different from that of the other provinces" (Quebec 1968: 362). Quebec sought sole authority over a wide range of social, cultural, industrial, and regional development policy areas, and made it clear that its position in no way depended upon what other provinces chose to do. If they followed Quebec's lead, the federation would become much more decentralized. If not, Quebec would have special status. Either alternative would meet Quebec's needs.

Meanwhile, as an opposition party, the Quebec Liberals moved to an even more explicit endorsement of special status for Quebec. They presented a view of Quebec as a "distinct society" (a phrase that would become the focus of intense controversy twenty years later) and argued that constitutional revision of the division of powers and the structure of institutions was essential if Quebec was to retain its distinctiveness in a modern context (Quebec Liberal Federation 1968). They were virtually of one mind with the UN regarding the range of policy areas in which Quebec would require exclusive authority in order to "ensure the growth and maturity of Quebec's collective personality" (ibid.). Special status was, for the Liberals, the only alternative to independence for Quebec, and it was the alternative that, on pragmatic grounds, they deemed preferable.

For the growing separatist movement in Quebec, however, the complete political independence of Quebec from the rest of Canada was clearly the goal. The Parti québécois was formed in 1968 through the merger of a number of separatist groups, under the leadership of René Lévesque, a former journalist and Liberal cabinet minister and a member of the generation of intellectuals liberated by the passing of the Duplessis regime. The PQ used language and concepts similar to those of the UN and the Liberals (and vice versa). "We are a nation within a country where there are two nations," Lévesque declared. "We must secure once and for all . . . the safety of our collective personality" (Reading 2–1).

The PQ, like the Liberals and the UN, sought expanded powers for Quebec, emphasizing areas of social, cultural, and industrial policy. Unlike the other two parties, however, the PQ saw no possibility of achieving these powers within the Canadian federation within any reasonable time. It argued that attempting to accommodate the aspirations of French and English Canada within a single federation was a "waste of energy," and that both "nations" would be better off within two sovereign states joined in an economic union.

In October 1970 the attention of the nation was dramatically focused on the radical fringe of the separatist movement, with the kidnapping of a British diplomat and the kidnapping and murder of a Quebec cabinet minister by two cells of the Front de libération du Québec. The federal government, with the support of the Liberal government of Quebec, responded swiftly and decisively to invoke the War Measures Act, under which it assumed wide powers of search, seizure, and detention. The Trudeau government's action received broad public support, despite much criticism from the left; and the actions of the FLQ were denounced by "mainstream" Quebec separatists, including René Lévesque and the Parti québécois (Posgate and McRoberts 1976: 190).

The lasting effect of the "October Crisis," however, was not to discredit the separatist movement. Rather, it was to jolt Canadians, both within and outside of Quebec, into an awareness of the explosive potential of Quebec separatism, and hence to legitimize vehicles (notably the PQ) through which separatist energies could be channelled into the democratic electoral process. The rise of the separatist and social-democratic PQ dramatically transformed the Quebec provincial party system. The Union nationale disappeared over the course of the 1970s, and the PQ and the Liberals became the principal protagonists in a two-party system. Neither party, moreover, could ignore separatist sentiment. Public support for some form of political independence for Quebec, according to various polls in the early 1970s, hovered at about 30 percent of the francophone Quebec electorate, with about 50 percent opposed and about 20 percent undecided.[2] The Liberals, indeed, appropriated several PQ slogans to describe their own policies in office in the early 1970s (McRoberts 1988: 223–24).

Although their "constitutional radicalism" drove the constitutional agenda in the 1960s and early 1970s, Quebec governments were not, of course, the only participants in the debate. Counterposed to Quebec was the federal government. Under Liberal Prime Minister Lester Pearson from 1964 to 1968, the federal government had sought to respond to Quebec's demands for special status by pursuing a policy of "cooperative federalism." Such a policy rested upon *administrative* flexibility and ongoing federal-provincial negotiation. Federal programs in areas such as regional development were adapted to the particular needs of individual provinces as articulated by provincial governments. As noted above, provisions were made for provincial "opting-out" of federal programs. Key to this policy was that flexibility was to apply, at least in theory, to *all* provinces, although in practice Quebec was much more likely to avail itself of such provisions. While extending this administrative flexibility, however, Ottawa resisted any "special transfer" of jurisdiction under which Quebec would have more constitutional power than any other province (Reading 2–2).

Pierre Trudeau, who succeeded Pearson as Liberal leader and prime minister in 1968, was if anything less sympathetic to Quebec demands for special status. To him, and to the other Quebec federalists in his cabinet, the concept resonated with the Quebec nationalism that they had dedicated their political lives to combat. Trudeau sought to countervail Quebec's demands for increased jurisdiction with an attempt to enhance the ability of federal institutions to promote "national unity." As part of this approach, the Trudeau government undertook an extensive program of bilingualization in the federal civil service. On the constitutional front Trudeau pressed for the entrenchment of a Charter of Rights, including language rights, to establish a national set of standards governing the relationship between individuals and the state.

Ottawa-Quebec tensions virtually defined the agenda of constitutional politics in the 1960s, with the other provinces playing an essentially reactive role. In the 1970s, however, other provinces began to bring their own agenda items to the table. As international commodity prices increased, the western provinces pressed for increased powers over natural resources, and hence for a broader set of instruments through which they could share in resource rents (Chapter 6). The western provinces also sought a reform of federal institutions, particularly the Senate, to counterbalance the power accorded to central Canada in those institutions through the sheer weight of population and electoral strength. British Columbia, for its part, advocated a "five-region" concept—the regions being British Columbia, the prairie provinces, Ontario, Quebec, and the Atlantic provinces—for purposes of the design of federal institutions. Even Newfoundland and Nova Scotia, who with the other Atlantic provinces had traditionally defended federal powers as instruments of inter-regional redistribution, sought some measure of increased jurisdiction, particularly over offshore resources and fisheries.

Ontario, the largest and most federally oriented province (Chapter 1), was generally supportive of the federal government's position in this period. The Ontario government supported the concept of an entrenched Charter of Rights and sought little in the way of increased provincial jurisdiction. (Along with Quebec, however, it did seek increased jurisdiction over family law.) As an energy-consuming province, Ontario resisted changes that would increase the powers of the resource-producing provinces over pricing and distribution of energy resources (Chapter 6). Ontario had traditionally cast itself in the role of the "honest broker" of Confederation—mediating between Quebec and the rest of English Canada and between Ottawa and the provinces. Its ability to play a mediating role in each of these respects the 1970s, however, was constrained, on the one hand, by its unwillingness to accept the entrenchment of French as an "official language" of Ontario (Chapter 7) and, on the other hand, by its conflict with the western provinces over energy.

Process

Throughout the 1970s constitutional politics were contained within the nexus of federal-provincial governmental negotiations but were played out against a background of rising separatist sentiment in Quebec and increasing interregional tensions. In June 1971 a first ministers' conference on constitutional change was convened in Victoria, British Columbia. The conference had been preceded by a series of bilateral negotiations between Ottawa and each of the provinces; and the federal government came to the conference with a fully fleshed proposal for patriating the constitution, setting out an amendment formula, and entrenching a Charter of Rights. Quebec's demands for a revision of the division of powers over social policy were relegated by the federal government to the "non-constitutional" category of agenda items. In a pattern that was to be repeated several times in the next two decades, the first ministers met in closed marathon sessions (fourteen consecutive hours for premiers, longer for some officials) to hammer out an agreement. The result was the "Victoria Charter," endorsed by all eleven first ministers. It comprised a Charter of Rights and a regionally based amending formula that gave a veto to any province with at least 25 percent of the population of Canada (that is, in the foreseeable future, to Ontario and Quebec). In a nod to Quebec, it also contained an ambiguously worded provision requiring the federal government to consult with the provinces before enacting certain income security measures in areas of shared jurisdiction.

Consistent with the model of executive federalism within which they were operating, the first ministers established a twelve-day period within which they would seek approval of the Victoria Charter from their respective cabinets. In Quebec the proposal met its demise. The Quebec cabinet came to the conclusion that acceptance of the Victoria Charter implied acceptance of the entire written constitution, which it viewed as fundamentally flawed. If Quebec agreed to patriation, and an amending formula and a Charter of Rights, it would in effect allow the federal government, the only other major protagonist in the constitutional politics of the early 1970s, to accomplish its own agenda and would hence remove any incentive to meet Quebec's demands for changes in the division of powers. Quebec's announced rationale for rejection was narrower, however, and ironically presaged arguments that would contribute to the defeat of Quebec's agenda almost twenty years later. It argued that the language regarding the federal-provincial division of powers over income security was not sufficiently precise and would inevitably need to be interpreted by the courts, hence transferring to the judiciary "a responsibility that belongs pre-eminently . . . to those elected by the people" (Government of Quebec communique, quoted in Morin 1976: 68).

The opposition of Quebec effectively doomed the Victoria Charter, and efforts at constitutional reform entered a brief period of hiatus. Meanwhile, however, the constitutional agendas of provinces other than Quebec were expanding, as discussed above. An attempt by Prime Minister Trudeau in 1975 to call a conference based on the restricted agenda of the amendment formula necessary to achieve patriation was rejected by all provinces (Russell 1988: 16–17).

By 1976 the federal government was prepared to offer a slightly enhanced version of the Victoria Charter, while the provinces responded with a loosely defined "shopping list" of demands for increased jurisdiction. In that year, however, the floundering politics of constitutional reform were given new vigour with the election of a Parti québécois government in Quebec. The Péquistes could not claim a mandate for separation: They had won a majority of seats with 41 percent of the popular vote, and they had campaigned on a promise to hold a referendum before proceeding to negotiate political independence for Quebec within an economic union with what would remain of Canada. Nonetheless, their victory gave the spectre of Quebec separation a new reality in the eyes of the rest of Canada.

The period from 1976 to 1982 was one of intense debate at the elite level, through numerous conferences and other forums, over constitutional issues. A federal task force, jointly chaired by a former federal Liberal cabinet minister and a former Conservative Ontario premier, held hearings across the country in 1978. Decision-making power, however, remained closely held by federal and provincial executives, whose negotiations intensified. In 1978 the federal government, frustrated by the lack of progress of these negotiations, embarked on a bold strategy: It sought to divide the process of constitutional change into two phases. The first phase would involve changes to federal institutions and hence, under section 91(1) of the British North America Act, could be undertaken unilaterally by the federal government. The second phase would involve changes to the division of powers, patriation, and an amending formula, and would require provincial consent.

Accordingly, the federal government introduced legislation, bill C-60, which included a charter of rights, including linguistic rights, applying to the federal government (with a provision for provinces to opt in) and a sweeping reform of the Senate, which would be transformed into a House of the Federation composed of both federal and provincial appointees. This strategy dissolved in a flood of provincial protest, however. Among other things, the provinces maintained that the federal government's proposals, especially with regard to the Senate, extended well beyond its unilateral amendment powers under section 91(1). The federal government referred the legislation to the Supreme Court, which held (in the *Senate Reference*) that the Senate, because of its role in protecting regional interests, fell outside the scope of the federal government's authority to amend its own "constitution." By the time the Court ruled in December

1979, however, bill C-60 had already been allowed to die on the order paper, and the federal government had abandoned its two-stage strategy.

In 1978 and 1979 a series of premiers' conferences and first ministers' conferences addressed the broadest range of constitutional issues yet considered in such forums. The federal government produced an "Agenda for Change," comprising fourteen items that included proposals for both institutional reform and changes in the division of powers. In the period between conferences in November 1978 and February 1979 issues were delegated to a Continuing Committee of Ministers on the Constitution (CCMC), composed primarily of justice and intergovernmental affairs ministers, who were charged with preparing a "best efforts" draft. The small-group dynamics of the CCMC were crucial to the process of reaching agreement (Romanow, Whyte, and Leeson 1984: 22–24), and the group was able to present to the first ministers conference in February 1979 a draft that "enjoyed the support of most governments, for almost all matters" (ibid.: 24).

This level of consensus, however, was not enough. No agreement could be reached on an amending formula—the vetoes for Ontario and Quebec under the Victoria Charter proposals were no longer acceptable to most other provinces. The 1978–79 round ultimately foundered, however, on the opposition of Quebec. Pending its promised referendum on the fundamental issue of the relationship between Quebec and the rest of Canada, the PQ government felt constrained from agreeing to any specific lists of constitutional amendments. And because, as in earlier rounds, unanimity was taken for granted as the ground rule for agreement, Quebec's opposition amounted to a veto (ibid.: 53).

On an issue that went so deeply to the core of Canadian conceptions of political community—the relationship of Quebec to the rest of Canada—processes of elite accommodation were not sufficient to resolve conflict. A direct appeal to the electorate was necessary to break the impasse among elites. Accordingly, after the failure of the 1978–79 round, the constitutional energies of the federal and Quebec governments were almost entirely directed to contesting Quebec's referendum on "sovereignty-association," announced in December 1979 and held in May 1980. Significantly, the option put to the Quebec electorate was complex and hedged about with qualifications. It was presented as political independence for Quebec, within an economic association with the rest of Canada. Voters were asked to approve not the sovereignty-association model directly, but rather a mandate for the Quebec government to negotiate such a model. Another referendum to approve the results of these negotiations was promised (Reading 2–3).

The referendum campaign was passionately waged. Trudeau and Lévesque were the towering protagonists on the "non" and the "oui" sides, respectively, but all members of the Quebec political elite were vitally engaged. Members of the federal cabinet and Parliament from Quebec stumped the province for the "non" side, as did the Quebec Liberals in opposition at the provincial level. Throughout the campaign Trudeau pledged constitutional reforms (without being specific as to their content), and the provincial Quebec Liberals presented a more fully delineated decentralized federal model, abandoning their earlier support for special status for Quebec in favour of increased powers for all provinces.

In the end the proposal was defeated by a margin of almost 60 percent. Even among francophones a bare majority voted against it. Like the question itself, however, the meaning of the referendum result was ambiguous. Numerous polls taken around the referendum period, however, indicated that Quebec voters were not opting for the status quo. Less than one-third favoured existing arrangements, but those who favoured change were divided as to whether change should take the form of a more decentralized federation, special status for Quebec, sovereignty-association, or the severing of all political and economic ties between Quebec and Canada (Gibbins 1982: 182–84; Kornberg and Archer 1984: 74–78).

The results of the Quebec referendum gave new impetus to constitutional reform but also guaranteed that the process would be conflictual. Trudeau appeared to believe that the failure of the PQ government to win endorsement of sovereignty-association had given his own administration a mandate to protect the strength of the central government (Romanow, Whyte, and Leeson 1984: 102–3). After yet another failed first ministers' conference on constitutional reform in September 1980, the federal government prepared to act unilaterally to patriate the constitution, introducing a parliamentary resolution in effect requesting the British Parliament to pass the appropriate legislation.

The federal resolution provided for patriation with an entrenched Charter of Rights and Freedoms and a regionally based amending formula modelled on the earlier Victoria Charter. Unlike the Victoria Charter, however, this amendment procedure provided that provincial consent could be given *either* by provincial legislatures *or* by provincial electorates through a nationwide referendum.[3] The proposal for a referendum route flew in the face of the Canadian tradition of elite accommodation in constitutional matters and had never been discussed in first ministers' conferences. It reflected in large part Trudeau's exasperation with the process of intergovernmental negotiation and his success in the Quebec referendum. In effect, this formula would have given Quebec (as well as Ontario) a veto over constitutional change but would have allowed Ottawa to appeal over the heads of the Quebec National Assembly to the Quebec populace to influence the exercise of that veto.

In the hearings conducted by a special parliamentary committee on the federal resolution, the process was opened up for the first time to participants beyond the closed circle of intergovernmental decision making. Most of the ensuing activity centred on the charter, as various groups sought increased charter protection. In response, the clause making charter rights subject to "reasonable limits" (Chapter 1) was somewhat modified and increased protection was provided for aboriginal rights and for nondiscrimination on the basis of gender.

While these hearings were being held at the federal level, provincial opposition was coalescing. Three provinces launched court challenges contesting the right of the federal government to patriate the constitution with a unilateral request to Britain. In April 1981 eight provinces (all except Ontario and New Brunswick), who came to be known as the "gang of eight," signed an alternative patriation plan under which provinces would be able to opt out of any constitutional amendment derogating from provincial powers—a proposal first made in 1936 and resurrected by Alberta in the late 1970s. Unlike the 1936 proposal, however, the "gang of eight" plan would entitle opting-out provinces to fiscal compensation.

The provincial legal challenges quickly reached the Supreme Court of Canada, whose ruling provides a highly instructive example of the nature of Canadian constitutionalism. The Court held by a 7–2 majority that the federal government had the strict legal authority to proceed unilaterally as it had intended. But by a 6–3 majority the Court also held that there was a *conventional* requirement for the federal government to obtain a "substantial degree" of provincial consent regarding proposed changes to federal-provincial relationships and provincial powers before taking such a request to the United Kingdom. Since the federal request to Britain included an amending formula, a charter of rights that would apply to both levels of government, and provisions regarding the reductions of regional fiscal disparities, it clearly entailed federal-provincial relations and provincial powers and hence fell under the conventional requirement of provincial consent.

In the face of this ruling the federal government again began negotiations with the provinces to obtain the unspecified "substantial degree" of consent. As three of the participants put it, "The First Ministers' Conference on 2 November 1981 was convened in a mixed mood of grudging necessity, persistent mistrust and modest hope" (Romanow, Whyte, and Leeson 1984: 193). After a week of intense, private, and often informal meetings, agreement had been reached between the federal government and all provincial governments except that of Quebec regarding the content of a proposed constitution act.

The package of reforms finally agreed to by ten first ministers differed in several important respects from the 1980 federal proposal. The amending formula reverted firmly to a governmental base—the referendum alternative was removed, as Russell (1988: 18) notes, "without a whimper of public protest." The formula was based, not on the Victoria Charter, but on principles drawn from earlier models. Like the Fulton-Favreau formula of the 1960s, it divided constitutional matters into categories for purposes of amendment and established a "7/50" requirement as the general rule. Under the general category, that is, amendments required the approval of the federal Parliament and two-thirds (seven of ten) of the provinces representing 50 percent of the Canadian population. This level of approval had to be reached within three years from the time at which the first legislature approved the amendment. The formula also established a category of matters, such as the composition of the Supreme Court, bilingualism in federal institutions, and the amending procedure itself, for which unanimity would be required (but no time limit applied).

Notably, the federal-provincial division of powers was *not* assigned to the category of matters requiring unanimity. Rather, the first ministers agreed to allow dissenting provinces to opt out of amendments derogating from provincial powers, as had been proposed by the "gang of eight." Entitlement to "reasonable compensation" for opting-out provinces would, however, apply only with regard to amendments dealing with educational and cultural matters. This limitation of compensation for dissenting provinces was one of Quebec's major sticking points.

Given that the federal and provincial governments were attempting to reach agreement on the amending procedure without having reached agreement on the division of powers, these opting-out provisions made sense. There was, indeed, only one area in which the division of powers was altered in the 1982 constitutional package: As part of the price of the agreement of the western premiers, the provinces gained increased authority over natural resources (Chapter 6). Much of the broad agenda of the 1978–79 negotiations remained unresolved.

The other major change in the 1981 constitutional package concerned the Charter of Rights and Freedoms (Chapter 1). To overcome the deeply held concerns on the part of the western premiers, especially Sterling Lyon of Manitoba, that an entrenched charter would undermine the principle of parliamentary supremacy, a section was added to the charter that would allow federal or provincial legislatures to expressly override the charter by providing that specific pieces of legislation would have effect "notwithstanding" charter provisions. Such overrides, which could last for renewable five-year periods, could be applied to fundamental freedoms, legal rights, and equality rights, but (at Trudeau's insistence) not to democratic, mobility, or language rights. This "notwithstanding clause" (Reading 2–4) was a crucial component of the so-called kitchen accord negotiated by the federal justice minister and the attorneys general of Ontario and Saskatchewan during the first ministers' conference of November 1981. In an intensely distilled version of the Canadian practice of small-group elite negotiation, these three men had met in a small kitchen apart from the general conference room to produce, "scribbled on a notepad" (Romanow, Whyte, and Leeson 1984: 208), the bare bones of the agreement that resulted in the 1982 constitutional package. That no Quebec government representative was present in the "kitchen" is testimony to the reluctant conclusion on the part of the other provinces that no accommodation between Trudeau and Lévesque was possible.

The consent of nine of the ten provincial premiers having been obtained, the federal government proceeded to pass, with the support of all federal political parties, a resolution requesting Britain to take the legislative action necessary to patriate the Canadian constitution. The British Parliament accordingly passed the Canada Act, 1982, which "signed off" on British authority to legislate for Canada. The Constitution Act, 1982 (included as a schedule to the Canada Act) was proclaimed by the queen in her capacity as Queen of Canada on April 17, 1982, and henceforth could be amended only by Canadian legislative action.

Consequences

On the day that the Constitution Act, 1982, was proclaimed, Premier René Lévesque ordered that Quebec's flag be flown at half-staff. The process of removing an embarrassing vestige of colonialism had led, not to a restructured federation, but to the persistence of the same federal institutions, essentially the same division of powers, and the adoption of a centralizing Charter of Rights and Freedoms. After twenty years of constitutional ferment the Quebec government had been faced with the prospect, not merely of living under a federal constitution that it viewed as fundamentally flawed, but of *reassenting* to it. And under the 1982 constitution the Quebec government lost power. It was constrained by the charter, and neither the process of patriating the constitution nor the new amending formula had accorded Quebec the veto that Quebec governments had exercised in the past over constitutional change. The Quebec government withheld its consent from the 1982 agreement but this action in itself was a symbolic one—it did not exempt Quebec from the application of the constitution.

The struggle for patriation had been a contest among elites—in which contending Quebec-based elites had played the largest roles. The constitution "rejected" by the Quebec government bore the profound imprint of the Quebec native-son Prime Minister Trudeau and was supported by all Quebec members of the federal parliament. Public opinion polls throughout the process revealed continuing irresolution and division of opinion in Quebec about the variety of constitutional options. And elite conflict continued as the Quebec government sought to insulate itself as much possible from the application of the Constitution Act, 1982. Quebec launched a court challenge to the act, on the grounds that the consent of Quebec formed an essential component of the "substantial" provincial consent that the Supreme Court had held, in the *Patriation Reference*, to be conventionally required for constitutional changes affecting provincial powers. Quebec argued, in other words, that by convention it possessed a veto over constitutional change. The Supreme Court of Canada, however, rejected this argument. The Quebec government also invoked the "notwithstanding" clause on a blanket basis in June 1982 to exempt all existing Quebec legislation from the charter's guarantees of fundamental freedoms and legal and equality rights, and subsequently invoked the clause on a routine basis in new legislation (Chapter 7). Finally, the Quebec government refused to participate in further constitutional discussions.

As long as the Trudeau and Lévesque governments were in power, with their fundamentally different views of the relationship between Quebec and the rest of Canada, there was little hope of resolving the impasse between Ottawa and Quebec City. In the mid-1980s, however, two elections rekindled the process of constitutional negotiation. In September 1984 a Conservative government was elected with a massive majority at the federal level (including fifty-eight of Quebec's seventy-five seats) under a bilingual anglophone Quebecker, Brian Mulroney. Mulroney's Quebec caucus had a strong Quebec nationalist streak: A number of its members, including some of those who were to assume important cabinet positions, had worked for the "oui" side in the 1980 referendum on sovereignty-association. In December 1985 a majority Liberal government was elected in Quebec under Robert Bourassa. The Quebec Liberals were generally federalist, albeit with a history of supporting special status for Quebec within Canadian confederation (Reading 2–5). Their "neoliberal" economic and social agenda, moreover, meant that they were less committed than the PQ to building up the Quebec state (McRoberts 1988: 393). Although further constitutional reform was not a high priority for the other provincial governments, the presence of the Bourassa Liberals in power in Quebec City and the Mulroney Conservatives in Ottawa augured well for a constitutional accommodation with the Quebec government.

The Quebec Liberals, while in opposition, had developed a list of five constitutional changes that they viewed as the "minimum conditions" for Quebec's willing acceptance of the federal constitutional framework: recognition of Quebec as a "distinct society," limitations on the federal spending power, increased powers for Quebec over immigration, participation by Quebec in the selection of three of the nine judges of the Supreme Court of Canada, and a Quebec veto over constitutional changes affecting federal institutional and provincial powers. In terms of the scope of its implications for the federal-provincial division of powers, this list of conditions was more modest than those of Quebec governments of the preceding twenty years (Union nationale, Liberal, and Péquiste) which had included, *inter alia,* demands for paramountcy for Quebec in broad areas of social policy and regional development.

Even before the 1985 Quebec election, officials of the federal Conservative government had engaged in bilateral shuttle diplomacy with the other provinces to lay the groundwork for negotiations that might translate the Quebec Liberals' five conditions into a constitutional amendment package. When the Liberals came to power in Quebec, the process took on increased momentum and culminated in a first ministers' meeting at Meech Lake, in the Gatineau hills near the national capital, at the end of April 1987. From that meeting (yet another marathon negotiating session) emerged the so-called Meech Lake Accord, a package of proposed constitutional amendments. Another meeting one month later finalized the language of the accord (Reading 2–6).

Although Canadian elites were being inexorably drawn to specify more than ever the constitutional framework within which they would operate, they still sought refuge in ambiguity. The Meech Lake Accord was written in the language of compromise and equivocation. It had essentially five provisions, corresponding to the five "minimum conditions" of the Quebec government.

First, an interpretation clause was to be added to the constitution recognizing Quebec as a "distinct society" and recognizing the existence, *and the regional concentration,* of French- and English-speaking Canadians as "fundamental characteristics of Canada." All governments, federal and provincial, were to "preserve" this "fundamental characteristic" of the nation, while the Quebec government was given the additional responsibility to "preserve and promote" the "distinct identity" of Quebec. The language of "distinctiveness" had been part of the Quebec political lexicon for at least twenty years, shared by nationalists and federalists. The PQ had spoken of a "collective personality" as being the "distinctive feature" of the French-Canadian nation (Lévesque 1968: 21). The Liberals had characterized Quebec as a distinct society, first to argue for special status for Quebec (Quebec Liberal Federation 1968) and later to argue for a more decentralized federation (Reading 2–5). In the rest of Canada, however, the term had not gained currency and was, at least at first, less threatening than the concept of "special status." Premiers of the English-speaking provinces, in presenting the accord, insisted that the distinct-society clause would not give Quebec special status (that is, more powers). A Gallup poll of June 18, 1987, reported that, of a national sample, 38 percent approved of the proposed distinct-society clause, 40 percent disapproved, and 22 percent were undecided.[4] These mixed results contrasted sharply with the overwhelming rejection of special status for Quebec in public opinion ten years earlier.[5]

A second major set of provisions of the accord concerned the federal spending power. The accord would have constitutionally recognized for the first time the power of the federal government to establish shared-cost programs in areas of exclusive provincial jurisdiction. But it also granted any province that chose not to participate in such a program the constitutional right to "reasonable compensation," provided that it established a "provincial program or initiative that is compatible with the national objectives." The accord would, that is, have constitutionalized a generalized version of the opting-out provisions of federal social programs of the 1960s, discussed above.

The wording of these proposed amendments ("reasonable compensation," "compatible with the national objectives") allowed considerable scope for interpretation. It was the result of intense negotiation among the first ministers. The phrasing "national standards," for example, was rejected, primarily at Quebec's insistence, as tying provincial entitlements to compensation to too specific a correspondence between provincial and national programs. The reference to provincial "initiatives" was added for the same reason. This very ambiguity, however, still constituted a limitation upon the federal government's current discretion to attach conditions to shared-cost programs, since as a matter of *constitutional* interpretation it would ultimately be for the courts, and not for the federal government, to determine whether a provincial program complied with "national objectives," and if so, what constituted "reasonable compensation."

In response to Quebec's demand for a constitutional veto, a third set of provisions in the accord extended the range of matters requiring unanimity for amendment (thus granting *each* province a potential veto). Accordingly, for example, amendments related to provincial representation in the Senate, and the creation of new provinces, would henceforth require unanimous consent. The federal-provincial division of powers was still not included in this category; but compensation to provinces who dissented from amendments affecting their powers was extended to all matters, not only those dealing with education and culture.

A fourth set of provisions in the accord dealt with the Supreme Court of Canada. It entrenched essential features of the Supreme Court,[6] including the requirement that three of its nine members be from Quebec, and further required that appointees to the Court be drawn from lists of nominees submitted by provincial governments. In the same spirit, and pending the reform of the Senate sought by western premiers, the accord required that appointments to the Senate also be drawn from provincial lists. Fifth, in response to Quebec's demand for increased constitutional powers over immigration, it gave constitutional status to an existing agreement between Quebec and the federal government, and it provided for the negotiation of such agreements with the other provinces. Finally, the accord entrenched requirements for annual first ministers' conferences on economic and constitutional matters.

The Meech Lake Accord, then, sought to meet the Quebec government's five "minimum conditions" for signing the Canadian constitution largely by applying to *all* provinces the provisions (with the exception of distinct-society status) that Quebec had demanded for itself. It reflected a considerably more decentralized vision of the federation than that which infused the Constitution Act of 1982, and it was initially negotiated with much less rancour. The differences, both in tenor and in substance, between the negotiations leading to the 1982 constitutional package and those leading to the Meech Lake Accord were largely attributable to the fact that the incumbents of the elite roles had changed. Notably, the Quebec premiership was no longer occupied by an avowed separatist; and the prime ministership was in the hands, no longer of a visionary centralist, but of a former labour lawyer who prided himself on his negotiating skills and who headed a Conservative party of a more decentralist bent than the federal Liberals.

Although the incumbents had changed, however, the process of constitutional decision making had remained much the same. The process of negotiating the Meech Lake Accord was a quintessential display of executive federalism. The eleven first ministers, meeting in private, agreed to proposals that among other things enhanced the powers of provincial political executives over appointments to national institutions by the national political executive, and entrenched the primary institutions of executive federalism, the first ministers' meetings. Furthermore, in presenting these proposals to their respective legislatures for ratification, the first ministers announced that they would accept no changes other than those necessary to correct "egregious errors" in drafting.

In negotiating a package of proposed amendments, the first ministers bound themselves to a ratification requirement more stringent than any individual component of the package would have attracted by itself. Under the Constitution Act, 1982, the accord's distinct-society, spending power, and immigration provisions fell under the general amending formula, which required the consent of the federal parliament and the legislatures of seven provinces representing 50 percent of the Canadian population *within three years* from the time at which the first legislature approved the amendment. The provisions regarding the Supreme Court and the amending procedure itself fell into the category of constitutional matters requiring *unanimous* consent, but subject to no time limit. Because the accord constituted a "seamless web," the first ministers presented it as a package whose adoption required *unanimous consent to be obtained within a three-year period* from first approval. A resolution approving the accord and hence starting the clock ticking on the three-year amendment process was quickly passed by the Quebec legislature (with the PQ opposition dissenting) on June 23, 1987—one day before Quebec's "national" holiday, St. Jean-Baptiste Day. At the federal level the Liberal and NDP caucuses were divided over support of the accord. Both Liberal and NDP leaders endorsed it, however; and in the end it was approved by the House of Commons on June 22, 1988, with only seven dissenting votes.

As the package was laid before the various legislatures, the implications of the changed rules of constitutional amendment under the 1982 constitution began to become apparent. For the first time the final say with respect to constitutional change lay with provincial as well as federal legislatures. The accord was submitted to eleven legislatures, of different political complexions and legislative agendas, and at varying stages of their electoral cycles. Notwithstanding the insistence of the first ministers that they would accept no changes, the accord was laid bare to public scrutiny during legislative hearings at both levels of government. And under the pressure of that scrutiny the ambiguous language of the accord began to fracture into shards of competing interpretations.

In retrospect, the eleventh-hour involvement of interest groups in the process leading to the 1982 constitution, through the parliamentary hearings on the federal government's unilateral proposal as discussed above, had presaged the change in constitutional politics that would occur under the new amendment procedure. Legislative hearings on the Meech Lake Accord provided a focus for mobilization against the amendment package. Groups enjoying charter protection, notably women's and civil liberties groups, which had won changes late in the 1980–81 process, sought to have the accord altered to make it clear that the distinct-society clause could not trump charter rights. Those cleaving to a more centralized vision of the federation, including Pierre Trudeau, now a private citizen, passionately attacked the decentralist thrust of the accord (Reading 2-7). Others, pointing to the accord's pervasive ambiguity, argued that it would have the effect of turning over to the courts the resolution of issues that ought to be resolved by elected representatives. And, perhaps most importantly, the process through which the accord was negotiated became itself a matter of controversy: The closed nature of the Meech Lake negotiations and the insistence of the signatories that no changes would be accepted appeared to make a mockery of the requirement for legislative ratification.

Would-be defenders of the accord (principally the signatories) in English Canada were in a difficult predicament. They had agreed to language that was acceptable to Quebec but that was capable of being interpreted to mean that little of significance was being changed. The distinct-society provision, for example, could be seen as simply a recognition of reality—indeed, the courts had already considered Quebec's need to preserve its "distinctiveness" as one factor that might justify "reasonable limits" on Charter rights (Chapter 7). The spending power provisions could be interpreted as the first explicit constitutional affirmation of the federal government's right to spend and to set conditions on its spending in areas of provincial jurisdiction. And the extension of the requirement for unanimous consent for constitutional amendment could be seen as a recognition of prevailing practice—a practice abridged in 1982 at considerable cost to the social fabric of the country. To make at least some of these arguments explicitly, however, could only be interpreted within Quebec as derogating from the significance of the accord. The fact that the accord was capable of different interpretations in different parts of Canada was what had made the agreement possible—public attempts to "explain" it risked unravelling that agreement.

Nonetheless, if the accord could have been approved quickly, it would have succeeded. All of the signatories headed majority governments, and the substance of the accord was little attended to by the electorate. But the intensity of the commitment of most provincial premiers to the accord was considerably less than that of the Quebec premier and the federal prime minister: They had more pressing items on their legislative agendas. One, the NDP premier of Manitoba, entertained lingering doubts about the decentralizing aspects of the accord and delayed laying it before the legislature until he was defeated in the April 1988 provincial election, which brought a minority Conservative government to power. Similarly, in New Brunswick, the October 1987 election intervened before the accord had been submitted to the legislature.

The newly elected premier of New Brunswick announced his opposition to the accord and became a lightning rod for other opponents. In Manitoba the opposition parties, both the Liberals and (under a new leader) the NDP, also declared their disagreement and became another focus for mobilization. As the process of approval in these two provinces was dragged out, opposition across the country began to build. Representatives of linguistic groups other than English and French wanted multiculturalism recognized as a fundamental characteristic of Canada; native groups demanded such recognition for Canada's aboriginal heritage. A number of groups opposed the rigidity of the extended unanimity provisions for constitutional amendments—notably those, largely in the western provinces, who sought Senate reform, and residents of the Northwest Territories and the Yukon, who saw such provisions as virtually insurmountable obstacles to their acquisition of provincial status.

The death-knell of the Meech Lake Accord was sounded, however, by an event that finally gave content, in the minds of many English-speaking Canadians, to its ambiguous distinct-society provision. In December 1988, in response to a Supreme Court ruling that certain clauses of Quebec's language legislation contravened the freedom-of-expression guarantees of both the Quebec Charter of Human Rights and Freedoms and the Canadian Charter of Rights and Freedoms, the Bourassa government invoked the override clauses in both charters (Chapter 7). Bourassa justified his action on the grounds that such legislation was necessary to preserve the "French face" of Quebec in the anglophone sea of North America.

Opponents of Meech Lake seized upon the Quebec government's action to make their point. If Bourassa was prepared to tread on individual rights in the interests of Quebec's collective distinctiveness even in the absence of constitutional status for Quebec as a distinct society, how much further would he and successive Quebec premiers go once that status was assured? Yet another provincial election, in Newfoundland in April 1989, brought another nonsignatory to power. Clyde Wells, the new Liberal premier, had been a constitutional advisor to Pierre Trudeau. He immediately announced his opposition to the accord and his intention to have the Newfoundland legislature rescind its approval, as it was constitutionally entitled to do before the accord had been proclaimed. (The Newfoundland legislature rescinded its approval in April 1990.) In October 1989 the New Brunswick and Manitoba legislatures issued reports outlining the changes upon which their approval would be contingent. Quebec, however, was adamant that there could be no retrenchment from its five minimum conditions as incorporated in the accord and insisted that the accord not be amended. Ironically, the very moderation of the Quebec government's demands had left it virtually no room to manoeuvre, and what had begun as an historic feat of mediation came to be perceived as the rigid defence of a polar position. Meanwhile, the dissident premiers were buoyed by the growing public opposition to the accord outside Quebec. As the various political executives defended their positions publicly, they became increasingly locked into a politics of "face" (Gusfield 1963) and lost much of the flexibility that traditional closed federal-provincial negotiations had afforded.

Another round of shuttle diplomacy and constitutional soul-searching ensued in the spring of 1990, culminating in a seven-day meeting of the first ministers in Ottawa at the beginning of June. The meeting was deliberately delayed by the prime minister to heighten the pressure of the June 23 deadline upon the dissident premiers. This strategy amounted to an exploitation of, rather than a respect for, the processes of executive federalism—it was a labour negotiator's attempt to force the parties to an agreement in the shadow of a crisis. And the result was a caricature of executive federalism: The eleven first ministers met in private in ten-hour sessions, while the media and crowds of demonstrators thronged outside the conference building, waiting for the comments of the exhausted and occasionally testy first ministers as they emerged. At the end of their meeting the first ministers briefly went into public session to announce what amounted to yet another layer of ambiguity over the accord. The dissident premiers undertook to submit the accord, intact, for "appropriate legislative or public consideration" and to "use every possible effort to achieve decision" before June 23. Clyde Wells made this undertaking while stating that he personally remained opposed to the accord, but that he would not "seek to cause the legislators or the people of Newfoundland and Labrador to reject" it. The first ministers also agreed that, once the accord had been passed, a number of "additional" amendments would be made, such as shielding gender equality rights in a limited way from the interpretive reach of the distinct-society clause, and adding a number of issues (notably, aboriginal issues) to the agendas of future constitutional conferences. The first ministers also agreed to consider a number of other possible future constitutional amendments, including a "Canada clause" recognizing a number of dimensions (such as an aboriginal heritage and a multicultural social fabric) as fundamental characteristics of Canada. (One wag noted that this would constitute Canada's "we, the peoples" clause, in contrast to the opening words of the American constitution, "we, the people.") An agreement to pursue reform of the Senate was also made. Finally, the contentious distinct-society clause was not changed, but in an innovation that took Canada's constitutional ambiguity to what must be its limit, a legal opinion regarding the impact of the clause, signed by six constitutional lawyers, was appended to the first ministers' communique but was not endorsed by the first ministers themselves.

Despite Premier Wells's clearly stated continuing personal opposition to the accord and the necessity of negotiating legislative approval processes in three provinces within a very tight time frame, a rather bizarre "signing ceremony" marked by self-congratulatory speeches and "welcomes" to Quebec was held at the conclusion of the first ministers' meeting. Very shortly thereafter, however, it became apparent that the accord had not been salvaged.

In the end the accord expired in a flurry of tactical manoeuvres. The New Brunswick legislature passed the accord in the week following the first ministers' meeting. But in Manitoba, in a penultimate twist to the tale, the sole aboriginal member of the Manitoba Legislative Assembly opposed the accord on the grounds that it did not give constitutional recognition to aboriginal peoples. He was able to use procedural techniques to delay the introduction of the accord until it was impossible for legislatively required public hearings to be completed. In response, the federal government, having insisted for three years that the June 23 deadline was immutable and having used the pressure of that deadline to attain the June 1990 agreement, announced on June 22 that it would refer the issue of the deadline to the Supreme Court of Canada. It alleged that the constitutional requirement for ratification within three years was in fact ambiguous: It could be interpreted to mean that ratification could be achieved with three years of passage by any legislature and did not necessarily date from the *first* legislative passage of a ratification resolution. The federal government stated, however, that it would refer this question to the Court only if Newfoundland passed the accord before June 23, in which case Manitoba would be left as the only province that had not ratified the accord and that lacked only the time to do so. This desperate appeal to constitutional ambiguity failed, however. Premier Wells of Newfoundland, incensed at this final federal attempt to bring pressure to bear on him, adjourned debate in the Newfoundland legislature, and the accord lapsed into death (Reading 2-8).

The Meech Lake Accord was a creative attempt to accommodate the differing balances of bilingualism and multiculturalism, centralization and decentralization, and individualism and collectivism that make up competing visions of the Canadian political community. But, in the end, it simply lacked the level of public support necessary to carry it through an extended process of legislative approval by all governments. Though Newfoundland accounted for just over 2 percent of the Canadian population and aboriginal people less than 2 percent, their leaders were strengthened in their final stands against the accord not only by their firm convictions but also by widespread public dissatisfaction with the agreement.

The effects of the protracted Meech Lake episode were several. On the one hand, the extended public debate on the accord exacerbated linguistic, ethnic, and regional tensions. As the prime minister said at the conclusion of the June 1990 first ministers' meeting, "In the conference foreground, the Meech Lake debate has been about commas and colons and interpretive clauses and preambles. But in the national background, it has been about bilingualism and multiculturalism and about alienation, favouritism and rejection." Separatist sentiment in Quebec, as measured in public opinion polls, rose dramatically. By May 1990, as tensions leading up to the first ministers' meeting in June were reaching their height, support for Quebec's becoming an "independent country" was variously measured at 42 and 48 percent in Quebec (Gallup Canada May 3, 1990; Adams and Dasko 1990). On the other hand, even in the context of extensive dissatisfaction with the accord, the fear that its failure would result in the breakup of the country had made many Canadians hesitant to see it rejected. As in the case of the 1988 Free Trade Agreement with the United States, another highly controversial agreement that bore upon Canadians' self-definition (Chapter 5), a plurality of Canadians (even in Quebec) would have preferred a renegotiation of the accord to either its acceptance or its rejection (ibid.). After the June 1990 first ministers' meeting a national poll suggested that 56 percent of the population believed that the agreement reached was "not very good but probably the best that could be done in the circumstance," and 55 percent believed that the accord should be passed as a result (Southam News 1990). In the wake of the accord's failure, a sense of frustration and exhaustion with constitutional wrangles and debates about the nature of the political community pervaded the country.

The very failure of the accord, however, meant that these issues could not be laid to rest. Even before the official deadline for the approval of the accord had passed, the Quebec Liberal government had begun reviewing its constitutional options. The premier and the minister of intergovernmental affairs had speculated in public about some sort of "supranational" structure and alluded to the model of the European Economic

Community. Prominent *québécois* representatives of business had begun for the first time to consider the possibility of "divorce" from the rest of Canada should the accord fail. With the failure of the accord, Quebec began to move in the short term toward consolidating and advancing its de facto special status, and in the longer term toward a new constitutional arrangement between Quebec and the rest of Canada. The Quebec premier announced that Quebec would henceforth deal on a bilateral basis with Ottawa and with other provinces. (Ontario is the most likely candidate for bilateral arrangements and joint projects with Quebec.) He announced that the government of Quebec would no longer engage in multilateral discussions of constitutional issues among the eleven first ministers, although it might participate in other conferences in which Quebec's interests were involved. At the federal level six Conservative members of Parliament from Quebec (including a key cabinet minister) and two Liberal members resigned from their respective caucuses to sit as members of a newly-formed Bloc québécois, an ideologically diverse group united only by its objective to "represent the interests of Quebec in Ottawa." A ninth Bloc québécois member was elected as such in a Quebec by-election. Meanwhile, minor parties formed in the mid-1980s on platforms of promoting the interests of regions other than Quebec (notably the Reform Party) gained in popular support, particularly in the west. In the spring of 1991 two major reports were issued in Quebec, one by a committee of the provincial Liberal party, and one by a special legislative commission (popularly referred to by the names of their chairs as the Allaire report and the Bélanger-Campeau report, respectively). Each called for a massive decentralization of powers from Ottawa to Quebec as the only alternative to Quebec independence. In the wake of these reports the Quebec National Assembly passed legislation, over the opposition of the PQ, requiring a referendum to be held in Quebec on the issue of Quebec sovereignty in October 1992, but allowing the referendum to be held instead on a federal offer of constitutional reform if an offer judged acceptable by a committee of the Quebec legislature were to be made by before that date. Meanwhile, committees and task forces at the federal level and in several provinces sought to establish their own positions on constitutional issues.

As Canada entered the 1990s, then, constitutional change remained on the political agenda. In this latest phase, a continuing Quebec boycott of "conventional" constitutional discussions is likely. And in any event, the lesson of Meech Lake is that the conventional processes of executive federalism are less and less viable in the constitutional arena under the changed rules adopted in 1982. Those rules entail delay, which always risks the unravelling of initial agreement, especially when levels of intensity of commitment to that agreement vary. And they open up the process beyond the boundaries of executive federalism—to a range of groups beyond governmental actors, and to public scrutiny and debate. The careful ambiguity necessary to reconcile fundamentally different views of the political community is much more difficult to maintain in the broader politics of this new process.

Nonetheless, it would be a mistake to infer from the heated reactions to the failure of the Meech Lake Accord that polarization has replaced ambivalence as the motif of Canadian constitutional debate. Indeed, ambivalence was a common theme in interpretations of opinion polls and in journalistic commentary in the post-Meech era. One major poll conducted in April 1991, for example, found that 47 percent of Quebec respondents indicated a preference that Quebec become a sovereign country or a sovereign country with an economic association with Canada, while of those outside Quebec only 13 percent held such views and 68 percent preferred that Quebec remain a province within Canada with its current set of powers. At the same time, however, 83 percent of Quebec respondents and 89 percent of those outside Quebec agreed that "Canada is the best country in the world to live in," 78 percent in Quebec and 89 percent outside Quebec agreed that "it's worth the effort to try again to resolve the problem of national unity," and 64 percent in Quebec and 72 percent outside Quebec disagreed with the view that "Quebec and the rest of Canada really don't have much in common" (Winsor 1991).

Nor should the death of executive federalism in the constitutional arena be prematurely proclaimed. It is remarkable, indeed, given the complexion of public opinion, that the processes of executive federalism generated as much intergovernmental consensus around the Meech Lake Accord as they did. Had these processes not been so patently exploited by the federal government in the last stages of the episode, it is possible, though not likely, that they might have succeeded. Quebec's moves toward bilateral discussions, moreover, likely presage a transmuted form of executive federalism in the relationships between Quebec and the rest of Canada, as further discussed in Chapter 8. Meanwhile, ironically, the very failure of executive federalism to resolve "once and for all" the division of powers between federal and provincial governments means that political executives will continue to negotiate that balance in virtually all policy arenas as new issues arise.

Readings

2-1.   THE PÉQUISTE MANIFESTO*

In 1968 René Lévesque broke from the Quebec Liberal Party to found the separatist Parti québécois (PQ). His book Option Québec *(whose English title was* An Option for Quebec*) constituted the PQ's founding manifesto. The following excerpts are taken from the book's outline of Quebec's "basic minimums."*

We are a nation within a country where there are two nations. . . .

Two nations in a single country: this means, as well, that in fact there are *two majorities,* two "complete societies" quite distinct from each other trying to get along within a common framework. That [French Canadians are] in a minority position makes no difference: just as a civilized society will never condemn a little man to feel inferior beside a bigger man, civilized relations among nations demand that they treat each other as equals in law and in fact.

Now we believe it to be evident that the hundred-year-old framework of Canada can hardly have any effect other than to create increasing difficulties between the two parties insofar as their mutual respect and understanding are concerned, as well as impeding the changes and progress so essential to both.

It is useless to go back over the balance sheet of the century just past, listing the advantages it undoubtedly has brought us and the obstacles and injustices it even more unquestionably has set in our way.

The important thing for today and for tomorrow is that both sides realize that this regime has had its day, and that it is a matter of urgency either to modify it profoundly or to build a new one.

*René Lévesque, *An Option for Quebec* (Toronto: McClellan and Stewart, 1968), pp. 20–24.

As we are the ones who have put up with its main disadvantages, it is natural that we also should be in the greatest hurry to get rid of it; the more so because it is we who are menaced most dangerously by its current paralysis. . . .

First, we must secure once and for all, in accordance with the complex and urgent necessities of our time, the safety of our collective "personality." This is the distinctive feature of the nation, of this majority that we constitute in Quebec—the only true fatherland left us by events, by our own possibilities, and by the incomprehension and frequent hostility of others.

The prerequisite to this is, among other things, the power for unfettered action (which does not exclude cooperation) in fields as varied as those of citizenship, immigration, and employment; the great instruments of "mass culture"—films, radio, and television; and the kind of international relations that alone permit a people to breathe the air of a changing and stimulating world, and to learn to see beyond itself. Such relations are especially imperative for a group whose cultural connections in the world are as evident and important as ours.

Our collective security requires also that we settle a host of questions made so thorny by the present regime that each is more impossible than the next. Let us only mention as examples the integrity of Quebec's territory, off-shore rights, the evident inacceptibility of an institution like the Supreme Court, and Quebec's need to shape freely what we might term its internal constitution.

That collective personality which constitutes a nation also cannot tolerate that social security and welfare—which affect it directly in the most intimate ways—should be conceived and directed from outside. This refers to the oft-repeated demand for the repatriation of old-age pensions, family allowances, and, when it comes into being, medicare.

By the same token, and even more so, it relates to the most obvious needs of efficiency and administrative responsibility. In this whole vast area there are overlapping laws, regulations and organizations whose main effect is to perpetuate confusion and, behind this screen, to paralyze change and progress. . . .

Mutatis mutandis, we find similar situations with equally disastrous results in a multitude of other arenas: the administration of justice, jurisdiction in fields such as insurance, corporations, bankruptcies, financial institutions, and, in a general way, all economic activities which have become the most constant preoccupations of all men today and also the aspect of society in which modern states have seen their spheres of action grow most dramatically in the last couple of generations. . . .

In this up-dating of political structures that are completely overtaxed by an economic role they cannot refuse to play, the action demanded of the Quebec government, to be specific, would require at the very least new jurisdictions over industrial and commercial corporations, fiduciary and savings institutions, and all the internal agencies of development and industrialization, as well as the power to exercise a reasonable control over the movement and investment of our own capital.

So as not to belabour the obvious, we shall mention only for the record the massive transfer of fiscal resources that would be needed for all the tasks this State of Quebec should undertake in our name—not counting the tasks it already has, tasks that daily grow more out of proportion to its inadequate means: i.e., the insatiable needs of education, urban problems without number, and the meagreness or tragic non-existence of the tools of science and industrial research.

Very sketchily, this would seem to be the basic minimum of change that Quebec should force the present Canadian regime to accept in order to reach both the collective security and the opportunity for progress which its best minds consider indispensable.

We could certainly add to the list. But nothing could be struck from it easily.

For us, this is, in fact, a true minimum.

2-2.   THE FEDERAL RESPONSE TO QUEBEC'S CONSTITUTIONAL AGENDA*

In this 1967 address Prime Minister Lester Pearson expressed the not yet firmly formulated response of the Canadian federal government to the growing pressure in Quebec for constitutional change. The wrestling with language that characterizes Canadian constitutional debate is apparent in these excerpts.

I am confident that when Canadians in Quebec have fully measured the gains and losses from separating themselves from the rest of Canada

---

*Lester B. Pearson, "Changing Canadian Federalism," an address to the conference on the Economics of Canadian Unity, Banff, Alberta, October 15, 1967. Reprinted in J. Peter Meekison, *Canadian Federalism: Myth or Reality* (Toronto: Methuen, 1968), pp. 406–12.

in the atmosphere of tension and hostility which would prevail, they will not regret having chosen Confederation and Canada. But with this choice, can there not be a particular, a special status for Quebec inside Confederation? Many moderate people and good Canadians ask this question.

The answer, of course, depends on what is meant by particular status. If it means that the special position in Canada of the French-Canadian language and culture and tradition must be officially recognized and protected; that the unique national characteristics of French-Canadian people should be encouraged to develop, then I respond with warmth and with understanding to this direction for Canadian federalism.

To me, indeed, this approach is implicit in the B.N.A. Act that made Canada possible in the first place.

It is not being soft or "giving in" to Quebec to agree that Quebec is not a province like the others, and that Canadians should recognize this fact. This is already being done in many ways. Where federal programmes impinge upon or affect the special characteristics of French-Canadian society, they can be and have been adapted to that society. The CBC [Canadian Broadcasting Corporation], for instance, has a French network. The National Film Board produces films for French-Canadians as well as English-Canadians. The ARDA [Agricultural and Regional Development Program] programme is being planned differently in Quebec than in Nova Scotia. Other examples could be given.

Examples could be given, too, of the adaptation of federal programmes to the needs of other provinces and regions: the Atlantic Development Fund for the Atlantic Provinces; the coal-mining phase-out programme in Nova Scotia; the Prairie Farm Rehabilitation Administration for the Prairies; harbour developments in British Columbia.

There is a considerable scope for further changes of this kind. Federal governments may have been too slow in adapting their programmes and their administration to the different regions in Canada. But progress is being made.

I have no difficulty in accepting this kind of "particular status", which affects Quebec most directly but is not exclusive to Quebec. Indeed, it represents the kind of federalism which is not only essential generally to a country so vast and regionally disparate as Canada; it is also an essential ingredient of the two-societies concept of Confederation.

But to some others, "particular status" is more than this. It is defined to mean a special transfer of federal jurisdiction in certain fields to the

provincial government of Quebec. This, in effect, would give more constitutional power to the Government of Quebec than that enjoyed by other
provinces, including the largest province in Canada, Ontario.

The corollary is that the influence of Members of the Federal Parliament and ministers in the federal government from Quebec would be
reduced in comparison with that of members and ministers from the rest
of Canada. This kind of "particular status" could lead to a "separate
state", a result that cannot be accepted.

We should be very clear, therefore, about what we mean when we talk
about special or particular status. . . .

The same difficulty arises over the use of the expression "two nations",
or *deux nations*.

These words have come to mean so many different things to so many
different people that their real meaning has often been lost in sterile
semantics.

One thing, however, is clear and unequivocal. There do exist in Canada
two distinct cultural and linguistic societies, one English-speaking, one
French-speaking, with each including members of other cultural and
ethnic groups.

The English-speaking society is less homogeneous, less cohesive,
than the French-speaking one, but there is a common strand running
through it. . . .

It is not a question, I repeat as to whether there *should* be or *will* be,
a French-Canadian society. There is one *now;* and it will exist so long
as French Canadians have a will to survive, with their own language and
traditions and culture. If English-speaking Canada tries to isolate this
French-Canadian society, whether by design or, more likely, by indiffer-
ence, it will simply encourage separatism.

So we are left with a clear and simple question: what price are we
prepared to pay to preserve our total identity as Canadians; in a country
which history has built on a "dual foundation"? . . .

Social action is often more difficult than individual action. Yet it is
social action we must take. It will involve, for many English-speaking
Canadians, a change in attitude and approach to, and a greater respect
for "the French fact" in our country, in our Confederation.

It means that we must make all Canada, and not merely Quebec, a
homeland for all French-Canadians and to take the steps necessary for
that purpose.

2-3.   THE QUEBEC REFERENDUM

This question was put to the Quebec electorate in December 1979 and voted on in May 1980. Its tortuous and "editorializing" phrasing (McWhinney 1982: 29) is a quintessential example of the tendency to qualify even the most fundamental statements in Canadian constitutional politics.

The government of Quebec has made public its proposal to negotiate a new agreement with the rest of Canada, based on the equality of nations.

This agreement would enable Quebec to acquire the exclusive power to make its laws, administer its taxes and establish relations abroad—in other words, sovereignty—and at the same time, to maintain with Canada an economic association including a common currency.

Any change in political status resulting from these negotiations will be submitted to the people through a referendum.

On these terms, do you agree to give the government the mandate to negotiate the proposed agreement between Quebec and Canada?

YES ☐
NO ☐

2-4.   ENTRENCHED RIGHTS VERSUS
        PARLIAMENTARY SUPREMACY *

These are the sections of the Canadian Charter of Rights and Freedoms that are meant to reconcile the principle of entrenched rights with the principle of parliamentary supremacy. Legislative debate is part of the "demonstration" envisaged in section 1, and legislatures are granted an override in section 33.

Guarantee of Rights and Freedoms

1. The *Canadian Charter of Rights and Freedoms* guarantees the rights and freedoms set out in it subject only to such reasonable limits prescribed by law as can be demonstrably justified in a free and democratic society. . . .

*The Constitution Act, 1982, Schedule B, sections 1 and 33.

33. (1) Parliament or the legislature of a province may expressly declare in an Act of Parliament or of the legislature, as the case may be, that the Act or a provision thereof shall operate notwithstanding a provision included in section 2 [fundamental freedoms] or sections 7 to 15 [legal and equality rights] of this Charter.

(2) An Act or a provision of an Act in respect of which a declaration made under this section is in effect shall have such operation as it would have but for the provision of this Charter referred to in the declaration.

(3) A declaration made under subsection (1) shall cease to have effect five years after it comes into force or on such earlier date as may be specified in the declaration.

(4) Parliament or the legislature of a province may re-enact a declaration made under subsection (1).

(5) Subsection (3) applies in respect of a re-enactment made under subsection (4).

2-5.   THE QUEBEC LIBERALS' CONSTITUTIONAL POSITION
        DURING THE 1980 REFERENDUM CAMPAIGN*

In opposition during the Quebec referendum campaign, the Quebec Liberal party set forth a constitutional position in contradistinction to that of the governing PQ. This report echoed earlier Quebec Liberal documents with its emphasis on Quebec as a "distinct society." Unlike earlier Liberal statements, however, this one did not make reference to "special status" for Quebec; rather, it argued for a considerable decentralization of power to all provinces. These excerpts discuss the "distinct society" and outline the developments of the 1960s in Quebec.

For Quebec, life within the Canadian union has not always been easy. Because of its language and culture, it remained for many years a stranger to the centres of political and economic power. A Quebecker, to succeed in the wider world of Canadian affairs, was required to leave his own language and culture at home. For many years Quebec's participation in the development of important national policies was more a matter of appearance than reality.

Despite these obstacles, the population of Quebec has remained homo-

*Constitution Committee of the Quebec Liberal Party, *Report*, January 1980

geneous since 1867, and its provincial government has provided it in recent years with a lifestyle and a network of institutions which fully express its distinct culture. Quebec's laws, judicial system, municipal and provincial institutions, volunteer organizations, media, arts and letters, teaching system, social and sanitary service networks, religious institutions, and small savings institutions are preponderantly French, both in terms of their language and of the culture which inspires them. . . .

In effect, Quebec forms within the Canadian federation a society which is distinct in terms of its languages, its culture, its institutions and its way of life. Quebec is also the home of a large Anglophone community and numerous ethnic groups, concentrated mainly in Montreal. These communities and their institutions make up an essential dimension of Quebec life. But in general, Quebec sees itself and expresses itself as a society which is French, in language and in spirit. Within the Canadian political family, Quebec society has all the characteristics of a distinct national community. . . .

In 1960, Jean Lesage and his team undertook to modernize Quebec's governmental structure and to exercise their responsibility in all of the jurisdictions which were accorded to Quebec in the BNA Act. In a number of these initiatives, they opposed themselves unhesitatingly to federal bureaucrats and politicians who had developed conflicting or parallel programs.

The multiplicity of government intrusions in different fields, characteristic of the period between 1960 and 1975, greatly increased the opportunities for overlapping between the two orders of government. In a number of sectors we were witness to a veritable frenzy of interventionism by one level of government or the other. Not surprisingly the risk of conflict grew accordingly.

By 1965, Jean Lesage had become convinced that a substantial realignment of powers within the federation was necessary in order to satisfy Quebec's aspirations. In June 1965, Mr. Lesage itemized the five basic principles which would guide him in this reform:

1) Quebec is the provincial expression of French Canada, and her role is that of a mother country for those in Canada who speak French;

2) Quebec has particular traits which it has the right to develop and the responsibility to protect;

3) The constitutional framework must permit the national francophone

community to achieve, in its own way, the objectives which it establishes for itself;

4) Quebec must possess and control to the fullest extent possible the economic, social, administrative and political levers which will allow it to realize the legitimate aspirations of a mature people;

5) Quebec's actions must be exercised in peace and harmony, taking into account the North American reality, the new bonds which attach Quebec to the French-speaking world, and the Canadian federal dimension.

These principles, enunciated at the beginning of the Quiet Revolution, have continued to inspire the actions of the successive governments of Quebec. Each of the latter, with differing overtones, has come to consider itself not only as the government of a province but also, and above all, as having the primary responsibility at the political level for the cultural self-realization and affirmation of that distinct society, of that original national community which has its principal home in Quebec and important extensions in the other Canadian provinces. From 1960 onward, the expression "State of Quebec" became more and more commonly used. This change of vocabulary is not a semantic accident; it reveals a change of perception. More and more people became aware of the distinctive nature of Quebec society and the historic challenges which it had to meet. More and more people decided that this society, in order to survive and prosper, had to control the major levers of its development. More and more people came to the conclusion that the government of Quebec was the privileged instrument by which the people of Quebec could ensure their cultural self-realization, make their own statement, in their own way.

This was a major change of perspective. It would give rise to Quebec's quest for broader powers and lead it to question the validity of the political balance established in 1867 by the British North America Act. For some, this question of the validity of the political balance would translate directly into separatism. For others, presently much more numerous, the aim became the revision in depth of the federal regime. One thing is certain: the desire for change became, from 1960 onward, a widely spread political reality.

2-6.   THE MEECH LAKE ACCORD (EXCERPTS)*

The Meech Lake Accord was unanimously agreed to by the first ministers on April 30, 1987, and its language was finalized at a subsequent meeting on June 3. (Most of the changes made to the language of the accord at the June meeting were technical. At least one, however, had important symbolic significance. The initial wording of section 2 referred to "French-speaking Canada" and "English-speaking Canada." At the June meeting the collectivist flavour of this clause was tempered, and the language was modified to refer, in more individualistic terms, to "French-speaking Canadians" and "English-speaking Canadians.") The following excerpts relate to the central and most controversial elements of the accord. In comparison with the demands of the PQ and of previous Liberal governments such as that of Premier Jean Lesage in the 1960s (Readings 2-1 and 2-5), the provisions of the accord can be seen to entail relatively modest changes to the status quo.

1. The *Constitution Act, 1867* is amended by adding thereto, immediately after section 1 thereof, the following section:

2. (1) The Constitution of Canada shall be interpreted in a manner consistent with

- (a) the recognition that the existence of French-speaking Canadians, centred in Quebec but also present elsewhere in Canada, and English-speaking Canadians, concentrated outside Quebec but also present in Quebec, constitutes a fundamental characteristic of Canada; and
- (b) the recognition that Quebec constitutes within Canada a distinct society.

(2) The role of the Parliament of Canada and the provincial legislatures to preserve the fundamental characteristics of Canada referred to in paragraph (1)(a) is affirmed.

(3) The role of the legislature and Government of Quebec to preserve and promote the distinct identity of Quebec referred to in paragraph (1)(b) is affirmed.

(4) Nothing in this section derogates from the powers, rights or privi-

*"The Constitutional Amendment, 1987," in Government of Canada, *Strengthening the Canadian Federation*. (Ottawa: Government of Canada, August 1987), pp. 10–19.

leges of Parliament or the Government of Canada, or of the legislatures or governments of the provinces, including any powers, rights or privileges relating to language. . . .

7. The said Act is further amended by adding thereto, immediately after section 106 thereof, the following section:

106A. (1) The Government of Canada shall provide reasonable compensation to the government of a province that chooses not to participate in a national shared-cost program that is established by the Government of Canada after the coming into force of this section in an area of exclusive provincial jurisdiction, if the province carries on a program or initiative that is compatible with the national objectives.

(2) Nothing in this section extends the legislative powers of the Parliament of Canada or of the legislatures of the provinces. . . .

9. Sections 40 to 42 of the *Constitution Act, 1982* [relating to the amendment procedure] are repealed and the following substituted therefor:

40. Where an amendment is made under subsection 38(1) [requiring the approval of the legislatures of seven provinces with 50 percent of the Canadian population, and the federal parliament] that transfers legislative powers from provincial legislatures to Parliament, Canada shall provide reasonable compensation to any province to which the amendment does not apply.

41. An amendment to the Constitution of Canada in relation to the following matters may be made by proclamation issued by the Governor General under the Great Seal of Canada only where authorized by resolutions of the Senate and House of Commons and of the legislative assembly of each province:

(*a*) the office of the Queen, the Governor General and the Lieutenant Governor of a province;

(*b*) the powers of the Senate and the method of selecting Senators;

(*c*) the number of members by which a province is entitled to be represented in the Senate and the residence qualifications of Senators;

(*d*) the right of a province to a number of members in the House of Commons not less than the number of Senators by which the province was entitled to be represented on April 17, 1982;

(*e*) the principle of proportionate representation of the provinces in the House of Commons prescribed by the Constitution of Canada;

(*f*) subject to section 43, the use of the English or the French language;

(g) the Supreme Court of Canada;
(h) the extension of existing provinces into the territories;
(i) notwithstanding any other law or practice, the establishment of
      new provinces; and
(j) an amendment to this Part.

2-7.   TRUDEAU'S CRITICISM OF THE ACCORD*

*The Meech Lake Accord, with its decentralist thrust and its recognition
of Quebec as a "distinct society," stood in contrast to the centralism and
the resistance to any special treatment of Quebec that had characterized
federal constitutional policy under Prime Minister Pierre Trudeau. In May
1988 Trudeau, then a lawyer in private practice, emerged from political
retirement to criticize the accord scathingly in the press and in testimony
before a parliamentary joint committee holding public hearings on the
accord. Trudeau's comments were edited into book form by a former member of the federal Liberal cabinet under Trudeau, Donald Johnston, an
anglophone Quebecker. The following excerpts are from Trudeau's testimony before the joint committee. Trudeau refers to Henri Bourassa, a
federal Liberal politician and journalist from Quebec in the late nineteenth
and early twentieth centuries, who strongly supported Quebec interests
within Confederation and opposed British influence. Trudeau also invokes
the name of an anglophone Canadian politician of the late nineteenth
century—Edward Blake, a Liberal premier of Ontario who subsequently
entered federal politics.*

I will . . . begin by quoting two of the most brilliant parliamentarians
Canada has ever known. Edward Blake, some half-dozen years after the
beginning of Confederation, said:

The future of Canada depends very largely upon the cultivation of a
national spirit. We must find some common ground on which to unite,
some common aspiration to be shared, and I think it can be found
alone in the cultivation of that national spirit to which I have referred.

And, almost half a century later, the great Henri Bourassa observed that
there was, in Canada, a distinctive patriotism among people living in

*Donald Johnston, ed., *With a Bang, Not a Whimper: Pierre Trudeau Speaks Out*
(Toronto: Stoddart, 1988), pp. 32–35.

Ontario, another in Quebec, and yet another among Westerners. But, he said, "there is no Canadian patriotism; and as long as we have no Canadian patriotism, there will be no Canadian nation."

. . . I am simply suggesting that Meech Lake will allow people to say: "Yes, we have our own provincial patriotism back home." It is a case of the interest of one province coming before the common good of all Canada. And that was certainly not the wish of Henri Bourassa when he said: We will have to create a Canadian nation by developing Canadian patriotism.

Finally, I come to what is perhaps the most important point of all: the one dealing with Quebec as a distinct society. I hasten to say right from the outset that this is indeed a sociological reality, and that I see no harm in our thinking it to be true, or even expressing the thought verbally or in writing, if we so choose. But let us also recognize right from the start that when we talk about a distinct society, and particularly when we enshrine that into the Constitution as an operative clause, we are, by definition, by the actual meaning of the terms, working towards or promoting a provincialist view of Canada. Not national patriotism, not the national spirit that Blake was talking about!

Is that regrettable or not? Time will tell. But certainly, if that amendment is added to all the others, you have a massive shift towards provincial patriotisms, towards the idea that Canada is a nice "country," but it is made up of a collection of provinces, no more no less, and that our provincial loyalties will be enough to hold us together as one nation.

Well, many people do not think so, and I am one of them. I think that if we want to have a federal and not a confederal country, we have to have a national government, a national parliament that can speak for all Canadians, since the House of Commons is indeed the only legislature in the country whose members are elected by all Canadians rather than by separate regions called provinces.

. . . Either the phrase "distinct society" means nothing, or it means something. . . . If this phrase is meaningless, has no constitutional impact, well, it is rather insulting for Quebec to be told, "Okay, you are a distinct society, but you shall have no more powers than the others, basically you are no more distinct than the others." Because Newfoundland also claims to be a distinct province, and certainly British Columbia and many others. So you Quebeckers will be told that you constitute a distinct society, but do not count on the Constitution to give you powers to preserve or develop or protect this distinct society.

When you are told in subsection 3 of section 2:

> The role of the legislature and government of Quebec to preserve and promote the distinct identity of Quebec . . . is affirmed.

all you are being told is that it is your duty, your role, to govern the province well. The other provinces do not have to be told that, because they are sensible enough to govern themselves properly without being told.

Well, all I can tell you, ladies and gentlemen, is that if you take that view of the interpretative clause, you are in for some nasty surprises later on. Because you just have to read what the representatives of the Quebec government have said to their constituents publicly, in the National Assembly and in the newspapers. They see things differently; they feel that if the lawmakers, and all the more so the Constitution writers, say something, they want their words to have meaning. And personally, I cannot blame Quebeckers for thinking so. It is an old legal principle that legislators do not engage in empty rhetoric. That can happen, but not when writing laws.

Thus, we have to examine the hypothesis that "distinct society" means something. And what does it mean? Obviously there is much disagreement about that. You have only to read the testimony of some people, of the Premier of Quebec, of his Minister of Intergovernmental Affairs, Mr. Rémillard, and you will see that they give it a pretty broad meaning.

Apply the distinct society clause to the Canadian Charter of Rights, for example. The crucial importance of the Charter meant that we all share a set of common values and that all Canadians are thence on an equal footing; whether they be Quebeckers, Albertans, French, English, Jewish, Hindu, they all have the same rights. No one is special. All Canadians are equal, and that equality flows from the Charter.

As soon as you say, "Well, Quebec is unique under the Constitution, we can administer ourselves, we do not need this Charter" . . . and I think that is the effect of the distinct society clause . . . what do you do? You eat away and undermine further the Canadian spirit that is so essential to unity, as Blake told us. . . .

So, we have made peace, but how? First, by giving the provinces everything they wanted. I assure you that I could have had peace, that Mackenzie King could have had peace with the provinces, that John A. Macdonald could have had peace with the provinces, if they had given them everything they asked for. So that peace has been dearly bought. And I predict that it will be a temporary peace, because the next federal-provincial conference already has on its agenda further transfers of powers to the provinces. Newfoundland in particular. All the provinces will say, "Me too, gimme!" And that will be the story in the future: Provincialism triumphant.

Second, we have made peace with Quebec by letting it believe that "distinct society" means Two Nations. If the courts hold that it does have that meaning, Canada is doomed. If they hold otherwise, Quebec will have been tricked, and the howls of protest will strengthen separatism. One way or another, Meech Lake may mean the peace of the grave for the Canada we know and love.

2-8.   ONE LEGISLATOR'S AMBIVALENCE*

Premier Clyde Wells submitted the Meech Lake Accord to the Newfoundland legislature for ratification, while expressing his own continued opposition to the accord, after returning from the first ministers' meeting in Ottawa in the first week of June 1990, as discussed in the text. Although a number of the major protagonists in the debate had taken increasingly polarized positions on the accord in the weeks leading up to the first ministers' meeting, Ms. Duff's comments reflect the extent to which a number of legislators had to wrestle with their own ambivalence about the accord and the issues it raised.

Meech Lake has preoccupied my thoughts and a great deal of my free time for months. . . .

I have read extensively and thought out opposing views. I have talked to people in my District and in other parts of Canada. I have sought to talk to people in Quebec, because this is very important for the people of Quebec, and I wanted to understand the significance of this decision for them.

I confess I have strong positive feelings for the Province of Quebec. I lived there for seven years. One of my children was born there, and I still maintain links of friendship in that province. I believe that our linguistic duality is an important part of our Canadian identity and I believe that Canada and Canadians are immensely enriched by the culture and heritage of Quebec.

*Excerpts from an address by Shannie Duff, Member for St. John's East, to the Newfoundland House of Assembly, June 22, 1990. Published in Newfoundland House of Assembly, *Verbatim Report* 41, no. 57(A), pp. 2–10.

I also believe that Quebec has not been always easy to live with or to understand. I am offended as a Newfoundlander by some of the comments about my Province by Quebecers and other Canadians, as I am offended by some of the actions and words of English Canadians in Canada and in Newfoundland related to Quebec. I want Quebec to find a comfortable place in Canada, but not at the expense of other rights and not at the expense of our recognition of our multicultural diversity.

I have asked myself how these issues are affected by the Meech Lake Accord. Slowly and painfully, over many months, I have come to an opinion, but not a conclusion or a total conviction that the best path for many reasons, the greatest good, would be to adopt the Meech Lake Accord. . . . I lean to accept based on my own examination and re-examination of the substance of the Accord, and my appraisal of the consequences of accept or reject.

I am tempted to reject, based on the opinions of the majority of my constituents, many of whom have given the most thoughtful consideration to the Accord. I am tempted to reject on the fact that Meech is not a perfect document; on my concerns with the process; on anger with the Prime Minister for the handling of the seven days in Ottawa and his subsequent statements.

I have changed my mind daily as new concerns have been raised by my constituents and in debate. I have followed these concerns up. I have phoned Ottawa. I have phoned various places looking for answers so that I could be sure that my judgement was correct. I have asked more questions. I have doubted my judgement. I have been somewhat reassured by answers to the questions. I have argued with myself. I have fought with my friends and members of my family, and I have been reassured by others. . . . I have found, Mr. Premier, a fundamental difference of vision for the future of Canada. There is a strong centralist vision and the vision of an evolution to a more confederal Canada, through a devolution of Federal power to the Provinces. This is an honest and fundamental difference of opinion. It is not a fundamental flaw.

Constitutions may guide our future and changes to the structures of Government may influence our evolution, but they are not the only determinant. We must evolve if we are to grow. Which vision best accommodates our strong desire for a whole and united Canada? I am not sure which one is right, or which one wrong, or even if there is a right or a wrong. For those who see this as a pivotal issue in this debate, there will remain a strong difference of opinion.

Meech Lake moves Canada toward the confederal vision. For those who support the Accord it is a more tolerant vision, more accommodating of diversity. It redefines the relationship between provinces and the Federal Government within a united Canada. For those who oppose the Accord it is a recipe for the entrenchment of economic disparity and continued disunity. We can only base our judgements on an assessment of probability and an evaluation of risk.

Notes

1. Quebec's attempt to defend its legislation establishing French as the official language of its governmental institutions in the late 1970s, on the ground that this was a matter relating only to the constitution of Quebec, was rejected by the courts (Chapter 7). The federal government's proposal to make changes to the Senate was held *ultra vires* by the Supreme Court in the *Reference regarding the Upper House* in 1978.

2. Measures of separatist sentiment in Quebec are a matter of dispute among public opinion researchers. Pinard (1975) maintains that Quebec respondents do not necessarily consider "independence" to mean "separation." Support for the latter, as measured by surveys, was considerably lower (less than 20 percent in the late 1960s and early 1980s) than support for the former. When "independence" was somewhat clarified to mean Quebec's becoming an "independent country," Gallup polls indicated fairly modest levels of support in the 1970s but tracked a fairly steady rise in support from 11 percent of all Quebec respondents in the late 1960s to 18 percent in 1979. The interpretation of support for Quebec "sovereignty" in public opinion polls is similarly clouded.

3. Under either the legislative or the referendum route the consent of each province with at least 25 percent of the population, at least two Atlantic provinces, and at least two western provinces was required. Under the referendum provision the decision of each province would be determined by a majority of those voting in that province.

4. Gallup did not provide a regional breakdown of opinion in its June 1987 report, but it can be assumed that Quebec respondents were more favourable to the distinct-society concept than those in the rest of Canada. In January 1989, as opposition to the concept was building outside Que-

bec, Gallup published another poll and this time reported separate figures for Quebec. At that time 36 percent of the national sample supported the constitutional recognition of Quebec as a distinct society, with 46 percent opposed and 18 percent undecided. In Quebec the approval level was 57 percent, with opposition at 13 percent and indecision at 30 percent (Gallup Canada June 18, 1987, January 16, 1989).

5. Simeon and Blake (1980: 105) report that, "when asked in July 1977 whether Quebec should have a 'special status', defined as 'more powers than the other provinces', fully 91 percent of Canadians outside Quebec expressed opposition." Simeon and Blake also note that 72 percent of Quebec residents were opposed to special status for Quebec and that, "even assuming most English Quebeckers are opposed to special status, this is still a large figure." However, it is important to recognize what Quebec residents considered to be the *alternative* to special status. Polls in 1980 indicated that 31 percent preferred "sovereignty-association" and 7 percent preferred complete independence from Canada. Thirty-one percent preferred more power for all provinces, and only 15 percent preferred the status quo (Gibbins 1982: 183–84).

6. The Constitution Act 1867 merely provided that Parliament may establish a general court of appeal. The Supreme Court was established by federal legislation in 1875. Legal opinion differed over the extent to which its structure and powers were constitutionally entrenched through the amendment formula established in the Constitution Act, 1982 (Russell 1987: 67–68). The Meech Lake amendments attempted to remove this ambiguity.

3 Health Care Delivery

Health care is Canada's social policy success story. The Canadian national health insurance program enjoys broad popular support and, increasingly, international acclaim. It provides universal, comprehensive first-dollar coverage of medical and hospital services, while incurring a rate of cost escalation that is moderate in international perspective (Table 3-1). Canadian health care expenditures (public and private) increased 70 percent faster than GDP from 1960 to 1985, while such expenditures increased 90 percent faster than GDP in OECD nations on average, 120 percent faster in Britain, 130 percent faster in the United States, and 200 percent faster in Sweden (Schieber and Poullier 1987). This level of performance has been achieved, as noted in a 1989 editorial in the *New England Journal of Medicine*, without either the "intrusive regulation" that has characterized the (unsuccessful) American approach to cost containment, or "nationalization" of the health care system on the British model (Relman 1989: 590). A 1988 cross-national public opinion survey found Canadians to be more satisfied with their health care system than are either Americans or Britons, and a large majority of Americans saw a Canadian-style system as preferable to their own (Blendon 1989).

The Canadian system of "private practice/public payment" (Naylor 1986) is consistent with a political system in which the public and private sectors wrestle for legitimate domain. The system, furthermore, combines national standards with provincial experimentation. It is both shaped by and respondent to the ambivalences that characterize the Canadian political system: It is a model of Canadian compromise, and it "works."

This glowing portrait of the Canadian system needs some qualification. Canada's level of per capita expenditure on health care was second only to the United States in the 1980s. As a proportion of GDP, Canada's

TABLE 3-1   Measures of Health Expenditures, Nine Nations and OECD
            Average, 1960–86

Nation	Public Health Expenditures as Percentage of Total Health Expenditures		Total Health Expenditures as Percentage of GDP	
	1960	1986	1960	1986
Australia	52.6	73.0	4.6	6.8
Canada	43.1	76.0	5.5	8.5
France	57.8	79.2	4.2	8.5
Germany	67.5	78.1	4.7	8.1
Italy	83.1	78.0	3.3	6.7
Japan	60.4	72.9	3.0	6.7
Sweden	72.6	90.9	4.7	9.1
United Kingdom	85.2	86.2	3.9	6.2
United States	24.7	40.8	5.2	11.1
OECD mean	61.8	76.7	4.1	7.2

Source: Schieber and Poullier 1988: exhibits 1 and 2.

total health expenditures were stable through most of the economic boom of the 1980s, but rose to 9 percent as GDP growth declined in the early 1990s. Medical and hospital services are covered by the public plan, but coverage of other goods and services, notably dental services and drugs provided outside hospitals, is not comprehensive and varies across provinces. Public expenditure accounted for 76.0 percent of total health care expenditures in 1986, near the OECD average of 76.7 percent. Competing concerns about cost escalation, underfunding, and rationing are periodically raised in the Canadian health care policy arena, but these expressed concerns need to be seen in context as part of the rhetoric of negotiation between providers of health care and governmental funding agencies. Finally, the impact of the health care delivery system on the *health* of Canadians is notoriously difficult to estimate. On one commonly used measure of health status, low infant mortality, Canada compares favourably with other OECD nations, ranking ninth of twenty-four— below the Nordic nations, Japan, Switzerland, and the Netherlands, but above Germany, France, the United States, and the United Kingdom (OECD 1987: table 8).

Notwithstanding these qualifications, the relative success of Canadian public policy in the health care arena is remarkable—all the more so because Canadian social policy more generally does not, when seen in comparative perspective, appear in such favourable terms. Because the most immediate comparison is with the United States, there is a tendency for Canadians to think of their social programs as generous. During the intense public debate over the Free Trade Agreement with the United States, for example, concerns that Canada's social programs would be jeopardized by a process of harmonization with American programs were vigorously voiced by opponents of the deal. In broader comparative and historical perspective, however, this impression of generosity diminishes.

The effect of Canadian ambivalence about state and market mechanisms is apparent in the social policy arena, as it is in others. A "European" view of social benefits as a right of citizenship has advocates within the political system, most notably within the New Democratic Party; and it competes with an "American" view of social benefits as constituting a "safety net" for those unfortunates who fall out of the market. Accordingly, the Canadian social security system comprises some universal elements (notably, old age security pensions and family allowances) on the European model. Increasingly, however, these universal benefits are being taxed back from higher-income recipients. Furthermore, the proportion of Canadian income-maintenance spending that goes to means-tested social assistance programs (as opposed to universal transfers or social insurance) is far above the OECD average (Banting 1987: 34–35).

Canada's public spending on social programs (income maintenance, health, and education) as a proportion of GDP has consistently been below the OECD average—even below average for the seven major OECD nations, which include the low-spending United States and Japan. (Canada's social spending/GDP ratio was estimated to be 22.3 percent in 1986, as compared with the OECD average of 24.7 percent and the average for the largest seven OECD nations of 23.3 percent.) Canada's proportionate spending on social programs has also been consistently but only marginally higher than that of the United States through most of the postwar period. In the 1980s this gap began to widen somewhat as Canadian social spending continued its gradual secular increase as a proportion of GDP, while the rate of increase in the U.S. social spending/GDP ratio levelled off (OECD 1989: 16–17).

It is Canada's relatively niggardly approach to income maintenance (other than unemployment insurance, or UI) that accounts for these relatively low social spending levels. Income transfers in general as a proportion of GDP are well below the OECD average (Banting 1987: 195). Canada's spending on public pensions (at 5.5 percent of GDP in 1986) was below not only the OECD average but also below that of the United States (OECD 1989: 16–17). In part, Canada's low spending on public pensions reflects its demographic composition, with a relatively large "baby boom" generation that has not yet reached retirement age. Primarily, however, it reflects the low level of pension benefits for the average retired worker. Because of its universal flat-rate benefit (old age security, or OAS) and means-tested supplements at the federal and at some provincial levels, the Canadian public pension system does relatively well at lifting elderly households out of poverty (Banting 1987: 51; Myles 1988: 269; Smeeding, Torrey, and Rein 1988: 11). Benefits under the contributory component of the public pension system (the Canada Pension Plan, or CPP), however, amount to a lower percentage of preretirement income than is the case in most other western industrial nations (Aldrich 1982). As a result "a substantial portion of middle-income Canadians who are dependent primarily on public pensions face a much sharper drop in their living standards when they retire than do their counterparts elsewhere in the western world" (Banting 1987: 51). For the *nonelderly* poor, moreover, Canada ranks relatively poorly among advanced industrial nations in the extent to which its income transfer programs move families out of poverty (Smeeding, Torrey, and Rein 1988: 111).

Canada's unemployment insurance program, however, is relatively generous—largely because of its eligibility requirements and the duration rather than the level of its benefits. The UI program, indeed, has come to play a redistributive role, both between income categories and between regions, beyond what might be expected of a contributory social insurance scheme (Banting 1987: 209). The unemployment insurance plan has been laden with redistributive objectives largely by default, given the difficulty of making changes in the federal-provincial fiscal arrangements that underlie other components of Canada's system of income security. The redistributive role of the UI plan became increasingly controversial in the 1980s, and changes made in 1990 reduced this role somewhat (Chapter 4).

Why has Canadian social policy provided significant benefits under a popular program in the health arena, but not in the arena of income maintenance? The answer lies, in this case as in others, in the intersection of state structures with the organization of interests that characterizes each of these arenas. In the health field policy has been shaped along two axes of conflict and accommodation: the medical profession–state axis and the federal–provincial axis.

Context

Constitutional jurisdiction over health care policy in Canada is clearly lodged at the provincial level. Nonetheless, the federal government's use of its spending power has made it a major participant in the health policy arena. The ambiguities inherent in this de facto overlapping of powers have made for an ongoing dynamic. Provincial governments have experimented with policy initiatives. The federal government has fostered the diffusion of those initiatives through the development of a national framework. The provinces in turn have developed their own particular programs within the national framework, and some of that continuing provincial experimentation has fed back into national policy change.

In addition to producing this dynamic of policy generation and diffusion, Canadian federalism has affected policy development in the health care arena in a second way. Changes in the temper of federal-provincial relations have alternately favoured or frustrated the development of national policies. This changing temper, then, has affected the *timing* of policy changes in the health care arena. And since the climate of policy ideas and the constellation of interests have varied over time, the timing of policy changes has been crucial in establishing the context in which they are made.

Until the 1940s neither federal nor provincial governments in Canada were significantly involved in the financing of health services. The rise of the socialist Cooperative Commonwealth Federation in the 1930s and 1940s, however, placed health insurance firmly on the political agenda. In 1944 the CCF came to power in Saskatchewan and almost immediately proposed the adoption of a governmental hospital insurance program. (There was some tradition of governmental financing of health care in the prairie provinces, under the "municipal doctor" programs in place since the early 1900s.)[1] Although not in power, the CCF also became a significant force in opposition at the federal level and in Ontario in this period, and it was seen as an electoral threat in particular by the federal Liberals. At least in part as a response to this threat, the federal Liberals moved to develop proposals for national health insurance (Taylor 1978: 8; Falcone and Mishler 1989: 11–12).

Beyond these partisan considerations, moreover, there existed in the immediate postwar period a remarkable consensus among medical, hospital, and insurance interests favourable to the establishment of a comprehensive health insurance plan in the public sector. Viewing national health insurance as "necessary, and . . . probably inevitable" (Taylor 1978: 23), these groups supported such a plan in principle and sought to maximize their influence in its development and implementation. The sense of necessity and inevitability arose in part from awareness of developments in other jurisdictions, notably Britain, where the National Health Service (NHS) was being born. Had national health insurance been adopted in Canada at that time, it would almost certainly have borne a closer resemblance to the NHS than did the program ultimately adopted (Taylor 1973: 33; Tuohy 1989: 144–45). The federal government did indeed present a set of proposals for a cost-shared national health insurance program at the Federal-Provincial Conference on Post-War Reconstruction in 1945. These proposals, however, ultimately sank to defeat under the weight of the larger package of intergovernmental financial arrangements to which they were bound, and the first propitious moment for the introduction of national health insurance was lost.

The resulting delay gave private health insurance plans time to develop and expand—plans that demonstrated to the medical, hospital, and insurance communities the viability of alternatives to government-sponsored health insurance. These developments blunted some of the general public pressure for government health insurance by providing coverage for the actuarially insurable. As a result, the strategic consensus in favour of a comprehensive public-sector plan began to unravel, to be replaced by a preference among medical, hospital, and insurance industry interests for government indemnification or partial subsidization of the uninsurable and the medically indigent, as a supplement to the private sector plans.

While the support for comprehensive health insurance among strategic interests in the health field was unravelling, however, a more favourable climate of federal-provincial relations was slowly developing. The provinces' postwar suspiciousness that the federal government would consolidate its wartime centralization of power had abated somewhat. Moreover, the "demonstration effect" of provincial hospital insurance plans in Saskatchewan and British Columbia, adopted unilaterally by those provinces in 1947 and 1948 after the collapse of the federal-provincial negotiations, added further impetus to provincial action. In 1957, accordingly, the climate of federal-provincial relations again dominated the politics of the health care field—this time with the result that a national hospital insurance program, cost shared between the federal and provincial governments,[2] was adopted in the face of the opposition of providers of hospital care and insurance.

With respect to the introduction of *medical* care insurance, the intersecting influences of federalism, partisanship, and organized interests are even more apparent. It was the social democratic CCF/NDP, in a foothold provided by the provincial government of Saskatchewan, that in 1962 adopted a comprehensive public-sector medical care insurance program in the face of medical opposition culminating in a physicians' strike. The consequences of this pivotal episode were several. First, medical incomes increased dramatically in the first few years of the program, reducing the likelihood of militant medical opposition to the adoption of a similar program nationwide. Second, the physician's option to bill patients directly, at rates above the fee covered by the public plan, without jeopardizing the patient's right to reimbursement from the public plan was part of the strike-settling agreement—and was henceforth viewed by the medical profession as a hard-won right. Finally, physicians brought from Britain on contract by the Saskatchewan government to provide services during the strike remained to staff nascent community clinics—a development that further politicized the issue of alternative organizational forms of health care delivery (alternative, that is, to fee-for-service private practice).

The catharsis and the demonstration effect of the Saskatchewan program eased the introduction of national health insurance. A Royal Commission on Health Services had been appointed by the federal Conservative government in 1961; it reported to a minority Liberal government in 1964. It recommended a comprehensive national medical services insurance program, to be administered by the provinces and cost shared by the federal government, on the model of the hospital insurance plan already in place. While doing so, however, the royal commission emphasized the need to protect the principle of "free and self-governing professions" in the health care field (Reading 3-1). In 1965 the federal government introduced legislation that would establish a federally cost-shared, provincially administered medical services insurance program, based on four principles: comprehensive benefits, universal coverage, public administration, and portability between provinces.

The adoption of the program was not without conflict. Medical and insurance interests continued to favour government supplementation of private-sector programs. There was, moreover, no "major outcry" for medicare on the part of the Canadian populace (Taylor 1978: 367). The conflict was primarily among political elites, and it was again channelled along federal-provincial fault lines, not along partisan lines within the federal or provincial governments. The Medical Care Act was passed in 1966 under a minority government, with only two dissenting votes in Parliament. But the provincial level was the locus of considerable opposition. Ontario, for example, protested that its entry into the program was practically coerced by the federal imposition of a supplementary tax introduced to pay for it (ibid.: 375). Notwithstanding this opposition, the fiscal incentives of the scheme were such that, between 1968 and 1971, all provinces entered the plan.[3]

The adoption of national hospital and medical insurance (usually referred to as medicare) fundamentally altered the financing of health care delivery in Canada, but it left the *organization* of health care delivery unchanged. Indeed, by underwriting the costs of the system, the plan removed incentives for organizational change. The organization of health care delivery in the 1980s remained much as it was in the 1960s: that is, as a decentralized system based upon privately organized medical practices and hospitals governed by community boards.

The medicare system put in place in the 1960s and early 1970s, then, combined "centralized" and "public" payment (in the sense that provincial governments were "single payers" for medical and hospital services within their jurisdictions, although their costs were shared by the federal government) with "decentralized" and "private" decision making about the pattern and volume of health care delivery. In this sense the Canadian system contrasts with, for example, the relatively centralized payment and management system of the British NHS, the decentralized public payment and private delivery system of Germany, and the decentralized public–private payment and private delivery system of the United States. Out of the particular conjunction of centralized public payment and private delivery of the Canadian system evolved the agenda of Canadian health policy in the 1960s and 1980s.

Agenda

The implementation of medicare contained the seeds of future policy challenges. The underwriting of first hospital and then medical services, without changing the organization of health care delivery, had several implications. It reinforced an existing bias in the system toward the utilization of in-hospital services. It "froze" the existing structure of institutional and organizational interests in place. And, because it reimbursed physicians on a fee-for-service basis and hospitals on a per diem basis, it left the funding of health care services "open-ended." The agendas of governments and health care providers evolved in that context.

Establishing a program of universal coverage and making the federal and provincial governments responsible for its open-ended costs guaranteed that the primary emphasis of the governmental agenda would shift from a concern with ensuring access to a concern with controlling costs. This shift was reinforced by cross-national trends. In virtually all advanced industrial nations (although to varying degrees) the increasing proportion of GDP devoted to health care became a matter of growing public policy concern throughout the 1970s and 1980s (Schieber 1985). Cost control replaced access as the dominant theme of the international climate of policy ideas.

In Canada the challenge of controlling costs was felt most strongly at the provincial level. Because provincial governments administered the insurance plans, it was they who had access to the primary levers of cost control. The federal government, although it shared the costs of the program, had virtually no leverage on those costs. In the mid-1970s the federal government moved unilaterally to cap the open end of its financial commitment. The Established Programs Financing (EPF) arrangements, negotiated in 1977 under the shadow of unilateral federal action, limited the rate of increase in federal contributions to provincial health insurance plans to the rate of increase in nominal GNP and population.[4] These arrangements left provincial governments 100 percent at risk for cost increases in health care over and above the rate of increase in the general inflation rate, GNP, and population.

Canadian provincial governments had basically three types of leverage on the control of these costs (not including the transfer of costs to the private sector—an option discussed below). They could attempt to hold down price increases; they could restrict the supply of personnel, facilities, and services; and they could seek to improve the efficiency of the system through organizational change. The logic of policy development in the health care arena led to a consideration of each of these options in a cumulative progression.

Rather than paying the medical fees that were "usual and customary" in particular localities as did U.S. third-party payers, provincial governments at first agreed to pay physicians on the basis of the fee schedules set by the provincial medical associations, prorated by a given percentage. Soon, however, the schedule of payments was set through negotiations between the government and the medical association in each province. In most cases they negotiated overall increases in the payment schedule, leaving the allocation of these increases across individual items in the fee schedule (rewarding certain patterns of practice, or benefitting certain specialties) to be carried out internally by the medical associations themselves.

Under these negotiations professional fees declined in real terms in the 1970s but rose in the 1980s (Barer and Evans 1986: 80). Moreover, cross-provincial differences in fee schedules increased under medicare, reflecting the different accommodations between the profession and government across provinces. Physician *incomes*, however, depended not only upon fee levels but on the number and type of services provided (the so-called utilization factor). As a result of increasing utilization of services per physician, incomes declined more slowly and accelerated faster than medical fees. Furthermore, since utilization tended to rise faster in provinces with lower rates of increase in fee schedules, medical incomes varied less across provinces than did medical fees (ibid.: 88).

Measures to limit the supply of physicians, such as restrictions on the immigration of physicians and on medical school enrollments, were considered and implemented with limited success. The supply of physicians per capita continued to increase in Canada, as it did in all OECD nations in the 1970s. In 1971 the active civilian physician-to-population ratio was 1:659; by 1983 it was 1:512. (These levels, however, varied considerably across provinces [ibid.: 86].) Although the Canadian growth rate was lower than average for the OECD,[5] it presented policy challenges for increasingly cost-conscious governments. Given the limited success of policies aimed at controlling the supply of practitioners, provincial governments began to experiment with measures to control the number and type of services provided *per practitioner*—that is, to control utilization. As discussed below, some governments developed mechanisms for identifying and reducing payments to "overservicing" physicians; and some incorporated constraints based on projected utilization into their negotiated agreements on medical remuneration (Rachlis and Fooks 1988; Lomas et al. 1989).

In the hospital sector supply constraints were more apparent. In the early 1970s governments began to negotiate global operating budgets with hospitals on a prospective basis, rather than reimbursing them retrospectively on a per diem basis. Capital budgets required separate approval by the provincial government, which also provided, in most cases, a large part of the funding. This centralization of the hospital budgeting process at the provincial level meant that provincial governments retained considerable leverage over operating costs and over hospital expansion. This contrasts, for example, with the situation in the United States. There, hospitals were able to build both operating and capital costs into their rate structures; they had access to private capital markets; and the lack of centralized payment meant that costs could be shifted from one type of payer to another as the terms and conditions of reimbursement varied (Brown 1990; Evans et al. 1989). The Canadian system also provides greater capacity for hospital cost control than do decentralized public systems, such as the German model in which operating costs are borne by parapublic insurance funds, while capital funds are provided by state governments (Altenstetter 1989).[6] In Canada, as elsewhere, wage and unit price increases in the hospital sector outpaced general inflation through most of the 1970s. But overall costs did not increase proportionately, reflecting the fact that the actual level of hospital facilities—personnel, beds, supplies, and equipment—available per capita actually declined slightly toward the end of the 1970s (Bird 1981). By 1982 hospital admissions per capita were slightly below the OECD mean (see Table 3-2).

These attempts at restricting supply did not touch central issues of the organization and utilization of health care personnel—the third instrument of cost control noted above. Measures to reallocate health care functions among health care personnel (away from physicians to less "expensive" personnel) have been on the governmental agenda since at least the late 1960s. Major reviews and revisions of professional legislation were carried out in Ontario, Quebec, and Alberta in the 1970s, but their effects were largely on the structure of professional governance rather than on the reallocation of functions (Tuohy 1986). Experimentation with forms of health care delivery alternatives to private fee-for-service practice (such as clinics funded on a capitation or global budget basis) advanced further in some provinces (notably, Saskatchewan and Quebec) than in others, but such models remained peripheral to the mainstream health care delivery system.

The development of such alternative organizational forms has been hampered by constraints in existing funding mechanisms—partly by the sheer size of financial commitments to existing programs, which limited the funds available for innovation (Stoddart 1985: 5), and partly by the terms of federal cost sharing. The federal government agreed to share the costs of hospital services, not other institutional forms of care.

Furthermore, its sharing of the costs of hospital and medical services was conditional on these services' being provided on "uniform terms and conditions." Changes to the financing arrangements in 1977 eased these constraints somewhat by reducing the proportion of federal transfers that were conditional and by providing block grants for extended care services. Acute-care hospital beds were indeed reduced in the late 1970s, in favour of extended-care facilities,[7] although experimentation with alternative organizational forms for ambulatory care remained limited.

The logic of policy development in the health care arena in Canada in the 1970s and early 1980s, then, led provincial governments to an early and continuing concern with the price of medical services, to later restrictions on supply and utilization, and finally (in a limited way) to considerations of organizational change. Throughout this period, however, governments also had to address the appropriateness of a "safety valve" option that might mitigate the relentless logic of cost control. An alternative to constraining costs, as actors in the U.S. health care system have well learned, is to *shift* them. The federal government, by limiting its contributions under the EPF arrangements, essentially shifted risk for cost increases to the provincial governments. The provincial governments in turn faced the question of whether or not to shift costs to the private sector through various forms of "user fees."

In other publicly funded systems—in Germany, Sweden, Japan, and Britain, for example—user fees were instituted or extended for some services in this period. These fees, however, were uniform across providers and were set by the funding agencies. In Canada the most controversial form of "user fee" was charged at the discretion of the provider and contributed directly to the provider's own income, through the practice of "extra-billing" by physicians: that is, the practice of billing patients directly for an amount over and above the fee covered by governmental health insurance.

Extra-billing had been an issue of some significance on the Canadian health care policy agenda since the 1960s. It had been a major issue in the medical strikes over the introduction of medicare in Saskatchewan in 1962 and in Quebec in 1970. Throughout the history of Canadian governmental health insurance, "extra-billing" took a variety of forms and was practised to varying extents in different Canadian provinces. At a rough estimate, extra-billing amounted to about 1.3 percent of total physician billings for services insured under medicare in Canada; and this proportion varied from 0.1 percent to 2.4 percent in the six provinces in which extra-billing was practised (Tuohy 1988: 280). An estimated 10 percent of physicians extra-billed (Canada 1983: 12), but again this proportion varied across provinces and even more across localities. Indeed, the "clustering" of extra-billing physicians in particular specialties and districts gave the practice a distributive and political significance beyond that which would be implied by the overall rate, and the continuation of extra-billing under universal medicare remained contentious.

As the logic of health policy under medicare unfolded, bringing concerns with price, supply, organization, and extra-billing to prominence, providers of health services attempted to adapt to and to shape the developing agenda. Chief among these groups, in the structures preserved by medicare, was the medical profession. And what marked medical opinion was its ambivalence toward the state. This ambivalence can best be understood by considering, in cross-national perspective, the experience of the medical profession under state and market-oriented regimes.

Under national health service or insurance programs, the medical profession must negotiate with the state over budgetary and organizational matters, and the "entrepreneurial" discretion of individual physicians is accordingly constrained. But within these constraints, professional *clinical* discretion (that is, the ability to determine the quantity and type of service according to diagnostic and therapeutic requirements) is essentially preserved. Studies of medical decision making in West Germany, Britain, and Sweden have consistently observed that state control of broad regulatory and budgetary parameters has not threatened professional control over the content of medical practice (Stone 1977: 38; Schwartz and Aaron 1984: 52–56; Heidenheimer, Heclo, and Adams 1983: 61; Bjorkman 1985: 417).

In contrast, in the United States, in which, among major OECD nations, the private sector plays by far the largest role (accounting for almost two-thirds of health care expenditures), much recent literature suggests that professional autonomy and clinical discretion is severely threatened. The threat arises not so much from the state as from what Paul Starr (1982) has called "the coming of the corporation": the development of large for-profit multi-institutional chains. These chains represent a significant threat to the clinical as well as the economic discretion of physicians, and to the ability of governments to contain health costs. Price, quantity, and type of service are increasingly influenced by corporate managers who pursue sophisticated strategies maximizing reimbursement and access to capital markets (Pattison and Katz 1983; Lewin, Derzon, and Marguilies 1981). The competitive advantage of these chains lies largely in their ability to exploit the very complexity of the regulatory and financing systems that have grown up in default of national health insurance in the United States. Furthermore, large third-party payers in the private sector, and large industrial corporations who are turning to "self-insurance" to provide their employees' health benefits, are developing mechanisms for the close scrutiny of physicians' claims. These large corporate entities on the supply side and the demand side are intervening much more directly and specifically into medical decision making than governments, with their relatively budgetary constraints, have done in other nations (Naylor 1986: 251; Fuchs 1983).

For the medical profession, then, the state is an adversary in the battle over the control of health care costs. But it may well be an adversary more tolerant of clinical autonomy than the corporate adversaries whom the profession might face in the market. It is this recognition that underlies medical ambivalence toward the state in Canada. Nonetheless, medical opinion has diverged regarding the appropriate trade-offs to be made in defending entrepreneurial and clinical discretion, and regarding the relative threats of the state and the market.[8] The majority view continues to hold to the defence of entrepreneurial discretion—essentially, the defence of the institutions of private fee-for-service practice. The example of the United States is not lost on these physicians, however; and there are limits to their willingness to embrace the market. Only a minority, for example, would support private for-profit management of hospitals, or a return to voluntary and commercial control of the health sector (Stevenson, Vayda, and Williams 1987: 12). There is, moreover, a less obvious but more strategically situated minority whose opinions differ from the entrepreneurial majority in several important respects. Their central concern is the physician's clinical discretion subject to professionally determined standards, not the defence of the traditional institutions of fee-for-service practice. They are prepared to accept arrangements limiting the entrepreneurial discretion of *individual* physicians and groups of physicians (such as mechanisms of peer review of workloads, changes in methods of remuneration, and organizational change) in the interest of preserving professional and *collegial* mechanisms of control over the standards of medical practice. In a sense, this body of opinion represents a kind of "red toryism" (see Chapter 1) within the profession—a recognition that the status and the function of the medical profession carries with it a social obligation and a corporate responsibility to constrain its economic power.

The distinction between the "entrepreneurial majority" and this "strategic minority" has important institutional manifestations. Since the 1960s provincial governments have insisted upon enforcing a distinction between voluntary medical associations, representing the interests of physicians, and professional regulatory colleges (the provincial licensing bodies), endowed with the authority of the state and charged with the protection of the "public interest." A licence to practise medicine carries with it membership in the respective provincial college. The governing councils of the colleges are composed of elected representatives of the membership, appointees of the medical schools in the province, and, in most provinces, "lay representatives" appointed by the provincial governments.

The "entrepreneurial majority" is most likely to be represented by the voluntary associations, although the political stance of these associations may vary over time as the incumbents of elected executive positions change. The minority dedicated to the preservation of professional governance of the clinical discretion of physicians, however, is strategically situated in what might be termed the "core institutions" of medicine: that is, in the regulatory college–medical school axis.[9] As will be discussed shortly, the policies that these core institutions pursued over the 1970s and 1980s, with few exceptions, indicate a willingness to collaborate with governments, trading off some measure of the entrepreneurial discretion of individual physicians in order to maintain such professional control. In reaching such accommodations, however, these institutions have engendered considerable hostility within the profession (Tuohy 1988: 279).

The configuration of support for extra-billing within the medical profession needs to be understood in these terms. On average, the level of support was moderate and varied across provinces (Stevenson and Williams 1985: 513). Relatively few physicians actually extra-billed. Extra-billing was, however, seen as one way of increasing the total funds available to the health sector—as a mechanism for responding to the pressure for increased medical fees without reallocating funds from elsewhere in the system. Even physicians whose personal incomes were not increased by extra-billing nonetheless supported the practice as a way of obviating the supply restrictions that in their view increasingly threatened the technological base of medicine and the clinical discretion of physicians. In this way, the "entrepreneurial majority" and the "strategic minority" could make common cause. The formal presentations of voluntary medical associations tended to be phrased in these terms (Readings 3-2 and 3-3).

In addition to these pragmatic considerations, however, the issue took on important *symbolic* dimensions for the majority of the profession. At a time when entrepreneurial discretion was coming under increasing pressure, extra-billing came to symbolize "private" and "individualistic" practice (Tuohy 1988: 284–86) (Reading 3-3). Still, support for market mechanisms per se in the health care field was a matter of considerable ambivalence among Canadian physicians; and to the extent that extra-billing carried a "market" connotation, its symbolic attractiveness was somewhat tempered.

Another major set of provider interests in the health care arena is that of the hospitals, whose political bases lie primarily in the local community that they serve. Provincial hospital associations exist and provide a variety of technical services to their members, as well as dealing with provincial governments on common issues of concern. But the primary political resource that hospitals can bring to bear is community support; and their dealings with the provincial government tend to be on a bilateral basis, negotiating operating and capital budgets. The shift to global budgeting in the 1970s intensified this negotiation. Attempts by provincial governments in the 1970s to close beds or entire hospitals demonstrated the political strength of community support and met with only limited success. Hospitals learned this lesson well: Many proceeded to breach their global budgets and to maintain that, unless the provincial government covered the deficit, beds would have to be closed. In most cases governments responded by covering deficits, but the annual negotiations constituted a "rolling restraint" on hospital spending.

Perhaps because they wished to maintain their bases of community support vis-à-vis provincial governments, hospitals were generally not enthusiastic about user charges. Alberta hospitals, for example, did not take up an option granted them by the province in January 1984 to impose per diem charges on patients up to specified maximums; and the Catholic Health Association of Canada, representing Catholic hospitals, took an explicit policy position opposing user fees and extra-billing.

Groups of health care practitioners other than physicians also became increasingly active under medicare. The objective of most of these groups has been to reduce the "medical" biases inherent in both the medicare plan and the regulatory structure in the health field. For much of the period from the mid-1960s through the 1980s, various groups of health practitioners have lobbied strenuously in attempts to have their services made eligible for coverage under medicare and to expand their scopes of practice under regulatory legislation. Rather than reaching accommodations with provincial governments as the medical profession has done, a number of these groups have followed a strategy of whip-sawing, using concessions gained from one government to attempt to extract similar concessions from another (Tuohy 1989: 151–52).

In general, however, the attempts of nonmedical groups to loosen regulatory constraints on their scopes of practice have been ineffective. As is discussed later in this chapter, their effects have been tempered by the nature of the accommodation between the medical profession and the state. But as the issue of organizational change moves higher on the health policy agenda, the climate for substantial regulatory reform may improve.

With few exceptions, nonmedical health care provider groups have not linked their demands for regulatory change to the broader agenda of organizational change in the health field. In part, this is due to the relatively recent mobilization and the lack of political resources and sophistication of these groups. One important exception, however, is organized nursing, which has made organizational change an important part of its policy agenda, and which has played an active role in broader coalitions, such as that which developed in opposition to extra-billing (Reading 3-4).

One arena in which nurses and other hospital and institutional employees became much more mobilized in the period from the 1960s to the 1980s was the arena of collective bargaining. As discussed in Chapter 4, labour-relations legislation governing the public and parapublic sectors changed significantly in this period, and increasingly mobilized nursing and public sector unions representing health care workers demanded and obtained substantial "catch up" wage increases (Bird 1981; Barer and Evans 1986: 56). The "squeeze" between these arbitrated wage awards and the constraints of negotiated global hospital budgets contributed, as noted above, to reductions in supply in the hospital sector (Bird 1981; Detsky, Stacey, and Bombardier 1984) and to hospital deficits.

While governments and health care providers have been active in the health care arena, the diffuse consumer interest has, in this field as in others, been notoriously difficult to mobilize. Indeed, the problems of mobilizing consumer interest are exacerbated under a national health insurance scheme in which the consumer interest is fragmented: Those who consume health services do not, directly and proportionately, bear the costs. All but two provinces (Alberta and British Columbia) had eliminated premiums in favour of general revenues or payroll taxes as the mechanism of financing the system by the late 1980s, and even in those provinces premium revenues covered only a portion of health care costs.

Because the costs of the health system have been spread across the tax base, Canada has not seen the mobilization of business interests concerned about the rising cost of health care in employee benefit packages that has occurred in the United States. Nor does the Canadian system provide a base for the corporatist "concerted action" that has occurred under the German system of sickness insurance funds (Altenstetter 1989: 41; Katzenstein 1987: 33–35). The general popularity of the Canadian program has meant that consumers have been relatively quiescent and have mobilized only periodically regarding issues that touch them directly, such as the threatened closing or curtailing of local hospitals, or medical extra-billing.

Mobilization around the extra-billing issue was, indeed, more marked than around any issue in Canadian health policy in the previous twenty years; and public support for banning extra-billing was much stronger than it had been for the introduction of medicare twenty years earlier—despite the fact that the practice was confined to a small proportion of the medical profession and involved a minuscule proportion of overall health expenditures (Tuohy 1988). In part, this mobilization was due to the "clustered" distribution of extra-billing, which meant that its effects were concentrated in particular localities. More important, however, was the symbolic significance of the issue. If extra-billing came to symbolize private practice for physicians, it conversely came to symbolize a threat to the "universality" of medicare (and of Canadian social programs more generally) to the labour, welfare, and church-related groups who formed a "Medicare in Crisis" coalition (Reading 3-5). As is discussed in the following section, this symbolism was promoted by the federal Liberal party as part of a partisan strategy.

Process

The parameters of health policy in Canada have been set by the shifting climate of federal-provincial relations, and within those parameters policy has been shaped by processes of conflict and accommodation between the medical profession and the state. The balance of conflict and accommodation, and the terms of accommodation, have varied across provinces. A brief review of the profession-state relationship in three provinces—Quebec, British Columbia, and Ontario—can illustrate the extent of this variation.

In Quebec the terms of the accommodation have been most "statist." Quebec effectively banned extra-billing when it entered the national medicare plan in 1971. Extra-billing was one of the major issues in the strike of Quebec specialist physicians against the introduction of governmental health insurance. The government's response, enforced by back-to-work legislation, was to make extra-billing economically unfeasible. It refused to reimburse patients of extra-billing physicians for any portion of their costs and hence denied extra-billing physicians their market. The Quebec government also froze medical fees under its health insurance plan from 1971 to 1975. When physicians responded by increasing utilization, Quebec in 1976 became the first province to introduce constraints based on utilization into the negotiation of medical fee schedules, and it continues to have the most elaborate constraints. Negotiated agreements provide for the prorating of fee-for-service payments to individual general practitioners beyond a negotiated target income (based on projected utilization). Furthermore, overall limits on payments to general practitioners and to specialists (again based on projected utilization) are established. If these limits are exceeded in any given year, subsequent fee increases are reduced to recapture the excess (Lomas et al. 1989). Quebec was also one of the first provinces (with Ontario) to establish a utilization review committee to review the practice profiles of physicians and to reduce payments to physicians identified as "over-servicing." Unlike those in other provinces, moreover, Quebec's utilization review committee was located within the provincial agency administering the health insurance plan, not within the professional regulatory body.

Organizational change has also progressed furthest in Quebec. In the mid-1970s in response to the recommendations of a provincial commission (the Castonguay-Nepveu Commission) the provincial government instituted a sweeping set of organizational changes. Regional planning boards were established to oversee hospitals, other institutional facilities, and local community health and social service centres. The regional boards were composed of representatives of health and social service providers, universities and colleges, and business, labour, and community groups. They were granted not only planning authority but also, in phases, some executive functions as well, such as the funding and organization of home care and emergency services (Gosselin 1984: 12; Marcoux 1987: 64). The governing legislation also specified the representative composition of governing boards of hospitals and local centres. At the end of the 1980s there were more than 160 local community health and social service centres, providing a source of primary care alternative to private practitioners, emphasizing team care by a variety of professionals and paraprofessionals (Rachlis and Kushner 1989: 237). Fewer than 10 percent of Quebec physicians, however, practised in these centres. Furthermore, regional boards continued to be dominated by physicians and health care administrators (Desrosiers 1986: 214–15). Legislative changes proposed in 1990 would further increase the powers of regional boards and administrators, including the authority to accredit physicians to practise in a given region. The most contentious of these reforms were deferred pending further review, however, after fierce protest from the associations of medical specialists, general practitioners, interns and residents, and students was encountered. Quebec thus presents a potentially more coherent and a more innovative organizational structure for the management of the health care system than exists in other provinces, but in practice the impact of this structure has been modest.

Much the same can be said for the process of revising professional legislation in Quebec. In 1974, also in response to the Castonguay-Nepveu Commission, Quebec adopted an umbrella statute, the Professional Code, with which all professional regulatory bodies, including those for the health professions, were to comply. It also established an oversight agency, the Quebec Professions Board, to enforce the provisions of the code. These revisions focused largely on the structures and processes of professional regulation, providing for lay representation on professional governing councils, cabinet approval of professional regulations, the possibility of unilateral governmental regulatory action in default of action by the professional body, and mechanisms of appeal by nonmembers from decisions of professional bodies. These changes have had, to date, virtually no effect on the allocation of functions among health care personnel, although they have in some cases constrained the entrepreneurial discretion of individual professionals or the economic monopoly power of professional groups (Contandriopoulos, Laurier, and Trottier 1986).

Quebec's greater "statism" in the health field reflects a similar stance in other policy arenas. In this arena, moreover, the relative strength of the state is enhanced by the limited mobility of French-speaking physicians and other health care providers in the North American context, and by a split in the organization of the medical profession. Not only are the voluntary associations separate from the professional licensing "corporation," but (unlike other provinces) there are also *two* voluntary associations, one representing specialists, the other general practitioners. The 1970 strike call, for example, was issued only by the specialists' association.

In British Columbia, where provincial politics in general are populist and polarized, and where the ranks of the medical profession have been more heavily populated than in other provinces with "refugees" from the British National Health Service, the relationship between the medical profession and the state has been confrontational. Indeed, it shows elements of the highly adversarial labour relations of British Columbia (see Chapter 4), although the professional association is not formally certified as a bargaining agent. This adversarial relationship has yielded physicians in British Columbia one of the highest fee schedules in the country; but it has meant that the policy process in general has been marked by periodic confrontations, strike threats, professional boycotts of governmental bodies, and recourse to litigation. The attempt by the British Columbia government to limit billing numbers provides an illustration. In 1985 the government refused to issue new billing numbers (effectively denying payment under the provincial health insurance plan) to physicians who located in overserviced areas. The medical profession responded by boycotting the planning committees that were to determine the need for physicians in given areas, and by launching an ultimately successful court challenge to the policy on the grounds that it infringed physicians' rights under the Canadian Charter of Rights and Freedoms.

This adversarialism, however, has not negated the possibility of pragmatic collaboration between the government and the profession. Extrabilling was effectively prevented in British Columbia by agreement between the British Columbia Medical Association (BCMA) and government, until this agreement was superseded by legislation in 1981. Overall utilization constraints have been negotiated into fee schedule agreements under the governmental health insurance plan: Thresholds based on projected utilization are established and, if those thresholds are exceeded, the excess is partially recouped through a reduction in subsequent fee increases (Lomas et al. 1989: 88). A utilization review committee to review the practice profiles of "aberrant" physicians was established as a committee of the voluntary association, the BCMA, not the governmental insurance agency; and, on the basis of limited evidence, it would appear that this committee penalizes proportionately fewer physicians than either Quebec's governmental utilization review committee or Ontario's committee which (as discussed below) is located within the professional licensing body (Wilson, Chappell, and Lincoln 1986).

Organizational change in British Columbia has been very limited. Regional hospital boards for capital planning were established in the late 1960s but functioned more as "buffers" between local hospitals and the provincial government than as planning agencies (Crichton 1984: 15). A report on regional restructuring, along the lines that were being considered in Quebec, Ontario, and Saskatchewan at the same time, was commissioned by the New Democratic Party government in the early 1970s but was not implemented.

Ontario does not consistently exhibit either the statism of Quebec or the adversarialism of British Columbia. Rather, the dominant motif of the profession-state relationship is a tenuous accommodation, punctuated by periodic conflict. The linchpin of this accommodation is the relationship between the state and the "strategic minority" of physicians, primarily based in the medical schools and the licensing body, the College of Physicians and Surgeons of Ontario (CPSO).[10] These strategically placed physicians are prepared to collaborate with the state on the condition that clinical discretion and professional autonomy are preserved. Given the vagaries of medical politics, the position of this minority within the executive ranks of the Ontario Medical Association (OMA) has varied over time and so, accordingly, has the political stance of the OMA. This minority, however, remains well represented within the leadership of the CPSO and on the numerous advisory task forces established by the government on a variety of health policy issues. The Ontario Council of Health, a government-appointed standing committee advisory to the minister of health, which existed from 1966 to 1988, was chaired for the last eight years of its existence by a former dean of medicine at the University of Toronto. Throughout its existence its membership was drawn from medical academe as well as from other scientific and professional groups and from the "general public." When the model of a standing advisory council at the ministerial level was abandoned in the late 1980s in favour of a series of issue-oriented task forces and a high-profile Premier's Council on Health Strategy (PCHS), medical academics continued to be heavily represented. The thirty-one-member PCHS, chaired by the premier, included representatives of the provincial cabinet, the medical profession, other health disciplines, and business, labour, and consumer groups. Of the eight medical members, all had academic appointments (not including the deputy minister of health, a former academic physician, who sat on the council as secretary). In 1991, under the NDP government, the PCHS was restructured as the Premier's Council on Health, Well-being and Social Justice. Of the forty-two members on the new council, seven (including one medical student) were drawn from the medical profession. Of these seven, all but one had past or current affiliations with medical schools.

The development of a process of utilization review in Ontario illustrates the nature of the accommodation between the profession and government. In the early 1970s the government moved to establish a review committee within the Ministry of Health to review and investigate aberrant accounts, identified through its computerized billing system, that suggested overservicing by individual physicians. After protests from both the OMA and the CPSO, however, the Medical Review Committee was established within the structures of the licensing body, the CPSO. Although it appears that this committee does not penalize at the rate of the governmental utilization review committee in Quebec, it has been more punitive than the committee operated by the voluntary medical association in British Columbia (Wilson, Chappell, and Lincoln 1986; Tuohy 1982b). Utilization constraints were formally incorporated into medical remuneration agreements under the governmental insurance plan in 1991 (well after such constraints had been adopted in Quebec and British Columbia) as part of a broad "partnership" agreement between the OMA and the provincial government, discussed below.

The effects of this accommodation between government and the core institutions of the medical profession in Ontario can also be seen in the area of professional regulation. Reforms of the legislation relating to medicine, dentistry, nursing, pharmacy, and optometry in 1974 did not impinge upon the scope of medicine's exclusive right to practice. And although accountability mechanisms were introduced, the collegial authority of professional regulatory bodies remained essentially intact. Like the Quebec reforms instituted at the same time (but much more limited in the range of professions involved), the Ontario reforms established common procedures across professional governing bodies, providing for lay representation on governing boards, governmental approval and initiative for professional regulations, and mechanisms of appeal from the decisions of governing bodies. As in Quebec, the substantive effects of this legislation on the policies of professional bodies have been slight (Tuohy 1986: 414–15). Another review process, begun in 1982 and culminating in a 1989 report, could however have a more significant impact on scopes of practice. It recommended an innovative model of professional legislation under which particular "acts" would be licensed—and some acts would be licensed to more than one profession. In theory, this model offers greater regulatory flexibility. In practice, however, change is likely to be incremental.

Organizational change in Ontario has also been moderate: less than in Quebec, more than in British Columbia. A 1974 report of the Ontario Council of Health, recommending sweeping reforms somewhat similar to the Quebec model of local community centres and regional boards, was not implemented. Instead, district health councils, advisory bodies appointed by the minister of health to represent health care providers and consumers, were established as planning agencies. The effectiveness of these bodies in reallocating expenditures across institutional facilities in their respective districts has varied considerably (Dixon 1981). They have, however, performed the administratively and politically useful functions of compiling information and negotiating compromises at the local level. Without fiscal authority on the model of, for example, Swedish county councils, it is unlikely that they could play any greater role (Tuohy and Evans 1984).

The Ontario Health Insurance Plan (OHIP) has written contracts to fund a limited number of community health clinics, managed by lay boards, on a block-grant basis to provide health services. OHIP has also written contracts to fund health services organizations (HSOs), managed by professional boards, on a capitation basis. (In fact, the majority of HSOs are simply small group practices that have opted for capitation rather than fee-for-service payment [Griffith 1990].) At the end of the 1980s the numbers of community clinics and HSOs were small (fewer than seventy, in total, serving about 4 percent of the population of Ontario), and their contracts continued to be administered as a pilot project within the Ministry of Health.

Quebec, British Columbia, and Ontario, though illustrative, do not exhaust the range of cross-provincial variation. Other provinces present other models. In Alberta, for example, a laissez-faire approach has allowed not only individual physicians but also other health care providers considerable entrepreneurial discretion. In Nova Scotia a traditionally close and consensual relationship between the profession and government has persisted under medicare (Boase 1986). And in Saskatchewan the terms of the strike-settling accommodation after the introduction of medicare in 1962 have been respected (with one exception shortly to be noted): Ambitious organizational reform proposals were greatly scaled down, and pragmatic negotiations characterize the ongoing relationship between the profession and government.

These provincial-level accommodations intersect with federal-provincial politics in determining the shape of health policy in Canada. Nowhere was this more apparent than in the case of the banning of extra-billing through the passage of federal legislation, the Canada Health Act, in 1984. The fueling of the extra-billing episode, indeed, had more to do with federal-provincial and partisan competition for public support than it did with profession-state relations. Responding to provincial opposition to the changes made in federal cost sharing under Established Programs Financing by the federal Liberal government in 1977, and to the rapid (although, in retrospect, transitory) increase in rates of opting out and extra-billing following the end of the anti-inflation program controls in the late 1970s (Chapter 5), the Conservatives appointed a one-man commission of inquiry into the health care system during their brief period in office federally in 1979–80. The report of this inquiry in September 1980, delivered to the Liberal government, which had by then replaced the Conservatives, supported the contention of provincial governments that they were not diverting federal health contributions to other purposes but gave strong support to federal concerns by identifying extra-billing as a major potential distortion of universal health insurance.

In 1983 the federal Liberal government, declining in popularity and facing non-Liberal governments in each of the provinces, seized upon the extra-billing issue as a way of signifying its commitment to defend the "universality" of the country's most popular social program—and, by extension, of others. The general climate of federal-provincial relations was extremely sour. The federal government developed, with only the most perfunctory discussion with the provinces, legislation reducing federal cash transfers to any province allowing direct patient charges to be made for insured services. The federal transfers were to be reduced by an amount equal to the dollar amount of charges to patients for insured services above governmental insurance coverage—a "dollar for dollar penalty" for direct charges. In defence of the proposed legislation the federal government issued a position paper whose title, "Preserving Universal Medicare," clearly summarized its major theme (Reading 3-6).

In responding to this threat from the federal level, medical associations generally sought to defend the accommodations that they had reached with provincial governments. In its brief to the 1979–80 Hall commission of inquiry, the Ontario Medical Association argued that "a national identity for the Medicare program should be confined to broad and general principles" and should allow for flexibility at the provincial level (Reading 3-2). The President of the Canadian Medical Association in 1983 defended "provincial responsibility and prerogative" in the health field (Reading 3-3).

The medical profession had few supporters among other organized interests, however. Because of its implications regarding the commitment to universality, as well as its more specific distributive implications, the principle behind the proposed legislation drew support from a broad coalition of welfare, labour, and church-related groups (including the Catholic Health Association, the organization representing Catholic hospitals). It was also supported by a number of health professional groups, most actively by organized nursing. And, perhaps because of the relatively small overall financial stakes,[11] the groups that had supported the medical profession on medicare-related issues in the past—the insurance industry and business groups more generally—were not as active in this case.

The Liberal government's attack on extra-billing, symbolizing the defence of universality, was an attempt to win broad public support for the federal government vis-à-vis the provinces, and for the federal Liberal party vis-à-vis the opposition Progressive Conservatives. In the latter respect at least, the strategy misfired. The federal Conservatives responded by supporting the legislation despite the opposition of their provincial counterparts, thereby depriving the Liberals of an election issue. Like its predecessor, the Medical Care Act in 1966, the Canada Health Act was passed in April 1984 with the support of all parties at the federal level. It incorporated and clarified the principles of universal accessibility, comprehensive coverage, public administration, and portability; and, by prescribing the "dollar for dollar" penalties for user fees and extra-billing, it specified sanctions under the EPF arrangements for violating the principle of universality.

With the passage of the Canada Health Act, much political activity shifted to provincial arenas, although federal-provincial politics continued to be entailed. The act provided a three-year "grace period" (ending April 1987) during which the federal government would retain in trust the penalty funds withheld from a province and would release those funds to the province as soon as it ceased to allow direct patient charges.[12] Before the end of the grace period all provinces were in compliance with the Canada Health Act. Nova Scotia introduced a ban on charges above the government rate for insured services to coincide with the coming into force of the Canada Health Act on July 1, 1984. Manitoba and Saskatchewan came into compliance in 1985; Ontario, Alberta, and New Brunswick, in 1986.

The terms on which extra-billing was banned and the process by which the change was made varied considerably across these provinces, reflecting different government-profession accommodations (Hieber and Deber 1987; Tuohy 1988). But in general (with one exception) the process of negotiating the ban was relatively nonconflictual, and the medical profession achieved substantial gains in the form of fee schedule increases and binding arbitration mechanisms for future fee schedule disputes, in return for the sacrifice of extra-billing. The exceptional case was that of Ontario. There, the banning of extra-billing was marked by a period of unprecedented conflict between the government and the OMA, marked by a legal challenge by the OMA and the Canadian Medical Association (CMA) to the Canada Health Act, and culminating in a four-week doctors' strike in June and July 1986. The legislation banning extra-billing was passed midway through the strike, which ended with the profession's having achieved no immediate gains in return for the ban. The conflict was attributable largely to a change in government in Ontario, after more than forty years of Conservative rule. The OMA had had a well-established understanding with the Conservatives and misread for months the new minority Liberal government's intransigence on the issue of extra-billing. Compliance with the OMA's strike call varied considerably across specialties and localities, and was both passively and actively discouraged by the medical schools and the regulatory college. The actual reduction in service was marginal.[13] The episode poisoned the relationship between the government and the OMA for a time, but by 1990 the OMA had effectively withdrawn its legal challenge to the Canada Health Act and had adopted a position of reestablishing "partnership" with the provincial government (Reading 3-7). In 1991 a wide-ranging agreement between the OMA and the NDP government among other things adopted binding arbitration for fee schedule disputes, incorporated utilization constraints in the medical remuneration system, established a standing bipartite committee of medical and governmental representatives to make policy recommendations regarding the improvement of the cost-effectiveness of medical service delivery and the supply and distribution of physicians, and gave the OMA the right to collect dues from all practising physicians in the provinces, including nonmembers (a version of the Rand formula in the provincial industrial relations system as discussed in Chapter 4).

Like the introduction of medicare itself, the resolution of the extra-billing issue demonstrates that the structures of the Canadian state allow political elites to legislate and enforce common standards across provinces, even in the face of considerable cross-provincial variation in the relationship between the state and organized interests.[14] Indeed, the achievement (or the approximation) of national standards is possible only because the interpretation and application of these standards can be worked out through particular accommodations between government and health care providers at the provincial level.

Consequences

In the episodes of conflict that punctuate the general pattern of accommodation in the Canadian health care arena, the language of crisis abounds. Providers allege that the system is "under-funded"; government spokesmen maintain that costs are "out of control." These allegations need to be put in comparative perspective. Table 3-2 provides some measures of Canada's record regarding changes in the price of medical and hospital services, the supply of physicians and hospital beds, the utilization of medical and hospital services, and medical incomes, in comparison with other OECD nations. It is, on balance, a record of relative moderation. Like a number of nations, Canada held medical price increases below the general rate of inflation in the 1970s and early 1980s, but like most others it also experienced hospital price increases above the prevailing inflation rate. Changes in the supply of hospital beds were at the average for the OECD nations, and physician supply grew less rapidly than the OECD average. Measures of service intensity are in the moderate-to-high range. Relative physician incomes declined in Canada, as they did across OECD nations in the 1970s and early 1980s, but again they remain in the moderate-to-high range. This moderation may be the key to Canada's ability to combine relative success in overall cost control (as presented in Table 3-1) with universal coverage of medical and hospital services, high levels of public satisfaction with the medicare program, and a general accommodation (punctuated with episodes of conflict) between the medical profession and the state.

TABLE 3-2   Indicators of Price, Supply, and Utilization, and Physician Relative Incomes, Nine Nations and OECD average, 1970–1980s

Nation	Price—Average Annual Percent Change 1970–84			Supply—Average Annual Percent Change 1970–1980s		Outpatient Physician Consultations per Capita	Hospital Admissions per Capita	Hospital Expenditures per Admission*	Physician Incomes Relative to Average Employee Income	
	Consumer Prices	Medical Prices	Institutional Prices	Inpatient Beds	Physicians per Capita				1970	1981
Australia	21.5	31.8	30.0 (1983)	1.0 (1981)	4.6 (1981)	6.4 (1981)	21.0 (1980)	$1460	4.3	2.5
Canada	15.0	13.6	22.0	−0.1 (1982)	2.2 (1982)	5.5 (1981)	14.7 (1982)	3020	5.1	4.1
France	19.0	15.0	20.8	1.0 (1983)	5.3 (1983)	4.7 (1983)	11.8 (1983)	2380	4.8	3.3 (1979)
Germany	6.6	8.1	14.0 (1982)	−0.1 (1982)	4.2 (1982)	NA	18.1 (1982)	2050	6.4 (1971)	4.9 (1980)
Italy	43.0	36.4	68.7	−1.0 (1983)	13.8 (1983)	8.3 (1981)	15.4 (1983)	NA	1.4	1.1
Japan	8.7	7.8	6.1	1.4 (1983)	2.3 (1982)	14.2 (1978)	6.7 (1983)	3190	NA	4.7
Sweden	18.1	12.7	22.4	−0.5 (1983)	6.5 (1983)	2.7 (1983)	19.2 (1983)	NA	3.7	2.1
United Kingdom	27.8	27.7	39.6	−1.3 (1981)	3.0 (1981)	4.2 (1983)	12.7 (1981)	3490	—	2.4
United States	10.6	13.8	15.6	−2.3 (1981)	1.7 (1981)	4.6 (1981)	17.0 (1981)	3450	5.4	5.1
OECD	19.6**	20.01	28.0**	−0.1	4.8	NA	15.3	2600	3.5	2.8

Source: OECD 1987: tables 25, 26, 27, 30, 34, 38.

*Purchasing power parities with U.S. dollar.

**For sixteen countries for which comprehensive data are available.

Canada's social policy success story, however, contains a dilemma as it unfolds into the 1990s. Much of the "success" of Canadian health policy rests on the fact that it has not fundamentally changed the organizational arrangements that preserve the clinical discretion of health care providers and that continue to be popular with consumers. Almost all of the leverage over costs has been exercised by constraining the entrepreneurial discretion (largely with respect to price) of physicians and the supply of acute-care hospital beds. Increasingly, however, policymakers are being driven to consider more substantial organizational change in the health field.

Two forces are driving policymakers in this direction. One has to do with ongoing development in the international climate of policy ideas and with an ironic "demonstration effect" from the United States. In the 1960s, the organization of health care delivery in the United States was very similar to that in Canada. But whereas Canada's adoption of comprehensive national health insurance "froze" this system of health care delivery in place, in the United States a variety of vehicles for health care delivery evolved in response to the various incentives provided under fragmented financial and regulatory arrangements. Some of these organizational developments, such as for-profit multi-institutional chains, are viewed with alarm in Canada, as was apparent in the debate of the adoption of the Free Trade Agreement with the United States during the 1988 federal election (Chapter 5). One of the agreement's provisions was that each nation afford "national treatment" to the other's health care facilities management firms, except for purposes of government subsidy. Both Liberal and NDP politicians raised the spectre that this provision would erode the Canadian system by introducing managers accustomed to profit maximization (Fraser 1989).[15] Other American organizational developments, however, have drawn more favourable attention from Canadian policy analysts. Notably, the apparent ability of health maintenance organizations (HMOs) in the United States to reduce hospitalization rates (Luft 1981) sparked experimentation with and advocacy of similar "alternative modalities" in Canada (Stoddart 1985; Lomas and Barer 1986: 261–63). The advantages of HMO-type mechanisms may indeed be better realized within the framework of a publicly sponsored plan than within the fragmented U.S. system, in which, according to recent studies, competition between HMOs and traditional insurance plans may have the perverse effect of increasing medical inflation in local markets (Morone 1990: 138; Hollingsworth, Hage, and Hanneman 1990: 193).

A second and ultimately more driving force behind organizational change in the health care field in Canada is the logic of policy development itself, and the intersection of this logic with the motives of health care providers. With the end of extra-billing, the last (or nearly the last) of the individual physician's discretion over the price of services has been ceded. The negotiation of fee schedule increases still produces periodic conflict, but the primary issues of contention are now constraints on supply and utilization. And in this next phase the fee-for-service system will come under increasing pressure.

Attempts so far at constraining supply and utilization—across-the-board limits and attention to aberrant cases—have amounted to a strategy of "sitting on the lid" to contain health care costs. As long as these mechanisms are successful in keeping both costs and levels of service within politically acceptable limits, it is unlikely that experimentation with changes in organization and remuneration will go much further. But increased cost pressures are looming, not only with the advancement of medical technology but also, and more ominously, with the aging of Canada's population. With its particularly large baby-boom generation, Canada faces an even greater challenge than most OECD nations in controlling future health care costs arising from an aging population (OECD 1987: table 43).

As these pressures grow, existing cost-containment strategies are likely to be less successful. Future policy developments are likely to evolve along two interrelated tracks: more sophisticated measures to control utilization, and changes to the organization and financing of the health care delivery system. Utilization control will move beyond identifying aberrant cases, to attempts to redefine the professional norms as to what constitutes appropriate medical care. The key issues will be *who* defines these norms, under what aegis (governments, voluntary professional associations, or professional regulatory bodies), and what fiscal and regulatory sanctions will be used to enforce them. As early as 1979 a task force established by the federal-provincial conference of deputy ministers of health established guidelines for periodic health examinations, although their recommendations were not incorporated into payment schedules under provincial insurance plans. In 1986 the national professional certifying body for obstetrics and gynaecology developed guidelines for the performance of caesarean sections. In some provinces, notably Ontario, there has been considerable jockeying for position by the provincial government, the professional association, and the regulatory body over who may legitimately define practice norms. In Alberta explicit policies and proposals to "de-insure" services not regarded as medically "necessary" have presaged the broader future politics around these issues, as critics have again raised the spectre of "two-tier medicine."

So far, these measures to control utilization have respected the delicate accommodation between the profession and the state regarding the preservation of professional clinical discretion. It will be easier to preserve this discretion if the direct link between utilization and cost that exists under a fee-for-service system is decoupled—if doctors' decisions about the mix of service to be provided do not directly translate into costs. Various ways of capping or replacing the open-ended fee-for-service system, involving various degrees of financial and organizational change, are increasingly being considered. Falcone and Mishler (1989: 26), indeed, foresee a "public utility" model for the Canadian health care system. Under this model, regional management boards would be granted global operating budgets out of which allocations would be made to all health care providers in the region, and such boards would also advise the provincial government on capital expenditures. A full-blown public utility model would incorporate physicians and other "private" practitioners as well as institutional facilities under the budgetary authority of the management boards. It would, because of the global budget constraint, imply either significantly modifying the fee-for-service system to "cap" payments to fee-for-services practitioners or replacing the fee-for-service system with salary or capitation arrangements. Such a model would move the Canadian system somewhat closer to the British National Health Service model (even as Britain experiments with changes to that model) and would represent, in terms of the scope and the degree of the boards' authority, a phase of evolution well beyond the advisory district health councils of Ontario or even the regional health and social services councils of Quebec. Falcone and Mishler, indeed, predict that such a model is likely to evolve first in the institutional sector and would coexist with a continuing system of negotiated fee-for-service payments to practitioners.

In April 1989 the Ontario minister of health initiated a "pilot project" program to test the feasibility of a model very similar to Falcone and Mishler's public utility model, to be known as the Comprehensive Health Organization (CHO). Under this model, community management boards would be funded on a capitation basis and would contract with hospitals, other institutional facilities, and practitioners to provide comprehensive care for each person enrolled with the board. These management boards, as and when they develop, may well have a hospital base—hospitals formed the nucleus of most groups expressing interest in developing pilot CHOs under the program. Although such pilot projects do not constitute major change, they may indicate the direction of change.

Both the direction and the pace of change will be greatly influenced, in the future as in the past, by accommodations between governments and health care providers, and hence will vary somewhat across provinces. It must be kept in mind that price, supply, and utilization indicators vary considerably across provinces. British Columbia, for example, has had a relatively rich medical fee schedule; Ontario, Quebec, and British Columbia have relatively high physician-to-population ratios; and Saskatchewan and Alberta have the largest supply of hospital beds per capita. Overall spending levels have varied as well. Indeed, Barer and Evans have made the startling calculation that "had Canada as a whole [in the period 1971–82] followed the growth experience of the three western provinces, total health care costs in 1982 would have been 10.5 to 13.4 percent above their actual levels, or from 9.3 to 9.6 percent of GNP—almost halving the difference with the US. Had Canada followed the growth pattern of Nova Scotia or Newfoundland since 1971, we might now be spending as large a share as the US or more" (1986: 72). Organizational arrangements also vary across provinces and are likely to vary even more as a result of provincial-level experimentation in the 1990s within the broad parameters established by the terms of the Canada Health Act and the cost-sharing arrangements thereunder (Stoddart 1985; Tuohy 1989: 156; Falcone and Mishler 1989: 21–22). Beginning in 1986 the federal government unilaterally reduced and then froze the rate of increase in per capita EPF transfers to the provinces, a policy that increases provincial incentives to control costs but limits the funds available for experimentation with policy options.[16]

Organizational experimentation will be constrained and shaped by these factors, but it will not be forestalled. Even the "entrepreneurial majority" of the medical profession is coming to accept and support organizational change, as long as fee-for-service practice remains an option in the system (see, for example, McAdam 1983). And it is unlikely in the extreme that any change in the 1990s would foreclose the fee-for-service option entirely. What is more likely is the gradual development of "alternative modalities" and increasing constraints on fee-for-service practice through various forms of caps on total payments and through utilization constraints.

Future policy developments in the health care policy arena are likely also to be affected by yet another change in the international climate of policy ideas: the growing emphasis on "healthy policy"—that is, on shifting the focus of health policy from health care delivery systems to the broad range of factors influencing the health of populations. Canada, indeed, received early international attention in this regard with the publication of the "Lalonde Report" by the Department of National Health and Welfare under health minister Marc Lalonde in 1974. The report set out a four-quadrant model of factors affecting health, including environmental, lifestyle, and technological factors as well as health care delivery. Despite its international acclaim, however, the report had little influence on Canadian health policy. Indeed, it was seen by some provincial officials and medical professionals as a federal attempt to provide a rationale for reducing financial contributions to medicare funding. Its emphasis has been institutionalized to a limited extent in the establishment of "health promotion" branches in federal and provincial health bureaucracies, and in some community clinics, which have taken an active role in environmental and occupational health issues at the local level. The problem with developing an institutional focus for "healthy policy," however, is that assigning it to established bureaucracies concerned with health care delivery will inevitably narrow its focus and marginalize its status. Attempting to establish a more broadly based institutional focus, on the other hand, entails problems of definition: there is a risk that "health" will become a synonym for the elusive concept of "social welfare" (Evans 1984: 4). Ontario has made an attempt to establish such a central institutional focus in the Premier's Council on Health Strategy and its successor, the Premier's Council on Health, Well-being and Social Justice, noted above.

The Ontario Premier's Council on Health Strategy institutionalized a process of consultation and investigation that was apparent in all provinces to varying degrees in the late 1980s and early 1990s. In that period temporary task forces or commissions of inquiry were established in each province to give broad policy advice to governments in the health field. Although their emphases varied, there were a number of common themes in the reports and documents issued by these bodies, including a focus on a broad set of determinants of health (beyond the health care delivery system), a shift from institutionally based to community-based care, a reallocation of functions among health care personnel, and a decentralization of decision making to regional councils representing a variety of interests in the health field (Reading 3-8). These themes echoed those of similar policy documents of the mid-1970s, and their incorporation into actual policy change is likely to be gradual and heavily conditioned by the existing accommodation of interests. Nonetheless, the existence of these various provincial commissions provided a mechanism and an opportunity for interprovincial communication, not only among the commissions themselves but among the groups potentially affected by their deliberations.

A consideration of the dense population of interests in the health field, and the predominance of the medical profession within that population, brings us back to the question posed at the outset of this chapter. Why is Canadian social policy characterized by a relatively generous and popular social program in the area of health care but relatively niggardly or controversial programs in the area of income maintenance? One possible answer is that there may be a broader political constituency of support for universal health care than for income maintenance. But there was no groundswell of public support for medicare when it was first introduced in Canada. And public pensions remain at relatively low levels in Canada despite a significant constituency of support—manifested in a successful protest against proposals in the 1985 federal budget to de-index OAS pensions. A fuller answer to this question lies in the intersection of state structures and organized interests.

As in the health care arena, a number of income-maintenance programs involve complex federal-provincial cost-sharing arrangements.[17] The mobilization of "provider" or "consumer" groups in the income-maintenance arena (with the exception of unemployment insurance), however, is very limited. In particular, because these programs are primarily concerned with the direct transfer of income rather than the provision of services, there is no central group of service providers comparable to the medical profession. In the absence of such mobilized groups, the relative significance of the interests of "governments as governments" is correspondingly greater (Banting 1987: 43, 51). Since change in these programs entails a complex set of implications for the fiscal responsibilities of various levels of government, these governmental interests have accordingly acted as a brake on policy development. The federally administered UI program, as we see in the next chapter, is an exception to this general characterization.

In the health care arena, on the other hand, governments must deal with highly mobilized provider groups. The health insurance system works because it allows for provincial-level accommodation between governments and these highly mobilized groups within a general national framework. The development of the national framework, from the introduction of national hospital and medical insurance through the 1977 EPF arrangements to the Canada Health Act, had more to do with federal-provincial fiscal manoeuvering than it did with group-government relationships. The ongoing interpretation of the framework, however, has been worked out between providers and governments at the provincial level. These relationships have varied across provinces. But the interests of the major provider groups—physicians and hospitals—are fundamentally similar across provinces, and under medicare they militate in favour of the diffusion of a relatively generous "national standard" around which provincial experimentation can take place. The potential opposition of the medical profession to governmental involvement is, moreover, muted by its own ambivalence toward the market and the state, and by the presence of a strategically placed group of primarily academic physicians who can mediate between the broader profession and the state.

In the health care delivery arena, then, a sophisticated network of organized interests acts in conjunction (if not always in collaboration) with the state to realize the genius of Canadian federalism—to innovate, to moderate, and to disseminate. In no other arena treated in this book does this federal genius accord so well with the nature of the policy challenges faced. And in no other arena does a conjunction of interests and institutions so conducive to realizing the potential of this genius occur.

Readings

3-1.   A HEALTH CHARTER FOR CANADIANS *

This royal commission, chaired by Justice Emmett Hall, laid the groundwork for the adoption of universal comprehensive governmental medical

*Royal Commission on Health Services (1964), *Report*, vol. 1 (Ottawa: Queen's Printer), pp. 11–12.

insurance in Canada. The following excerpts set out the elements of the proposed program, in the form of a "Health Charter for Canadians."

The achievement of the highest possible health standards for all our people must become a primary objective of national policy and a cohesive factor contributing to national unity, involving individual and community responsibilities and actions. This objective can best be achieved through a comprehensive, universal Health Services Programme for the Canadian people, IMPLEMENTED in accordance with Canada's evolving constitutional arrangements; BASED upon freedom of choice, and upon free and self-governing professions and institutions; FINANCED through prepayment arrangements; ACCOMPLISHED through the full co-operation of the general public, the health professions, voluntary agencies, all political parties, and governments, federal, provincial and municipal; DIRECTED towards the most effective use of the nation's health resources to attain the highest possible levels of physical and mental well-being.

1. "Comprehensive" includes all health services, preventive, diagnostic, curative and rehabilitative, that modern medical and other sciences can provide.

2. "Universal" means that adequate health services shall be available to all Canadians wherever they reside and whatever their financial resources may be, within the limitations imposed by geographic factors.

3. "Health Services Programme" consists of legislative enactments and administrative arrangements to organize comprehensive universal health care including prepayment arrangements for financing personal health services introduced in stages. Such a programme will provide complete health care with due regard to human factors and the spiritual, social, economic and regional forces intrinsic in the Canadian way of life.

4. "Canada's evolving constitutional arrangements" take into account the primary jurisdiction of provincial governments with respect to health matters including staging, scope and administration of health services, as well as the necessity for federal financial assistance to enable each of the provinces to implement a comprehensive, universal Health Services Programme.

5. "Freedom of choice" means the right of a patient to select his physician or dentist and the right of the practitioner to accept or not to accept a patient except in emergency or on humanitarian grounds.

6. "Free and self-governing professions" means the right of members of health professions to practise within the law, to free choice of location and type of practice, and to professional self-government. With respect to

"institutions" it means academic freedom for medical, dental and other professional schools, and for hospitals, freedom from political control or domination and encouragement of administration at the local level.

7. "Prepayment arrangements" means (a) financing within a province by means of premiums, subsidized premiums, sales or other taxes, supplements from provincial general revenues and (b) by federal grants taking into account provincial fiscal need.

8. "Full co-operation" means

(a) the responsibility of the individual to observe good health practices and to use available health services prudently;

(b) the responsibility of the individual to allocate a reasonable share of his income (by way of taxes or premiums or both) for health purposes;

(c) the methods of remuneration of health personnel—fee-for-service, salary or other arrangements—and the rates thereof should be as agreed upon by the professional associations and the administrative agencies and not by arbitrary decision, with an appeal procedure in the event of inability to agree;

(d) the maintenance of the close relationship between those who provide and those who receive health services, safeguarding the confidential nature of that relationship;

(e) the provision of educational facilities of the highest standards and the removal of financial barriers to education and training to enable all those capable and desirous of so doing to pursue health service careers;

(f) the adequate support of health research and its application;

(g) the necessity of retaining and developing further the indispensable work of voluntary agencies in the health care field;

(h) the efforts to improve the quality and availability of health services must be supplemented by a wide range of other measures concerned with such matters as housing, nutrition, cigarette smoking, water and air pollution, motor vehicle and other accidents, alcoholism and drug addiction;

(i) the development of representative health planning agencies at all levels of government, federal, provincial, regional and municipal, and integration of health planning.

3-2.   GOVERNMENTAL INSURANCE AND
CLINICAL JUDGEMENT: A MEDICAL VIEW*

In 1979–80 Justice Emmett Hall was commissioned by the federal government to review the operation of the Canadian health insurance system, in response to controversy over the federal-provincial balance under cost-sharing arrangements and over the practice of extra-billing by physicians in some provinces. In these excerpts from its brief to the Hall review, the Ontario Medical Association argues for a limited federal role and for extra-billing as a means of supplementing public expenditure on health care, and hence of avoiding what it sees as otherwise inevitable constraints on clinical judgement.

What is emerging is an increasing awareness that inevitably fiscal responsibility and budgetary decision-making bump into clinical judgment. There are early indications that government is considering the establishment of centrally determined criteria or standards by which to measure the performance—or more precisely the judgments—of physicians with a view to creating distribution norms.

In defence of government, the current system really allows no choice. Finite resources and the need for equitable distribution require distribution controls. The current spate of problems is merely the result of the need for hastily applied fiscal constraints and the increasing sophistication of the bureaucracy. There is inherent conflict between state medicine and personal freedom of choice and perhaps we are fortunate in that the rapid evolution of a bureaucraticized health-care system in Canada over the past few years has led to the identification of the dilemma early in its development.

The very personal and variable nature of health-care needs and the rapidly changing nature of biomedical information suggest that even the most sophisticated bureaucracy must founder in such an exercise. To be frank, creativity and precision have not been a benchmark of large public undertakings. Indirectly, through domination of the conditions of practice, governments could well impose standardization patterns of medical investigation and treatment which could hamstring the efforts of conscientious physicians.

In the Report of the Royal Commission on Health Services, under

*Ontario Medical Association, "Brief to the Health Services Review" (1979).

Health Charter for Canadians, it is stated that the objective of a health services program can best be achieved if it is based upon freedom of choice, and upon free and self-governing professions and institutions. Given recent developments in government's approach to health-care planning, these freedoms appear to be in serious jeopardy. The twin nemeses of under-funding and over-control can present impossible hurdles. . . .

The doctor must continue as a free and independent professional advocate for his patient, and a free and independent adviser/critic to government as opposed to becoming an employee of the state.

The "safety valve" effect of opting-out must be retained as it provides a more socially acceptable sanction than any formal withdrawal of services. To deny Plan benefits to patients of opted-out doctors is to de facto prohibit opting-out.

Provincial governments should devise ways to encourage the introduction of private money to provide a buffer against the predictable inadequacies of government benefit levels for physicians' services. . . .

A national identity for the Medicare program should be confined to broad and general principles. Monitoring by the federal Government should be benevolent as opposed to punitive and should be supported by sufficient flexibility and financial arrangements as to assist provinces with financial difficulties.

3-3.   THE CANADIAN MEDICAL ASSOCIATION AND CANADIAN MEDICARE*

In this address the president of the Canadian Medical Association outlined the association's disagreement with the federal legislative proposals that were ultimately to take the form of the Canada Health Act. He rested the case heavily on opposition to increased federal activity in the health field, reflecting the fact that the CMA's constituent provincial medical associations had by and large worked out satisfactory accommodations with their respective provincial governments. It is also noteworthy that the CMA supported the basic structure of Canadian medicare, while viewing the abolition of extra-billing as tantamount to "state medicine."

The government of Canada has made major contributions to health care. It has been a major supporter of hospital construction and hospi-

---

*Marc A. Baltzan, "Why CMA Opposes Canada Health Act," *Ontario Medical Review* (July 1983).

tal insurance, to medicare and to the health of Canadians. In return it has received considerable criticism and little in the way of recognition or credit. That's not fair and it's time that it was corrected. . . .

We support proposals that would provide the federal government with appropriate recognition and credit for its contribution to health care. We also *support* the proposal that provinces provide Ottawa with reasonable aggregate data on health care expenditures.

We *oppose* provinces being required to provide detailed information on a community-by-community, on a hospital-by-hospital, or a physician-by-discipline basis. Health care is a provincial responsibility and prerogative, and should remain so. Provincial governments must be allowed to run their own affairs and to be held responsible for them. The federal government should not try to convert provincial governments into branch offices. Provincial governments should not be subjected to financial control and direction by the government of Canada.

The CMA supports attempts to make health care insurance truly portable from province to province. And there is no objection or concern regarding public administration.

I mention these items to indicate that there are several proposals for the Canada Health Act that we support.

Where do we disagree? We disagree with proposals that . . . will destroy one of the better and most cost-efficient health care systems in the world. They will inevitably result in a decline in the availability and the quality of health care. . . .

The CMA has known for three or four years that Canada's major problem in health care is underfunding—especially in mental health, chronic care and our acute-care hospitals. The problem is particularly serious in our tertiary-care hospitals where more sophisticated and expensive medical care is provided. Our underfunding concerns generally do not relate to payment levels for physicians. There are a number of noteworthy exceptions, but in general and under current economic conditions, physicians are paid reasonably for their services. . . .

From whatever source, we want to see sufficient monies allocated to health care to provide the facilities, equipment and personnel needed to provide our patients with quality care. We want the freedom to practise medicine as independent, patient-employed professionals responsible to our patients. We want reasonable compensation for our services. . . .

We *do not want* to practise state medicine as employees responsible to government, not patients.

3-4.   THE CANADIAN NURSES ASSOCIATION
AND CANADIAN MEDICARE*

In these excerpts from its brief to the Health Services Review noted in Reading 3-2, the Canadian Nurses Association recommended changes in the organization of health care delivery. In other statements (for example, "Health Services and the Poor," June 1970, and "The Social Policy Function," February 1985), the CNA has taken a broad view of the socioeconomic determinants of health to advocate changes in social policy beyond the health care delivery arena.

In the preparation of this submission, the Canadian Nurses Association has reviewed the overall picture of health care in Canada in light of the *Charter of Health for Canadians*, a valuable guide since its proposal by the Royal Commission on Health Services in 1964. The CNA has always supported the principles on which the Charter was based, considering it a document ahead of its time and one capable of providing a framework for the evolution of Canadian hospital and medical insurance programs into a health insurance program. For the future, CNA advocates the development of a health care system that will allow the initiation of programs to promote primary health care, new points of entry into the system, more efficient use of all qualified health personnel, while ensuring the continuing improvement of programs to meet the needs of the ill. The following recommendations are presented in this context.

Recommendation 1: That the existing legislation underlying the hospital and medical insurance programs be revised to allow the emergence of a health insurance program which would stimulate the development of primary health care services, permit the introduction of new entry points and promote the appropriate utilization of qualified health personnel.

The promotion of the appropriate utilization of qualified health personnel will require other legislative revisions to enable nurses and other prepared health personnel to undertake activities which currently are legally defined as the exclusive domain of medicine.

*Canadian Nurses Association, "Putting Health into Health Care," submission to the Health Services Review (1979).

Recommendation 2: That provincial legislation be revised to enable qualified nurses and other prepared health personnel to undertake activities currently defined as medical acts.

The immediate corollary to the foregoing recommendations is the need to institute a mechanism for remunerating all health personnel by salary. This submission illustrates how the fee-for-service payment scheme for physicians, together with their guardian role of the gates of the system, cannot but increase the use of costly acute care services, whether necessary or not.

Recommendation 3: That remuneration of all health personnel be by salary.

. . . New points of entry, as recommended by CNA, refer to the recognition of innovative uses of existing facilities and organizations, rather than the building of costly new structures.

Recommendation 4: That Health Services Review '79 strongly support the initiation of better preventive, diagnostic and ambulatory care programs through various community-based points of entry. . . .

The basic principles of the Charter of Health are the uniting force which transforms ten provincial systems of health care into a national system. It is essential that criteria be developed by the federal and provincial governments, in concert with non-governmental organizations to ensure that these principles are honored.

Recommendation 5: That the federal and provincial governments, together with relevant non-governmental organizations, develop criteria to ensure that the underlying principles of the Canadian Health Insurance System are being upheld.

3-5.   A CONSUMERS' COALITION SEEKS A COMMUNITY-BASED HEALTH PLAN*

The Medicare in Crisis Coalition comprised labour, social service, church-related, nursing, and consumer groups, and was organized by

*Medicare in Crisis Coalition, "Brief Presented to the Ontario Cabinet" (December 13, 1979).

the Ontario Federation of Labour. The issue that galvanized the mobilization of the coalition was the increase in the incidence of extra-billing by Ontario physicians in the late 1970s. The concerns expressed in this brief, however, went well beyond that issue to embrace recommendations for organizational change in health care delivery, including community-based administration. As is apparent in these excerpts, this brief, like all of the documents presented with this chapter, expressed the basic pride and satisfaction of all parties with Canadian medicare, but also the fear that the program was in jeopardy.

Public health insurance—popularly called medicare—is one of this country's proudest social achievements. It has freed Canadians from all walks of life from the financial burden of illness. Our health system has made us the envy of our American neighbours. Yet medicare in Ontario finds itself under attack.

The provincial government's failure to arrive at an agreement over appropriate physician fee schedules has led large numbers of doctors to opt out of OHIP, leaving patients to face substantial out-of-pocket expenses for routine medical procedures. Government imposed hospital budget restraints have threatened our traditionally high standards of institutional health care.

Few Canadians would have us return to the bad old days of profit motive health care. Yet this is the route your government is taking.

. . . The health care of our people must be promoted through a comprehensive care system which treats the whole individual as he or she lives. Experience has taught us that the problems which affect individuals and families can not be neatly divided into health, social, economic, legal, education, employment or housing areas. Among examples of this sort are drug and alcohol abuse, alienation between parents and children and many problems associated with aging. It follows then, that treating people where they live, work and play means that social and health services must be integrated.

. . . We believe the best vehicle to effect this needed change is the Community Support Centre (C.S.C.). The C.S.C. would provide access through one door to health and social services on a treatment or referral basis. Basic teams of medical, dental and social service workers would provide those services dictated by the particular characteristics of the surrounding community or neighbourhood. (For instance, a C.S.C. in a neighbourhood adjacent to a lead smelter would obviously have an occupational health and safety nurse or doctor on staff equipped to meet this problem.) Laboratory, x-ray and pharmaceutical services would also be made available.

. . . We believe a community's residents should have input into programming and budget allocation—a reasonable role based on the truism that people know better than any government the needs of their own community. This does not, however, mean a surrender of the Ministry's important role in setting standards and allocating funding. It does mean ensuring that the system is accountable to the community it serves.

. . . We are not being overly melodramatic in saying that adoption of the C.S.C. is critical to the long-term health and wellbeing of the people of our province. Your government is concerned with health care spending. So are we. Too much money is misapplied to support defects in the existing system. These funds could go to improve and expand medicare in this province. The C.S.C. makes good sense from a health care point of view. With the integration of key services under one roof operating on a preventive rather than curative basis, it makes even better sense from a fiscal point of view.

. . . Mr. Premier, the Ontario Federation of Labour and its medicare coalition partners are proud of our public health care system. All the more so when we see that even with OHIP's structural faults, this province and this country spends less of its G.N.P. on health care than does the United States with its private-based profit-motive health care system. Indeed, medicare is but a part of the Canadian tradition of public enterprise that culturally distinguishes us from our American neighbours.

3-6.   EXTRA-BILLING AND THE UNIVERSALITY
        OF SOCIAL PROGRAMS *

Preserving Universal Medicare, *issued by the federal government as part of the process leading to the Canada Health Act, clearly indicates the tying of the extra-billing issue to the broader symbol of universality of social programs.*

The Government of Canada invites concerned Canadians and provincial governments to work together to preserve Medicare. . . . Through-

*Government of Canada, *Preserving Universal Medicare* (Ottawa: Minister of National Health and Welfare, 1983), pp. 7–8.

out this discussion there is one common thread: a vision of Canada as a humane and caring society, a society that has undertaken to care for all its people through a comprehensive social security program system. Throughout the economic crisis, which is now passing, we have preserved programs such as the Old Age Security and Guaranteed Income Supplement, Family Allowances, and the Canada Assistance Program. Now the challenge is Medicare.

3-7.   THE MEDICAL PROFESSION SEEKS A PARTNERSHIP WITH GOVERNMENT*

After a period of considerable tension between the Ontario Medical Association and the Ontario government in the wake of the banning of extra-billing and the medical strike of June and July 1986, the OMA sought to reestablish a collaborative relationship across a range of issues. The OMA also sought to restructure the framework within which it acted as the bargaining agent for the profession on matters of medical remuneration. Notably, it sought a binding arbitration mechanism, such as had been established in a number of other provinces with the banning of extra-billing.

The most significant issue is to manage efficiently the health-care system while not endangering the fundamental elements of medicare. Every resident of this province must be concerned with the escalating costs of providing health services. Society cannot let the cost of care exceed its ability to pay. We must, however, be equally concerned that the quality and accessibility of care will not be jeopardized because of cost controls.

To reconcile these issues will require new and creative approaches, and a willingness by everyone to accept change, including the medical profession and the government.

The profession must be prepared to work constructively in partnership with government, and to actively participate in policy planning and program implementation. We must be prepared to co-operate positively in the management of medical services.

The medical profession must not allow itself to be regarded as a force

*Ontario Medical Association, "Toward a Partnership for the 1990s," OMA position paper published in the *Ontario Medical Review* (May 1990), excerpts.

resistant to positive change. We are prepared to leave old dogmas behind, and shed outdated ideas that only serve to impede innovative thinking and constructive change.

But government also needs to change. It must listen and not dictate. It must be prepared to co-operate and not act unilaterally. Most important, it must stop blaming the medical profession for problems in the health-care system, because it is this action, as much as any other, that has contributed to the worsening of relations.

For its part, the Ontario Medical Association is prepared to meet the challenge. Specifically, we share with government many of its goals for the health-care system:

- We support utilization management that will increase efficiency and avoid waste in the health-care system;
- We support proper physician resource planning in co-operation with government and all other interested parties;
- We support quality-assurance techniques as the way to guarantee that the medical care provided for patients will have a positive effect on their health. Medical care must be based on the best current professional knowledge;
- We support the evaluation and use of alternative forms of physician remuneration and new structures of health-care delivery, provided doctors have the freedom to choose the system in which they practise, and patients have the freedom to choose the system in which they receive care;
- We support expanded roles for other health-care professionals where this is clinically responsible;
- We support properly developed guidelines for medical practice to guarantee consistency and accountability in medical practices;
- We support the establishment of an innovative forum that will institutionalize a new partnership between government and the medical profession in the management of medical services. We are prepared to embark on a comprehensive and high-level co-operative process in the management of medical services.

We have one important principle, however, that we will not sacrifice in any new partnership with government. While we will work for improved efficiency and better management of the health-care system, we will not be a party to any reduction in the provision of needed services. We will vigorously and publicly defend and preserve the universality, accessibility, and quality of our health-care system.

This new relationship between government and the medical profession requires a fair and rational process to settle disputes. . . .

We accept that individual doctors will not again have the ability to unilaterally set fees in the medicare system. Therefore, we accept and support Justice Hall's landmark conclusion that an end to extra-billing must be accompanied by fair and independent binding arbitration, and that the two cannot be separated. . . . After the bitter disputes of 1986, the OMA began legal actions that challenged the constitutional validity of the ban on extra-billing, and the constitutionality of the Canada Health Act.

We have determined that the continued pursuit of these actions is not consistent with the adoption of a new, constructive approach for the 1990s. We see the acceptance by both government and the medical profession of the principles of the Canada Health Act and the Hall report regarding binding arbitration and banning extra-billing as being an integral component of a new partnership.

Therefore, the Board of Directors of the OMA will recommend to the OMA Council that these legal actions be deferred, and ultimately withdrawn, when fair and independent binding arbitration, as recommended by Mr. Justice Hall, is achieved. [Ed. note: This proposal was approved by the OMA Council in June 1990.]

3-8.   THE POLICY AGENDA OF THE 1990S
AT THE PROVINCIAL LEVEL *

This report was one of the most comprehensive and detailed reports emanating from the various commissions established at the provincial level in Canada in the late 1980s and early 1990s. The themes set out in this excerpt are representative of those that characterize the reports of the other provincial commissions, and they reflect an elaboration of the original principles underlying Canadian medicare as set out in Reading 3-1. Note also the emphasis on the need for distinctive provincial approaches within the overall national framework.

*Saskatchewan Commission on Directions in Health Care, *Future Directions for Health Care in Saskatchewan* (Regina: Government of Saskatchewan, 1990), pp. 28–30.

The health care system born and nurtured in Saskatchewan has been enshrined nationally in *The Canada Health Act*. The Commission supports the principles of that Act, and has founded its redesigned system on them and on the health care ideals that Saskatchewan people determined long ago and still hold dear today: universality, comprehensiveness, accessibility, public administration, quality, freedom of choice and responsibility.

Universality ensures that everyone has an equal opportunity to receive health services and the most effective treatment, regardless of their economic and social needs and circumstances.

Comprehensiveness promises that a full range of essential health services is provided to Saskatchewan citizens, as has traditionally been done.

Today, *accessibility* means that each citizen is able to receive quality care appropriate to his or her legitimate needs with a minimum of inconvenience.

Public administration means that health care programs and services should be the responsibility of public authorities at the federal, provincial and local levels and should be administered and operated on a non-profit basis.

Quality means that health care services are provided in keeping with the advances made in professional training, expertise and technology, and in a sensitive and caring way. It does not mean quantity.

Freedom of choice means that within appropriate limits, a consumer has the right to seek out health care in a way that does not limit him or her to a prescribed place or kind of treatment.

Responsibility means that all citizens practise lifestyles which contribute to their own health and that of others and work jointly for a clean environment, and that both consumers and health care practitioners are responsible in their use and provision of services, respectively.

The Commission accepts those same principles as vital to the new health care system for the 1990s and 21st century. However, after it listened to the briefs presented to it across the province, it was convinced these principles must be expanded, taking into account the projections for the future and the successes and problems of the present system. The new health care system must stand on the twin bases of principles that have been proven over the long term and new ones that respond directly to the situations of today and tomorrow.

Sense of Ownership   The health care system must be owned by the people it serves; this is the first and most vital principle. Throughout its public meetings and in many of the briefs it received, the Commission was told of the need for local ownership of the system. That means it must be decentralized, giving local people influence and authority over it, control of it, and responsibility and accountability for it.

A Provincial System   In terms of its objectives, the services it provides and the standards it ensures, the health care system of Saskatchewan must have a provincial dimension and direction. A distinctly Saskatchewan system with a unique character, it acts as a unifying force among the locally-controlled regions.

Focus on Health   Health care must focus more on health and less on sickness. A true health care system for the 1990s and beyond will emphasize personal and community responsibility for health, health promotion and care of the environment, with a wide range of efforts aimed at disease prevention, and quality care in time of sickness.

Continuity of Care   Tomorrow's health system must be unified, with unbreakable links among its various facets. No longer can it be chopped into acute and long-term institutional care, home care, community services, mental health services. A unified system will provide people with the services they need and ensure there are no cracks for them to fall between.

Quality of Life   The system must provide for more independence for health care consumers and aim at reducing dependence on institutional care and professional services. It must start from the belief that people, when they become sick, disabled or old, will be encouraged to live privately and independently for as long as possible, supported by community services as needed.

Professional Teamwork   Professional services must be delivered through interdisciplinary teams whose members share responsibility and authority, who work interdependently and cooperatively, and whose roles complement each other.

Effectiveness   This old principle takes on a new meaning: the health care system must be outcomes-oriented. The crucial question must always be, what will be the outcome for the person of this treatment, this medicine, this therapy?

Adaptability   The health care system must be flexible and able to adapt to changing times and circumstances in a huge and varied province. This very diversity must be seen as an opportunity to develop new ways of improving health and delivering services, to explore options and alternatives.

Affordability   Ensuring a health care system is affordable means making it streamlined, efficient and effective, reducing open-endedness and abuses, and relating it to provincial resources. It does not mean lower quality or less adaptability and innovation, but it does mean the subtraction of programs and services which do not achieve their goals.

Consultation   Those who manage the health care system, at every level, must consult with their local communities, consumer groups, and with health care professionals. Such consultation can be time-consuming, but it helps to ensure the rightness of the choices and the commitment of the entire community to those choices.

Notes

1. Under these programs, provincial legislation permitted municipalities to subsidize doctors and establish municipal hospitals (Taylor 1978: 70–74; Falcone and Mishler 1989: 10–11).

2. The original cost-sharing formula under national hospital insurance had a regionally redistributive component. Federal contributions to each province were calculated as follows: (25 percent of the national average per capita cost + 25 percent of the provincial average per capita cost) × the number of insured persons in the province. Hence federal funding in poorer provinces spending less on hospital services was moved toward the national average.

3. Cost-sharing arrangements under medical insurance were even more regionally redistributive than those under hospital insurance, since

no reference to actual provincial costs was made. The federal contribution was calculated as 50 percent of the average national per capita cost × the number of insured persons in the province. The federal government also instituted a 2 percent "social development" surtax on income in 1968 to launch the program; hence taxpayers were made aware that they were supporting the program whether or not their own provinces participated.

4. Under the EPF arrangements federal contributions to the provinces are partly in the form of conditional cash transfers and partly in the form of unconditional transfers of tax "points." The formula for calculating federal contributions is complex and has been changed somewhat over time. Essentially, these arrangements limited the rate of increase in total federal contributions (cash plus tax points) to increases in population and nominal GNP. Beginning in 1986 the GNP escalator was reduced by a set percentage; beginning in 1990 it was temporarily frozen.

5. The average annual percentage growth in the number of physicians per capita between 1970 and the early 1980s in Canada was 2.2 percent, well below the OECD average of 4.8, but above the 1.7 rate in the United States. Other OECD nations were in fact catching up with and in some cases surpassing Canada and the United States in terms of medical supply. Physician:population ratios in both Canada and the United States in the early 1980s were virtually identical with the OECD average (OECD 1987: table 34).

6. Nonetheless, health care expenditures in West Germany remained fairly stable as a proportion of GDP during the 1980s, in part as a result of constraints on payments to ambulatory care (non-hospital-based) physicians (Kirkman-Liff 1990).

7. In 1975, 46.9 percent of Canadian health expenditures went to hospitals and 9.2 percent to extended-care facilities. By 1982 these proportions were 41.4 percent and 13.7 percent, respectively (Falcone and Mishler 1989: 22).

8. This discussion of Canadian medical opinion is largely drawn from earlier analyses of data from two physician surveys in Ontario in the 1970s, reported in Wolfson and Tuohy 1980 and Tuohy 1982b. These findings are supplemented with reference to a 1983 five-province survey reported in Stevenson and Williams 1985 and a subsequent 1986 nationwide survey reported in Stevenson, Vayda, and Williams 1987.

9. This strategic minority is composed largely, though not exclusively, of academically based physicians (Tuohy 1982b: 190–95). The linkages

between the medical schools and the regulatory Colleges are both functional (deriving from a common interest in entry standards to the profession) and structural (deriving from the representation of medical schools on the governing councils of the Colleges).

10. See note 9 regarding the linkages between the medical schools and the regulatory colleges. Ontario, moreover, has the highest concentration of medical schools in Canada. Five of Canada's sixteen medical schools are in Ontario, four in Quebec, two in Alberta, and one in each of British Columbia, Saskatchewan, Manitoba, Nova Scotia, and Newfoundland.

11. It should also be noted that in the two largest provinces, Ontario and Quebec, the provincial health insurance legislation prohibited private insurance companies from insuring services that were covered by public insurance; hence the coverage of extra-billing, or billing totally outside the governmental system in Quebec, did not provide a market for private insurance.

12. The budgetary implications of these penalties for provincial governments were relatively small. In Ontario, the province in which these penalties constituted the largest proportion of the health budget, that proportion was still only .6 percent in FY1984–85.

13. The reduction in service has been estimated at less than 20 percent in the first part of the strike period, dwindling to about 5 percent toward the end (Tuohy 1988: 292).

14. To be sure, the statement that the resolution of the extra-billing issue achieved a "common standard" needs some qualification. Physicians in some provinces increased the practice of charging "administrative fees" to cover such allegedly "uninsured" services as giving telephone advice, providing certificates, and the like. "Guidelines" for such charges were issued by some provincial medical associations, and as of 1991 they were still being tolerated by both federal and provincial governments.

15. It should be noted that the actual scope of this provision is fairly narrow, and it is likely to have only a very marginal effect on the health care delivery system in Canada. An acceptance of for-profit health care delivery in Canada would require a sweeping reorientation of funding mechanisms and policy objectives, far beyond anything the Free Trade Agreement implies for the health care sector.

16. Under the EPF formula, these cuts also hasten the rate at which the conditional cash component of federal transfers will disappear and all federal EPF transfers will be composed of unconditional tax points.

This gave rise to concern that the federal government would no longer be able to enforce the general principles of the national framework set out in the Canada Health Act. The federal government responded to these concerns in 1991 by introducing legislation allowing it to deduct penalties for transgressing the Canada Health Act from federal transfers to the provinces under other programs.

17. Under the 1867 constitution the provinces were granted exclusive authority in the income-maintenance arena. The federal government, however, has acquired an important presence in that arena, both under constitutional amendments in 1940 (unemployment insurance) and 1951 and 1964 (old age pensions and supplementary benefits), and also through the use of its spending power (social assistance and family allowances). Some central elements of the Canadian income-security system involve federal-provincial arrangement or other forms of interrelated policymaking. Legislation establishing the contributory Canada Pension Plan, for example, provides that any province may opt out of its provisions with compensation (only Quebec has done so), and that substantive amendments must be approved by two-thirds of the provincial governments representing two-thirds of the population. The needs-tested Canada Assistance Plan (the major social assistance program) is cost shared by federal, provincial, and municipal governments. Both federal and some provincial governments, moreover, administer needs-tested income supplements to the universal federal old age security payment.

4 Industrial Relations and Labour-Market Policy

One of the most remarkable phenomena of North American industrial relations is the divergence between the Canadian and the American experience in the past twenty-five years. Despite the considerable integration of the two economies, the significance in Canada of U.S.-based firms and unions, and the early emulation of U.S. industrial-relations models in Canadian public policy, the Canadian labour movement has maintained its organizational strength during a period in which organized labour in the United States has been in precipitous decline. In 1961 union density (union membership as a percentage of all wage and salary earners) stood at 30 percent in both Canada and the United States. By 1985 union density had declined to 18 percent in the United States but had risen to 37 percent in Canada (Kumar, Coates, and Arrowsmith 1987: 364).

In the same period, however, Canadian unemployment rates were, on average, relatively high. From 1960 to 1987 Canadian unemployment averaged 7.0 percent of the labour force annually, compared with an annual average of 4.5 percent in the six other large OECD economies.[1] Unemployment in Canada cannot be attributed to wage rigidities, as it has been in Europe (OECD 1986: 22). Canadian real wages have adjusted much more quickly to changing economic conditions: High annual increases during the resource boom of the 1970s quickly decelerated in the 1980s. Rather, Canada's high average rates of unemployment reflect the vulnerability of its economy, and especially of its resource sectors, to international swings. This vulnerability has created strong pressures for structural change in the economy, and for policies that would improve

159

the flexibility of the labour market and facilitate shifts of labour between sectors.

The survival of organized labour in Canada, in the context of pressures for structural adjustment, places the labour movement at a crossroads. It is powerful enough that it can constrain the policymaking capacity of both business and the state. But it lacks the comprehensive organization and the internal consensus to demand a policy price for its coopera-tion, particularly in terms of full employment policies. Where cohesively organized labour interests collaborate with business and the state in "cor-poratist" policymaking structures, as in Austria and Sweden, adjustment policies premised on the maintenance of full employment are more likely to be followed (Schmidt 1982; Cameron 1984; Goldthorpe 1984; Martin 1986). Power within the Canadian labour movement, however, is decen-tralized to individual unions and indeed to locals within unions. Further-more, the influences of British immigrants and American unions and of syndicalism in Quebec, and Canada's own turbulent history of indus-trial relations, have combined to produce an inclination to adversarialism within organized labour. Collaborative strategies do not come naturally or easily to such a labour movement.

The characteristics of business interests also militate against collabo-rative strategies. Business is fragmented along a number of dimensions, including those of sector, region, and international versus domestic ori-entation (Chapter 1); and business culture is decidedly "firm-centred" (Chapter 5). Furthermore, like labour, business interests are accustomed to adversarialism in industrial relations. Nonetheless, pressures toward structural adjustment are leading them to consider collaborative models.

This chapter examines the role of organized labour, business interests, and the state in the two interrelated arenas in which labour and busi-ness interests most immediately confront each other—industrial relations and labour-market policy. It is the survival of organized labour in the industrial-relations arena that has positioned it to play a role in labour-market policy. The institutional characteristics of these two arenas are quite different, however. In the industrial-relations arena constitutional authority rests primarily at the provincial level, and provincial-level ac-commodations of interests have allowed, as in the health care field, for considerable experimentation. In the arena of labour-market policy, how-ever, control over the relevant policy instruments is much more evenly divided among levels of government. More important, these issues, like other issues of economic adjustment to be discussed in the next chapter, involve interregional conflicts. Given the regionalized structure of Canada's economy, shifts between sectors may well involve shifts between regions. As we see again in Chapter 5, neither state structures nor social interests are well organized to mediate such interregional conflicts. In the absence of comprehensive and cohesively organized labour and business associations at the national level, and of mechanisms of intrastate federalism, the burden of dealing with interregional disputes has fallen upon political executives. Given a fundamental lack of consensus about the priority to be given to the mitigation of regional economic disparities as opposed to the promotion of national economic development, political executives have focused more on bureaucratic reorganizations and the repackaging of programs than on substantive policy development.

In the 1980s there were intimations of change in the labour-market policy arena. Frustrated by the lack of governmental action, business and (especially) labour representatives began to press for "bipartite" (that is, joint labour-management) policymaking mechanisms. Both parties, however, made these proposals with great ambivalence. Labour organizations, in particular, pressed simultaneously for the preservation of an adversarial model of industrial relations at the workplace level and for labour participation in central collaborative mechanisms of labour-market policy development.

Context

The roots of adversarialism in Canadian industrial relations are many and deep. In the Canadian context the confrontational bread-and-butter unionism of the U.S.-based internationals has blended with the political militancy carried by immigrant British union activists and with the influence of Catholic syndicalism in Quebec. Canada's poor record with respect to working days lost because of strikes (discussed below) reflects not so much the number of work stoppages as the fact that strikes, when they occur, tend to be large, long, and hostile. These large strikes have entered into the history, the collective experience, and the mythology of Canadian industrial relations, and they have contributed to a cultural archetype of bitter labour strife.

The Canadian labour movement is fragmented and decentralized. Historically, it has divided along craft-industrial and national-international lines. The development of the labour movement in Quebec, moreover, followed a different and ideologically more fractious trajectory than elsewhere in Canada. More recently, public-private sector divisions have further exacerbated tensions within and among labour organizations.

As in the United States, craft unions were earlier to develop in Canada than were industrial unions. Tensions between craft and industrial unions continued throughout the history of the labour movement. To a large extent, these conflicts were directly imported through the significant presence of U.S.-based unions in Canada. The major labour federations of craft and industrial unions in Canada have always been affiliated with their U.S. counterparts. In 1938 the split of the Congress of Industrial Organizations (CIO) from the American Federation of Labor (AFL) in the United States was quickly replicated in Canada. The major Canadian labour federation, the Trades and Labour Congress (TLC), was compelled to expel CIO unions from its ranks in Canada or face the severing of the TLC-AFL affiliation. The CIO in Canada then merged with another central composed primarily of national and international industrial unions to form the Canadian Congress of Labour (CCL) in 1940. Not until after the 1955 AFL-CIO merger in the United States did craft and industrial unions combine in a national federation in Canada: In 1956 the TLC and the CCL combined to form the Canadian Labour Congress (CLC).

The political strategies followed by the craft and industrial wings of the labour movement differed considerably, reflecting and magnifying differences in the United States. The craft unions of the TLC were more disposed to "business unionism" and less to political action or "social unionism." The CCL, with its more solidaristic industrial bases and the strains of nationalism within its membership, was more politically oriented. In 1943, shortly after its founding, the CCL established an organizational link with the socialist party, the CCF, which had been established in 1933. The successors to the CCL and the CCF, the CLC and the NDP, respectively, have maintained this link, as discussed in Chapter 1.

More radical ideologies have characterized other segments of the labour movement. Communist strains have been effectively marginalized. After World War II the CCL in convention adopted resolutions condemning "World Communism" and expelled or suspended a number of unions as allegedly communist dominated. Syndicalism, a doctrine that abjured labour participation in the structures of the state and emphasized decentralized economic action at the level of the workplace and the community, took root in British Columbia and Quebec. British Columbia shares with the Pacific Northwest of the United States the syndicalist tradition of the International Workers of the World (the "Wobblies"), which flourished in the first two decades of the twentieth century but foundered thereafter. In Quebec syndicalism is more deeply rooted—arguably because its elitist but decentralized organizational philosophy resonated in a culture accustomed to the paternalistic, parish-based organization of the Roman Catholic church. Indeed, the clearest bearer of syndicalism in Canada in the postwar period has been the Confédération des syndicats nationaux (CSN), or, in English, the Confederation of National Trade Unions (CNTU). The CSN is a Quebec-based central that has undergone much ideological ferment and radicalization over time, but that traces its lineage back to the conservative Confédération des travailleurs catholique du Canada (CTCC), founded in 1921.

Quebec presents the most extreme case of ideological diversity in the Canadian labour movement, but ideological divisions persist throughout the country. In very general terms the public-sector unions, the industrial unions, and the craft unions range along the ideological spectrum from left to right, respectively; but there are divisions within these broad categories on matters such as historical grievances and Canadian and Quebec nationalism. Moreover, the organizational decentralization of Canadian labour also militates against the adoption of common strategies—not only by increasing the "transactions costs" of developing such strategies but also by building in resistance to them. Common strategies imply, in the eyes of individual unions and union locals, a shift of power away from themselves toward the central federations.

The decentralization of the Canadian labour movement is reinforced by the decentralization of the other major actors in the industrial relations arena: the business community and the state. Canada's firm-centred business culture and the lack of a comprehensive "peak association" of business (Chapter 5) has meant that Canadian business is organizationally equipped to deal with industrial relations issues at the level of the firm, or at most the industry.

The Canadian state, moreover, is extraordinarily decentralized with respect to authority over industrial relations. As Weiler (1980: 10) puts it, "to Americans, it is almost inconceivable that the State of Michigan, for example, would have the authority to govern the relationship between General Motors and the United Auto Workers, as the Province of Ontario has done for over thirty years." Inconceivable or not, most authority over industrial relations rests at the provincial level in Canada. The Constitution Act, 1867, was silent on the federal-provincial division of power over industrial relations, and until 1927 the field was primarily occupied by the federal government. In that year, however, a decision of the Judicial Committee of the Privy Council interpreted industrial relations to be essentially a matter of employment contract and hence subject to provincial authority over property and civil rights. Subsequent legislative and judicial decisions established the present division of authority: The federal government may regulate industrial relations in all industries under federal jurisdiction, but general authority over industrial relations rests with the provinces. During World War II, however, the federal government exercised its general emergency power to regulate industrial relations by a federal order-in-council, P.C. 1003. P.C. 1003 brought to Canada the model of the Wagner Act, the industrial-relations legislation adopted by the U.S. federal government in 1935.[2] After the war the provinces began to adopt legislation modelled on P.C. 1003 (with distinctive provincial variations), and by the early 1950s Wagner-type legislation had been adopted in all provinces except Prince Edward Island (Adams 1988: 19). In Quebec, however, the Wagner model was more ostensible than real; in practice the Duplessis government exercised arbitrary power and often did so repressively (Lipsig-Mumme 1984)—a situation that did not change until the ascension of a progressive Liberal government in 1960 and the revision of the Quebec Labour Code in 1964–65.

The Wagner model is essentially one of regulated and delimited adversarialism. It thus contrasts with the codetermination models of Germany and Sweden, which imply the participation of workers in managerial decision making through structures of industrial democracy such as works councils and employee representation on corporate boards. Under the Wagner model, labour and management recognize each other as legitimate adversaries. Conflict between them is to be regulated through agreed-upon rules and structures, which they are to respect in "good faith." The role of government is to enforce these rules for the regulation of conflict and to act as arbiter in disputes that cannot be resolved through negotiation. This role, moreover, is to be performed largely by administrative tribunals (labour-relations boards) rather than by the courts. The model assumes that labour-relations boards, with membership drawn from those with expertise in industrial relations and less bound by principles of judicial interpretation, offer greater potential for devising pragmatic solutions to industrial-relations problems (Weiler 1985; Riddell 1986a: 16). Labour-relations boards have been established in all provinces and at the federal level, although the jurisdictions vary in the extent to which they consign matters to the boards or to the courts.

In the 1960s the Wagner model began to be extended from the private to the public sector in Canada. The establishment of collective-bargaining rights ran against the British tradition that "the crown does not bargain," and the more general problem of reconciling the sovereignty of the state with the concept of the state as an employer like any other under the Wagner model. Nonetheless, in Canada as in most other western industrial jurisdictions in the postwar period, these traditional restrictions gave way with the blurring of public-private sector boundaries. Canada, indeed, surpassed both Britain (from which it inherited the concepts of parliamentary supremacy and crown prerogative) and the United States (with which it shared the Wagner model in the private sector) in the granting of collective-bargaining rights to public servants. Statutory limitations on the right to strike and on the scope of negotiable issues are considerably less stringent at both federal and provincial levels in Canada than are statutory limitations in American jurisdictions or conventional and administrative limitations in Britain (Riddell 1986a: 18).

The bulk of legislative change extending collective-bargaining rights to public-sector employees occurred from the mid-1960s to the late 1970s.[3] Quebec amended its Labour Code to provide for collective bargaining for public employees in 1964, and comprehensive legislation at the federal level (the Public Service Staff Relations Act) was enacted in 1966. By the end of the 1970s collective-bargaining structures were in place in the public sector in all provinces, although the scope of bargaining and restrictions on the right to strike varied considerably. By 1984 three-quarters of employees in public administration were covered by collective agreements, and two-thirds were union members (Kumar, Coates, and Arrowsmith 1986: 308). Collective bargaining was also extended in the health and education fields in this period: By 1984, 81 percent of paid employees in teaching and related occupations and 71 percent of paid employees in health care were covered by collective agreements (74 percent and 64 percent, respectively, were unionized) (ibid.: 309).

The Wagner model, as implemented in Canada, has a number of important political implications. As a result of the combination of provincial authority over industrial relations with the Wagner model of plant-level certification, Canada has one of the most decentralized legal frameworks for collective bargaining among western industrial nations (Riddell 1986a: 15; Ergas and Shafer 1987–88). As Kumar (1986: 98) reports, "because of the dominant pattern of single plant/single union bargaining, there are more than 22,000 collective agreements, covering varying numbers of employees, between nearly 200 national and international unions and nearly 40,000 employers."

It should be noted, however, that although single plant–single union bargaining remains the rule, there was a considerable increase in multi-plant and multi-employer bargaining in the late 1970s and early 1980s. In most provinces industrywide bargaining structures in construction were established in the 1970s. Quebec and British Columbia went further in facilitating the recognition of associations of employers and councils of trade unions for purposes of collective bargaining in other sectors (Davies 1986: 218–19). Quebec, moreover, beginning in the 1930s, developed structures in a number of sectors under which the terms of a basic agreement were negotiated by "comités paritaire" composed of union and employer representatives, and were then decreed by the state to cover all workers, organized and unorganized, in the sector. Nationally, however, the earlier trend toward larger units showed signs of reversing in the mid-1980s. In several significant sectors such as pulp and paper in British Columbia, national railways, and the public sector in Quebec, established patterns of centralized bargaining were modified or abandoned (Kumar, Coates, and Arrowsmith 1986: 73).

Certification of unions at the level of the plant limits the scope of their impact on the terms of employment and the working conditions of workers outside their own membership. In Canada approximately 39 percent of wage and salary earners were union members in 1985; the proportion of those covered by collective agreements at the time has been estimated at 46 percent (Riddell 1986a: 5). In the Federal Republic of Germany, in contrast, where collective agreements are negotiated for entire industries, the proportion of wage and salary earners who were union members was about 40 percent in 1979, and more than 90 percent were covered by collective agreements (ibid.: 83n.).

The decentralization of collective bargaining, together with the strong currents of business unionism and syndicalism in different segments of the labour movement, has militated against the participation of labour in central decision-making about labour-market policy. Similarly, the firm-centred culture of business (Chapter 5) has meant that concerns with the broader labour market have been left to the state. And within the structures of the state the development of labour-market policies has been constrained by the federal-provincial distribution of authority and the necessity to mediate interregional conflicts.

Historically, the key component of Canada's labour-market strategy was immigration policy, an area of concurrent federal and provincial constitutional authority. The immigration of skilled workers was essential to Canada's industrializing economy in the late 1800s and first half of the twentieth century. Since the 1960s, however, immigration policy has become relatively less important as a component of labour-market strategy, and vice versa. The composition of immigrant cohorts has shifted over time. The proportion of "independent" immigrants (the category in which skilled workers are concentrated) declined from 61.1 percent of all immigrants in 1965 to 23.2 percent in 1979 (Employment and Immigration Canada 1981: 180).

Another instrument of labour-market policy, job creation, overlaps with industrial assistance and regional development policy (Chapter 5). Federal and provincial direct job-creation programs were peripheral to labour-market policy until the late 1960s. In 1968 federal spending on job-creation programs amounted to .03 percent of GDP. By 1977 this proportion had risen to .23 percent (ibid.: 31), but it declined again to .02 percent by 1987 (OECD 1988: 86).

The major instruments of labour-market policy since the 1960s have been unemployment insurance and training programs. In each of these areas policy development has been fraught with federal-provincial tensions and marked by a lack of consensus over the objectives and the design of policy. After an earlier federal attempt to establish a national UI scheme was ruled *ultra vires* by the courts, the federal government acquired the constitutional authority to establish such a program through a constitutional amendment in 1940. The amendment had the unanimous approval of the provinces (Chapter 2), but the UI program itself has been the subject of federal-provincial as well as partisan dispute, leading to periodic large- and small-scale revisions.

The disputes over unemployment insurance have essentially turned upon the question of whether the program was to operate basically as a mechanism of income security or as a tool of labour-market management. As discussed in Chapter 3, Canadian income-maintenance programs are relatively modest in international perspective. Furthermore, changes to these programs are likely to be incremental, given that they entail a web of federal-provincial agreements. Unemployment insurance, on the other hand, is funded largely through employer-employee contributions. It is nominally administered by a tripartite Unemployment Insurance Commission representing business, labour, and government, but overall policy direction remains effectively in the hands of the federal cabinet (Pal 1985: 77–78). Because it is thus relatively free of federal-provincial complications, it holds tempting potential to serve income-maintenance purposes.

This temptation was clearly at work in the liberalization of the UI program that occurred in 1971. This liberalization occurred in the context of failed attempts at both the bureaucratic and political levels to gain broad cabinet support for guaranteed annual income or negative income tax proposals. Despite, or perhaps because of, that context, it caused remarkably little dissension. The program was made universal.[4] Regional considerations were built into the schedule of eligibility requirements and benefit periods, which were designed to be more liberal in regions where levels of unemployment were high. The federal government, out of general revenue, bore the costs of regionally extended benefits and regular benefits attributable to national unemployment rates above 4 percent. Special sickness, maternity, and retirement benefits were added to the program. The reforms left the program complex, indeed "baroque" (ibid.: 83) and on balance much more generous. (The program's generosity related to the ease of qualification for benefits and the length of time for which benefits could be drawn, not to the level of the benefits.)[5] UI thus provided a safety valve for pressures for increased income security, which could not be accommodated within income-maintenance programs established under federal-provincial agreements. But the UI program, in its generosity, contained the seeds of future conflicts, as it was made to bear an income-maintenance burden ultimately inconsistent with its function as an instrument of labour-market policy.

UI, however generous, constituted an essentially passive response to the failure of labour markets to clear. More active measures, notably training programs, were not part of the arsenal of labour-market instruments in Canadian public policy until the 1960s.[6] Since then they have assumed more importance, but their continual repackaging over time attests to the lack of consensus regarding the appropriate locus of responsibility for training and the appropriate goals and targets of training programs. Federal provision of training programs raises issues of federal-provincial jurisdiction, since it encroaches on provincial power over education. One result of federal-provincial negotiations in this arena was the favouring of institutional rather than on-the-job training, as provincial governments, at least until the 1980s, sought to have federal training funds channelled to provincial educational institutions (Muszynski 1986: 265). Canadian industry, for its part, resisted on-the-job training, whether or not it was governmentally assisted. As of the late 1980s, private-sector spending on training in Canada, relative to the size of the labour force, was only about 20 percent of that in the United States. The emphasis of government training programs, moreover, tended to be on new entrants to the labour force and on the long-term unemployed; little was done for workers employed in declining industries or for recently laid-off workers. The focus on the long-term unemployed was reinforced by regional considerations: Long-term unemployment tended to be most heavily concentrated in Quebec and the Atlantic provinces (Shaw 1985: 146–47).

Agenda

In the United States the unravelling of the so-called Labor Accord that established the Wagner model began in the 1950s but was greatly accelerated in the economically troubled times of the mid-1970s and early 1980s. Explicit policies of de-unionization replaced good-faith dealing. In some cases employers used the provisions of the law itself to frustrate union organizing, by technically drawing out the certification process and using the delay to campaign against unionization (Adams 1988: 17). In other cases resistance to unionization also involved deliberate noncompliance with the law, for which penalties were often light or nonexistent (Weiler 1983). The success rate in certification "elections" (discussed below) declined from 80 percent in the 1940s to under 50 percent in 1980 (ibid.: 1774). Even after certification some unions faced continued resistance from employers. The proportion of newly certified unions gaining first contracts declined from 86 percent in 1955 to 63 percent in 1980 (Weiler 1984: 353–54).

Apart from these attempts to abrogate the Labor Accord, there were attempts by some employers to rework it, to abandon adversarial "hard bargaining" strategies (in which managerial prerogatives, on the one hand, and union "job control" and seniority systems, on the other, were fairly clearly defined) in favour of more cooperative, "high trust" strategies based on the Japanese model of flexible task definition, informal dispute resolution, and a distinction between lifetime core employees and peripheral employees who may be laid off arbitrarily by the employer (Adams 1988: 9). Experiments with "quality circles" and "quality of working life" (QWL) programs began to proliferate (Riddell 1986b: 16–20; Kochan, Katz, and Mower 1984).

These developments in the United States had important implications for the agenda of industrial relations in Canada. In very general terms business sought in various ways to emulate U.S. developments; unions sought to resist them; and governments were concerned with industrial peace, economic stability, and, increasingly, with their own roles as employers.

The incidence of unfair labour practices and deliberate skirting or flouting of labour law by employers was considerably less in Canada than in the United States (Adams 1988: 22). Rather, Canadian employers in the economic climate of the 1980s aggressively pressed a "hard bargaining" strategy consistent with the Wagner model. They began to demand and in some cases to win at the bargaining table a variety of provisions, such as two-tier wage structures for new and existing employees, lump-sum payments, and profit-sharing plans, designed to make compensation more flexible. They also pressed, with somewhat less success, for changes in collective agreements eliminating restrictive work rules and permitting greater use of part-time employment and subcontracting. Reductions in nonwage benefits, such as sick leave and paid holidays, were rare; indeed, such benefits, including job-security provisions, were generally increased (Kumar, Coates, and Arrowsmith 1986: 69–73).

The greatest impact of harder bargaining by employers, however, was on wages. Wage gains, which were large in the 1970s during the boom in commodity prices, decelerated rapidly in the 1980s. Indeed, the OECD (1986: 22) reports that "Canada reported the fastest deceleration in wage inflation of any OECD country in 1982 and 1983." The deceleration began in early 1982 and became "pronounced and widespread" in 1983, and wage settlements reached a record low in 1984–85 (Kumar, Coates, and Arrowsmith 1986: 69). The annual average for effective base rate adjustments in new settlements between 1978 and 1982 was 10.3 percent; between 1983 and 1985 it was 3.9 percent—below the prevailing rate of inflation.

In the political arena business groups also pressed for greater "flexibility" in labour-management relations. In their briefs to the Macdonald Royal Commission in 1983 (discussed in Chapter 5), both the Business Council on National Issues and the Canadian Manufacturers Association were careful to emphasize the legitimacy of organized labour. They decried the adversarialism of Canadian industrial relations, however, and praised experiments in labour-management cooperation at the workplace and the central level, which they saw as vehicles for improving productivity (Readings 4-1 and 4-2).

The governmental agenda in this period turned to economic stability and industrial peace, and particularly to wage restraint and the control of work stoppages in the public sector. After 1965 both inflation and levels of strike activity began to climb in Canada. The problem of inflation was one that Canada shared with other western industrial nations: Canadian inflation rates were high in historical but not in international perspective. With regard to strike and lockout activity, however, Canadian levels were high in both respects. In terms of limiting the number of *working days* lost because of industrial disputes, Canada's relative position among eleven industrial nations declined from seventh in 1948–57 to ninth in 1958–67 to tenth in 1968–81. The granting of the right to strike to public-sector employees after 1965 contributed to this phenomenon. Not only did it expand the pool of workers eligible to strike, but also public sector workers were slightly more strike prone than were private sector workers (Riddell 1986a: 35–36). Public-sector wage increases in the early 1970s also outpaced those in the private sector—largely, if not entirely, as a result of the greater union density of the public sector and the flexing of its newly gained bargaining power (ibid.: 26–27).

Dealing with these problems forced governments to confront the potential conflict between their roles as economic managers and their roles as employers. Was public-sector wage restraint an instrument of incomes policy or a mechanism for reducing governmental expenditure budgets? Were restrictions on strikes in the public sector instruments of industrial peace, or a unilateral abrogation of collective-bargaining rights by governmental employers? In grappling with these issues, some governments, especially the federal Liberal government under Pierre Trudeau, began to look to European models: centralized bargaining structures involving business, government, and labour and covering both public and private sectors on the Swedish model; or, more favourably, information exchange and collaboration through less formal networks on the model of West German concerted action. In general, and with some exceptions to be noted below, the governmental agenda of the 1970s and 1980s moved in the direction of a greater role for the state in the industrial-relations arena, as employer, as pace-setter, and as "guarantor" of the industrial-relations system, whether or not these roles could be satisfactorily resolved.

Throughout the 1970s and 1980s organized labour perceived itself as under assault by both private and public-sector employers (Panitch and Swartz 1984). In its brief to the Macdonald Commission, the CLC dealt with this threat as one of the two major themes of its presentation. In the face of this assault, and despite its ideological divisions, organized labour was virtually united on the need to preserve the Wagner model and to build broad-based coalitions on issues of social policy including but extending beyond workplace matters. As discussed in other chapters, labour entered into coalitions with welfare, women's, church, and community groups on issues such as medicare (Chapter 3) and free trade with the United States (Chapter 5). There was also little division over assigning increasing priority to issues of occupational health and safety. In this respect the Canadian labour movement reflected the international climate of increased concern over occupational health issues, as scientific evidence of occupational illnesses with long latency periods (particularly cancers) became widely available (Ashford 1976).

On other issues, however, labour opinion was more divided. Particularly troublesome was the question of how far the Wagner model could be stretched to accommodate more collaborative "high trust" relationships. At the workplace level, reactions to management proposals for QWL programs, "quality circles," and the like ranged from tentative participation to skepticism to hostility. At the level of central decision making, organized labour was even more divided over the issue of participating in tripartite policymaking structures.

Other issues divided the unions and the federations as well. One was the tension between Canadian and U.S.-based unions. This tension was manifested in a number of forms: in rivalry between individual unions, in conflict within the CLC, in conflict between the CLC and the "all-Canadian" federations such as the CNTU and the Confederation of Canadian Unions, and within the international unions themselves as the issue of Canadian autonomy from U.S. parents continued to simmer. Between 1972 and 1986 thirteen breakaways of Canadian from American-based unions occurred, involving more than 300,000 members (Kumar, Coates, and Arrowsmith 1986: 336–36). The largest of these was the secession of the 136,000-member Canadian wing of the United Auto Workers to become the Canadian Auto Workers in 1986. In addition, a number of international unions modified their structures and constitutions to recognize a greater degree of Canadian autonomy.

On the organizing front interunion raiding continued to weaken labour solidarity. Such raiding was fostered in part by the threat of a declining membership base, in part by tensions between national and international unions (such as the almost incessant raiding between the Canadian Association of Industrial, Mechanical and Allied Workers and the United

Steelworkers of American, especially in British Columbia)—and in part by public policy. In the late 1960s and early 1970s, for example, Quebec governments moved toward establishing centralized bargaining structures by industry (particularly construction) in which the bargaining agent was to be the labour central that was supported by a majority of unionized workers in the sector. This policy had the effect of "setting the centrals into really brutal competition for majority affiliation in those sectors in which they had traditionally divided membership" (Lipsig-Mumme 1984: 304). In the public sector, however, the Quebec Federation of Labour (QFL), the CNTU, and a teachers' federation, the CEQ, fairly successfully maintained a common front for bargaining with government in the 1970s and 1980s.

Interunion rivalry in the Quebec construction sector contributed to the 1981 split of twelve U.S.-based building trades unions, with a total membership of about 355,000, from the CLC. The unions withheld dues from the CLC and were accordingly suspended. Nine of the unions then proceeded to form the Canadian Federation of Labour (CFL). Indeed, the split of the building trades from the CLC illustrates in microcosm most of the major tensions within the Canadian labour movement: between national and international, public and private sectors, industrial and craft unions, and Quebec and the rest of Canada (Rose 1983). The catalyst for the split was the refusal of the CLC's Quebec arm, the QFL, to expel construction locals that had broken away from international unions—a decision that was motivated largely by a fear of losing majority support, and hence exclusive bargaining-agent status, in the construction sector. The CLC supported (or at least did not discipline) the QFL. The CLC had since 1974 granted the QFL even greater autonomy than other provincial federations, recognizing the need for the QFL to present a strong *québécois* image in competition with its rival federations in Quebec. The dispute was also fed by the building trades' resentment of the overrepresentation of public-sector unions in CLC conventions.[7] Finally, it drew upon the long-standing political differences between craft and industrial unions, and pitted a business unionist heading the Canadian Building Trades Executive Board against an NDP-stalwart social unionist in the presidency of the CLC (ibid.: 89).

While these changes in the industrial-relations field were occurring, the agenda of labour-market policy was also evolving. The cost projections of the designers of the 1971 unemployment insurance reforms were soon proved very wide of the mark. The increase in benefit payments for 1972 had been projected to be 4.03 percent; the actual increase was 110.17 percent (Pal 1985: 82). Although this rate of cost escalation did not continue, cost increases were well above projections. In response, the program's requirements were progressively tightened between 1972 and 1978, as the measured unemployment rate continued to climb. Concerns about "work disincentives," expressed only by the opposition Progressive Conservatives at the time of the 1971 changes, became an important part of the Liberal rationale for the 1972–78 tightening (ibid.: 80–88; Muszynski 1986: 274). The program remained generous, however—not in the level of its benefits but in the ease of qualification for UI and the duration of the period for which it could be drawn. "Developmental" uses for UI funds were also incorporated at this time. On the German model, but on a much more modest scale, provisions for work sharing and allowances for UI recipients in approved training and job-creation programs were adopted. The take-up of these provisions was limited, however. And the use of UI funds in this way came under strong criticism from business and labour as a plundering of an employer-employee fund for expenditures that should have come from general revenue (Muszynski 1986: 286).

Toward the end of the 1970s the orientation of training programs to basic skills, the long-term unemployed, and institutionally based methods came under increasing criticism. Representatives of industry urged a shift in focus to target key areas of skill shortages. Organized labour, for its part, argued for a greater responsibility on the part of employers to provide on-the-job training and advocated a grant-levy plan to provide the necessary incentive. Under such a scheme employers would pay a compulsory levy into a training fund, from which they could then draw training grants. Apart from labour's grant-levy proposal, the views of labour and business regarding an "active" labour-market policy emphasizing on-the-job training, skills upgrading, and labour-management collaboration were closer in this arena than in any other area of economic policy. This was the one area, indeed, in which the BCNI was prepared to admit the need for industrial policy.

Process

The process for dealing with issues of collective bargaining varied significantly across jurisdictions in Canada. The differences derived from the distinct historical legacies of particular regions and from the partisan complexions of provincial and federal governments. And they became even more apparent in the 1980s than they were in the 1970s. It is important to place these cross-provincial variations in context, however: The Wagner model survived in Canada as a whole to a much greater extent than in the United States. Indeed, in the 1970s the model was reinforced, and the role of the state (more specifically, of labour-relations boards) as guarantor was increased.

The two most significant differences between the Canadian and American legal frameworks for industrial relations, in terms of their impact on union activity, are provisions affecting union certification and the achieving of a first contract. In the United States the evolution of the law and the practice of the National Labor Relations Board (NLRB) has made certification more difficult. In both Canada and the United States labour boards will certify a union as the bargaining agent for a group of employees once the union has demonstrated that it has the support of a majority of those employees. In the United States, however, the measure of support is taken through a secret-ballot election conducted by the NLRB. Election procedures allow for considerable delay between the union's application to the NLRB and the vote, and allow campaigns to be waged by both union and management for the support of the workforce. In Canada the measure of support for the union is taken through signed membership cards gathered by union activists, although some provinces also require a vote if the majority demonstrated by membership cards is narrow (under 55 percent), or if the labour board has any reason to doubt the validity of the membership support has expressed through cards. Specialists in industrial relations generally agree that certification is facilitated by the "membership card" as opposed to the "secret ballot" model (Weiler 1980: 37–49).

Attaining recognition and certification is only the first hurdle faced in establishing collective bargaining in a workplace; the second arises in winning a first contract. As noted above, substantial employer resistance to first contracts has been encountered by unions in the United States. In Canada legislation at the federal level and in five provinces allows the respective labour-relations boards to require arbitration of the terms of a first contract in the face of an impasse in bargaining. The jurisdictions vary somewhat, however, as to the conditions under which the board may intervene (for example, whether or not "bad faith" must be demonstrated). Even in jurisdictions without first-contract arbitration, labour boards have levied more severe sanctions than have been levied in the United States against employers refusing to bargain in good faith to negotiate first contracts (Rose and Chaison 1985; Meltz 1985; Adams 1988: 22).

Another feature of Canadian labour law of advantage to unions is the so-called Rand formula, a version of the closed-shop principle, whereby unions may negotiate an automatic checkoff of union dues from all members of a bargaining unit, whether or not they are union members. Such provisions are expressly prohibited in "right-to-work" states in the United States. The legitimacy of such requests was first recognized in Canada by Justice Rand in the settlement of a lengthy strike at the Ford Motor Company in Windsor, Ontario, in 1945. By the mid-1980s the federal government and four provinces had enacted legislation *requiring* employers to adopt the Rand formula at the request of the union.

Significantly, these provisions regarding certification requirements, first-contract arbitration, and the Rand formula were made or reaffirmed in the 1970s and 1980s in Canada—at a time of rapid erosion of the legislative and administrative underpinnings of the Wagner model in the United States. The difference between the two nations is attributable in part to the strength of social democratic parties—the NDP and the Parti québécois—at the provincial level in Canada in this period.

Social democratic governments generally, and most notably the NDP government of British Columbia from 1972 to 1975, led the way in the strengthening of provisions for collective bargaining in the 1970s, and governments of other political stripes followed their lead. The first three jurisdictions to adopt first-contract arbitration legislation had social democratic governments at the time: British Columbia (NDP) in 1973, Manitoba (NDP) in 1976, and Quebec (PQ) in 1977. In one jurisdiction (Ontario in 1986) first-contract legislation was adopted by a minority Liberal government under the terms of an "accord" under which the NDP agreed to support the Liberals in power. Of the remaining two cases of the adoption of such legislation, one was under a Liberal government (the federal government in 1978), and one under a Progressive Conservative government in Newfoundland in 1985. Similarly, the strongest anti-scab legislation in Canada was enacted by the PQ in Quebec in 1977, although restrictions on professional strike breakers were also adopted in the early 1980s by the conservative populist Social Credit government of British Columbia and a majority Progressive Conservative government in Ontario. The pattern in the case of legislative provisions for the imposition of the Rand formula at the request of unions is less somewhat clear. The first such legislation was adopted in 1977 by the social democratic

PQ in Quebec and the Social Credit government of British Columbia. Subsequently, Rand requirements were adopted by a minority Progressive Conservative government (with the NDP playing a strong role in opposition) in Ontario in 1980, the federal Liberal government in 1983, and the Progressive Conservative government of Newfoundland in 1985.

Even while governments were shoring up the Wagner model in the private sector, however, tensions were increasing between public-sector unions and governments as employers. Although most legislation granting public-sector employees the right to strike attempted to confine its exercise to "nonessential services," governments were faced, de jure or de facto, with having to decide in each case whether a strike disrupted or threatened to disrupt "essential services." At the federal level positions "essential to the safety and security of the public" may be designated by the government before a strike begins, and employees in those positions may not strike.[8] Provincial governments continued to wrestle with definitions and changes to definitions of essential services in their labour-relations legislation throughout the 1970s. In an increasing number of cases governments resorted to back-to-work legislation. Total instances of the use of this instrument rose from one in the 1950–54 period to nineteen in the 1980–84 period. Much of this increase occurred at the provincial level and was attributable to the use of back-to-work legislation in public-sector disputes (Riddell 1986a: 20).

Tensions between governments and public-sector unions were exacerbated in the 1980s as governments undertook programs of fiscal restraint. In 1982 the federal government unilaterally restricted wage increases in the federal public sector to 6 percent in the first year of a two-year period beginning in June 1982 and 5 percent in the following year. Existing agreements were extended for two years and "rolled back" where necessary to meet the 6 and 5 limits. The extension of existing agreements had the effect of preventing public employees from striking, since under Canadian labour law strikes are illegal during the term of a contract.

Following upon the federal action, eight provinces enacted similar time-limited public-sector wage-restraint legislation. The governments of these provinces spanned the ideological spectrum, from the social democratic PQ government of Quebec to the conservative populist Social Credit government of British Columbia. Relations between public-sector unions and the Quebec government, indeed, were as turbulent and confrontational under the PQ as they had been under previous Union nationale and Liberal governments. In 1983 the PQ government unilaterally restrained public-sector wage increases and made changes to provisions regarding job security and working conditions (Panitch and Swartz 1984: 135). In 1985 the PQ government enacted new legislation governing collective bargaining in the public sector, the major effect of which was to decentralize certain aspects of the centralized bargaining process.

The Social Credit government of British Columbia went even further. It followed temporary wage controls imposed in 1982 with proposed legislation expanding the power of public-sector employers to dismiss employees, extending the wage-control program indefinitely, and restricting the scope of bargaining. Opposition to these and other features of the government's broader restraint program culminated in public-sector strikes and the mobilization of a "Solidarity Coalition" embracing not only public and private-sector unions but also tenants, welfare, and human rights groups. Ultimately, an accord was reached (albeit one highly contested within the British Columbia Federation of Labour) that effectively preserved seniority and job-security rights, while allowing government to reduce the size of the public sector.

In the period of sustained economic growth of the mid- to late 1980s, such public-sector restraint programs did not recur. But tensions between governments and public-sector unions, though diminished, continued. In 1986, for example, the Conservative government of Saskatchewan passed back-to-work legislation to end a sixteen-month rotating strike by government employees. The legislation imposed the terms of a collective agreement that had earlier been recommended by a conciliator; and, in what was arguably its most controversial feature, it invoked the "notwithstanding" clause of the Canadian Charter of Rights and Freedoms to exempt the legislation from the charter's guarantee of freedom of association. And in the economic downturn of the early 1990s governments once again adopted unilateral programs restraining public-sector wages. In its 1991 budget, for example, the federal government announced a one-year freeze on public-service salaries, followed by a 3 percent cap in each of the two following years—to be enforced by legislation if the public-service unions did not agree to these terms at the bargaining table. Some observers have seen in such public-sector restraint programs, together with increasing restrictions on public-sector strikes, a trend toward "permanent exceptionalism"—that is, toward making exceptions to the Wagner model on a continuing basis (Panitch and Swartz 1984).

Apart from public-sector restraint programs, moreover, there were some cases of more lasting legislative change that made the establishment of collective bargaining more difficult. And whereas social democratic governments had led the way in reinforcing the Wagner model, the major instances of retrenchment occurred under conservative governments. In 1979, for example, the Conservative government of Nova Scotia enacted legislation requiring that a union obtain the support of a majority of the workers at *all locations* at which an employer carried on business in order to be certified to bargain collectively with the employer. The development and passage of the legislation was precipitated by the drive of the United Auto Workers to organize employees of Michelin Tire Corporation (hence the legislation's colloquial name, the "Michelin bill"), and it effectively frustrated not only that unionization drive but also others in the province. In 1983 the Conservative government of Alberta passed a set of amendments to its Labour Relations Act that, at least in the view of organized labour, would have made it easier for unionized employers to set up nonunion subsidiaries. In the face of massive opposition by unions, these amendments were not proclaimed.

The most controversial example of retrenchment occurred with the passage of British Columbia's "bill 19" by the Social Credit government in 1987. Several changes to the province's Labour Code, opposed by organized labour, had already been made in 1984. Bill 19, among other things, further restricted picketing, facilitated decertification, and constrained strikes and lockout in certain circumstances (Kumar, Coates, and Arrowsmith 1987: 24). The legislation also replaced the Labour Relations Board with a reorganized Industrial Relations Council having increased powers. In protest, organized labour boycotted the new council for several months but shortly found that it had no choice but to participate in the industrial-relations system. And even with the changes of the 1980s, the NDP's industrial relations legacy is such that British Columbia remains one of the firmest bastions of the Wagner model in North America.

Legislative changes did not go unchallenged, especially as both labour and business seized the new instruments made available to them by the passage of the Canadian Charter of Rights and Freedoms. After 1982 issues of charter rights began to be raised in the industrial relations arena, as in virtually all other arenas of Canadian public policy. As of 1989 there had been approximately eighty court cases (entailing more than one hundred decisions at various levels) invoking the charter in matters related to work (Weiler 1990: 120). Employers and unions seized the charter to attack legislation that they respectively believed to be unfriendly. And individual employees asserted charter rights against both employers and unions. By and large, each of these groups has been unsuccessful in these attempts (ibid.: 166–67). Unions were ultimately unsuccessful before the Supreme Court of Canada in asserting a right to strike or a right to picket under the charter's freedom-of-association and freedom-of-expression guarantees.[9] Employers, for their part, were unsuccessful at the Ontario Supreme Court level in appealing to the freedom-of-association guarantee to challenge the "closed shop"[10] provisions of collective agreements negotiated under Ontario legislation governing industrywide bargaining in the major construction industry. Challenges to mandatory retirement requirements brought by individual employees, on the grounds that they contravened charter provisions against age discrimination, were turned down by the Supreme Court of Canada.[11] Other cases have pitted individual employees against unions. One of the most celebrated of these cases was the attempt by an Ontario public servant to contest the links between unions and the NDP, on the grounds that his right to freedom of association was infringed because a portion of his compulsory dues to the Ontario Public Service Employees Union went to support political activities of which he disapproved. This attempt was ultimately unsuccessful before the Supreme Court of Canada. Employees did succeed at the Supreme Court of Canada, however, in arguing that restrictions on the political activity of civil servants infringed their rights to freedom of association.

The existence of the charter, then, has added another incentive to adversarialism in Canadian industrial relations. With its orientation to the courts rather than to labour-relations boards,[12] however, charter litigation diverges from the Wagner model. There has also been speculation that the charter will exert a centralizing influence on Canadian labour law and limit the scope of provincial diversity (Riddell 1986a: 16), but judicial self-restraint in this arena suggests that this influence will be limited (Weiler 1990: 167).

Although adversarialism continued to be the dominant motif in labour-management relations in the 1970s and 1980s, there were some experiments with more collaborative models, particularly with regard to occupational health and safety, and to a lesser extent in the labour-market policy arena. In the case of occupational health and safety the social democratic influence is clear. Almost all Canadian jurisdictions made major changes to such legislation in the 1970s and 1980s, but it was the influence of social democratic parties in office in Saskatchewan, British Columbia, and Quebec, and in opposition in minority governments in Ontario, that led the way on key provisions such as the right to refuse hazardous work and the establishment of workplace joint health and safety committees. By the late 1980s labour-management health and safety committees at the workplace level were provided for in legislation in the federal jurisdiction and in all provinces except Nova Scotia and Prince Edward Island. These committees were Canada's closest approximation to European works councils and structures of codetermination. With their purely advisory status and limited mandates, however, they were pale shadows of those European mechanisms. At the central level collaborative mechanisms with advisory or even executive status were established in a number of provinces. Tripartite boards were set up to administer occupational health and safety regulations in Quebec and New Brunswick. Advisory councils drawn from labour, business, and other (primarily academic) communities were established in Alberta, Saskatchewan, Manitoba, Ontario, and Prince Edward Island. In 1990 Ontario replaced its multipartite advisory council with a bipartite (business and labour) agency with executive authority over health and safety training programs.

On other issues attempts to develop tripartite mechanisms of consultation followed a more tortuous path. During the 1970s the federal government attempted to involve business and labour representatives in tripartite mechanisms of consultation on a range of economic policy issues, including incomes and labour-market policies. The subsequent history of these initiatives was one of considerable instability: Labour boycotts of joint bodies, analogous to the use of the strike at the workplace level, were fairly common.

In 1974–75 in the context of historically high inflation rates, the federal finance minister launched a round of consultations with business and labour with the purpose of developing agreement on voluntary restraint of wages and prices. In the absence of comprehensive peak associations, the representation of business and labour in these discussions was selective: Officials of the CLC represented labour, and business was represented by corporate executives chosen by the minister of finance. A Canada Labour Relations Council, comprising equal numbers of labour and business representatives with the minister of labour as chair, was also established for a brief period in 1975.

Consensus, however, was not forthcoming. It was, in fact, neither institutionally nor politically possible for the CLC to agree to wage guidelines in the face of opposition from union locals who held the effective power in the collective-bargaining system (Waldie 1986: 169). In October 1975 the federal government unilaterally announced the imposition of wage and price controls, to be administered by a tripartite Anti-Inflation Board. In protest the CLC (as well as the CNTU) refused to nominate representatives to the board (Fournier 1986: 297). The CLC also withdrew from formal participation in the two federal governmental bodies in which it was involved: the Economic Council of Canada (Chapter 5) and the short-lived Canada Labour Relations Council.

Throughout the life of the controls program, from 1975 to 1978, however, the question of mechanisms of tripartite collaboration continued to be debated. At its biennial convention in May 1976 the CLC adopted a "manifesto" (Reading 4-3) that broke new ground in calling for a full partnership of organized labour with business and government in the making of economic and social policy decisions, although the language of the manifesto was testimony to the tensions and disagreement within the CLC about this shift from the traditional path of adversarialism. The manifesto also faced head-on the issue of the centralization of power that such a strategy would involve and called upon all affiliates to support the CLC executive. In July 1986 the CLC followed up its manifesto with more concrete proposals for a tripartite social and economic planning council, with parity representation of business and labour and a government chair, and a similarly constituted labour-market board with administrative and regulatory as well as planning functions (Waldie 1986: 171).

Business was also mobilizing for participation in more centralized structures of decision making at this time. In 1976 the BCNI was established as the self-styled "senior voice of business in Canada," representing primarily large businesses (Chapter 1). The BCNI was more open than other business organizations to the development of mechanisms of ongoing consultation with labour and government (Coleman 1988: 83). The federal government, for its part, proposed a model of consensus building through a purely advisory national consultative forum whose members would be drawn from labour, business, and other constituencies.

While these proposals were in the air, a series of bilateral meetings were held in 1976 and 1977 between government and business (coordinated by the BCNI), government and the CLC (and on one occasion between government and the CNTU), and the BCNI and the CLC. From these meetings there developed two parallel types of processes: one bipartite between the BCNI and the CLC, and one tripartite, involving the

BCNI, the CLC, and the federal government. The tripartite stream, peri-odically boycotted by the CLC, included such initiatives as the Tier I and Tier II exercises discussed in Chapter 5, and the establishment of the Canadian Centre for Occupational Health and Safety, an information-gathering and disseminating body governed by a tripartite board and funded by government.[13] Governmental proposals for parallel centres for the quality of working life and for collective bargaining information did not come to fruition, although the latter proposal reached the stage of a legislative bill introduced in the federal parliament in 1979.

The major development within the bipartite stream was the establish-ment of the Canadian Labour Market Productivity Centre (CLMPC), an agency funded by the federal government but governed by a joint business-labour board. The CLMPC resulted largely from CLC-BCNI negotiations and joint pressure upon the federal government. It was estab-lished in 1984 with a broad mandate to conduct research and analysis related to economic adjustment, and an annual budgetary allocation from the federal government. The governing board of the CLMPC was bipar-tite, with twelve members from labour (nine from the CLC and three from the CFL)[14] and twelve from business; federal and provincial gov-ernment representatives had observer status only. The board could not reach consensus on the translation of the broad objectives of the centre into concrete research projects, however, and in 1986 it decided to trans-form the CLMPC from a research institute to a central labour-business policy forum for the discussion of broad public policy issues.

Some experiments with tripartite consultations on labour-relations issues were also undertaken at the provincial level in this period (Four-nier 1986: 303–11). In Quebec the Parti québecois launched a round of sectoral conferences and economic "summits" shortly after assuming office in 1976. The PQ's rationale was more explicitly corporatist than that of any other government in Canada, but it was also the most statist. Although the QFL was an important ally of the PQ in these undertakings, the other Quebec union centrals were highly suspicious, and the em-ployers' federation, the CPQ, was a wary participant. No ongoing institu-tionalized process of "concertation" for dealing with industrial relations materialized. Only in the arena of occupational health and safety, as noted above, was a tripartite structure institutionalized.

Another provincial-level experiment was undertaken in Ontario, where an informal Labour Management Study Group (LMSG) evolved from an advisory committee established to oversee a number of pilot QWL projects. The group was chaired by the deputy minister of labour and composed initially of three representatives of labour organizations and four representatives of business, the latter selected by the deputy minister. The rationale was clearly to develop, in a small-group setting, a body of shared information and a nucleus of support among opinion leaders in labour and business for strategies of concertation. The process, however, unlike the European models that it sought to emulate, lacked a supporting structure of comprehensively organized interests. It was heavily dependent upon the personal commitment of and relationships among its "charter members." With different incumbents in the positions of deputy minister of labour and president of the Ontario Federation of Labour (OFL) after 1986, the LMSG fell into abeyance.

These experiments at both federal and provincial levels were essentially experiments in *process*, however, and they yielded very little by way of substantive change. This pattern of structural and procedural change without changes in substance was even more pronounced in the labour-market policy arena. There, bureaucratic and program reorganizations substituted for substantive policy development. The Unemployment Insurance Commission (UIC), having lost some of its functions to a newly created Department of Manpower and Immigration in 1966, was integrated with that department in a restructuring in 1977–78. A new Canada Employment and Immigration Commission (CEIC) was created, retaining the tripartite structure of the old UIC, attached to a renamed and reorganized Department of Employment and Immigration. In 1979, as part of the elaboration of central agencies discussed in Chapter 1, the Liberal government established the Ministry of State for Economic Development (MSED) and the Ministry of State for Social Development (MSSD). In a significant recognition of the social security emphasis of labour-market policy, the Department of Employment and Immigration was placed under MSSD.

In 1980–81 the federal government appointed internal task forces to review its labour-market policies and undertook consultation with outside interests post hoc—just the pattern to which business and labour had been objecting in the late 1970s. The reports of both of these task forces, issued in July 1981, clearly opted for a facilitation of structural shifts in the interests of national economic development, and for decreased reliance upon income-support measures, notably, unemployment insurance. These reports were swiftly attacked, even from within the governing Liberal party, and few of their recommendations were adopted. The one exception was the establishment of the Critical Trades Skills Training program (CTST), under which federal labour-market analysts designated certain critical areas of skill shortages, and these designations guided the allocation of federal training funds. That program in turn came under criticism, not only as a result of the limitations of labour-market analysis in identifying shortages, but also as a result of the inevitable disputes between federal and provincial governments over the designation of needs in particular regions.

The market orientation of the federal Conservative government elected in 1984, and particularly its pursuit of a strategy of liberalized trade with the United States (Chapter 5), implied the facilitation of labour mobility. Existing programs of relocation assistance were limited, however; and training programs, with their focus on entry-level training and on the long-term unemployed, were not adapted to facilitating shifts from job to job. But these programs were embedded in the structure of unemployment in Canada, in regional sensitivities, and in federal-provincial relations; and they were resistant to anything more than superficial change.

The Conservative government in its first term did little to address these problems. Rather than making immediate changes to the UI program, the government appointed a commission of inquiry, headed by a prominent Liberal, an economist and former social affairs minister in the Quebec cabinet, Claude Forget. The Forget Commission was appointed in July 1985 and reported in December 1986. It recommended a radical simplification of the UI program, treating it as an *insurance* program and shearing it of both its broader income support and its "developmental" components. The two labour representatives on the commission dissented vehemently from the report. The Forget report was sharply criticized by the parliamentary Standing Committee on Labour, Employment and Immigration, however, and the government announced that the program would not be changed (Kumar, Coates, and Arrowsmith 1987: 31–32).

In 1985 the federal government reorganized federal training and job-creation programs into six streams under a "Canadian Jobs Strategy" (CJS), intended to shift funds from short-term job creation to training programs, and to allow for greater private-sector participation in the administration of programs. The CJS, however, was fraught with ambivalence. The announced intention was to "help build the skilled, resilient labour force the economy needs for greater productivity and international competitiveness" (Employment and Immigration Canada 1985: 4). If anything, however, it reinforced the orientation of these programs to those "most in need"—that is, the long-term unemployed and disadvantaged groups such as youth, women reentering the workforce, and workers in communities in economic decline (Premier's Council 1989: 140–41; Advisory Council on Adjustment 1989: 47–51). The CJS was criticized by both a parliamentary standing committee and the Canadian Labour Market Productivity Centre for encouraging training only in low-level, nontransferable skills and for its lack of an anticipatory strategy (Muszynski and Wolfe 1989: 260).

The implementation of the CJS was rocky. Allocated budgets for the CJS were underspent (Auditor General for Canada 1987: 14,15), in part as a result of the transition from old to new programs, restrictive eligibility criteria under the CJS, and the concomitant reorganization of the Department of Employment and Immigration. Moreover, the slow start-up of the CJS was exacerbated by federal-provincial relations, as the federal government attempted to integrate its purchase of places in provincial institutions (including apprenticeship places)[15] under five of the six streams of the CJS. Much dispute and some delay surrounded the negotiation of the initial federal-provincial agreements in this area in 1986, and both the format and the content of the agreements varied across provinces.

Federal-provincial relations also slowed the implementation of a second Conservative initiative, the Program for Older Worker Adjustment (POWA), announced in 1986. POWA replaced a federally funded program adopted by the previous Liberal government to provide a financial bridge from unemployment insurance to public pensions for unemployed workers aged fifty-five to sixty-four in designated areas of high unemployment. Under POWA bridging benefits were to be available to workers aged fifty-five to sixty-four who were affected by specific *lay-offs* (not by regional levels of unemployment). Qualifying lay-offs would be jointly designated under agreements between the federal and the respective provincial government, who would share the costs of the program. The wheels of federal-provincial negotiation ground slow, however, as the provinces protested the replacement of a federally funded program with a cost-shared program and pressed for increases in the federal share. By 1991 seven provinces had signed POWA agreements.

In the period leading up to the adoption of the Free Trade Agreement in 1988, Canadian labour-market policy again came under criticism. Business decried the lack of focus on the "higher-level" skills that would be essential in the more competitive market, and labour criticized the inadequacy of Canadian labour-market measures to respond to the dislocations that free trade would entail. The Conservative government responded by appointing an Advisory Council on Adjustment, chaired by a prominent businessman and member of the BCNI executive, Jean de Grandpré, to review and make recommendations about adjustment policies. Organized labour, as part of its protest against the Conservatives' free trade agenda, refused to participate in the council. The report of the de Grandpré council in March 1989 (Reading 4-4) recommended a shift of expenditures from the "safety net" components of labour-market policy to what it termed the "trampoline" components—training allowances for UI recipients, and three streams of the CJS directed toward those recently unemployed or threatened by lay-offs, skills in short supply, and community development. It also proposed the establishment of a bipartite business-labour group to advise on how this shift might be accomplished and endorsed a form of grant-levy system for private-sector training in the form of a tax that would be offset by a firm's expenditures for training.

Shortly thereafter the federal government proposed changes to the UI program that were consistent with the thrust of the de Grandpré recommendations. Under these changes UI was to be funded entirely from employer and employee contributions, and the current federal contribution from general revenue would be reallocated to training programs. Contributions from employers and employees would not increase, however, since the UI program was to be tightened, particularly in areas of relatively low unemployment.[16] The implementing legislation for these changes was delayed for more than a year by the Senate and was finally passed only after the Conservatives gained sufficient strength in the Senate in October 1990. In the meantime, given the controversiality of these proposals and the prospect of renewing expiring agreements with the provinces under the CJS, the federal government commissioned the bipartite CLMPC to conduct a consultative exercise that would lead to yet another integrative framework, a new labour-market development strategy. This exercise culminated in the establishment of a Labour Force Development Board, on a modified bipartite model. The board is composed of eight business representatives, eight labour representatives, and six members representing educational institutions and disadvantaged groups; it is charged with setting training priorities and establishing budgets for a range of training programs.

At the provincial level the repackaging of bureaucratic units and programs also characterized the labour-market policy arena. From the late

1970s to the late 1980s, for example, the Ontario government experimented with various mechanisms for developing and coordinating training and job-creation programs. In 1979 it established the Ontario Manpower Commission (OMC), which was composed of business, labour, and academic representatives and a government chair, and staffed by administrative units transferred from the Ministry of Labour. In 1985 the OMC was combined with certain units from the Ministry of Colleges and Universities and elsewhere to form a new Ministry of Skills Development (MSD). In 1986 a new policy package, the Ontario Training Strategy (OTS), was initiated, doubling the provincial budgetary allocation for training programs (not including apprenticeship) to $100 million. It was designed in explicit contrast to the federal CJS: It was directed primarily at employed as opposed to unemployed workers, it subsidized employers' training costs as opposed to wages, and it offered a consulting service for employers. Despite Ontario's criticisms of "shortcomings in the industrial and competitiveness aspects of national training programs" (Premier's Council 1989: 145), however, its own training programs continued to focus primarily upon basic or firm-specific skills. Problems of intra- and intergovernmental coordination, moreover, continued to hobble training programs in Ontario as elsewhere (Reading 4-5).

In large part because of the congeries of programs with which MSD was charged—some focused on employers, others on individual workers —and its liaison role between the federal government and provincial educational institutions, MSD did not develop a distinct clientele. Nor, in such circumstances, could it articulate a coherent model of labour-market development under which its variegated mandate could be seen as a coherent whole. It remained a minor portfolio, held either by a senior minister in combination with another portfolio or by a junior minister. In 1989 and 1990 its dismantling began and its various components were dispersed to different ministries, while proposals for a bipartite labour-management Ontario Training and Adjustment Board gathered momentum (see below). The pattern of institutional change without substantive policy development continued.

Consequences

Between 1961 and 1981 Canada experienced a greater growth in union membership than six other western industrial nations with which it is often compared (Table 4-1). It is true that the Canadian labour force was also growing rapidly in this period, but union organizing activity was

TABLE 4-1   Union Membership Changes 1961–84 and
             Union Density, 1984, Seven OECD Nations

Nation	Percent Change in Union Membership		Union Members as Percentage of Wage and Salary Earners, 1984
	1961–81	1981–84	
Australia	58.0	1.2	57
Canada	141.0	4.7	38
Japan	51.5	0.02	29
Sweden	79.8	5.5	95
United Kingdom	13.3	−9.2	53
United States	26.6	−11.3	19
West Germany	48.1	−3.4	42

Source: Calculated from Kumar, Coates, and Arrowsmith 1987:364.

more than able to keep pace with the growth of the labour force. Union density thus increased in Canada in this period, while it declined in the United States, Japan, and Australia. Furthermore, Canadian unions survived the 1981–82 recession rather better than their counterparts in all of these nations except Sweden.

Labour's ability to maintain its base is attributable in large part to a relatively favourable legislative environment (Kumar 1986: 126–39; Riddell 1986a: 8–10; Bruce 1989); and that environment in turn is attributable largely to the strength of social democratic parties at the provincial level, in a context in which provincial governments have primary authority over industrial relations. There has, in fact, been a process of reciprocal reinforcement at work. Social democratic parties have been fairly strong, either in government or in opposition, and as an electoral threat to the government of the day in British Columbia, Quebec, and Ontario. Hence the three largest provinces in Canada have provided a relatively favourable climate for union growth. This fact has been crucial in maintaining the union base, 36.1 percent of which was located in Ontario, 29.1 percent in Quebec, and 12.4 percent in British Columbia as of 1984 (calculated from Kumar, Coates, and Arrowsmith 1986: 313–15).[17] As long as unions were not fundamentally threatened in these three provinces, then, more than three-quarters of the union base was protected from substantial erosion. From this base, moreover, unions and union centrals have been able to continue to engage in political activity at the federal level. The effect of social democratic governments in smaller jurisdictions such as Saskatchewan has been largely (outside the jurisdictions themselves) a demonstration effect. Saskatchewan's occupational health and safety legislation, for example, was emulated, depending on the balance of political forces, in other provinces and eventually at the federal level.

There are some indications, however, that Canadian unions will be under severe pressure in the 1990s to maintain current levels of membership, let alone past growth rates. Certification activity in fact peaked in the early 1970s; and decertifications, though proportionately much less significant in number, have been increasing in the 1980s, especially in British Columbia (Kumar, Coates, and Arrowsmith 1987: 380). (It should be noted that not all decertifications imply a loss of union membership; a significant but unreported number involve employee groups who choose to change unions. The increased decertification activity in the 1980s hence undoubtedly reflects the increased competition for union membership in that period.) Furthermore, employment in some of the sectors in which unions have been strongest—public administration, major manufacturing, mining, and forestry—is not likely to increase greatly. In a number of the sectors that are likely to expand—such as financial institutions and retail trade—past union organizing efforts have been unsuccessful (Kumar 1986: 142ff.).

Social democratic governments, moreover, have not been the only experimenters with change in this arena: In the 1980s conservative governments attempted various forms of retrenchment. The structures of the Canadian state, by providing footholds for both social democratic and conservative parties in provincial governments with substantial powers in the industrial relations arena, have both fostered and constrained the economic and political power of labour. They have allowed for considerable variation and innovation across jurisdictions, while still essentially maintaining the Wagner model of collective-bargaining structures.

The survival of organized labour in the industrial-relations arena has positioned it to play a role in broader arenas of economic and social policy, particularly in the labour-market policy arena. Labour has been internally divided and ambivalent about pursuing collaborative labour-market strategies, while continuing to hold to its traditional adversarialism in industrial relations. In fact, however, this very ambivalence may slowly be yielding a distinctively Canadian resolution. If in Japan in the postwar period "the hostility between business and labour at the national level has been mitigated by cooperation and coordination at the level of the individual firm" (Pempel 1982: 98), the emerging model in

Canada may be the obverse. The power of labour may continue to be grounded in its adversarial relationship with management at the level of the firm and institutionalized in the Wagner model. But from this power base labour may enter into collaborative arrangements for making labour-market policy at the central level, both federally and provincially.

There are indications, moreover, that these arrangements are more likely to be bipartite than tripartite in structure, albeit with governmental financial involvement (Fournier 1986: 327–28). Bipartism comes more naturally to labour and business interests, who share a skepticism about the state and who are accustomed to bipartite structures of collective bargaining. (Indeed, these bipartite structures as they evolve are likely to be marked not only by collaboration but also by adversarial features such as boycotts and bloc voting [Tuohy 1990]). The federal Labour Force Development Board, though not strictly bipartite, accords greater representation to each of its business and labour components than to all other interests together. In the latter half of the 1980s several bipartite business-labour initiatives were taken at the sectoral level, most notably in the steel industry (Reading 4-4).

At the provincial level proposals for bipartite structures to deal with labour-market issues have also been made. The Ontario Federation of Labour, at its 1988 convention, adopted a statement advocating "co-determination of the training process" (Reading 4-6). But these proposals were paired with demands for a strengthening of the collective-bargaining system on the Wagner model. The leadership of organized labour appeared to be dealing with its ambivalence toward adversarialism and collaboration by seeing the one as dependent upon the other: that is, by maintaining that collaborative mechanisms at the central and sectoral levels would be effective only if labour entered those arrangements from a base of strength in the collective-bargaining system.

At the end of the 1980s collaborative arrangements were still in their infancy and had had virtually no effect on policy. The general pattern of spending on labour-market policies from 1968 to 1987 showed a buildup in spending in the 1970s, especially on unemployment insurance after the 1971 reforms, and some decline in the 1980s, especially on job-creation programs (Table 4-2). By 1987 there had been little change in the overall profile of public spending on labour-market programs since the mid-1970s (with the exception of a decrease in spending on job-creation programs), despite changes in institutional and program configuration. In this sense, Canada is similar to most European countries (OECD 1988:

TABLE 4-2   Public Spending on Labour-Market Programs as Percentage of GDP, 1987

	Canada 1968*	Canada 1977*	Canada 1987	Australia	France	Germany	Italy	Japan	Sweden	United Kingdom	United States
Employment promotion:	0.35	0.73	0.57	0.32	0.74	0.99	0.46	0.17	1.86	0.89	0.24
Training	0.26	0.30	0.22	0.03	0.27	0.29	0.01	0.03	0.49	0.11	0.11
Job creation	0.03	0.23	0.02	0.10	0.06	0.20	—	0.10	0.26	0.31	0.01
Youth and disabled	0.06 ⎱	0.19 ⎱	0.12	0.08	0.29	0.27	0.37	0.01	0.90	0.31	0.06
Employment services	⎰	⎰	0.21	0.11	0.12	0.23	0.08	0.03	0.21	0.16	0.06
Income maintenance:	0.005**	1.9	1.68	1.21	2.33	1.35	0.81	0.42	0.80	1.68	0.59
Unemployment insurance	0.005**	1.9	1.69	1.21	1.26	1.33	0.49	0.42	0.70	1.66	0.59
Early Retirement	—	—	—	—	1.07	0.02	0.32	—	0.10	0.02	—
Total labour-market programs	0.36	2.63	2.24	1.53	3.07	2.34	1.27	0.59	2.66	2.57	0.83
Income maintenance as percentage of total	1.4**	72.2	75.0	79.1	75.8	57.7	63.8	71.2	30.1	65.4	71.1
Unemployment rate	4.5	8.1	8.9	8.1	10.5	7.9	11.0	2.8	1.9	10.3	6.2

Note: For Canada 1968 and 1977, the "Youth and disabled" and "Employment services" figures are bracketed together as a single combined value (0.06 and 0.19 respectively).

Sources: OECD, 1988: 86; Employment and Immigrantion Canada 1981; Statistics Canada 1986: table II.

* 1968 and 1977 data refer to GNP.

** Unemployment insurance data are from 1966; hence, the measure of UI spending as a percentage of total must be taken as an estimate. There were no significant UI program changes between 1966 and 1968.

90). Canada's overall level of spending on labour-market programs also approaches European levels (Table 4-2). But Canada's *profile* of spending is more heavily weighted toward income maintenance, particularly unemployment insurance, than is the case in most European nations. The UI program has borne the burden of Canadian ambivalence about national versus regional development and about state versus market solutions. Laden by default with mandates of income redistribution between classes and regions, it has been the focus of continual controversy and periodic expansion and contraction.

Although Canada's spending on training compares favourably with European levels, Canadian programs have been more heavily concentrated on the long-term unemployed, despite the fact that long-term (over six months) unemployment is lower, as a percentage of total employment, in Canada than in most OECD nations (OECD 1985: 3). Long-term unemployment, furthermore, has proved relatively intractable; it involves "relatively small numbers of individuals who experience recurrent spells" (Shaw 1985: 146). A number of factors have nonetheless conspired to produce this focus upon the long-term unemployed. Long-term unemployment is regionally concentrated in Quebec and the Atlantic provinces; hence, it carries greater political weight than if it were more evenly distributed across regions. Even more fundamentally, this focus was a result of Canada's institutionalized ambivalence toward the state and the market. Since federal and provincial governments, with their interrelated instruments and their different partisan complexions, could not agree on who should intervene in the market, in what ways, by how much, and in whose interest, they focused instead on compensating the market's most obvious casualties.

Readings

4-1 and 4-2. THE BUSINESS VIEW OF LABOUR-MANAGEMENT
              COOPERATION*

The BCNI and the CMA each presented briefs to the Royal Commission on the Economic Union and Development Prospects for Canada (the

---

*Business Council on National Issues, *National Priorities*, a submission to the Royal Commission on the Economic Union and Development Prospects for Canada (Decem-

Macdonald Commission) in 1983. The following excerpts deal with industrial relations and labour-market policy issues. The influence of American "high trust" models of labour relations, downplaying the importance of collective bargaining, is apparent here. Although the emphasis on productivity and the support for policies such as profit sharing placed these submissions at some distance from the views of organized labour, both briefs adopted a temperate tone in dealing with the union movement. The CMA recognized organized labour as "a significant economic and social partner in Canada's future," and the BCNI went further to suggest bipartite policymaking bodies—noting in particular the proposals for what later became the Centre for Labour Market Productivity, discussed in the text.

BCNI

With one of the worst strike records and the most dismal productivity performance in the Western world, it is abundantly clear that all is not well in the area of labour-management relations in Canada. The determinedly adversarial character of Canadian industrial relations has often been identified as one of the causes of our deteriorating economic and productivity performance. The mistrust and conflict that bedevil industrial relations throughout the country also breed resistance to change and adaptation, and this must be overcome if Canada is to reach its economic potential in the future.

Determining that Canada has suffered from poor labour-management relations is a simple task. Far more difficult is the development of workable proposals to improve the climate and reality of industrial relations. Several options have been proposed by observers of the industrial relations scene to diminish conflict and deal positively with the competitive challenges facing Canadian businesses and workers. Some have argued that permanent wage and price controls are needed to ensure that wage increases are kept in line with productivity gains and do not precipitate inflation. According to Barber and McCallum, for example, countries that have been more successful in reducing inflation are characterized by a high degree of "social consensus." Because Canada has lacked such consensus, an approach to fighting inflation that relies on voluntary compliance with guidelines and other stated goals will fail, and thus a system

ber 12, 1983), pp. 26–29; and Canadian Manufacturers' Association, *Future Making: The Era of Human Resources*, a submission to the Royal Commission on the Economic Union and Development Prospects for Canada (September 6, 1983), pp. 37–40.

of mandatory price and wage controls is the only means by which Canada can have lower inflation. A second possible approach toward improving industrial relations, productivity and economic performance would be to construct some kind of formal national tripartite mechanism whereby business, labour and government would regularly sit down to discuss and bargain over major economic decisions for the country. Under this system, these three major groups would presumably be expected to tackle and resolve such difficult questions as which industries should grow and which should be allowed to decline, what level of wage increases should be adopted across the country, and where investments should be directed.

The Business Council is not in favour of either of these alternatives. We fear that a system of permanent price and wage controls would lead to the gradual accumulation of crippling rigidities and distortions throughout the economy and reduce the flexibility of our economy to respond and adapt to change. It would also continually impose on government the onerous responsibility of determining what levels of price and wage increases are appropriate in the various sectors of the economy. Nor are we convinced that the existence of a formal, national tripartite institution would offer workable solutions to Canada's economic problems. Tripartism also raises difficult problems because of the tendency to exclude certain elements of society not formally represented in existing business, labour and government institutions.

Rather than a grand, national tripartite body, we believe that more modest and smaller scale co-operative initiatives involving business and labour—and in some cases governments as well—may be the most effective way to improve industrial relations in Canada. Studies have shown that labour-management co-operation at the firm and industry level can lead to significant productivity and quality improvements. Union leaders and employees increasingly recognize that their jobs can only be secured and their interests served by making sure that their companies and industries are competitive and productive. True, traditional adversarial attitudes and practices are not likely to disappear as a result of labour-management co-operation within firms and industries, but such initiatives can contribute to a better understanding of the shared destiny of workers and employers in the private sector.

In addition to encouraging more labour-management co-operation at the level of firms and industries, the Business Council favours the establishment of national institutions designed to facilitate dialogue and discussion with labour on a variety of key problems. These institutions should have restricted, clearly defined mandates and areas of responsibility; and they need not necessarily include governments, except perhaps in an ex-officio capacity. What we have in mind is *not* a national tripartite body that would make plans for the economy as a whole or divide up the nation's "economic pie" among business, labour and government, but rather something more modest. In fact, several concrete steps have already been taken in this direction. In 1979, the tripartite Ontario Manpower Commission was established to study and identify issues of concern to labour and management in the area of manpower policy. Another example of the type of initiative we favour is the Industrial Labour Market Institute, which the Business Council and the Canadian Labour Congress jointly endeavoured to bring to fruition. As mentioned earlier in this submission, establishment of the Institute was recently announced, but its full implementation has been held up so that consideration can be given as to how the Institute's mandate might be merged with that of the National Centre for Productivity and Employment Growth proposed by the Minister of Finance in his April budget. Both of these proposed institutions would bring labour and business together to consider a number of carefully defined economic and labour market problems, and would hopefully lead to the development of useful policy recommendations. Government would also be involved, but neither body would be subject to government control.

Other suggestions for improving industrial relations in Canada also deserve consideration. For example, many believe that employees must be given opportunities to participate in their companies to a greater extent than is the case today. One way to achieve this would be to move in the direction of voluntary profit sharing, whereby workers directly share in the success of their companies. Some companies have already introduced profit sharing, but in many cases union leaders have expressed strong opposition to the idea. This is unfortunate. It is our belief that business should be encouraged to increase employees' stake in their companies, for this is likely to result in higher productivity and better labour-management relations. We suggest that unions re-examine their traditional opposition to profit sharing. Other ways to increase the scope for participation by workers in their firms also need to be seriously examined by business, labour and government.

CMA

Increasingly, human resources will be Canada's greatest asset in competing in the global village. If we are to accelerate the adoption of a flexible production system and reap the benefits which our highly educated work force can provide, then government, management and labour must find ways of developing a more collaborative relationship. In particular, management and labour must develop a mutual commitment to improving productivity and Canada's industrial competitiveness.

There must be a greater willingness by unions and management to solve problems during the term of the collective agreement. Continuous problem solving should result in fewer unresolved matters for collective bargaining, and the more constructive relationship between the parties should contribute to a faster resolution of the items which remain for bargaining. Further, unions and employers must consider approaches to minimize strikes or lockouts, or to ensure that work stoppages are not unduly prolonged. Management has a responsibility to find ways of sharing decision-making in the work place and linking compensation systems to productivity improvement.

Management should involve employees in the affairs of the company by means of participation on committees dealing with operational matters, where the company's goals, its competitive position, the problems which must be overcome, and the results obtained are openly discussed. Further, employee involvement can also take the form of participation in the financial side of the business. This might involve profit sharing or productivity bonuses, items which have the potential of adding to direct compensation at periodic intervals. Employees might be given the opportunity to purchase shares in the company in the expectation that, with a financial stake in the business, they will be committed to its success. . . .

Human resources planning is the first and critical step in employee development. It is the basis for employer decisions on the training, retraining and upgrading of employees, as well as for the policies of unions, governments and educational institutions. Employers should first look to their current employees in meeting their anticipated needs. Because job requirements are expected to change several times during an individual's working career, employers will have to continually evaluate the skills of their work force against anticipated needs, and take the appropriate steps to meet these needs. Training approaches must be flexible, and may involve short-term training on the job, longer-term job training combined with academic upgrading, release of the individual from work for varying periods of time for retraining, and career counselling.

As far as the future role of unions is concerned, while there is no doubt that they will continue to be a significant economic and social partner in Canada's future, we see the following issues as important determinants of their future effectiveness. First and foremost, unions will have to recognize the need for technical advance and capital accumulation as the basis for future job creation. Second, unions will have to recognize the imperatives of international competition and the consequent need to tie pay increases to productivity increases. Third, the simple and traditional role of unions as adversaries of management must be seen as too simple and inflexible a posture. Unions must be prepared to work with management to develop a new, more collaborative relationship.

As for governments, they should act in a facilitative and supportive role to employers and unions, avoiding the temptation to solve every actual or potential work place issue by legislation and regulation. In practice this means greater leadership in developing and maintaining initiatives that build greater understanding. Governments should approach issues with the objective of obtaining a consensus, and generally avoid acting unilaterally. Canada's . . . governments must attempt to simplify the legislation applicable to the work place. They should undertake at least to agree upon legislative principles of general application, which could then be elaborated according to special provincial or federal requirements.

4-3.   LABOUR'S APPROACH TO SOCIAL PARTNERSHIP*

This manifesto, with its proposals for labour to become a "full partner" in a "system of national social and economic planning," was hotly contested within the CLC. The adversarial tone represents in part a need to recognize the concerns of those with the CLC who viewed tripartism as cooptation. It also reflects labour's strong opposition to wage and price control program of 1975–78.

Canada has clearly reached a stage in its history when our future economic growth cannot be secured without the cooperation of organized labour in national economic and social policies. The present government wants the kind of cooperation in which we *willingly* accept reductions in our wages. They want us to go along with an anti-inflation programme which is based on the argument that labour costs are undermining our international competitive position; which has stimulated an attack on social programmes; which ignores the serious problems of unemploy-

*Canadian Labour Congress, *Labour's Manifesto for Canada* (Ottawa: Canadian Labour Congress, 1976), pp. 12–13.

ment and income distribution; and which fails to control prices or attack the structural causes of inflation in the three chief elements of the family budget—housing, food and energy. They want us to cooperate in rolling back our historic achievements.

We have made it clear that we will not cooperate with a programme of wage controls; to do so would be to reject the fundamental principles of our movement. We will not be a party to an attack on the incomes and rights of working people and the economically defenseless. . . . What is required is change in the way that important economic and social decisions are made. Business and government must now share their power with labour. If labour's cooperation is required to lead us out of our economic difficulties then it can only be on the basis of a programme

- which recognizes the right to employment for a living wage as the cornerstone of a productive and equitable society;
- which recognizes the need to create jobs as the first economic priority;
- which contains a commitment to protect those who suffer from inflation by taxing those who benefit;
- which includes a commitment to redress this country's unacceptable record in redistributing income;
- which recognizes that an equitable society can only be achieved if the power of corporations to set prices is constrained to match the constraint which is imposed on the price of labour by the collective bargaining process;
- which recognizes that private investment decisions must serve the interests of ordinary people.

Organized labour is committed to these objectives and principles. The only guarantee that they will be honoured in our national economic and social decisions is if organized labour is a full partner in making those decisions.

What is required is a system of national social and economic planning. . . .

Our fight *against* wage controls must become a fight *for* a just and equitable society based on:

- the right to employment at a wage which will meet basic needs;
- the right to freely associate with your fellow workers;
- the right to bargain collectively with your employer.

What is required now is a programme of action to *defeat* wage controls and *achieve* national social and economic planning. Only with such a programme can we honour our historic commitment to equality, justice and freedom for all and play our full part in securing the economic and social future of this country.

Progressive change can grow out of the *need* for change, that is the price of our cooperation. To win in this struggle every trade unionist in our movement and every affiliate of this Congress will have to commit themselves to mobilizing our strength and coordinating our resources in a way which has never been done before.

4-4.   GOVERNMENT AS A CATALYST IN LABOUR-MANAGEMENT COOPERATION*

The Advisory Council on Adjustment, boycotted and severely criticized by organized labour, endorsed collaborative initiatives by business and labour, with government acting as a "catalyst," to deal with adjustment issues at the level of the firm and the industrial sector. It recognized, however, that such undertakings had occurred on a very limited scale. One of these initiatives, the Canadian Steel Trade and Employment Congress (CSTEC), was established in 1984 as a bipartite sectoral association comprising twenty steel companies and the respective locals of the United Steelworkers of America. In 1987, with a commitment of up to $20 million from the Department of Employment and Immigration under the Canadian Jobs Strategy, the CSTEC undertook essentially to administer adjustment measures for laid-off workers in the steel industry.

Better cooperation between workers and management, leading to constructive efforts to adjust to change, is, in the view of the Council, a fundamental part of a skills strategy. The Council fully supports the views expressed in a recent British North American Committee publication: "the politics of confrontation cannot accommodate the changes needed in the relationship between labour and management to help them to solve the difficult problems created by today's international economy and new technology." Although increased cooperation remains a private sector responsibility, the Council concludes that the government must foster such cooperativeness.

*Advisory Council on Adjustment, *Adjusting to Win* (Ottawa, March 1989), pp. 38–41.

The Council encourages innovative approaches. For example, an Employment and Immigration Canada (EIC) project with the Canadian Steel Trade and Employment Congress (CSTEC) is an experiment to foster both increased labour-management cooperation and industry-led adjustment measures for laid-off workers in the steel industry; in the Council's opinion, this experiment should be carefully followed up. Under the Innovations program, EIC agreed to assist the CSTEC financially to develop and implement adjustment measures. The CSTEC approach hinges on improved labour-management relations. CSTEC's first requirement is, indeed, that a joint labour-management committee be formed at any plant where workers are going to be laid off. This, in some cases, involves breaching a confrontational attitude.

The Council applauds the thrust of such government initiatives. It believes that governments can be a catalyst in fostering worker-management cooperation and notes that increased resources are required. However, it wants to stress that, to meet the challenges and opportunities of technological change and the increasing globalization of the economy, business and labour will have to try to eradicate the lingering politics of confrontation. . . .

The Council would like to see human resources planning by both business and labour across the economy. This planning must permeate all industrial levels and must become an essential element of a national agenda to increase competitiveness. Strengthening the role of the Canadian Labour Market and Productivity Centre (CLMPC) could be one way to facilitate such planning. At the industry level, the Council is encouraged by the activities of organizations such as the Canadian Automotive Repair and Service Council or the Canadian Electric and Electronics Manufacturing Association. At the firm level, human resource planning should be intimately linked to the firm's business plan or corporate strategy, since it is part of the necessary future orientation of any enterprise, as firms such as IBM Canada or the Xerox Corporation demonstrate.

The Council believes that human resource planning remains primarily a joint responsibility of business and labour. It is of the view that in this area also the government should play a catalytic role by making Canadians more aware of the benefits of such planning and by providing support services. The Council noted some promising examples of government initiatives in this area. Employment and Immigration Canada entered into agreements with private sector organizations to help the private sector identify their current and future skill requirements and to ensure that training provided by firms and educational institutions meets their needs. Agreements with the Canadian Electrical and Electronics Manufacturing Association and with the Aerospace Industries Association of Canada are two such examples. . . .

The government in its programs could also play an important role in human resource planning by putting greater emphasis on government training in areas where opportunities and problems are emerging. In this respect, the Council identified an EIC program which emphasizes linking upside and downside development. The Continuing Employment Option of the Skill Investment program was implemented in July 1988. This option provides financial assistance to help defray workplace-based training costs, wages, and other costs incurred by new or expanding employers when they hire and train workers recently laid off or whose job is threatened because of technology or market change (an IAS [Industrial Adjustment Service—see Reading 4-5] certification is required for eligibility). Although the thrust of this option appears promising, it has been introduced too recently for further assessment. The Council also noted that the funding for this option is limited, some $4 million for 1988/89.

4-5. AN EVALUATION OF GOVERNMENT ADJUSTMENT ASSISTANCE*

The Ontario Premier's Council, an advisory body described in Chapter 5, issued a report in 1989 that evaluated adjustment assistance available to Ontario firms and workers in comparison with other jurisdictions. In these excerpts the Council gave examples of the problems of intra- and intergovernmental coordination that characterize Canadian training programs.

Canada's industrial policies and programs to assist labour adjustment and industrial restructuring have often been piecemeal and reactive— usually responding to a problem only after it has reached a critical stage. This has resulted in relatively short-term strategies, often lasting only a few years, combined with an emphasis on bailouts to salvage ailing companies. Although labour adjustment programs have traditionally con-

*Ontario Premier's Council, *Competing in the Global Economy*, vol. 3 (Toronto: Queen's Printer for Ontario, 1989), pp. 42–48.

centrated on assisting workers to find new jobs rather than providing them with new skills for changing markets, training is now receiving more attention from governments.

At the federal level, industrial programs for labour adjustment are run primarily through the Industrial Adjustment Service (IAS). The Service, which was established in 1983 as Manpower Consultative Services, acts as a catalyst in developing strategies at the plant level to assist workers to adjust to layoffs or redeployment. The IAS can become involved in cases involving plant closure, threat of layoff, technological change, worker transfer, high labour turnover and, more recently, plant expansion.

The IAS encourages management and labour to co-operate in easing labour adjustment to economic or technological change. To achieve this, it assists the two parties to form a bilateral committee to oversee the development of a strategy to deal with the problems involved. . . . The IAS also plays a consultative role in the adjustment process, particularly with respect to available labour market programs. However, its role is clearly restricted to being a facilitator. It is up to the parties themselves to devise the solutions.

The IAS has an annual budget of $10 million, $2 million of which is spent in Ontario. In 1986–87, 527 new agreements were signed involving 330,000 employees. Contributions by the Canada Employment and Immigration Commission amounted to $113 per worker.

The federal government also offers assistance for workers who wish to relocate in order to get a job. The Canadian Manpower Mobility Program helps workers who are unemployed, underemployed, or about to become unemployed look for work elsewhere . . . During 1985–86, $8.9 million was used to help workers under the program. . . .

Training is another mechanism in the government's strategy to assist adjustment. Since 1984, all federal training programs have been subsumed within the six streams of the Canadian Jobs Strategy. Typically, people laid off from a job might use the direct purchase option for training, which is provided in a community college. For those affected by technological change or plant expansion, the Skill Investment or Skills Shortages programs are available. These programs defray the wages and training costs of participating employees—25 percent of total weekly wages if undertaken while on the job, and 60 percent off the job, to a maximum of $350 a week, plus reimbursement of training costs. In 1985, training benefits amounted to $235 million for these participants; the 88,900 unemployment insurance claimant trainees received average weekly benefits of $166 for participating. . . . In 1980, the Minister of Finance announced a special allocation of $350 million for the Industrial Labour Adjustment Program (ILAP) to promote industrial restructuring, manpower retraining, and mobility in areas of particular need. The following year, four communities—among them Windsor, Ontario—were declared eligible. . . .

However, ILAP contained several fundamental flaws that prevented it from assisting laid-off workers effectively. Response to the portable wage subsidy was limited, largely because workers who were re-employed by their previous employers could not use the voucher, and employers felt that the time and paperwork involved in making a claim were not worth the effort.

The relocation assistance was also poorly utilized. By the end of the first year of the program, only 18 relocation grants had been authorized. This was largely because of a 17 month time lag between the original announcement of Windsor's designation under the program and the eventual implementation of the plan. Many workers' unwillingness to relocate further hampered the assistance effort. Furthermore, another federal program, the Canada Manpower Mobility Program, already provided such assistance, thereby reducing the utility of the ILAP relocation initiative.

Two other components of ILAP, the Labour Adjustment Benefit and the Enhanced Training Allowances, also suffered from the delay in putting the program into action.

Ontario's Experience   The Employment Adjustment Branch of Ontario's Ministry of Labour represents the government's main vehicle for helping employees adjust to the effects of restructuring. The branch monitors large-scale cutbacks and closures, provides consultative assistance to employees and employers on the provisions of the Employment Standards legislation, and co-ordinates the involvement of other provincial agencies.

The primary function of the branch is to prepare people for the job placement activities of the Industrial Adjustment Service of the federal government. Its focus has shifted during the last 10 years from one of ensuring that employers provide severance pay to taking a more active counselling role. Employees affected by permanent job loss are given professional assistance in job search techniques, career assessment, access to training, and retirement and financial advice. The programs are delivered by staff at community colleges.

Several problems are evident in Ontario's approach to labour adjustment. First, the adjustment branch, like federal agencies, becomes involved only when a crisis has already arrived. Second, there is no coordinated government approach that links appropriate ministries together when such events occur. For example, in the case of two recent plant closures—Firestone and Richardson Vicks—efforts by the Ministry of Labour to obtain retraining money before the closures occurred met with little success. Ontario's Ministry of Skills Development matches eligible industrial training spending by employers. However, an employer shutting down a plant is hardly likely to have money available for training. Furthermore, most federal programs require that employees be laid off for up to six months before training funds become available. . . .

The British Columbia Experience   British Columbia appointed a Commissioner of Critical Industries in 1985 with a two-year mandate to help rejuvenate the province's hard-hit resource industries by restarting operations that had been shut down and maintaining employment where firms were in difficulty. The process was a voluntary one; the Commissioner gathered all parties involved and tried to achieve a compromise on ways to reduce costs in order to restore and maintain jobs. The Commissioner's budget was $1.1 million, but only $435,000 was spent, mostly on consultants and accountants.

The program did achieve some successes, however. The Commissioner oversaw the drafting of economic plans for 11 operations employing 2,600 people throughout British Columbia. Six of those plans were developed for forestry industry operations, four for mining operations, and one for primary steel industries. The Commissioner helped companies avoid closures by negotiating concessions from creditors, unions, governments, and Crown corporations. These concessions included such measures as debt restructuring, profit sharing, and reduced property taxes, wages, benefits, and electricity taxes.

4-6.   LABOUR ON COLLECTIVE BARGAINING
AND LABOUR-MARKET POLICY *

These excerpts from an Ontario Federation of Labour convention resolution illustrate the labour strategy of pursuing the strengthening of the ad-

*Ontario Federation of Labour, "Economic Restructuring and the Unequal Society," statement adopted by the 32nd annual convention (November 28–December 1, 1988), pp. 7–8.

versarial Wagner model for collective bargaining while developing mechanisms of "codetermination" for the development and administration of labour-market policy. The OFL subsequently made a submission to the Ontario cabinet fleshing out the proposals presented here, including more specific recommendations for changes to labour legislation and for the establishment of bipartite sectoral training boards under an umbrella bipartite training commission.

To be denied training is to be given a one-way ticket to low wages and insecure employment. To be denied training is to be channeled to the margins of the work force. To be denied training is to be forced to pay the price of economic restructuring without sharing in its benefits. And to talk about economic restructuring without talking about training is to treat workers like disposable "factors of production". A serious programme of economic restructuring must include a serious commitment to worker retraining. For us that means:

- adoption of a levy-grant system,
- co-determination of the training process, and
- support for trade union administered training. . . .

In the corporate view restructuring is to be achieved by giving more weight to market pressures—especially in fixing the terms of employment. Their neo-conservative programme is little more than 19th century trickle-down theory in modern dress.

Giving market forces more weight will make the economy more competitive, but it will produce that competitive edge by cutting wages and diminishing the rights of ordinary Canadians at the workplace. In a neo-conservative Canada workers' living standards will be sacrificed. What will "recover" will be profits and the economic share of those whom the market already serves well.

The American future that the corporations offer Canadians is already in the making. . . . Our alternative strategy has three elements:

- reversing de-industrialisation by imposing social controls on the investment process,
- ensuring an equitable distribution of the gains that flow from that restructuring by widening the scope for collective bargaining, and,
- building skills training into the fabric of the economy.

We therefore adopt the following eight-point programme.

1. A Political Commitment to Jobs as the Number One Priority: *The provincial government must commit itself to a Jobs* Budget. In such a budget the government will state the number of workers without jobs, the number of workers confined to low-wage, casual or part-time jobs and the job creation steps that the government will take along with their expected effect on the jobs deficit.

2. Equality and Fairness for Visible Minorities: In its job creation programmes and its training programmes the provincial government must show its commitment to affirmative action. . . .

3. A Guarantee of Training: *The provincial government must make training a legal obligation on employers and an enforceable right of workers.* The provincial government must demonstrate a serious commitment to re-training by adopting a levy-grant system.

4. A Fair and Equal Chance to Bargain: The provincial government must demonstrate by reforming labour legislation that it understands the link between the kind of economic restructuring we have in this province and the bargaining power of ordinary working people at their work place.

The provincial government must legislate real recognition of the right to organise and to bargain collectively. Specifically the provincial government must amend the Ontario Labour Relations Act:

(a) to make successor rights absolute,
(b) to prohibit the use of scab labour, and
(c) to bar contracting out during the life of a collective agreement.

5. Development Funds: *The provincial government must support the creation of development funds that will give workers and our communities an effective say in investment decisions.*

6. Collective Bargaining in the Small Employer Sector: *In order to extend collective bargaining into the small and middle employer sector the provincial government must adopt legislation that would establish collective bargaining on a sectoral basis when that was desired by the representative unions.* Such legislation would build on the experience of Quebec whose labour legislation allows for the extension of a collective agreement's economic terms to all employers in a designated sector.

7. Using the Provincial Government to Build an Independent and Self-Reliant Economy: . . .

8. Restoring and Strengthening the Public Sector: . . . .

Notes

1. Derived from Table 5-1.

2. Some Canadian provinces had earlier adopted legislation roughly modelled on the Wagner Act, but these statutes lacked administrative teeth (Adams 1988: 19).

3. Saskatchewan, however, provided for collective bargaining by public-sector employees as early as 1944, and collective bargaining was fairly extensive at the municipal level in Canada by the 1960s (Riddell 1986a: 17).

4. As originally established, the program covered 42 percent of the labour force. By 1970 coverage had reached 80 percent of wage and salary earners; under the 1971 changes it was increased to 96 percent (Pal 1985: 81).

5. Even after periodic tightening of the program as discussed below, as of mid-1989 claimants could qualify for benefits with between ten and fourteen weeks of employment in the previous fifty-two-week period, or since the start of the last UI claim. The duration of benefits depended upon the individual's employment history, but it was capped at thirty-eight weeks in regions of low unemployment (4 percent or less). Extended benefit periods of up to fifty weeks were allowed in other regions, depending upon the regional rate of unemployment. Benefits were set at 60 percent of previous insurable earnings up to a maximum payment (C$339 a week in 1989).

6. Apprenticeship programs, first introduced in Ontario in 1928, may be considered an exception to this statement, although they have essentially functioned as part of the educational system. Apprenticeship is administered by the provincial governments, and the federal government has made substantial financial contributions to the institutional portion of these programs since the mid-1940s.

7. Representation of locals at the CLC convention is proportionate to membership, with the important proviso that each local is entitled to at least one delegate, and each delegate has one vote. This arrangement tends to overrepresent unions with large numbers of locals. In 1981, the year of the split, for example, the Canadian Union of Public Employees had 1,629 locals and 267,000 members, whereas the building trades had 689 locals and 355,000 members (Rose 1983: 89–90).

8. The governmental designations may be appealed to the Public Service Staff Relations Board. Panitch and Swartz (1984: 150) have noted a shift to a wider use of these designations following a 1982 Supreme Court judgement giving a relatively broad interpretation to "safety and security." They describe this shift as part of a trend toward "permanent exceptionalism" in Canadian labour relations, as discussed below.

9. The Supreme Court did not address the issue of a right to strike under the charter until 1987. In 1986 the fact that the issue had not been resolved prompted the Saskatchewan government to shield its back-to-work legislation from the charter by invoking the override clause, as noted above.

10. In a closed shop only union members may be hired.

11. The Court ruled that mandatory retirement provisions constituted "reasonable limits" (under section 1 of the charter) on the right not to be discriminated against on the basis of age.

12. Weiler (1990: 166) reports that more than twenty-five labour board cases had involved interpretations of the charter by 1989. The constitutional issue of the charter jurisdiction of administrative tribunals, however, had yet to be resolved by the Supreme Court of Canada (ibid.: 5n).

13. In 1989 the federal government proposed to make successive reductions in the centre's budget with a view to making it self-sustaining.

14. With a membership one-tenth the size of that of the CLC, the CFL was overrepresented on the board of the CLMPC. Its support for increasing productivity as a "common objective" of business and labour (Fournier 1986: 322), however, undoubtedly made it an attractive participant from the point of view of business—and from the point of view of a federal government desiring to see the CLMPC established as a consensus-building body. The CNTU, with a membership approximately the same size as that of the CFL but with a much more adversarial ideology, was not represented on the CLMPC board.

15. The attempted integration of apprenticeship funding under the CJS was particularly contentious. Apprenticeship was traditionally a provincially administered (albeit primarily federally funded) program, and the provinces resisted the potential screening of apprentices through CJS criteria.

16. The 1990 changes raised qualifying periods and shortened maximum benefit periods. The basic qualifying period was raised from fourteen to twenty weeks, and the basic maximum benefit period was short-

ened from thirty-eight to thirty-five weeks. Furthermore, the graduated unemployment rate thresholds at which regional extended benefits would apply were also raised. Previously, for example, reduced qualifying periods and longer maximum benefit periods began to be available where unemployment exceeded 4 percent; the 1990 changes raised this threshold to 6 percent.

17. As of 1984, 39 percent of the employed paid labour force was located in Ontario, 25 percent in Quebec, and 11 percent in British Columbia (calculated from Kumar, Coates, and Arrowsmith 1986: 313–15).

5 Economic Development and Adjustment

Like all other western industrial nations, Canada faced major challenges of economic adjustment in the late twentieth century. The globalization of markets, the rise of regional trading blocs, the increasing competitiveness of the Asia-Pacific region, the wide fluctuations of commodity prices of which the oil price shocks of the 1970s are the starkest examples, and the collapse of the Bretton Woods regime of fixed exchange rates all conspired to shift international market shares and to increase economic uncertainty. In comparative perspective, Canadian economic performance since the 1960s, at least on some indicators, has been impressive. The growth of real GDP has been above the average of both large and small states, as indicated in Table 5-1. From 1968 to 1980, Canada led OECD nations in terms of employment growth (job creation) and was second only to the United States in the 1981–87 period. Inflation was moderate in the 1960–80 period, although it was above average from 1981 to 1987. But as noted in the preceding chapter, persistent high unemployment rates have been telling symptoms of the need for structural adjustment.

The range of policies with implications for economic development and adjustment is very broad—in addition to labour-market policies, discussed in Chapter 4, it extends to policies directed toward flows of capital as well as trade, and policies of regional and industrial assistance. This chapter, although it makes passing reference to the adjustment implications of other policies, focuses primarily upon trade policy, and industrial and regional assistance. In these areas, a fundamental lack of consensus about state-market and national-regional balances has retarded the progress and constrained the scope of policy. As in the case of labour-market policies, the reorganization of institutions and the repackaging of

TABLE 5-1 Indicators of Economic Performance, 1960–87

	Real GDP Growth[a]		Employment Growth[a]		Unemployment as Percentage of Labour Force		Change in Consumer Prices[a]	
	1960–80	1981–87	1968–80	1981–87	1960–80	1981–87	1960–80	1981–87
United States	3.5	2.8	2.3	1.8	5.5	7.8	5.3	4.7
United Kingdom	2.3	2.5	0.1	0.1	2.8	10.8	8.8	6.3
West Germany	3.7	1.5	0.1	-0.2	1.7	7.4	3.9	2.8
France	4.6	1.7	0.6	-0.2	2.8	9.3	6.8	7.7
Japan	7.7	3.8	0.9	0.9	1.5	2.6	7.4	2.0
Italy	3.8[b]	2.1	0.4	0.6	5.9[b]	9.4	11.4	11.3
Large States Average	4.3	2.4	0.7	0.5	3.4	7.9	7.3	5.8
Canada	5.1	3.1	2.8	1.6	6.0	10.1	4.6	6.6
Switzerland	3.0	1.7	0.3	0.4	0.1	0.7	4.2	3.4
Netherlands	4.0	1.2	0.4	-0.2	2.1	13.1	5.6	2.9
Belgium	4.1	1.1	0.4	-0.4	3.3	11.7	5.2	5.4
Sweden	3.3	1.8	0.9	0.5	1.9	2.4	6.6	7.6
Denmark	3.4	2.2	0.6	1.1	2.8	9.2	7.9	6.8
Norway	4.4	3.1	1.4	1.6	1.8	2.6	6.4	8.7
Austria	4.2	1.4	0.2	0.1	1.7	3.3	4.9	3.9
Small States Average	3.8	1.8	0.6	0.4	2.0	6.1	5.8	5.5

Sources: Katzenstein 1985: 194; calculations from OECD 1988, tables R.1, R.16, R.18, R.11.
[a] Average annual % change
[b] Figures are for 1968–80.

programs has substituted for substantive policy development. The ability to develop and implement adjustment policies has been constrained by the significance of U.S. trade and investment in the Canadian economy, and by the fact that economic performance, and the costs and benefits of economic policies, vary widely across regions. Because it entails these fundamental tensions of Canadian political life, the challenge of economic adjustment is as much a political as an economic problem.

These tensions have made for an ambivalence in Canada about the appropriate roles of the state and the market in leading economic development and adjustment. The integration of the Canadian and U.S. economies constrains the extent to which Canada can deviate from the state-market mix adopted in the United States. Closer integration, indeed, implies increased access for Canadian products to the larger U.S. market. But the Canadian desire to preserve its distinctiveness from the United States argues for the counterpoising of state to market pressure. Canadian regionalism also entails an ambivalence toward the market and the state. The "hinterland" regions have been highly critical of the state at the federal level, arguing that federal trade and monetary policies favour central Canadian manufacturing. Nonetheless, they have depended on the federal state to organize interregional transfers.

In matters of health policy and industrial relations, as discussed in Chapters 3 and 4, the strong role of provincial governments within the Canadian federation has allowed for different balances of interests to be struck at the provincial level, whereas the organization of interests and the existence of certain policy instruments in federal hands have allowed for policy diffusion. Where interregional conflicts have been at issue, however, as in the labour-market policy arena discussed in Chapter 4 and in the broader arena of economic adjustment policies discussed in this chapter, the federal system has been less successful in coping with ambivalence. Although provincial economic development and adjustment policies are marked by different state-market mixes, these provincial differences have not resolved the broader question of balancing regional and national economic development and adjustment, and the role of the state and the market in achieving that balance.

This lack of consensus extends to the very diagnosis of Canada's economic problems and the appropriate strategies of response. Has the problem been the fact that industry in Canada, alone among the seven major OECD economies, has lacked free access to a market of at least 120 million people? Has the problem, rather, been the lack of development of high-technology industries because of Canada's reliance on resource exploitation and because of the existence of a "branch plant" economy in which most research and development occurs offshore? Should solutions focus on strategies of national development in which regional economies play specialized roles and national wealth is redistributed across regions? Or should strategies of regional development be pursued, in which regional economies themselves are to become diversified and self-sustaining? The definition of the problem and the choice of solution imply different degrees and kinds of state intervention, and different weightings of national and regional concerns.

Canada is not alone in lacking consensus on policies of economic adjustment. In Britain, for example, as in Canada, the appropriate balance of state and market forces in this arena is highly contested (Grant and Wilks 1983: 16; Green 1981: 334; Chandler 1986: 178). Even in nations in which state activity in this arena is fully legitimate, there may be disagreement about the direction of that activity. Pempel reports, for example, that within Japan's hegemonic conservative coalition, "the more specific the goal, the less the level of full-scale conservative agreement" (1982: 55).

Nor is Canada alone in the significance of regional considerations in industrial policy. Indeed, the virtually ubiquitous support for regionally concentrated industries such as textiles, shipbuilding, and steel is testimony to the strength of regional considerations in unitary as well as federal states (Blais 1986a: 28–31). Furthermore, Canadian levels of interregional labour mobility are higher than European levels, though not as high as those in the United States (OECD 1986a: 22). The Canadian case, however, is marked by a unique *conjunction* of factors: a fundamental lack of consensus regarding the role of the state, regional disparities and sensitivities, strong regional (provincial) governments, and the lack of a mechanism to mediate interregional disputes.

A comparison of Canada and the Federal Republic of Germany is instructive in this respect. Regional concerns played a significant role in West German industrial adjustment policy, notably with respect to coal mining in the 1960s and 1970s and the declining steel industries of the Saar and Ruhr valleys in the 1970s and 1980s (Esser, Fach, and Dyson 1984; Katzenstein 1987: 101–102; Chandler 1986: 181). And regional (Land) governments, though less powerfully endowed with policy instruments than their Canadian counterparts, participated actively in the development and implementation of industrial strategies of response.

Indeed, even within regions, adjustment policies of Land governments depended upon the cooperation of local governments (Katzenstein 1987: 56). But nowhere is the contrast between the policy processes of Germany and Canada, noted in Chapter 1, more apparent than in the arena of economic-adjustment policy. The operation of Germany's "decentralized state" is facilitated, in this arena as in others, by its "centralized society"—its complex networks of organized industrial, financial, and labour interests—and by institutional features of the state-society relationship. Notable among these features are a centripetal party politics, flexible federal arrangements, and a range of parapublic institutions bringing major interests (particularly business and labour) together in administrative arms of the state. Canada shares only one of these characteristics—constitutional flexibility. In contrast to Germany's multilayered institutional linkages, moreover, Canada's constitutional flexibility depends heavily upon the relations among political executives. And Canada's party system, with its sharp distinctions between the federal and provincial levels, means that partisanship does not provide a strong basis upon which interregional alliances among executives can be struck. Furthermore, Canada lacks Germany's intrastate federalism: In the absence of an effective senate representing territorial interests, regional ministers in the federal cabinet have borne the major burden of regional representation within the federal government.

As a result, the state's role in economic adjustment policy is determined primarily through intra- and intergovernmental contests. These contests are marked not only by turf battles for jurisdiction but by disputes about the appropriate role of the state itself. Different views of the balance between national and regional development and between state and market instruments find proponents within these contests, but there are no natural mediators. Little of substance, accordingly, has been resolved: Policies have remained both controversial and essentially unchanged.

Context

Canada was a relatively late industrializer. Unlike other late industrializers such as Germany, Japan, and Sweden, however, Canada developed neither an industrial banking system nor a strong steering role for the state. The reasons for this anomaly lie in the two dominant relationships in Canada's economic and political history: the relationships with Britain and with the United States.

Until the late nineteenth century, by far the dominant engine of economic development in Canada was "resource appropriation": the fur trade, fishing, and lumbering (Manzer 1985: 22–29). In this period first the British and then the Canadian governments played an important role in securing access to resources through defence and foreign policies and through investments in transportation infrastructure. Railways were heavily subsidized, especially by land grants. The lumber industry developed within the protection of the high tariff walls imposed by the British in the early nineteenth century. Throughout this period, however, governments relied on monopolistic private enterprise, rather than public enterprise or public administration, as instruments of development. From the monopoly charters and property rights granted to fur-trading companies in the seventeenth, eighteenth, and nineteenth centuries to the subsidization of the transcontinental Canadian Pacific Railway, completed in 1885, large private corporations were fostered by government policies.

In the late nineteenth century Canada, like other nations industrializing in this period, faced the need to catch up to earlier industrializers, to adopt technology requiring a large capital investment. In Germany this challenge forged strong and lasting links between finance and industrial capital, as banks became major sources of equity capital for industrial firms (Katzenstein 1987: 84–85; Gerschenkron 1962). In Japan the state took an early and active role in establishing large industrial firms and then withdrew from ownership to perform a steering role (Pempel 1982: 48–49). In Sweden an initial period of industrial strife led to the building of a social democratic coalition under whose hegemony private capital accumulation was fostered and consensual economic management proceeded (Heclo and Madsen 1987: 46–50).

Canada followed none of these paths. A major role for the state in the direct subsidization or outright ownership of large corporations was generally confined to infrastructure (notably transportation, communication, and utilities), not other industries. Resource industries received more indirect forms of state subsidy, such as low stumpage fees on crown land in the case of the timber industry, or low freight rates for certain commodities. The Canadian banking system had developed throughout the nineteenth century under the strong influence of the British model of commercial banks; hence, by the late nineteenth century it became a source of short-term financing, not long-term investment. For their long-term capital requirements, Canadian industrial firms had essentially three sources: the bond market, retained earnings, and equity investment (Atkinson and Coleman 1989: 60–65). The main source of direct investment was Canada's earlier-industrializing neighbour, the United States.

The distinction between "financial" and "real" sectors on the Anglo-American model was reinforced throughout the twentieth century in Canada by governmental regulation; only in the mid-1980s, in concert with global trends, did Canadian governments begin to loosen these restrictions. As a result, as Atkinson and Coleman put it, "the financial system which has emerged in Canada places financial institutions, industrial corporations and government in distinct spheres" (1989: 65). On the one hand, this system constrained the ability of the state to undertake "anticipatory" industrial policy. On the other, by enhancing the autonomy of industrial corporations, it contributed to a "firm-centred industry culture" (ibid.: 66).

The organization of business and labour interests also limits their ability to participate in central policymaking structures. In the absence of a comprehensive consensus-building peak association of business at the national level, business groups find it difficult to collaborate on cross-sectoral strategies, although strong organizations in some sectors (especially in highly concentrated sectors such as steel) allow for collaboration at the sectoral level. As for labour, its decentralized organizational structure, together with its historical aversion to collaborative mechanisms as discussed in Chapter 4, also militates against participation in the development and implementation of cross-sectoral strategies. Again, however, this structure makes possible union participation in particular sectors (such as textiles and steel) or at the local level.

The role of the state in this arena is complicated by the federal-provincial division of powers. The federal government possesses the fullest panoply of powers related to economic development and adjustment policy, including monetary and tariff instruments, indirect and direct taxation, public ownership, loans, investments, and direct payments to firms, in addition to the instruments of labour-market policy discussed in the preceding chapter. The provinces lack control over interest and exchange rates, tariffs, and indirect taxation;[1] but like the federal government they control instruments of direct taxation, public ownership, financial assistance to firms, and certain regulatory instruments, such as health and safety and environmental standards, which may become indirect instruments of industrial policy. These powers are sometimes used in outright intergovernmental competition and conflict, as in the case of the conflict between Ottawa and the western provinces over energy policy in the late 1970s and early 1980s (Chapter 6). The general problem created by the division of powers, however, is less one of deliberately countervailing policies than of lack of coordination (Tupper 1986: 147).

The predominant role in adjustment policy is nonetheless played by the federal government. Not only is the range of its instruments broader but in a number of areas of shared jurisdiction the level of its financial commitment is greater. In the area of industrial assistance, for example, federal spending in the early 1980s was about three times as great as that of the provinces combined (Jenkin 1983: 171; Blais 1986a: 8).

One of the federal government's major instruments for responding to challenges from the international economy is trade policy. Policies on tariffs and trade have played an important role in Canadian economic policy since before confederation. And throughout, the issue of free trade with the United States has waxed and waned in importance. The economic threat posed by the demise of a reciprocal trade agreement with the United States was one of the motivating forces behind confederation, but the concept of reviving such an agreement continued to enjoy support (and to draw opposition) in the half-century thereafter. In general (in an alignment to be dramatically reversed more than one hundred years later) Liberals and labour supported free trade, and Conservatives and business opposed it. In 1874 a reciprocal trade treaty negotiated by the Liberal government was rejected by the American Senate. The "National Policy" of the subsequent Conservative government, elected in 1878, emphasized tariff protection for Canadian industry, the completion of the transcontinental railway, and increased immigration. In 1911 the Liberal government under Prime Minister Wilfred Laurier negotiated an agreement with Washington for a reciprocal lowering of tariffs on a broad range of commodities and some manufactured goods. However, when the Liberals, badly divided on the issue, lost the ensuing election, the implementing legislation for the reciprocity agreement was never passed.

Since the 1930s Canadian trade policy has followed two parallel tracks: one emphasizing multilateralism, the other emphasizing bilateral agreements, especially with the United States (Carmichael, Macmillan, and York 1989: 47). The primary example of the former is, of course, Canada's participation in the General Agreement on Trade and Tariffs in the postwar period; another example is the series of multilateral agreements since the 1960s limiting imports of textiles and clothing from low-cost countries. The primary example of bilateralism, until the negotiation of the more comprehensive Canada-U.S. Free Trade Agreement in the late 1980s, was the Auto Pact agreement with the United States implemented in 1965.[2] The Auto Pact allowed for the duty-free import of auto parts and finished vehicles into Canada provided that the importing firms met essentially two conditions: that they produced in Canada (approximately) as many cars as they sold in Canada, and that the Canadian value-added was at least 60 percent of the value of automobiles sold in Canada (Wonnacott 1988: 269).[3] The impact of the Auto Pact was dramatic. Largely as a result of the exploitation of economies of scale made possible by access to the larger American market, labour productivity in the automobile industry grew on average by 7 percent annually in the ten years following the Auto Pact, as opposed to 3 percent in other manufacturing industries (OECD 1988: 60). Automotive trade between the two countries increased by a factor of 24 between 1965 and 1985 (Takefield 1988: 285), as compared with an 18-fold increase in total bilateral trade in merchandise.

The pursuit of the bilateral option became increasingly pressing for Canada as it became clear that the global economy was dividing into regional trading blocs. Trade within major regional blocs (North America, Asia-Pacific, Europe, and the East Bloc) increased from just under 40 percent to almost 43 percent of total world trade from 1970 to 1986. The North American share of total exports declined by five points from 18.7 percent to 13.7 percent, while the Asia-Pacific share rose over eight points from 10.7 to 19.0 (GATT 1987: 177–78).

The issue of Canada-U.S. bilateralism, however, had important implications for another set of concerns that have been central to economic development and adjustment policy in Canada—concerns about regional development. Since the days of the National Policy, trade policies have favoured manufacturing and hence primarily central Canada. Rates of price protection (defined as the potential increase in domestic prices made possible by trade barriers, including tariffs, quantitative restrictions, and federal government procurement) have been generally higher for manufactured goods than for natural resources. In 1987 these rates ranged from less than 1 percent in the mining, fishing, and forestry sectors to more than 19 percent for clothing and for knitting mills (OECD 1988: 79).[4]

Macroeconomic policies, especially monetary policy, have also arguably exacerbated regional economic disparity. As Carmichael notes, "there is only one Bank of Canada rate and only one exchange rate for the

Canadian dollar, and all regions must accept these rates even though they may have different impacts on interest-sensitive spending or on the competitiveness of particular exports" (1986: 12). The regional impact of the fiscal-monetary mix which the federal government pursued in the wake of the 1981–82 recession provides a case in point. High real interest rates exacerbated the problems of the west, by contributing to a slowdown in construction in provinces whose economies were already reeling from the effects of sharply reduced commodity prices. Furthermore, the fluctuation of the exchange rate has differential effects across regions, since regions compete in different international markets with different international competitors. In the 1980s, for example, Canada's real effective exchange rate fell by more than the rates of other industrial countries, but by considerably less than those of most other resource-exporting countries. This tended to favour central Canadian manufacturing while working to the disadvantage of the resource industries, which are relatively more important to the economies of the western and Atlantic provinces (ibid.: 13–14).[5]

Faced with the regional economic disparities described in Chapter 1, and with eastern and (especially) western resentment of the effects of federal macroeconomic and trade policies, successive federal governments have used their fiscal powers to soften these effects. Unlike monetary policy, federal fiscal policy can and does vary across regions. Taxation is a less flexible instrument than is spending, since the federal tax base is common across provinces (and all provinces except Quebec assess their own income taxes using the federal tax base).[6] Spending levels, however, vary widely. Accordingly, deficit spending, especially on the part of the federal government, is much deeper in some provinces (notably the Atlantic provinces) than others (Carmichael 1986: 15).

Increased federal spending in poorer provinces takes a number of forms: unconditional transfers of tax revenues under "equalization" policies developed over time and enshrined in the 1982 constitution; spending under social programs such as unemployment insurance and welfare, which tends to be greater on a per capita basis either by deliberate design or as a result of greater demand; and regional development programs. Indeed, federal spending on explicit programs of regional development (construed to include roads, highway, and public works projects) has amounted, over time, to less than 10 percent of total federal transfers to the provinces (Lithwick 1986: 150).

Federal spending for regional economic development has nonetheless been politically significant, because of its visibility and because of the controversy that inevitably surrounds it. Since the 1950s there has been continual change in the packaging of regional development programs and the institutional structures for their development and delivery. These institutions and programs have fluctuated in their focus and in their degree of centralization or decentralization. This continual change attests to the irresolution of political actors, not only about the appropriate balance between "national" and "regional" economic development but also about theories of economic development and their associated definitions of problems and implied solutions (Savoie 1986: chap. 1).

Apart from explicit regional development policies, but still suffused with regional concerns, have been a wide variety of programs and instances of aid to industry. Aid grew sharply in the 1965–71 period as a number of these programs were established, administered by the Department of Industry, which became the Department of Industry, Trade and Commerce (ITC) in 1969, and other line departments. There has, however, been no coherent industrial strategy: rather, Canadian industrial policy has been marked at the federal level by a "tangle of industrial grants and loans" (Tupper 1986: 349) and by ad hoc selective intervention to aid particular firms (Chandler 1986: 188–89). Specific programs of industrial assistance are primarily focused on small to medium-sized businesses; aid to large businesses tends to occur outside regular program structures, in the form of ad hoc "bail-outs" (Trebilcock et al. 1985).

All states, of course, undertake some degree of selective intervention outside a coherent policy framework. What varies is the weight of such activities as a proportion of all industrial policy activities. In Canada, as in Britain and the United States, such firm-specific aid is the dominant form of industrial assistance: It does not constitute, as in France, a stream apart from dirigiste planning (Green 1981), nor, as in Germany and Japan, an exception to sectoral policies. Federal aid to industry grew rapidly from 1965 to 1971 and then levelled off; but only in the 1980s, as discussed below, did Canada begin to experiment with aid tied to comprehensive restructuring on a sectoral basis.

Industrial assistance at the provincial level has been similarly focused on firms. As at the federal level, significant provincial involvement in programs of industrial assistance began in the 1960s and 1970s. All provinces established some mechanism for aiding industry with grants or loans. A common denominator of provincial policies has been "bidding" for industry through location incentives, sometimes with and sometimes without federal involvement, and occasionally in competition with each other (Savoie 1986: 100–101). Beyond this, there has been some variation across provinces in the types of firms favoured for assistance and the level of assistance, as might be expected, given their different economic structures and fiscal capacities. Alberta, Ontario, and especially Quebec have been most active in industrial assistance. In the 1970s Alberta sought to upgrade natural resources and to develop technology-based downstream industries such as petrochemicals, drawing in part on its Alberta Heritage Savings Trust Fund established in 1976 with windfall revenues resulting from the increase in oil prices after 1973 (Chapter 6). Ontario, through the Ontario Development Corporations and a variety of special assistance programs, administered a congeries of grants and loans to firms through the 1970s. Quebec sought to foster francophone business and finance, and established not only state lending and assistance agencies, the Société du développement industriel and the Société générale de financement, but also a major state-controlled investment fund, the Caisse de dépôt et placement, established in 1966, as part of the agenda of the "quiet revolution," to invest the assets of the Quebec Pension Plan. The Caisse, an innovation in Canadian industrial policy and an example of the greater activism of the Quebec state, was consciously modelled on western European funds such as the French Caisse des dépôts et consignations and the Swedish National Provident Fund for Retirement Pensions (Brooks and Tanguay 1985: 102–3). Like its western European counterparts, it has had to juggle its fiduciary mandate with objectives of economic development. Within these constraints, it has sought to favour small to medium francophone business. In a few notable instances, as in the food retailing industry, it has fostered some restructuring through mergers. It has also sought to extend its influence by appointing representatives to the boards of directors of the large corporations in which it invests, again on the European model, a practice that embroiled it in controversy with the anglophone business community and the federal government (Brooks and Tanguay 1985).

With regard to all of the instruments of economic adjustment and development—trade policy, industrial assistance, regional development—the institutional structures of policy development and program delivery, as well as the federal-provincial balance of power, were in a state of considerable flux during the 1960s and 1970s. In the 1950s and early 1960s a variety of relatively modest shared-cost programs of regional assistance, job creation, and training were administered by various federal line departments, in fairly close collaboration with their provincial counterparts, and "regional ministers" wielded considerable influence. The late 1960s and early 1970s, in contrast, constituted a period of federal activism, unilateralism, and sweeping institutional change. That period saw the consolidation and development of regional development programs at the federal level within a newly created Department of Regional Economic Expansion (DREE). A new Department of Industry, Trade and Commerce brought industry and trade under the same bureaucratic umbrella. These departments oversaw a number of federally funded programs, developed with little provincial input. In the mid-1970s the centralist thrust of these policies was tempered somewhat by increased collaboration between the relevant federal and provincial bureaucracies.

Agenda

In the late 1970s controversy over economic adjustment policy began to build. Regional conflicts were exacerbated by the differential effects of the first and second oil price shocks on the oil- and gas-rich west and energy-dependent central and eastern Canada. Internationally, the rise of regional trading blocs and the increasingly competitive newly industrializing countries (NICs) threatened Canadian markets and potential markets abroad. Unemployment rates hovered close to a postwar high of 8 percent—much higher in some regions. The fiscal climate shifted to one of constraint as governmental deficits inexorably widened at the federal level and in most provinces.[7] The agenda of economic adjustment policy became crowded, but no consensus emerged to deal with it.

The climate of federal-provincial relations was growing increasingly tense in this period. On other fronts the federal government had moved unilaterally in 1975 to cap the open end of its cost-sharing arrangement with the provinces for certain "established" programs such as medical and hospital insurance, and the provinces had been required to renegotiate these arrangements under the shadow of that unilateral action (Chapter 3). The federal government was also pressing ahead with its agenda for constitutional reform, including a proposed Charter of Rights and Freedoms, which a number of provincial governments saw as a centralizing force (Chapter 2).

In the industrial policy arena, federal-provincial and interprovincial tensions were increasingly apparent. Region clearly dominated partisanship in debates over the role of the state in this arena. The Conservative premier of Ontario declared in 1978, "To trade off competitive industrial development so as to achieve a better regional distribution of incomes is a terribly expensive strategy which we can no longer afford."[8] Meanwhile, governments of disadvantaged regions continued to maintain that regional development policy was only just compensation for the negative effects of other federal policies—for, in the words of Conservative premier Richard Hatfield of New Brunswick in 1980, "the bad policies or the policies that favoured [the more developed regions] years ago, and still do" (quoted in Savoie 1986: 4).

Meanwhile, another recurrent tension began to emerge. In the mid-1970s, even in the context of a current of economic nationalism that led to the implementation of a foreign-investment review process, the issue of free trade with the United States reappeared. In 1975 the Economic Council of Canada (an advisory body discussed in Chapter 4) tentatively raised the issue. In two reports issued in 1978 and 1982 the Senate Committee on Foreign Affairs strongly argued for the negotiation of a bilateral agreement, as Canada's virtually sole option in the face of regional trading blocs and increasing U.S. protectionism. In 1980 a discussion paper was published by the federal Department of External Affairs, which advocated the negotiation of sectoral trade liberalization agreements with the United States, while rejecting an across-the-board bilateral agreement.

At the same time an alternative position was being developed, emphasizing the need for Canada to develop "technological sovereignty" and hence the need for an active and anticipatory industrial policy on the part of the state that would foster high-technology industries. This position was most closely associated with the Science Council of Canada, a federal advisory body established in 1966 and composed of thirty representatives of the natural and social sciences appointed by the federal government (Science Council of Canada 1979).[9] Critics of this approach argued that in a "small" economy such as Canada's it was not in the interest of taxpayers to subsidize the development of technology that could be adopted and used without compensation offshore, and that Canada should rather adopt and internally diffuse foreign technology. In fact, Canada's "smallness" is a matter of perspective: Among the largest seven OECD economies, Canada ranks sixth (ahead of Italy) in research and development spending as a proportion of GDP (at just under 1.5 percent). Canadian spending is comparable to the middle range for considerably smaller economies (about the same as Belgium and Norway, and well below Sweden, Switzerland, and the Netherlands) (OECD 1986b:

15). However, as Blais notes, the "technological sovereignty" option appealed, in Canada as elsewhere, to national pride: the collective desire to achieve technological excellence (1986b: 65–66). In Canada, always sensitive to instances of its loss of talent to the United States, this appeal was all the stronger.

The mobilization of groups behind these two options (the free trade–continentalism–market orientation versus the technological sovereignty–nationalism–state orientation) was in its early stages in the late 1970s and early 1980s, and the alignment was not sharply defined. Indeed, these options did not dominate the political agenda in this period. The constitutional reform process (Chapter 2) increasingly preoccupied federal politicians and officials and, perforce, their provincial counterparts. Even in the economic policy arena, the general malaise about declining levels of growth and rising levels of unemployment had not yet crystallized around alternative solutions. The governing federal Liberal party itself was divided, the divisions reflecting the long-standing disputes between "nationalists" and "continentalists."

The only clear alignment was that of the "dominant coalition" of business (resource and resource-related manufacturing industries, finance, and "branch plant" manufacturers) behind the free-trade option, and the opposition of organized labour to what it perceived as a "general shift to the political right in the policy of government and in the political mood" (Canadian Labour Congress 1976: 7) and to market-based approaches. This alignment was apparent in the 1983 submissions of the BCNI and the CLC to the Macdonald Royal Commission, discussed below (Readings 5-1 and 5-2). Other business groups were more ambivalent. The Canadian Manufacturer's Association, for example, while sharing the BCNI's orientation to the market and its distrust of the state's ability to "pick winners," did not so clearly opt for the *continental* market. In its brief to the Macdonald Commission it endorsed a multilateral approach to trade policy and rejected comprehensive bilateral free trade while allowing that "investigation may reveal future opportunities for special arrangements in certain sectors." Nonetheless, it argued that "the objective of good Canada-US trade relations should be at the top of our agenda" (Canadian Manufacturers' Association 1983: 35–36).

Process

One effect of the irresolution and controversy around economic adjustment policy was the instability of institutional structures in this arena.

Having institutionally separated "regional development" from "industry and trade" policy in 1969 (in DREE and ITC, respectively), the federal government began to experiment in the late 1970s with structures to draw them together. When the Ministry of State for Economic Development was established in 1979 (Chapter 1), both DREE and ITC were brought under the MSED umbrella.

The ministries of state were intended to be a consensus-seeking bodies, but MSED inevitably came into conflict with the strong positions taken by line departments. In 1980 and 1981, in particular, under Herb Gray, one of the leaders of the nationalist wing of the Liberal party, ITC opted to promote the technological sovereignty–nationalist–interventionist approach to industrial policy against considerable cabinet opposition. MSED attempted to forge a compromise emphasizing "Canada's traditional comparative advantage in the production of basic commodities [and] related manufacturing products [as well as] high productivity, high technology goods" (quoted in Doern and Phidd 1983: 437).

In 1982–83 another major reorganization took place, creating a new blizzard of acronyms at the federal level. Both DREE and ITC were broken up: Responsibility for the industrial programs of each was given to a newly created Department of Regional and Industrial Expansion (DRIE); DREE's other programs went to various line departments; and ITC's trade responsibilities went to a reorganized Department of External Affairs (placing industrial assistance and trade policy once again in different portfolios). With the demise of DREE, the responsibility for coordinating regional economic policy in general was moved from the purview of a single line department and located at the cabinet level: The Ministry of State for Economic Development became the Ministry of State for Economic and Regional Development (MSERD), serving a Cabinet Committee on Economic and Regional Development.

These changes also moved in the direction of recentralizing power over regional economic development policy (Savoie 1986: 87). Federal Economic Development Coordinators (FEDCs), reporting to MSERD, were established in each region as *federal* (as opposed to provincial) articulators of regional interests. The tilt toward centralization did not imply greater coordination, however. Under these arrangements several powerful coalitions emerged among provincial and local officials and the respective FEDC and "regional minister" in the federal cabinet[10]— coalitions that were on occasion in competition with each other.

These changes in institutional and program configuration did not, by

and large, affect the orientation of industrial assistance, which continued
to focus on individual firms and localities, not on sectoral restructuring.
Some sectors (albeit with regional bases) were targeted for aid in "mod-
ernizing" in the late 1970s and 1980s (shipbuilding from 1975 to 1985;
pulp and paper from 1979 to 1984; and textiles from 1981 to 1986), but
the programs entailed subsidies to individual firms to modernize, not the
rationalization of capacity; and shipbuilding and textiles continued to be
protected by relatively high tariff and nontariff barriers after the termina-
tion of the programs (OECD 1988: 67–69). One exception, however, was
the case of the Atlantic fisheries. A special task force, established outside
the regular channels of regional and industrial assistance, negotiated federal and provincial aid tied to the merger and rationalization of five failing
fish companies (McCorquodale 1988: 140). This restructuring was successful in restoring profitability to the fishery, but it was accomplished
in the context of a crisis in an industry that is the economic mainstay
of Canada's most disadvantaged region, and it remained an exception.
Furthermore, the industry was soon faced with fresh crises: notably, the
depletion of cod stocks in the late 1980s.

   Structural experimentation in the late 1970s and 1980s was not confined to the governmental bureaucracy per se. This period was also
marked by experimentation with tripartite and bipartite mechanisms for
involving representatives of business and labour in the formulation of
economic policy, as discussed in Chapter 4 with regard to industrial
relations and labour-market policy. In 1977 and 1978 a large-scale consultative enterprise was undertaken under the aegis of the Department
of Industry, Trade and Commerce, comprising twenty-three sectoral task
forces (Tier I) and an overall "synthesizing" task force (Tier II). The process, particularly in its early stages, was primarily oriented toward ITC's
clientele, the business community. Organized labour's participation in
the Tier I process was relatively late, limited, and skeptical, but in the
Tier II process labour successfully demanded a bipartite structure with
parity representation for labour and business, and labour and business
cochairs. The impact of the Tier I and Tier II exercises was almost entirely on the process rather than on the substance of policy. It contributed
to the nascent development of bipartite collaboration between business
and labour, but it resulted in little governmental action.

   The bipartite model was also followed in two other significant undertakings. One, leading to the establishment of the CLMPC, is discussed
in Chapter 4. The other was a bipartite task force on the role of resource-

related "major projects" in Canadian industrial policy (known as the Blair-Carr task force, after its business and labour cochairs),[11] established in 1978 under the aegis of the federal-provincial industry ministers' conference. When the task force reported in 1981, the era of the National Energy Program (Chapter 6), a megaprojects strategy focusing upon energy and resources briefly became the centrepiece of proposed federal industrial and regional development policy. The government did not, however, embrace a Blair-Carr recommendation that a standing bipartite (business and labour) agency with regulatory authority over major projects be established and proposed to establish a bipartite board with advisory and research functions only (Waldie 1986: 190). As in the case of incomes policy (Chapter 4), the government's model of conflict resolution emphasized a sharing of information, not authority. Again, moreover, the lasting impact of the Blair-Carr task force was in contributing to a legacy of experience with bipartite processes, rather than in shaping policy. The task force recommendations were overtaken by events: With declining energy prices in the 1980s, enthusiasm for the megaprojects waned (Savoie 1986: 127). The proposed bipartite board was never established.

Notwithstanding these bipartite experiments, the major consultative enterprises of the 1980s took a more traditional form. In 1982 the federal government adopted a time-honoured response to the uncertainty and lack of consensus that prevailed in the economic policy arena: It appointed a commission of inquiry, highlighted with the cachet of designation as a "royal commission." The Royal Commission on the Economic Union and Development Prospects for Canada—better known by the name of its chairman, Donald Macdonald, a former member of the federal Liberal cabinet—was extraordinary in the scope of its mandate and the size of its membership. Its thirteen members were drawn primarily from business and academe; only one was a representative of organized labour. Its terms of reference required it in broad terms to address both economic goals and policies and institutional reform. It commissioned a massive review of the academic literature, ultimately publishing seventy-two volumes of background studies by Canadian academics. It held public hearings across the country and received more than fifteen hundred written briefs. The trade liberalization–market position was forcefully presented to the commission, primarily by business associations and firms. The technological sovereignty–interventionist option, linked to the need for consensus-building mechanisms of "social partnership," also had its advocates, primarily among state agencies (Drache and Cameron 1985: xiii). The technological-sovereignty option found some support in briefs from organized labour,[12] but in general labour briefs emphasized the need for full-employment policies and improvements to labour-relations legislation. Welfare state issues were generally taken up by voluntary associations and women's groups.

Not surprisingly, given its scope and size and the atmosphere of uncertainty and dissensus in which it was appointed, the Macdonald Commission did not quickly come to a central theme for its recommendations. An unfocused interim report published in 1983 merely set out issues and questions that had been raised in its consultations. But in the last eighteen months of its existence, the commission found its centrepiece: a recommendation for comprehensive trade liberalization with the United States as essential to a market-oriented strategy of economic development. Its report, released in September 1985,[13] quoted liberally from business briefs and academic studies in defence of this central recommendation (Reading 5-3).

The recommendations of the Macdonald Commission went well beyond trade issues to treat labour-market policy, stabilization policy, social policy, and institutional reform; but in general they were consistent with its general "market" orientation. The central recommendation with regard to labour-market policy was the reform of the unemployment insurance program: notably, the elimination of regional differentiation, the general tightening of eligibility requirements, and reductions in maximum benefit levels. But the commission also recommended increased spending on mobility and training assistance to unemployed individuals, and the replacement of a variety of income supports and social benefits with a modest version of a guaranteed annual income designed to remove the work disincentives inherent in the existing tax-transfer system. With regard to regional development programs, the commission's recommendations were predicated on a model of regional specialization and interregional mobility. The role of the federal government was hence not to undertake job-creation programs but rather to facilitate structural change.

The sole labour representative on the commission dissented from the report. His dissent focused on unemployment as "the major problem facing Canadians today" and criticized the commission for turning to "market based fantasies as a solution" (Reading 5-4). Rather than free trade, he advocated "promotion of import substitution and a direct role for government in an industrial strategy." The stage was set for political mobilization around the free-trade issue. And between the time that the Macdonald Commission had been appointed and the time of its report, the partisan context in which this mobilization would take place had changed dramatically.

The Conservative government elected at the federal level in September 1984 brought with it an orientation to the market, to limited government, and to decentralization, all in sharp and deliberate contrast to the Trudeau years. In November 1984 the finance minister issued a document entitled *A New Direction for Canada: An Agenda for Economic Renewal*. In some areas, notably energy policy and foreign investment, it made specific proposals; in others, such as regional development, trade, labour-market, and adjustment policies, it called existing policies into question and promised to review them (Carmichael, Macmillan, and York 1989: 22).

In the arenas of energy policy and foreign investment, the new government moved quickly to extinguish two symbols of the Liberal years, the National Energy Program (NEP) and the Foreign Investment Review Agency (FIRA). The dismantling of the NEP is discussed in the following chapter. In the case of FIRA, an agency established in 1974 to review the acquisition or the establishment of businesses in Canada by foreign investors, the changes were admittedly as much symbolic as substantive. The agency was given a modified mandate (essentially excluding small or new businesses) and a new name, Investment Canada. The government explicitly sought to counter the "negative signals [that FIRA sent] to domestic and foreign investors, leading them to think that Canada is ambivalent, if not hostile, to non-Canadian investment." [14]

The Conservative government did not find the centrepiece of its agenda for economic adjustment, however, until the release of the report of the Macdonald Commission. Ironically, the recommendations of the commission, which had been appointed by a Liberal government and headed by a former Liberal cabinet minister, meshed much better with the views of the governing Conservatives than it did with those of the Liberals in opposition. Furthermore, concerns about increasing U.S. protectionism under its existing trade law (Hawes 1988: 146–49), and about the prospect of more protectionist U.S. trade legislation in the future, provided momentum. In September 1985 Prime Minister Mulroney formally invited the U.S. government to enter into negotiations on such an agreement, and in May 1986 the negotiations began.

The free-trade option provided a focus not only for the Conservative agenda but also for opposition to market-oriented strategies. During the eighteen months in which negotiations on the Canada-U.S. Free Trade Agreement were underway, coalitions of interest groups increasingly mobilized and polarized around the issue. Business networks formed to support a comprehensive bilateral agreement; and provincial labour federations, through a series of grass-roots meetings, built alliances with women's groups, churches, and social agencies in opposition.

In October 1987 the Free Trade Agreement was concluded. The major features of the agreement are summarized in Table 5-2. Notably, the thorny issue of developing a code of acceptable subsidies that would not be subjected to countervailing duties was deferred to subsequent negotiations. Once negotiated, the subsidies code would be applied by a binding-arbitration mechanism—a bilateral disputes-resolution panel. In the interim the panel would apply the existing trade laws of both countries and would also review changes to those laws to determine whether those changes were consistent with the General Agreement on Tariffs and Trade (GATT) and with "the object and purpose" of the agreement." [15]

Faced with a text rather than a general principle, the opponents and proponents of the deal increased the intensity of their debate. Conflict on this issue, which so directly touched Canadian sensitivities about the U.S. relationship, could not be contained within the structures of the state. In contrast to the traditional patterns of elite accommodation in Canadian politics and to the experimentation with collaborative "social partnership" discussed above, the conflict over free trade took the classic pluralist form of interest-group mobilization, partisan competition, and public debate. Business and labour organizations formed the centres of coalitions of pro- and anti- free-trade coalitions, respectively. Within the business community, however, there was considerable diversity of opinion, including some opposition to the agreement. All of the national business associations—the BCNI, the Canadian Chamber of Commerce, the Canadian Manufacturers Association, and the Canadian Federation of Independent Business—endorsed the agreement. At the level of sectoral associations and individual firms, however, divisions were more apparent. Firms and industrial associations in the "dominant coalition" (resource industries exporting largely to the U.S. market, and subsidiaries of U.S.-based multinationals) looked forward to easier cross-border transfers under free trade. Other export-oriented firms that depended on a degree of mercantilism on the part of the state were more ambivalent.

TABLE 5-2   Summary of the Free Trade Agreement

	Main provisions
Manufactured goods	Removal of all bilateral tariffs starting on 1st January 1989, over a maximum period of 10 years.
Automotive	US-Canada Auto Pact continues. Canada's embargo on imports of used cars to be eliminated. Duty remissions to be phased out. To benefit from tariff exemption, at least 50 percent of the value of goods must originate in North America.
Agriculture	Elimination of tariffs on agricultural trade within 10 years and the agreement not to use direct export subsidies on bilateral agricultural trade.
Energy	Restrictions on exports of Canadian oil and gas can be imposed; however, any reduction in exports to the United States must be proportional to the total supply of oil and gas available in Canada, without price discrimination.
Banking	Canada to eliminate restrictions on acquisition of Canadian assets by US banks. Canadian banks will receive equal treatment under US Securities laws.
Financial Services	Improved access and competition; national treatment for financial institutions.
Road haulage, maritime and air transport	No change; but further restrictions ruled out.
Other services	Liberalised access of enhanced telecommunications, computer services, tourism and architectural services.
Government procurement	Exclusion of national preference on government contracts worth more than $25,000; exceptions for defence procurement.
Direct investment	Restriction on establishing new firms relaxed; extension of national treatment.
Technical standards	Harmonisation of technical standards based on the GATT code.
Emergency action and arbitration	More stringent standards for the application of arbitration emergency safeguards. Establishment of a dispute settlements mechanism and an independent arbitration panel.

Source: OECD 1988: 77.

Firms and industries in the "nationalist coalition," heavily dependent on state protection (such as cultural industries and agribusiness), were opposed (Atkinson and Coleman 1989: 83–84).

The CLC and its provincial arms, and the Quebec-based union centrals (the CNTU and the CSD) adamantly opposed the FTA. The CLC's attack on the agreement was two pronged: it argued that free trade would lead to a loss of jobs in Canada and to a loss of Canadian sovereignty (Canadian Labour Congress 1985). Notwithstanding a number of econometric studies estimating that real income would rise by up to 3.3 percent and net employment by 1.8 percent as a result of the agreement (OECD 1988: 80), the labour argument emphasized its implications for job loss with "no guarantees of comparable job increases" in newly competitive industries (Canadian Labour Congress 1985: 137). The CLC also feared that, under pressure from business, Canadian labour legislation would regress to the level of the American lowest common denominator. The CLC preferred sectorally based "managed trade" agreements on the model of the Auto Pact, with its guarantees of production (and hence jobs) in Canada.

Most provincial governments had also established positions on the issue within a few months of the conclusion of the agreement: The three westernmost provinces and Quebec were strongly supportive; the governments of the Atlantic provinces (except Prince Edward Island) gave more cautious approval, applauding the expansion of their markets but fearing potential constraints on the ability of the state to pursue regional development policies; and Manitoba, Ontario, and Prince Edward Island were strongly opposed. All Conservative (and Social Credit) governments supported the deal. The one NDP government (in Manitoba) opposed it. Manitoba's opposition lasted only as long as the tenure of the NDP in office; the Conservative government elected in Manitoba in April 1988 strongly supported the agreement. Reflecting the division within the Liberal party, Liberal provincial governments could be found on each side of the issue and took their stands with varying degrees of intensity. Quebec's Liberal government was a strong supporter; the Liberal government of New Brunswick offered lukewarm support after a period of indecision; and Liberal governments in Ontario and Prince Edward Island opposed it. Ontario's opposition, however, was to the terms of the Free Trade Agreement, not the principle of liberalized trade with the United States.

Constitutional ambiguity gave the provincial governments some legitimacy, but not necessarily formal authority in the free trade debate. The authority of the federal government to enter into international treaties and agreements was unquestionable. But authority to pass the legislation implementing the agreement depended on whether the matters dealt with fell under federal or provincial jurisdiction. The provincial governments had not been directly involved in the negotiations, although they were consistently briefed and consulted by the federal negotiators; and the agreement was carefully crafted to deal as much as possible with matters under federal jurisdiction. But some matters, such as energy supply and wine and beer pricing in local (provincial) markets, entailed provincial powers. Furthermore, article 103 of the agreement specifically required the Canadian and U.S. federal governments to "ensure that all necessary measures are taken in order to give effect to its provisions, including their observance . . . by state, provincial and local governments."

There was considerable debate as to whether the federal government's power over international and interprovincial trade and commerce or other more general heads of federal power would allow it to legislate in areas of provincial jurisdiction in order to give effect to the agreement (Pilkington 1988; Bernier 1988; Fairley 1988; Gibson 1988). Ontario, indeed, threatened a constitutional challenge. But Ontario would have been virtually isolated in taking such action: other provinces (except Prince Edward Island) supported the deal and, furthermore, did not wish to risk having the constitutional ambiguity resolved in favour of the federal government. In any event, the courts would likely have required that implementing legislation have actually been passed before a case could be heard; and before the legislation was passed these legal questions were overtaken by political considerations, as is discussed shortly.

The resolution of the free-trade issue proceeded not through structures of elite accommodation, federal-provincial or otherwise, but through a process of vigorous and passionate public debate, culminating in a national election that essentially became a referendum on the issue. As in the case of the debate over the Meech Lake constitutional reforms (Chapter 2), the battle for public opinion forced elites to sharpen their positions and to make extreme claims and counterclaims. The federal Conservatives, of course, supported the Free Trade Agreement. The NDP, like its labour allies, had been consistently opposed to a comprehensive bilateral agreement in principle. The Liberals, however, launched their harshest attacks once the agreement was public, attacking not so much the principle of bilateral free trade as the "bad deal" negotiated by the Conservative government.[16]

In response, as discussed in Chapter 1, public opinion showed increasing symptoms of ambivalence. Levels of indecision rose. Moreover, although opinion became more evenly divided between support and opposition, these positions were relatively "soft"; pollsters found that opinions could be made to change by raising considerations such as threats to social programs (for supporters) or lower prices (for opponents) (Johnston and Blais 1988). A plurality of support began to develop behind the option of renegotiating the agreement (an option that was not on the table at that time) (Adams 1988).

The Free Trade Agreement was discussed in public hearings before the External Affairs and Trade Committee of the House of Commons in November and December 1987. It was signed by Prime Minister Mulroney and President Reagan in January 1988, and the implementing legislation was introduced into the House of Commons. The party leaders' speeches during the final legislative debate in August 1988 summarized the themes and exemplify the impassioned rhetoric that characterized public discussion of the issue (Reading 5-4).

With a massive majority (210 of the then 282 seats in the House of Commons), the federal Conservative government might have been expected to ride out the storm of protest and pass the legislation. But once again Canada's ambiguous institutional structures provided a foothold for opposition. In July 1988 Liberal leader Turner asked the Liberal-dominated Senate to withhold approval of the implementing legislation pending a general election in which a public verdict on the deal could be rendered. As discussed in Chapter 1, the Senate has the formal authority to withhold approval of the legislation, but as an appointed body it lacks the legitimacy to thwart the will of the majority of elected representatives in the House of Commons. But in this case public and elite opinion was so clearly divided that Turner's request, and the Senate's compliance, did not provoke a constitutional crisis. The prime minister called an election for November 21, 1988, and the country entered into one of the most keenly fought and passionate election campaigns in its history. Partisan competition was mirrored in the alignment of interest groups. Opponents and proponents of the deal had, by the fall of 1988, formed formal coalitions, the Pro-Canada Network and the Canadian Alliance for Trade and Job Opportunities, respectively. Each undertook extensive media campaigns.

A critical point in the campaign was reached with the nationally televised leaders' debates in October 1988. In a striking indication of the volatility of public opinion on this issue, Liberal support as measured in polls rose dramatically, and both Conservative and NDP support declined immediately after a televised leaders' debate in which John Turner vigorously attacked Mulroney for having "sold out" the Canadian people. By the time of the election on November 21, however, the Conservatives had recovered: They received 43 percent of the popular vote, compared with

32 percent for the Liberals and 20 percent for the NDP. This plurality of the popular vote translated into a majority of seats, and the Liberals were faced with the necessity of honouring their precampaign pledge not to use the Senate to obstruct free trade legislation if the Conservatives were returned with a majority.

In fact, although the election functioned effectively as a referendum on free trade, the public judgement amounted to a "resounding maybe" (Johnston and Blais 1988). A slight majority of votes were, in fact, cast for parties opposed to the Free Trade Agreement. But the considerable indecision and "softness" on the free trade issue, and some inconsistency in translating opinion on free trade into party support, clouded the result. "In the end," as Johnston and Blais have put it, "the government's mandate [was] the traditional one, a reflection of the fact that in our system seats are the real currency of the parliamentary game" (ibid.). Accordingly, with its Conservative majority, the House of Commons passed the implementing legislation on December 24, 1988. The Senate immediately approved the legislation, and the Free Trade Agreement came into effect as scheduled on January 1, 1989.

Consequences

Liberalized trade is only one component of a strategy of economic adjustment, as the Macdonald Commission recognized. And it is the least organizationally demanding component for the Canadian state and societal interests to pursue (Atkinson and Coleman 1989: 51). The process of deciding to adopt the agreement entailed the mobilization of business and labour groups and their allies on an unprecedented scale. But, unlike more interventionist and anticipatory strategies, the implementation of the agreement itself does not require that a comprehensive cross-sectoral or sectoral organizational structures of business or labour, much less institutions of social partnership, be maintained. In this sense the free trade option was best suited to the pluralistic nature of the relationships between the state, business, and labour in Canada.

But trade liberalization did not preclude other components of adjustment policy; rather, it established the context in which they were to be pursued. In this context various political actors sought to recover the middle ground staked out by the Macdonald Commission and especially by some of its background research studies, but lost during the polarized free trade debate. For example, the Ontario Premier's Council, discussed below, argued that free trade "may accelerate, but will not fundamentally change" the demands upon the Ontario economy to adjust to international competition and proceeded to set forth an adjustment strategy focused on restructuring in traded sectors and building a science and technology infrastructure (Premier's Council 1989: 13–14). Furthermore, by hastening (or at least not artificially retarding) the adjustment process, the Free Trade Agreement increased the importance of labour-market policies facilitating the integration of displaced workers. It also increased the political legitimacy of those policies, as a response to the concerns of those who "lost" the free trade debate.

However, the conventional political processes that persisted alongside and in the wake of the adoption of the Free Trade Agreement continued to militate against fundamental change and in favour of institutional reorganization and the repackaging of programs. At the federal level the Conservative government accelerated the trends, begun under the Liberals, to reduce real spending on regional development grants and to shift from grants to tax incentives as instruments of industrial assistance (Doern 1986: 81–87). In 1988 the federal Conservatives terminated the umbrella Industrial and Regional Development Program (IRDP) under which a number of programs in this arena had been consolidated by the Liberals in 1983.

Accompanying these policy shifts was yet another round of institutional change. In 1987 three new regional development agencies were created—one for the Atlantic, one for the north, and one for the west—each reporting to a different "regional" cabinet minister. These changes left the Department of Regional Industrial Expansion shorn of most of its regional responsibilities, to be merged into a newly created Department of Industry, Science and Technology (Bakvis 1989: 125–27). Essentially, the institutional structure had come full circle to the pre-1969 period: Industry and trade remained in separate portfolios, and regional development mandates were again scattered across portfolios. "Regional ministers" continued to play key roles in the allocation of regional development funds and industrial assistance (ibid.).

At the end of the 1980s, then, despite two decades of institutional experimentation, there was no single focus of responsibility at the federal level for either industrial policy or for regional development, let alone for both. The result of this lack of institutional focus is not only an inability to coordinate policies and to resolve disagreements over appropriate policy goals and instruments—although those are clearly weaknesses of the policy process (Atkinson and Coleman 1989: 127–29). In addition, the lack of a central coordinating body means that there is little to buffer politicians against special pleading by particular regional or industrial interests (Chandler 1986: 198, 204).

As the federal government wrestled with these policy changes, the provinces became increasingly active in industrial policy. At the provincial level, too, however, institutional and program change has reflected a lack of consensus about the objectives of policy and a resulting lack of coherence in institutional and program structure. Quebec, with the most interventionist provincial government, provides something of an exception to this generalization. In addition to the Caisse de dépot et placement, discussed above, Quebec has used a range of instruments to speed and steer economic adjustment, including research and development tax incentives, strategic procurement, loans and loan guarantees, and investment incentives. Since 1987 the principal industrial assistance agency, the Société de développement industriel du Québec (SDI), has adopted a "venture loan formula . . . for high-risk businesses involved in strategic technologies or regional development" (Premier's Council 1989: 82). This activist industrial policy has contributed to the development of an indigenous francophone business elite supportive of greater autonomy, if not independence, for the Quebec state (Chapter 2).

Ontario, on the other hand, provides a more typical case. In the early 1980s the Conservative government began to shift marginally the focus of industrial assistance to high-technology firms and industries. It participated with the federal government in the establishment of a biotechnology firm, Allelix; it undertook strategic procurement in the computer industry (somewhat unsuccessfully);[17] and it began to experiment on a small scale with venture capital programs for innovative firms, and with the establishment of a network of "technology centres" intended to diffuse technology by training workers to train other workers in new technologies. The Liberal government, which succeeded the Conservatives in 1985, established a premier's council in April 1986 as a standing committee of business, labour, academic, and governmental representatives to advise on policies that would "steer Ontario into the forefront of economic leadership and technological innovation." [18] The council commissioned an extensive survey of industrial policies in Canada, West Germany, Sweden, Japan, the United States, Britain, the European Economic Community, Korea, and Singapore; and in 1989 it published a three-volume report generally advocating a more activist, comprehensive, and coordinated set of policies aimed at fostering higher value-added industries, restructuring industries in traded sectors, and "smoothing industrial restructuring" (Premier's Council 1989).

Experimentation with economic adjustment mechanisms has not been confined to governments. A few sectoral industry associations, either alone or in collaboration with the federal Department of Employment and Immigration, have undertaken labour-market planning programs (Advisory Council on Adjustment 1989: 40–41). The Canadian Chamber of Commerce has facilitated cooperative training arrangements among small companies (Employment and Immigration Canada 1989: 22). The Quebec Federation of Labour established a Solidarity Fund in 1984. Investors in the fund include QFL members and others—including employers, often under the terms of a collective agreement. The fund makes investments in Quebec businesses primarily for the purpose of job creation, but its purpose is also seen as increasing labour influence in economic decision making and stimulating the Quebec economy and the development of Quebec enterprises. As of January 1988, the fund had $135 million in assets and almost 50,000 investors, and it claimed credit for the creation of 11,000 jobs through investments in about forty enterprises (Le Fonds de Solidarité 1988: 6).

This experimentation with different adjustment mechanisms has been limited, however, and has resulted in little substantive change either in policies or in their impacts. At the federal level periodic bureaucratic reorganizations and program changes have not yielded an institutional focus for policy: National and regional concerns continue to compete with each other through whatever institutional channels are put in place, and "market" and "state" orientations have ebbed and flowed with partisan change. Industrial assistance has continued to flow to individual firms, with few experiments in sectoral restructuring; regional development assistance has flowed through federal-provincial agreements marked by greater and lesser degrees of formality and centralization.

The exception to this pattern was the adoption of the Free Trade Agreement with the United States, with its definitive option for the continental market. Significantly, this decision was made outside the processes of elite accommodation through which the Canadian system has dealth with ambivalence. Just as the contest over one of the fundamental tensions of Canadian political life—the relationship between Quebec and the rest of Canada—went to a referendum in Quebec in 1980, so the contest over an equally fundamental tension—the relationship between Canada and the United States—could be resolved only through the "referendum" of the 1988 general election. Free trade was embraced with a "resounding maybe." And like the Quebec referendum, the free trade decision left unanswered questions of institutional change.

The substantive impacts of the policies discussed in this chapter are difficult to assess but would also appear to be limited. Regional disparities in growth and unemployment rates, which have so complicated the making of industrial policy, continue to exist. Interregional disparities in personal income have narrowed, although a considerable portion of that narrowing is attributable to transfer programs (including, of course, unemployment insurance) and not to programs of economic development (Chapter 1). It could be argued that economic disparities would have worsened in the absence of policies of regional economic assistance; but, as Lithwick (1986: 141–42) notes, the technical models necessary to test such a hypothesis have not been developed. Experience under the Free Trade Agreement, which will not be fully implemented until 1998, is too recent to be assessed.

It is, indeed, primarily the failure to manage interregional conflict that has hobbled policymaking in this arena. Disputes about state- and market-oriented approaches are often bound up with arguments about which approach best serves a region's interests. And no interregional mediator has emerged in this arena. The balance of centralization or decentralization within the structures of executive federalism has varied widely over time. Mechanisms of intrastate federalism are lacking—"regional ministers" in the federal cabinet" are too closely associated with the patronage function of the governing party to be effective in this respect. Furthermore, there is no effective interregional network of business and labour interests to compensate for the inadequacy of inter- and intrastate mechanisms. Hence the unanswered questions of institutional change have to do not only with the structures of the state but also with the relationship between the state and economic interests. In the latter respect, experimentation with tripartite structures has been marked by instability, notably by labour boycotts and dissents. Bipartite (business-labour) experiments at the sectoral and central levels have been somewhat more successful, as noted in this chapter and in Chapter 4. The bipartite structures may be relatively more successful because they build upon a model of collective bargaining. Hence they allow participants (especially the leadership of organized labour) to reconcile a tradition of adversarialism with collaborative endeavours and also allow them to operate in some cases under the aegis of the state but without direct governmental participation. However, the focus of these bipartite experiments, especially at the central as opposed to the sectoral level, has been more procedural than substantive. Whether this experimentation can lead to a Canadian version of the parapublic network that helps to integrate German policymaking remains an open question, to which we return in Chapter 8.

Readings

5-1.   THE BCNI CRITIQUE OF CANADIAN INDUSTRIAL POLICY *

In its wide-ranging submission to the Macdonald Commission, the BCNI advocated, among other things, the pursuit of bilateral sectoral trade agreements with the United States. It also engaged in a sharp critique of Canadian industrial policy, noting the lack of consensus and policy inconsistencies that characterize this arena.

Concern is often expressed about the fact that Canada's share of global trade has declined from 5 percent in 1970 to 3.5 percent currently. This development is not surprising given that more countries are participating in world commerce. Far more worrisome from the standpoint of Canada's trade interests are two other trends: the rise of protectionism in some of our major export markets, and the growth of regional trade arrangements that discriminate against non-members. Both trends are clearly inimical to Canada's trade prospects. As one of the few industrial countries without free access to a market of at least 50 million people, Canada is particularly vulnerable to protectionist policies. This is especially true in the case of the United States, which accounts for some two-thirds of our exports and for about 80 percent of exports of finished products. . . .

Although some progress has been made in addressing these issues in the GATT, we believe that U.S.-Canada trade questions are so important to Canada that an intensification of bilateral negotiations is now

---

*Business Council on National Issues, *National Priorities*, a submission to the Royal Commission on the Economic Union and Development Prospects for Canada (December 12, 1983), pp. 18–21, 32–38.

required. . . . Contrary to what some appear to believe, focusing more attention on the bilateral trade relationship does *not* imply that Canada should eschew the search for wider markets in Europe, Japan and the Third World. Indeed, our heavy dependence on a single foreign market suggests that this search must, if anything, be intensified. It is essential to recognize, however, that the United States is and will remain by far our most important trading partner, and that U.S. trade policy has a major impact on Canadian economic welfare. In order to improve Canada's access to the American market and ensure that Canada is not harmed by U.S. actions directed against third country imports, we believe that Canada should be willing to negotiate mutually satisfactory bilateral trade arrangements in various industrial sectors, as the federal government is now seeking to do. We also believe that Canada should press for special bilateral accords that deal with such key issues as government procurement. Finally, we suggest that the negotiation of an across the board free trade agreement with the United States also be considered, although we recognize that achieving this goal is likely to take a long time.

. . . [A]s noted by the President of the Business Council in a speech delivered to the Carnegie Foundation for Peace and American Foreign Service Association in Washington last April, Canada's industrial policy record "displays . . . a tendency towards pragmatism at best and inconsistency and confusion at worst. Our problem is that we have not made up our minds about what we want."

Where do most Canadian business leaders lie in relation to the industrial policy debate? In general, they are suspicious of the argument that a group of policy planners in Ottawa can predict and direct the course of Canada's industrial development. As the President of the Business Council argued in the speech referred to above: "They are not prepared to entrust to government the selection of so-called 'winners and losers'. They know that the management of business by public officials makes little sense." We do not believe that a comprehensive national industrial strategy is either feasible or necessary. With respect to the question of feasibility, it must first be shown how an effective, co-ordinated industrial strategy could be developed and implemented on an ongoing basis in such a diverse nation as Canada, in which eleven governments are typically pursuing often divergent policies. Extensive decentralization of economic and industrial policy making powers is simply incompatible with the notion of a co-ordinated national industrial strategy. Most regions and provinces are in fact competing for all sorts of industries, and it is difficult to see how these different governments might reach agreement on such delicate questions as where high technology industry should be located. A further problem posed by the decentralized character of economic policy making in our federation is that it has proven very difficult to develop workable *national* policies in such areas as skills training and education, where changes would be critical if an industrial strategy were to have even a remote chance for success.

Another problem that must be addressed in assessing the feasibility of a Canadian industrial strategy is the absence of a clear consensus on what such a strategy would consist of, with the result that various advocates are constantly producing lists of worthy objectives that are in fundamental conflict with each other. One recent study of industrial policies in Quebec and Ontario highlights the marked propensity of industrial strategy planners to adopt conflicting and at times very confusing policy objectives. Industrial policy can have a wide array of economic, social, regional and symbolic goals, many of which are clearly contradictory. For example, policies that aim to boost employment may retard productivity growth; efforts to accelerate the phasing out of so-called "losing" industries may run smack into regional development objectives; and raising trade barriers to protect Canadian high-technology industries courts retaliatory action from trading partners and thus may reduce the prospects for export growth. . . .

There is one area where we believe a concerted effort to devise a more coherent and integrated national policy is imperative if Canada's industrial economy is to progress. . . . [W]e suggest that the federal and provincial governments spare no effort to devise a more coherent *national policy* in respect of education, skill training and retraining. The objective should be to reduce duplication, to cease training people for occupations not likely to be in demand, and to develop a truly national policy in this critical area to replace the current ineffective hodge-podge of policies. In our view this may be the most important industrial policy challenge of the next two decades. We urge Canadian policy makers to concentrate on reducing some of the institutional obstacles to effective national policy in such areas as human resource development and strive to ensure that Canadians can make effective use of the new technologies.

5-2.   LABOUR'S GOALS: FULL EMPLOYMENT
AND GREATER PUBLIC CONTROL*

At the time that this submission was made, it was not apparent that the Macdonald Commission would adopt liberalized trade with the United States as its central recommendation. The CLC hence did not focus on that option, but rather reiterated its opposition to "market-based" policies and emphasized the centrality of the goal of full employment. It saw public control over investment as a primary instrument of industrial policy.

We are in need of a new approach that takes full employment seriously as a goal. We must place greater emphasis on the public control of the resources and economic levers which are important for our economic future and the wellbeing of our citizens.

Without going into detail, some of the approaches that might be considered as part of a long term strategy to gain greater public accountability of the investment process might include the following:

- strengthening the Foreign Investment Review Agency, and harmonizing FIRA decisions with the overall outlines of an industrial strategy;
- rethinking the corporate tax/corporate grants system, with an increased emphasis on job creation as a major criterion for grants and tax incentives and with a policy of public equity in return for grants;
- increased control of the banking community, including the public ownership of a substantial portion of the banking industry and regulations which would ensure a larger proportion of bank loans go to projects which fit into an overall industrial strategy and which are geared to job creation;
- the creation of a publicly controlled investment fund, designed to meet regional development needs;
- changes in pension regulations that would give workers, through their trade unions, more control over pension fund investment, and that would guarantee that these pools of capital be used for industrial development in Canada; and,
- laws to ensure adequate notice to workers and communities affected

*Canadian Labour Congress, *Brief to the Macdonald Commission* (December 12, 1983), pp. 13–17.

by technological change and/or by plant shutdowns, together with some measure of public control over such changes.

5-3.   THE MACDONALD COMMISSION ON CANADA-U.S. TRADE*

This section of the Macdonald Commission's report sets out the centrepiece of its proposals, the liberalization of Canada-U.S. trade. An ambivalence toward the United States and a recognition of the need to address regional sensitivities in Canada are apparent in these excerpts.

Relations with the United States have consumed Canadian energies from our country's very beginning. Most Americans live their whole lives only dimly aware of Canada and its people, but Canadians in all provinces have always fretted about our neighbour to the south. It is not easy to live next door to the most powerful, energetic and wealthy nation in the world. One reason why Americans are wealthier than we are is that they comprise an economic union of 240 million people, while our economic union is made up of only 25 million people. In an age of specialization, a difference of such scale matters a great deal.

Whether our association with our neighbour is easy or not, we "need" the United States. It buys about a fifth of what we produce, and it sells us many of the products which make our own lives rich and varied. We watch American television, drive American cars, eat American vegetables, drink American orange juice, and wear American clothes. The United States, however, also needs us. It needs our iron ore to make cars, our paper to print newspapers, our subway cars to travel to work, and our lumber to build homes. We are not only their best customer, but also their principal supplier.

. . . The closeness of this relationship offers both tremendous benefit and risk of harm. We Canadians are wealthier because of the Americans, but we are also vulnerable to changes in their fortunes. In 1972, this vulnerability caused our federal government to find deliberate ways to differentiate ourselves and to strengthen our links with other trading partners. Our vulnerability, however, can also be reduced by strengthening the links we have with the United States. Canadian business has reached a stage where our domestic market can no longer assure our continued

*Royal Commission on the Economic Union and Development Prospects for Canada, *Report* (Ottawa: Minister of Supply and Services, 1985), 1: 299–300, 323–26.

growth, and where our access to foreign markets is no longer perceived to be secure enough to stimulate long-term, job-creating investment. One senior corporate executive has pointed out:

> *We, manufacturers, are caught in a catch 22 situation. On one hand, the tariffs in Canada are no longer high enough to offset the higher costs of producing solely for the Canadian market. On the other hand, even modest tariffs into the U.S. can make it difficult, if not impossible, to set up production in Canada to export into that market. When dealing on the location of a new production facility, why locate it on the small market side of the border especially when it's dependent on exports and faces the problems of the Non-Tariff Barriers[?] We need to be inside those safeguards.*

. . . Canada would gain several advantages by negotiating a free-trade agreement with the United States. In the first place, freer trade would reduce the exposure of Canadian exporters to American non-tariff barriers (NTBs) such as countervailing duties and, hence, increase our *security* of access to the U.S. market. Of all the major economies in the developed world, Canada is unique in its lack of a large internal market like that of the United States or Japan and of access to a market of over 100 million people through a bilateral or other free-trade arrangement. . . .

Another advantage of Canada-U.S. free trade is that it would *improve* our access to the U.S. market in areas where that country now employs tariff and non-tariff-barrier (NTB) protection. While the U.S. economy has less tariff protection than Canada, there are important areas where American tariffs restrict the potential for increased Canadian exports. Certain steel products would fall into this category, as well as the petrochemical sector. This sector is especially important to producers in western Canada, but Canada's capacity to achieve improved access for petrochemicals in the multilateral Tokyo Round was circumscribed by the implications of this deal for U.S. trade with the European Community. In a bilateral agreement, Canada could negotiate for improved access to the U.S. market, in sectors like petrochemicals, without being constrained by the relations between the United States and its other trading partners. Although Commissioners believe that improved access is important for the export of certain commodities and services, Canada's goals should not be interpreted as a desire to become even more dependent on trade with the United States. Paradoxically, we believe that improved and secure access to that market will, in the long run, be the best means to achieve greater diversity of our economic and trade relations. To clarify this contention, we turn to the third advantage.

The most important advantage to Canadians of a free-trade agreement with the United States would be its effect on productivity and thus, in particular, on the competitiveness of our manufacturing sector. Improved and more stable access would create opportunities for Canadian business and increase the tendency toward specialization and rationalization of Canadian production.

. . . Since Confederation, trade policy and regional interests have been closely linked. Both our eastern and western provinces have long considered that central Canada has used the tariff to its own advantage by forcing itself on them as a trading partner, rather than leaving them the option to trade with more competitive foreign suppliers. They see the tariff largely as an instrument for protecting manufactured products, which are produced in central Canada. The tariff supposedly forces hinterland regions to pay higher prices for manufactured imports, produces large volumes of interprovincial trade and smaller volumes of international trade, and transfers income to central Canadian manufacturing industries from hinterland consuming regions.

Irrespective of whether or not this perception is true, it has proved over the years to exercise subtle influence over the conduct and formation of our trade policies. It has generally been assumed that western and eastern provinces would welcome any move towards freer trade, whether this be unilateral, through a negotiated arrangement with the Americans, or multilateral, through GATT negotiations. Equally, it has been assumed that both Ontario and Quebec would oppose any such moves.

During the course of this Commission's hearings, however, we have been impressed by the degree to which this traditional heartland-hinterland view of Canadian trade policy is now being challenged from several quarters. Both the very concept of a region and the notion of how regions are affected by changes in trade policies are central to any discussion of interregional effects of those policies. If factors of production are mobile between regions, however, as they now appear to be, how can it be determined whether a given region gains or loses from a change in trade policies? Some of the residents will be affected, but if workers move in and out of regions in response to changes in trade policy, the size of a region is not fixed, and interregional effects of trade policies become hard to "nail down".

Again, who owns interregional assets? And how does their ownership affect analysis of interregional effects of trade policies? Through pension funds, stock ownership, and other forms of financial intermediation, for instance, residents (say, of Ontario) will own assets that are located in other provinces (say, Alberta). . . . Moreover, the threat from contingent protection in the United States applies to industries in all regions, and the estimates of benefits from bilateral free trade with the Americans seem to suggest that the advantages will be spread broadly throughout our economy.

Commissioners therefore believe that the regional divisions on the free-trade issue that have been prominent in the past should not occur in the same way today. While some regions may anticipate adverse effects from free trade, we believe that the likelihood is that all regions will benefit, and that Canadians everywhere will be able to enjoy a higher standard of living. To put an even finer point on this conviction, we believe that freer trade with the United States would make a major contribution to Canada's regional development and to national competitiveness and overall confidence.

5-4.   LABOUR'S FOCUS ON FULL EMPLOYMENT*

Docquier, the Canadian national director of the United Steelworkers of America and the sole representative of organized labour on the Macdonald Commission, dissented strongly from a number of its key recommendations, arguing instead for an emphasis on full employment.

With a view towards contributing to the debate over the economic future of Canada, I wish to submit for the public record a statement on the parts of the Final Report of the Royal Commission on the Economic Union and Development Prospects for Canada with which I dissent.

There are at least four areas with which I cannot agree—some in total and some in part. These are: the lack of a serious effort to eliminate unemployment; the advocacy of U.S.-Canada bilateral free trade; proposals to roll back the Unemployment Insurance Program; and some recommendations on labour-management relations. . . .

The economic philosophy of the Report is expressed in its Introduction:

*E. Gerard Docquier, Dissent from *Report* of the Royal Commission on the Economic Union and Development Prospects for Canada (Ottawa: Minister of Supply and Services, 1985), 3: 527–37.

We seek a new relationship between the political system and the economy and society within which incentives will induce the making of choices compatible with social goals.

I disagree fundamentally with this principle. Our social goals are clear. They have not changed. Indeed they should not change. Canadians want to work. *Our goal is to create jobs for those that have been deprived of employment.* At the same time, we want to take care of those amongst us who are incapable of caring for themselves. We have long accepted the moral and ethical responsibility to protect those least able to fend for themselves. This is the legacy of the Canadian experience. Our commitment is to full employment and to social justice.

The major concern in the current political environment should be to allocate our financial resources for the attainment of these social goals. *The task of economic management should serve social development.* The biggest single problem which threatens to retard both our economic and our social development is unemployment. . . .

There is an alternative to the free trade option and that is promotion of import substitution and a direct role for government in an industrial strategy. This does not have to mean that a bureaucrat in Ottawa picks the country's economic winners and losers. The Commission recommends free trade as a solution to unemployment and growth. The research work extensively and repeatedly claims that there will be an increase in income and employment as the result of free trade. What all the studies and computer simulations cannot tell us is when these presumed benefits are to flow and to whom. . . . The Report has endorsed market based fantasies as a solution to our nearly two million unemployed. Instead, I advocate the continued responsibility of government to manage the economic environment and to encourage new forms of popular participation in public institutions.

5-5.   THE COMMONS DEBATE ON THE FREE TRADE AGREEMENT*

In the final Commons debate on the federal legislation necessary to implement the Canada-U.S. Free Trade Agreement, Prime Minister Mul-

*Excerpts from speeches by Prime Minister Brian Mulroney (PC), Opposition Leader John Turner (Liberal), and NDP leader Edward Broadbent in the House of Commons, August 30, 1988.

roney emphasized the economic benefits of the deal and projected an image of a strong and confident Canada that would be all the more able to maintain its distinctiveness with the wealth that would flow from liberalized trade. Liberal leader Turner sought the centre in this debate, arguing that he was neither anti-American nor opposed to market mechanisms, but that the Free Trade Agreement "sold out" Canadian sovereignty and threatened Canada's commitment to a mixed economy. NDP leader Broadbent drew upon similar themes, although his speech was somewhat less nationalist and more socialist in tone, with greater emphasis upon the "market" ideology underlying the deal and the threat to Canadian social programs and cultural industries.

It is not possible in this space to enter into a discussion of the validity of these claims. (For a detailed review of various sections of the agreement, see Gold and Leyton-Brown 1988). It should be noted, however, that it is very difficult to substantiate the claim that the agreement itself threatens Canadian social programs and cultural industries. These areas are almost entirely exempt from the agreement. (In the health field, Canada and the United States agreed to give "national treatment" to each other's health care facilities management firms and commercial laboratories. This treatment does not extend, however, to governmental procurement or subsidy, and the impact of this part of the agreement in the Canadian health care delivery field is likely to be marginal [Tuohy 1988].) Broadbent also alluded to the danger that social programs could be threatened as unfair subsidies under the code to be negotiated over the ensuing five to seven years. It is unlikely, however, that social programs would be seen as any less legitimate "subsidies" under a bilateral agreement than they are under GATT. (A possible exception is the program of regionally extended unemployment insurance benefits, particularly as it affects the fishing industry.)

Brian Mulroney

The idea of a free trade agreement is older than Confederation itself, and one whose time has finally come. It is in the national interest.

The agreement is necessary to secure access to our most vital market. It will bring economic benefit to Canadians from coast to coast. Free trade will mean lower prices for Canadian consumers, better jobs and greater individual opportunity. Free trade will help the regions of this country. And it will do so by creating a broader and deeper pool of national wealth, not just by redistributing existing resources. . . .

Almost 75 percent of our exports, worth $108 billion, go to the United

States. Millions of jobs are dependent on the success of this economic relationship. And that rich market, on which so many Canadian jobs depend, was turning inward and protectionist. About 40 percent of total exports to the United States were subject to quotas, "voluntary" restraint and other restrictions. . . .

Most fundamentally, the agreement will replace the politics of trade with the rule of law, a feature that is of particular value to the smaller of the two partners. From now on, any U.S. trade legislation affecting Canada will have to be consistent with the free trade agreement.

From now on, final decisions on disputes regarding access to that vital market will be taken, not just by Americans, as they have been all too often up to now, but by Americans and Canadians together. . . .

I recognize that the concept of free trade itself troubles some Canadians.

We hear fears expressed about a "loss of sovereignty" that "our identity is at risk" or that "our social programs will vanish." Let history and experience be our guide. Canada is surer of its identity today than it ever was before. Canada's international personality in the global community is more mature and we express ourselves more independently than ever in the past. . . .

Similarly, as Canada-U.S. trade grew steadily in importance over the years, successive Canadian governments brought in the Old Age Pension Plan, Family Allowances, National Health Care, the Canada Pension Plan, all uniquely Canadian initiatives. . . . If anything, the prosperity the free trade agreement will bring will make these and other social programs easier to sustain.

I believe that, if anything, the Americans are far more likely to emulate some of our programs, most notably in areas such as medical care.

John Turner

This debate is about the future of this country.

We love this country. And because we love this country, we will not allow it to be thrown away by this government. What this government is telling us to do in this trade deal is to close our eyes and sign away our future and give up our sovereignty.

It is unarguably a very attractive sales pitch: "Free Trade." Positive words, seductive words. But Canadians know there is no free lunch. There is always a price. And the price of this deal is just too high and is unacceptable.

The price is our sovereignty—the freedom to make our own choices, to decide what is right for us, to go on building the kind of country we want. But that is what this government wants to give away—our freedom to be different, our freedom to be ourselves, to do things our own way, not the American way.

We admire the Americans. We share many of the same hopes and goals. We are fortunate to have them as neighbours, we're proud to have them as friends. But as much as we respect and admire our American friends, we don't want to become Americans.

The United States is certainly the most powerful democracy in the world, but it isn't the only democracy.

We have chosen to make a separate place for ourselves on the northern half of this continent, and we have chosen to do it in a different way.

The Americans put all their faith in market forces, we in fairness and sharing in a mixed economy.

We have a parliamentary tradition. Theirs is a presidential system with a separation of powers.

When we oppose this trade deal, we are not being anti-American; we are pro-Canadian. And we don't like being sold out. . . .

This agreement talks about the free flow of market forces. I believe in the market system, in competition, in private enterprise, and in the need to reward success. But this country was not built on free market forces alone. Free market forces alone would not have given us public housing, a public transportation network, or the best medical care system in the world.

What I am saying is not anti-American. It is pro-Canadian.

We reject this deal because it turns us into little more than a colony of the United States.

Edward Broadbent

I believe we have before us a deal that does not protect our water or regional development programs, gives away control over energy, puts in jeopardy for the next five to seven years and beyond our social programs, is indifferent to foreign ownership and ignores the claims of Canadian culture, precisely because these matters are totally subordinate to the claims of the market place for the present government. . . .

It follows from this kind of thinking that the only criteria brought to bear by this government in assessing the historical implications of this deal are market criteria.

If you understand the Canadian national essence in such a limited way, it is no wonder that you will blithely sign a deal that will permit, over time, that essence to disintegrate. . . .

Our vision of Canada includes a strong but fair trading relationship with our largest trading partner, the United States.

Our vision of Canada encompasses enhanced trade with the world: with our traditional partners in the European Community and those of the Pacific Rim.

But most of all, our vision of Canada goes beyond mere matters of trade.

It retains Canadians' sovereign ability to determine our own destiny: to ensure Canadians retain control to make the decisions about the kind of society we want.

Notes

1. Except in the area of nonrenewable resources, as provided in a 1982 constitutional amendment discussed in Chapter 6.

2. Another significant example of bilateralism were the agreements between Canada and Japan limiting Japanese auto imports to Canada. These agreements expired in 1987.

3. Firms covered by the Auto Pact in Canada could import duty-free from any country, not just the United States. But, as Takefield reports, "the United States limited duty free entry from Canada to vehicles meeting a 59 per cent North American (United States plus Canada) content requirement to prevent third countries from avoiding US tariffs by shipping through Canada" (1988: 285).

4. Textiles and clothing are also subject to quantitative restrictions under the multilateral agreements noted above.

5. The real effective exchange rate is "real" in that it has been adjusted for differences in inflation across countries and is "effective" in that it is a weighted average of a country's bilateral exchange rates with its major competitors.

6. Nonetheless, tax policy has been used as an instrument of regional development, as in the case of regionally differentiated investment and employment tax credits.

7. These widening deficits occurred largely as a result of the economic

slowdown but also as a result of a 1974 decision to index marginal personal income tax rates and personal exemptions to the rate of inflation, depriving governments of the "inflation dividend" available when nominal increases in income push taxpayers into higher tax brackets. Because provincial income taxes are calculated as a percentage of federal tax, these effects were felt at the provincial level as well. Marginal rates and personal exemptions were partially de-indexed in 1985.

8. Hon. William Davis, "Notes for an Opening Statement to the Conference of First Ministers on the Economy," November 27–29, 1978. Quoted in Savoie 1986: 179n.

9. For a discussion of the Science Council's document, see Blais 1986b.

10. As noted in Chapter 1, there is a long-standing practice in Canadian cabinet government of having ministers from particular regions speak for those regions and participate in decisions about federal grants and projects in those regions regardless of their cabinet portfolios. The MSERD/FEDC structure provided further institutional support for this practice (Bakvis 1989: 123).

11. Robert Blair of Nova Corporation, formerly Alberta Gas Trunkline (AGTL), and Shirley Carr of the CLC.

12. See, for example, the brief of the Quebec Federation of Teachers, as excerpted in Drache and Cameron (1985: 121–28).

13. For reviews of the commission's report, see "The Macdonald Report: Twelve Reviews," *Canadian Public Policy* 12, Supplement (February 1986).

14. Hon. Sinclair Stevens, quoted in Baker (1985: 50).

15. The Canada-U.S. Free Trade Agreement, article 1902. The object and purpose of the agreement were defined as follows: "to establish fair and predictable conditions for the progressive liberalization of trade between the two countries while maintaining effective disciplines on unfair trade practices, such object and purpose to be ascertained from the provisions of the Agreement, its preamble and objectives, and the practices of the Parties."

16. A Liberal policy document entitled *Reaching Out: A Liberal Alternative to the Canada-US Trade Agreement*, while not ruling out liberalized trade with the United States, emphasized first the importance of multilateral relations through GATT and also endorsed the technological sovereignty–social partnership option discussed above.

17. The Ministry of Education and the Ministry of Industry, Trade and

Technology undertook to foster an indigenous educational hardware and software industry in Ontario by procuring such equipment for Ontario schools from Ontario manufacturers. The specifications were so specific to Ontario, however, that attempts to market the resulting ICON hardware and software in other jurisdictions failed (Premier's Council 1989: 76–78).

18. Business had a plurality on the council, with thirteen representatives. Other representation was as follows: academic and professional, six; labour, three; and seven cabinet ministers, including the premier as chair. In June 1991, under the NDP government, the council was restructured as the Premier's Council on the Economy and Quality of Life. The proportionate representation of business, labour, government, and other groups on the new council was similar to that of its predecessor.

6 Oil and Gas Policy

In the 1970s all western industrialized nations were confronted with the necessity of dealing with the economic shocks of two rapid escalations in international oil prices. In countries such as Canada and the United States, which were producers as well as importers of oil, the effects of these price shocks were twofold. On the one hand, they disrupted the energy infrastructures of national economies, compounding the problems of economic adjustment discussed in the preceding chapter. They also, however, presented opportunities for domestic oil producers and issues of redistribution.

In Canada the effects of the oil price shocks within the energy policy arena touched some of the most sensitive nerves in Canadian politics. The regional concentration of energy resources and energy consumption meant that producer-consumer conflict was manifested as regional conflict, and thereby exacerbated. The heavy degree of foreign, especially American, investment in the oil and gas sector meant that the issue of American influence in the Canadian economy was inevitably entailed. In these respects, then, the oil price shocks presented particular challenges to the ability of the Canadian system to deal with economic crisis. Canada's policy responses, as in other arenas, were filtered through opposing partisan views of the appropriate roles of the market and the state, and were channelled through the structures of Canadian federalism.

Context

Canada is rich in energy resources. It produces about 4 percent of the world's primary energy supply, and among OECD nations it is second only to the United States in energy production. It accounts for about 4.6 percent of world production of natural gas and 15 percent of hydroelectric power, but only about 2.6 percent of world production of crude oil. Canada has been a net exporter of energy since 1969. For most of the postwar period, however, it was a net importer of crude oil. Energy trade amounted to 3.4 percent of GDP in 1986.[1] For crude oil, petroleum products, natural gas, and hydroelectricity, its virtually sole export market is the United States.[2] In 1986 Canadian exports accounted for 13 percent of U.S. crude oil and petroleum product imports, 99.7 percent of U.S. natural gas imports, and 99.3 percent of U.S. electricity imports (Energy, Mines and Resources Canada 1987: 5, 118).

In terms of domestic consumption Canada is the most energy-intensive industrialized nation in the world. This intensive consumption is partly attributable to geographic conditions: a northerly location and a continental span. But it also "reflects the impact Canada's ample resource endowment and relatively low prices has [*sic*] had on the evolution of its industrial sector" (ibid.: 9). In part, these factors have encouraged the development of energy-intensive industries such as pulp and paper. But they have also dampened the incentives for industry in general to develop energy-efficient technologies. As in most industrialized nations, however, the pattern of energy consumption shows a marked shift from coal to oil in the 1950s, and a diversification after the oil shocks of the 1970s.

Energy resources are highly concentrated within regions in Canada. Nonrenewable sources of energy are heavily concentrated in the west, especially in Alberta, which produces more than 85 percent of Canada's oil and natural gas and almost one-half of its coal. Ontario, Newfoundland (Labrador), British Columbia, and especially Quebec have been able to draw upon their abundant inland water sources for the generation of hydroelectricity. Consumption of energy is also regionally concentrated, reflecting to a large degree the regional concentration of population and industry. Ontario consumes about 36 percent of all energy in Canada and Quebec about 22 percent, whereas the western provinces together consume about 35 percent and the Atlantic provinces about 7 percent. Methods used to generate electricity reflect these regional patterns of resource endowments and consumption. Quebec, Newfoundland, and British Columbia rely almost exclusively on hydro, and Alberta almost exclusively on thermal sources. Ontario, with its heavy demand, has drawn upon thermal, hydro, and nuclear modes of electricity generation (Statistics Canada 1985: tables 11.4, 11.6, 11.10, 11.15).

Energy industries in Canada therefore constitute both a leading sector of the economy and a crucial component of infrastructure. The development of energy policy in Canada has been complicated, however, not only by the regional concentration of production and consumption but also by the complex structure of federal-provincial authority over natural resources.

The state in Canada exercises authority over energy sources both as proprietor and legislator. Under the Constitution Act, 1867, the original provinces of the confederation retained ownership of all "lands, mines, minerals and royalties" belonging to them at the time of confederation. The remainder of present-day Canada was in 1867 still effectively held by the Hudson's Bay Company under a seventeenth-century charter from the British crown. In 1869 the federal government, with the aid of a loan underwritten by the British government, purchased most of the Hudson's Bay Company lands. As the western provinces were carved out of these territories, the federal government retained title to the public lands therein. Not until 1930, and after considerable pressure, did the federal government cede these public lands to the western provinces. The federal government continued to retain title to the public land in the Yukon and Northwest Territories (the "Canada lands") and to offshore resources.

The exploitation of oil and gas resources has been largely in the hands of private-sector enterprises. Since most of these resources are on public lands, however, these private enterprises pay royalties to the government owners. Royalties were traditionally calculated as a percentage of gross revenues, although they have been more finely tuned in the 1970s and 1980s to serve more discrete policy purposes (Energy, Mines and Resources Canada 1987: 99–100).

Federal and provincial governments have authority over natural resources other than that deriving from ownership. Until the 1982 changes to be discussed below, provincial powers were essentially limited to direct taxation and regulation within provincial boundaries. Federal powers are more extensive: They include unlimited taxing powers and powers over international and interprovincial trade, and authority over works and undertakings (such as pipelines) extending across provincial boundaries. Furthermore, the federal government possesses "emergency" powers and the power to declare a work (such as a mine or pipeline) to be for the general advantage of Canada and thus under federal regulation even if it lies within a single province. Finally, as in other arenas, Ottawa's spending power enables it to make payments for purposes beyond those for which it has legislative authority.

Issues pertaining to resource exploitation have encapsulated tensions between regionalism, nationalism, and continentalism perhaps more than any other component of economic development policy. Remarkably, however, in the period between the first major discovery of oil by the American-based Imperial Oil Company at Leduc, Alberta, in 1947 and the first international oil price shock in 1973,[3] the energy policy arena was marked by consensus, with only periodic eruptions of conflict and rumblings of discontent. The prevailing consensus concerned the need to develop the resource industry; the periodic conflict had to do with questions of transportation and distribution; and the rumblings of discontent were related to the heavy concentration of American capital in the nonrenewable resource sector (Reading 6-1).

As Doern and Phidd (1983: 458) succinctly put it, from 1947 to 1961 Canadian energy policy was "intended to promote the rapid growth of a domestically sourced oil industry, and to facilitate the transformation from a coal-based to an oil-based economy. In general, this was to be done with a minimum of government intervention, save for suitable tax incentives and encouragement for the building of the proper transportation infrastructure." Within this consensus lay the seeds of conflict, however. The expansion of markets and the distribution of oil and gas beyond provincial boundaries raised questions of the priority to be given to domestic and export markets and enhanced the potential role of the federal government in the resolution of these questions.

The late 1940s and early 1950s was a period of extensive pipeline development. To some extent pipelines raised jurisdictional issues. In the early 1950s, as the federal government was approving interprovincial oil pipeline routes and fostering the development of a consortium to build an interprovincial gas pipeline, the Social Credit government of Alberta was engaging in what Richards and Pratt (1979) have called "defensive expansion" with the development of an intraprovincial gas-gathering system under the Alberta Gas Trunkline corporation (AGTL).[4]

Primarily, however, questions of the routing of pipelines pitted Canadian nationalism against the economic logic of the continental market. A fundamental issue had to do with whether pipeline routes should be "all-Canadian" or whether they should partially traverse U.S. territory. As Doern and Toner (1985: 70–71) summarize these concerns: " 'All-Canadian' routes had the advantage of being free from US interference . . . and would not be subject to pressure for excessive exports to the United States." On the other hand, "it was argued that the unit cost of transmitting Canadian fuels to Canadian markets could be lowered by building in an 'export component' to take advantage of economies of scale achieved through increased throughput volumes." In the event, the decisions taken were models of compromise: The resulting network of pipelines formed "what could be called either a quasi-national or a semi-continental pattern of fuel transportation and distribution" (McDougall 1983: 57).

In one of these cases, however—the building of the Trans-Canada pipeline for natural gas—the initial compromise floundered for a time in controversy. Faced with competing proposals from (ironically) a Canadian group proposing a route partially through the United States and an American group proposing an all-Canadian route, the federal Liberal government fostered the development of a consortium combining the two ventures. This compromise soon became controversial, however, when the consortium encountered financial difficulties and sought assistance from the federal government. The government's response was to grant the assistance and to establish a crown corporation for the building of the most difficult and expensive portion of the all-Canadian route. Furthermore, the Liberal government allowed American interests temporarily to hold a majority interest in the consortium. Controversy over these decisions came to a head in 1956, with the notorious "Pipeline Debate" in the federal Parliament, and the Liberals' invoking of closure to secure passage of the relevant legislation. To its opponents, the venture had by that point come to symbolize American domination of the Canadian economy, eastern financial domination of western interests within Canada, and the arrogance of a twenty-two-year-old federal Liberal government (Doern and Phidd 1983: 461).

In the ensuing election of 1957 the Liberals were defeated and a minority Conservative government under John Diefenbaker, a western populist, came to power. Its response to controversy, like many governments before and after it, was to establish a commission of inquiry, in this case the Royal Commission on Energy (the Borden Commission), in 1957. The recommendations of the Borden Commission, which echoed some of the recommendations of an earlier commission, the (Gordon) Royal Commission on Canada's Economic Prospects,[5] led to the creation of a national regulatory agency, the National Energy Board (NEB) in 1959 and the promulgation of a National Oil Policy (NOP) in 1961.

The NEB, which continues to the present, is an administrative tribunal with considerable technical expertise and with authority to approve pipelines and to decide issues of interprovincial and international trade in oil and gas. The NOP established the transportation infrastructure for oil and gas and established a domestic pricing structure that lasted until the first oil price shock. It appears in retrospect as an inspired political compromise among competing interests, but it was predicated upon the twin assumptions of abundant domestic supplies and cheap international supplies—predicates that were to change dramatically in the 1970s.

Essentially, the NOP divided the country into two markets: East of the Ottawa River (that is, in Quebec and the Atlantic provinces) consumers would be served by (relatively cheap) imported oil; west of the Ottawa (that is, in Ontario and the western provinces) they would consume higher-priced domestic oil, delivered by the Trans-Canada Pipeline. The NOP also had the effect of further integrating Canadian and American decision making, at both government and industry levels, about oil pricing and marketing. The Canadian crude oil price was established by the industry on the basis of U.S. prices, which were protected by import quotas established by the United States in 1959. Canadian oil was exempted from these quotas, in return for voluntary constraints on Canadian exports. The "Ottawa River line" prevented Canada from being used as a conduit for through which oil from third-party countries could circumvent U.S. import quotas.

As a classic Canadian compromise, then, the NOP entailed some national integration (the penetration of the Ontario market by western producers), some continental integration, some sensitivity to the economically disadvantaged east (which received cheaper foreign oil), and some cross-regional subsidization (of western producers by Ontario consumers). The only "losers" under the NOP were Ontario consumers. But with their access to plentiful hydroelectric power, and as long as oil and gas were still relatively cheap and abundant, their resistance to bearing some of the costs of developing a domestic oil industry was not great.

Spurred by the development of the transportation infrastructure and by the guarantee of Canadian market west of the Ottawa River and the access to the American market under the NOP, the oil industry grew rapidly after 1960. Production increased from 543,000 to 2.1 million barrels per day between 1960 and 1973, and exports increased from 23 percent to 66 percent of domestic production in the same period (Energy, Mines and Resources Canada 1987: 12). The attention of the major oil companies began to turn to new sources of oil—from nonconventional sources, notably the Alberta oil sands, and in frontier areas in the Canada lands and offshore. The U.S.-owned Suncor pioneered in oil sands production, establishing its first plant in 1968, and another U.S. subsidiary, Esso Resources, began exploration in the Beaufort Sea.

The natural gas industry also grew rapidly in this period. Production increased fivefold and exports tenfold between 1960 and 1973. In the course of frontier explorations for oil, large natural gas reserves were discovered in the Mackenzie Delta and the Beaufort Sea in the late 1960s, sparking proposals for major gas pipelines to bring natural gas out of the Arctic. These proposals raised the ghosts of earlier conflicts as a Canadian group proposed a route partly through the United States, and a group composed largely of foreign-controlled companies proposed a route through Canada. A small Canadian-controlled consortium, led by Alberta Gas Trunkline, proposed to transport Alaskan gas across Alaska, the Yukon, and northern British Columbia to Alberta (with a possible lateral connection to bring Canadian Mackenzie delta gas south as well). A second group, comprising several of the multinationals as well as eastern Canadian financial interests, proposed to bring Mackenzie delta gas directly along the Mackenzie River corridor through Canada. These familiar conflicts were further complicated in this case by the dawning consciousness of the potential impacts of megaprojects on the environment and on aboriginal cultures. In 1977 a governmental commission of inquiry recommended a ten-year moratorium on the Mackenzie River route. The government ultimately opted for the route from Alaska, but recommended a ten-year moratorium. As a result of the rapid expansion of gas reserves in conventional areas of western Canada, the project effectively went into abeyance.

In terms of their industrial and political organization, oil and gas producers divide along several dimensions, although these cleavages are for the most part superimposed. Two of these dimensions have to do with ownership, dividing the predominantly U.S.-based multinationals from Canadian-owned firms and private-sector corporations from crown corporations—notably (until 1991) Petro-Canada, a federal crown corporation established in 1975 as discussed below. Another dimension involves size: Large firms include multinationals and a number of Canadian firms including Petro-Canada, but there are many smaller firms, both Canadian and foreign. A final dimension concerns the range of activities in which firms are involved. The large "integrated" companies combine downstream (refining and marketing) with upstream (production and exploration) activities. This group has traditionally been dominated by multinationals. In the late 1970s and 1980s, however, there were two major

Canadian entrants into the ranks of the integrated companies: Alberta Gas Trunkline (AGTL, later Nova) acquired the integrated Husky Oil in 1979, and Petro-Canada gained refining and marketing assets through two major acquisitions of foreign firms in the early 1980s. Other large Canadian firms have focused on exploration and production, whereas smaller firms tend to focus on one or other of these activities.

Associations of oil and gas producers were relatively late additions to the constellation of resource-based associations in Canada, reflecting the fact that the development of the industry took off only in the late 1940s. The division between foreign- and domestically owned oil and gas producers is reproduced in the organization of industry associations: The Canadian Petroleum Association (CPA), established in 1952, is dominated by the multinationals; Canadian explorers and producers established the Independent Petroleum Association of Canada (IPAC) in 1960 (Coleman 1988: 23). It should also be remembered that the foreign multinational integrated companies form an important component of the "dominant coalition" of Canadian business whose associational vehicle is the BCNI, established in 1976 (Chapters 1 and 5).

Despite the fact that Canadian companies consider their interests sufficiently distinct from those of the multinationals to maintain a separate association, the political stances of these associations were similar on most major policy issues through the 1960s and 1970s. Even on an issue that might have been expected to pit the interests of the integrated firms against independent producers—the National Oil Policy of 1960—there was in fact little conflict. The integrated firms wished to use cheaper imported oil in their eastern refineries and hence supported the two-market concept of the NOP. Although the independents might have been expected to press for access to eastern markets, they were more concerned with expanding export markets in the United States—a goal also achieved through the NOP.

Agenda

The quadrupling of oil prices in 1973 swept away the underpinnings of the National Oil Policy. Under that policy Canada was both an oil-exporting nation (in the west) and an oil-importing nation (in the east). Like other exporting nations, Canada was faced with the problem of cushioning the price shock for domestic consumers while allowing producers to reap the gains of the world price increase. Ontario consumers, in particular, having paid higher than world prices to subsidize the domestic oil industry since 1961, now believed it was their turn to be subsidized by paying lower than world prices to the domestic producers who served their market. To that regional conflict was added the plight of the oil-importing regions, Quebec and the Atlantic provinces, now faced with sharply higher world prices.

The agenda of Canadian energy policy was also being shaped by developments in the United States, Canada's only existing export market for crude oil and natural gas. Despite "voluntary constraints," Canadian oil exports to the United States had increased rapidly in the 1960s and early 1970s. They more than doubled between 1965 and 1970, when, in response to pressure from U.S. producers and the failure of a variety of measures by both Canadian and U.S. governments to tighten constraints, the United States imposed import quotas on Canadian oil (Energy, Mines and Resources Canada 1987: 123). These quotas were no more successful at stemming the flow of imports than voluntary measures had been, and Canadian oil exports to the United States almost doubled again between 1970 and 1973 (ibid.; Plourde 1988: 235–36). In 1973 the response of the federal government to the first oil price shock was to replace its oil import quotas with oil import fees applying to Canadian as well as other foreign oil, to control the price of "old" domestic crude oil and natural gas, and to ration the artificially cheap domestic oil through an "entitlement" system for refiners. It also embarked upon a series of energy-conservation programs. These restrictions in Canada's export market (together with Canada's own imposition of an export tax, as discussed shortly) meant that, having just achieved the status of net oil exporter as the expansion of production peaked in the early 1970s, Canada again became a net oil importer in 1975.

The Canadian federal Liberal government also imposed price controls on domestic crude oil and natural gas in 1973 and 1974; but instead of rationing oil through import quotas and domestic allocations as in the United States, it chose to subsidize consumption. In part, this decision was based on a recognition of the particularly critical nature of oil price increases for Canada's energy-intensive industrial base. It also, however, reflected the *electoral* base of the Liberal federal government in the consumer regions of central and eastern Canada. Initially the federal government froze the price of domestic oil and announced the extension of the interprovincial oil pipeline to bring domestic oil to Montreal. In subsequent negotiations federal and provincial governments agreed on an administered price for Canadia oil. To aid consumers of imported oil, the federal government established the Oil Import Compensation Program (OICP) in 1974. Under OICP the federal government subsidized refiners of imported crude oil in the amount of the difference between their acquisition costs and the costs of acquiring domestic crude. The subsidies were to be funded by an export tax on crude oil that had been imposed just before the oil price shock in 1973. The federal government also introduced price controls on natural gas traded interprovincially, and on exported natural gas. The intention was to encourage the use of natural gas as a substitute for oil in Canada. Accordingly, the control of domestic and export prices was to ensure that the price of gas, which tends to track the price of oil, remained lower than oil prices in Canada, and that the regime of administered domestic prices did not lead producers to increase their export volumes.

In 1975 the federal government established a crown corporation, Petro-Canada, to engage in and to foster resource exploration. Petro-Canada also had another important purpose: The federal government was heavily dependent upon the resource industries for information, especially about Canadian reserves and the costs of exploration and production, and Petro-Canada was to function as a "window" on the petroleum industry (Doern and Phidd 1983: 466). Petro-Canada represented both a symbolic and a real increase in the level of state involvement in the energy field and was bitterly resented by the Conservative government of Alberta, not only as a federal incursion per se but as the statist offspring of a Liberal government. The federal Conservatives, who elected an Albertan, Joe Clark, as leader in 1976, also took aim at Petro-Canada.

One of the major interregional effects of the 1973 increase in international oil prices, however, had to do not with its immediate results for producers and consumers but with its implications for federal and provincial fiscal policies. The western provinces, especially Alberta, shared in the windfall gains to oil producers through the royalties they collected as the "landlords" of the oil industry. (In Alberta approximately 80 percent of petroleum and natural gas is produced from provincially owned lands.) Royalty rates were raised in the early 1970s, and again after 1973. To deal with its massive revenue flows, the Alberta government established an Alberta Heritage Fund to allow capital to be accumulated primarily for purposes of industrial policy (Chapter 5). Resource wealth was seen by all three westernmost provinces, and especially Alberta and Saskatchewan, as offering the means to diversify and to develop their economies.

As the western provinces benefitted, the federal government suffered in a number of ways. In general it saw the burgeoning of provincial treasuries as inevitably implying a devolution of effective power to the provincial level. Increasing oil prices also presented more specific fiscal problems for the federal government. The increasing fiscal disparity between the provinces required Ottawa to increase equalization payments to "have not" provinces, even though it was not sharing in the royalty boom in the west (Economic Council of Canada 1982). As the gap between the price of domestic and imported oil grew, and as Canadian exports to the United States declined, the federal oil export tax no longer covered the subsidy for eastern consumers. The increases in provincial royalty rates not only increased provincial revenue but also decreased Ottawa's, since royalties were deductible from corporate income for federal tax purposes. Ottawa retaliated by eliminating the deductibility of royalty payments.

The legal and constitutional dimensions of these tax wars are discussed below. What is relevant here is their contribution to the poisonous atmosphere of federal-provincial relations in the energy field in the latter half of the 1970s and their impact on the industry. In a context in which the industry, while reaping substantial profits, was also moving into highly risky capital-intensive ventures in exploring nonconventional sources and frontier areas, the squabbling between levels of government in Canada added another source of uncertainty, and the increase in state involvement a potential threat.

That threat was heightened by a renaissance of concern within the Liberal party and the NDP about the concentration of foreign (especially American) ownership in the petroleum industry. The federal Liberal government had established a Foreign Investment Review Agency in 1974. Concerns about the particular implications of foreign ownership in the energy sector had existed at least since the late 1950s, when they were reflected in the report of the Gordon Royal Commission on Energy. In the latter half of the 1970s they were heightened by the perception that a substantial proportion of the increasingly large profits generated by Canadian resources were accruing to non-Canadians. Although this is true, it is also true that the level of Canadian ownership and control of the industry was increasing in the late 1970s, as a result of the establishment of Petro-Canada and other crown corporations, and as a result of several acquisitions of foreign firms by Canadian private-sector enterprises (Energy, Mines and Resources Canada 1987: 67–68). The percentage of capital employed in the industry that was controlled by Canadians increased from 25 percent in 1974 to 45 percent in 1978.[6]

Reaction to these concerns was only one of a number of factors that led to the establishment of the BCNI in 1976, to bridge what corporate leaders perceived as a growing distance between the heights of business and government. Nonetheless, given the membership of most of the large foreign multinationals in the BCNI (as well as the absence from the BCNI of the large Canadian oil and gas producers), that association became an important vehicle for the expression of the interests of the multinationals.

Furthermore, the federal Conservatives became the champions of the west and, to a lesser extent, of the petroleum industry. In opposition, they severely criticized the degree of federal intervention in the industry and, during the 1979 election campaign, promised to privatize Petro-Canada. At the beginning of their brief period in office as a minority government in 1979–80, there was some expectation that, with Conservative governments at both levels, an Ottawa-Alberta agreement might be reached. The ground upon which the negotiations were being conducted soon shifted again, however, with the doubling of world prices after the Iranian revolution in 1979. Even so, the federal Conservatives had hopes of attaining an agreement whereby oil and gas prices would rise to 85 percent of world levels by 1984. In its budget of December 1979 the government proposed a set of measures based upon that assumption (Doern and Toner 1985: 103–5). Relative to the Liberal programs that were to follow, these measures would have led to greater revenue shares for the industry and the provincial governments, and less for the federal government (Romanow, Whyte, and Leeson 1984: 115). In the face of the combined opposition of the Liberals and the NDP, the Conservative minority government stood adamant on these proposals and was defeated by a nonconfidence motion on the budget.

In summary, at the end of the 1970s there were essentially two major issues on the energy policy agenda. One issue was how fast, and how closely, Canadian oil and gas prices would be allowed to approach world levels. Although, under federal-provincial agreements, the domestic price had been moving in increments toward the world price and had reached 80 percent of the world price by 1978, the second price shock effectively ended that relationship. This issue was further fueled by events in the United States. In 1979 President Jimmy Carter announced a phased schedule for increasing the price of domestic oil to world levels by 1981. Under 1978 U.S. legislation the price of natural gas was to be gradually and partially decontrolled between 1978 and 1985. The second major issue had to do with how the rents generated by increases in oil and gas prices would be shared between federal and provincial governments and the industry. Of only somewhat lesser concern were issues of ownership: the extent to which, if at all, crown corporations (especially federal crown corporations) should participate in oil and gas exploration and production; and the extent to which, if at all, foreign ownership of oil and gas companies should be controlled. And underlying all of these issues were questions of jurisdiction, as federal and provincial governments experimented with a variety of instruments whose constitutional status was unclear.

On each of these issues the division was similar. The federal Conservatives, the western provincial governments, and, of course, the industry favoured a more rapid and closer approach to world prices, a smaller federal share of revenues, the privatization of Petro-Canada, and a more liberal approach to foreign investment. The federal Liberals, the NDP, and the governments of consumer provinces favoured a slower and more constrained escalation in price, a larger share of federal revenues (largely at the expense of the industry rather than the western provinces), the maintenance and indeed the expansion of Petro-Canada, and restrictions on foreign investment. Even on jurisdictional issues the consumer provinces generally supported the federal government. There were, of course, some divisions within these general groupings. Oil and gas producers preferred a reduction in provincial as well as federal revenue shares but muted their opposition—especially to the Alberta government, which they saw as their champion in the negotiation of pricing arrangements. There was surprisingly little division between the multinationals and the Canadian firms on the issue of foreign ownership, a phenomenon that may be attributable in part to the general ideological conservatism of the industry, which led firms to resist governmental restrictions of all kinds (Doern and Toner 1985: 246).

The very cleanness of this division of interests did not bode well for the resolution of conflict. There was virtually no vehicle for mediation. The federal Liberal party was firmly based in central and eastern Canada and was in a particularly centralist mode under Trudeau. The federal Conservatives were just as clearly based in western Canada and in a particularly decentralist mode under Joe Clark. The presence of Conservative premiers in Alberta and Ontario might have been expected to enhance the role of the federal Conservatives as mediators, but the very decentralism of their approach weakened their ability to force compromises between the Ontario and Alberta governments. Petro-Canada had a foot in both camps, one in the industry and the other in the federal government. As discussed below, however, although it did attempt to play a mediating role, its lack of legitimacy in western eyes hampered its attempts. Only on jurisdictional issues was there some glimmer of the "ambivalence" necessary for compromise: Although the consumer provinces, notably Ontario, favoured strong central authority over specific energy matters, they were jealous of their own authority over natural resources.

Process

The seeds of drastic change in energy policy were sown in discussions within the federal Liberal caucus during its brief period in opposition in 1979–80. Upon returning to power in February 1980 with an electoral base almost entirely in central and eastern Canada, the Liberals were prepared to act unilaterally to break the impasse with Alberta over oil and gas pricing. As we have seen, there were examples of bold federal unilateralism in the early 1980s in the arenas of constitutional and health policy (Chapters 2 and 3), but nowhere was this more apparent than with regard to energy policy.

The NEP, announced in the federal budget of October 1980, has been described as "a centralist, nationalist and interventionalist political and policy initiative which at its core was intended to substantially restructure the key relationships of power and the sectoral and regional distribution of wealth in Canadian energy politics" (Toner and Bregha 1984: 105). It had essentially three announced goals: security of supply, Canadianization of the oil and gas industry, and interregional "equity" in pricing and revenue sharing (Canada 1980: 2).

To accomplish the first two of these objectives—security and Canadianization—the NEP established a system of incentive grants (replacing earlier tax incentives) under the Petroleum Incentive Program (PIP) to encourage exploration and development of oil reserves. The criteria for PIP grants favoured Canadian firms and exploration on federally owned Canada lands in the northern territories and offshore. The federal government also claimed a 25 percent interest or "back in" on every existing or new discovery on federally owned Canada lands. A 50 percent Canadian participation was mandated for any production on Canada lands. It also provided support for Petro-Canada to acquire several foreign firms. The NEP's stated objective was 50 percent ownership of Canadian oil and gas production (as measured by gross revenues)[7] by 1990, as compared with 27 percent in 1980. As a further measure to enhance energy security (but as a minor portion of the NEP budget) the program included off-oil initiatives and conservation incentives.

As for the interregional "equity" (in pricing and revenue sharing) objective, the NEP unilaterally established an administered price regime for oil and gas over a four-year period. A tax on natural gas and gas liquids, both domestically sold and exported, was introduced. It also introduced a new Petroleum and Gas Revenue Tax (PGRT). The PGRT was levied on a firm's gross production revenues net of operating expenses and hence "lay somewhere between a royalty on gross revenues and an income tax" (Energy, Mines and Resources Canada 1987: 102). The PGRT rate was initially set at 8 percent.

The process of developing the NEP was highly atypical. Although, despite its boldness, it did embody some clever compromises, these compromises were not worked out through normal channels of elite accommodation. There was virtually no consultation with the western provincial governments or with private industry groups in the initial development of the NEP. Rather, the compromises were crafted within a small group of senior officials and key ministers: officials from the Department of Energy, Mines and Resources and the Department of Finance, executives from Petro-Canada, and the prime minister, the minister of energy, and the minister of finance, all of whom were powerful figures within the Liberal cabinet. There was considerable support among bureaucratic officials and Petro-Canada executives for a move to world prices. In the case of Petro-Canada such a move would clearly enhance revenues; for the economists in Finance and Energy, Mines and Resources, it was a mechanism for enhancing efficiency in the use of energy sources (Doern and Toner 1985: 42). The politicians, with their central and eastern base, however, insisted upon a "blended" price that would maintain wellhead prices for domestic oil below world levels and blend the price of domestic and imported oil through a complex system of taxes and subsidies to create a single price to the consumer.

The reactions to the NEP by the governments of the producing provinces and the industry were swift and negative (Carmichael and Stewart 1983: 7–8; Doern and Toner 1985: chaps. 6 and 7). Premier Peter Lougheed of Alberta delivered a scathing attack on the policy in a radio and television address and announced a variety of retaliatory measures, most notably a cutback in oil production (Reading 6-2). The government of Alberta also held hostage two of the megaprojects that (briefly) formed the centrepiece of federal industrial policy at the time, by delaying the necessary approvals. The pricing and fiscal arrangements of the NEP also galvanized the industry into virtually unanimous opposition, despite the advantages that the NEP's Canadianization held for Canadian firms. Petro-Canada attempted to play a mediating role by continuing to press for price increases while defending the Canadianization provisions of the NEP. But because Petro-Canada executives had been involved in the formulation of the NEP, and because the crown corporation was a beneficiary of several of its Canadianization provisions, it lacked the legitimacy to undertake the program's defence. In October 1981, in response to the severe criticism of the NEP and of Petro-Canada itself by IPAC, the crown corporation withdrew from the industry association.

Under severe pressure from the industry, the governments of Canada, Alberta, Saskatchewan, and British Columbia reached a set of bilateral federal-provincial agreements in 1981, which modified pricing arrangements (essentially by distinguishing between "old" and "new" oil on the earlier American model). Apart from removing an export tax on natural gas, however, the agreements left the fiscal structure of the NEP largely in place.

The resulting administered price system was, like the National Oil Policy of 1960, an ingenious attempt at balancing opposing interests. It established a "blended" price for oil, to be achieved through a complex set of price schedules, taxes, and subsidies. Essentially, the wellhead price of "old" domestic oil (essentially, oil discovered before December 31, 1981) was allowed to increase to up to 75 percent of the price of imported oil. Producers of "new" domestic oil received a quality-adjusted average of the world price. Through tax and compensation arrangements, however, refiners effectively paid a "blended" price, calculated according to the volumes of old, new, and imported oil refined in Canada. As the proportion of "old" oil declined, the blended price would therefore move toward world levels. The NEP and subsequent federal-provincial agreements also made changes to the administered price system for natural gas to further encourage substitution and established joint arrangements for financing the extension of gas transportation networks (Energy, Mines and Resources Canada 1987: 101–3). In 1982 the federal government issued an "update" on the NEP setting out and defending the content of the program as revised (Reading 6-3).

In 1981 the federal government also responded to protest from the

U.S. government over Canadianization requirements by offering compensation for its "back-in" shares in discoveries on Canada lands. And according to one account, the Liberals early in 1982 dropped plans to give Canadian firms preference in gas exports (Clarkson 1982: 80).

Despite the ingenuity of the NEP and its subsequent amendments, it remained a bone of contention between the federal government, on the one hand, and the western provincial governments (especially Alberta), the petroleum industry, and the U.S. government, on the other.[8] The industry and the Alberta government continued to object not only to the content of the policy but also to the unilateral way it had been introduced. The industry, indeed, felt betrayed even by the government of Alberta, which it believed to have put Alberta's fiscal interests above the industry's concerns in negotiations with the federal government. Major firms withdrew from two megaprojects in Alberta in late 1981 and 1982. In large part these decisions had to do with what were perceived even then to be softening oil prices: These capital-intensive projects were highly sensitive to cash-flow problems in periods of price volatility (Energy, Mines and Resources Canada 1987: 15–16). The reasons given by the firms involved, however, highlighted the negative impacts of the pricing and tax structure of the NEP and the uncertainties created by the policy environment (Doern and Toner 1985: 210, 274, 363–64).

Almost as soon as the NEP was adopted, the economic conditions upon which it was based shifted dramatically. It was based, of course, upon the assumption of continuing high world oil prices. But the crude oil import price into Canada in fact peaked in 1981; it declined by more than 5 percent in 1982, and by almost 12 percent in 1983. After a plunge in 1986, to be discussed below, the crude oil import price stood at only 45 percent of its 1981 level.[9]

The National Energy Program had been the product of crisis, and with the abatement of the crisis the ground for compromise began to reemerge. In this case the mediating function was performed in large part by the BCNI, which was able to set the energy policy issue in the broader context of business-government relations. The BCNI devoted a section of its brief to the Macdonald Commission (see Chapter 5) to energy issues and strongly criticized both the unilateralism and the interventionism of the NEP (Reading 6-4). But it also reported that it had convened meetings of "business leaders with a stake in the development of energy policy," the premiers of Alberta and Ontario and their respective energy ministers, and the federal energy minister in November 1983. Toner (1986: 122) reports that these meetings continued into 1984: "The objective of these meetings, given the new international energy environment, was to forge a consensus . . . in order to hammer out a new energy policy framework which would form the basis for a new energy policy after the 1984 election. This new era of cooperation and civility was reflected by the fact that an informal agreement was reached that ensured that the private sector participants and the Premiers would not embarrass federal politicians by raising energy issues during the election campaign."

There could hardly be a better illustration of the reassertion of the pattern of elite accommodation in the energy field, even under the Liberals, than these closed meetings of representatives of the "dominant coalition" of Canadian business, the Liberal federal government, and the Conservative governments of producing and consuming provinces. But it must be emphasized that this "new era of cooperation and civility" was also an era of change in the international energy environment. Price schedules and tax rates under the NEP had been premised on rising world oil prices; in a period of declining world prices they proved to be unworkable and burdensome, and were continually readjusted (Energy, Mines and Resources Canada 1987: 105). Furthermore, as the administered price for Canadian oil began to converge with the world price as world prices declined,[10] the consuming provinces lost their enthusiasm for the administered price system. Indeed, given the deregulation of oil and gas prices under the Reagan administration in the United States, "the Ontario government and the major Ontario industrial oil and gas consumers . . . were actually championing deregulation of oil and gas prices in the hope that this would lead to the lower oil and gas prices enjoyed by their American competitors" (Toner 1986: 122).

The various instruments used by federal and provincial governments in the post-1973 period had raised constitutional issues of jurisdiction. But because these issues were treated within the general process of constitutional change as it developed in the late 1970s and early 1980s, their resolution proceeded in a manner quite different from that which characterized the NEP. The settlement of these constitutional issues, although hardly insulated from the atmosphere of crisis and conflict surrounding the NEP, exhibited a much more typical pattern of elite accommodation.

The constitutional division of ownership and authority sketched earlier in this chapter left unanswered questions of access to key policy instruments such as price regulation and various forms of taxation. This constitutional ambiguity allowed for, and indeed encouraged, considerable jousting between federal and provincial levels of government in the wake of the first oil price shock. As governments at each level made unprecedented use of various instruments, they tested each other's willingness to mount constitutional challenges and tested the flexibility of the constitution itself. Both the federal and the Alberta governments moved to establish their authority over price: Alberta with its Petroleum Marketing Commission in 1973 and the federal government with its emergency price freeze in 1973 and the Petroleum Administration Act in 1974. The federal-provincial conference was clearly the preferred mechanism for price setting, and it was the mechanism used to reach an eighteen-month pricing agreement in January 1974. The Petroleum Administration Act, however, asserted the federal government's authority to act unilaterally if agreement could not be reached. When the First Ministers' Conference of April 1975 foundered on Ontario's refusal to accept new price increases, the federal government did exert its unilateral authority to set an increased price—and Ontario asserted its own authority over price through the imposition of a ninety-day stay on the new prices in Ontario. In subsequent negotiations prices were set by agreement between Ottawa and the producing provinces.

Considerable jousting also occurred over issues of access to various forms of taxation. Some of this jousting took place in the courts. The constitutional ambiguity with regard to forms of taxation of natural resources (that is, as to what constitutes a "royalty," an indirect or a direct tax) was used by industrial interests to launch a legal challenge to legislation passed by the NDP government of Saskatchewan expropriating (with compensation) all freehold oil and gas rights and imposing a "royalty surcharge" on all crown production. The federal government joined in the challenge. In 1977 (in the *CIGOL* case) the Supreme Court of Canada ruled that the royalty surcharge constituted an indirect tax and hence lay exclusively within federal jurisdiction.[11] In another case outside the energy arena (the *Central Canada Potash* case), also dealing with Saskatchewan legislation, the Supreme Court of Canada ruled that provinces could not directly control international trade in natural resources.[12] But in a later case sparked by one of Alberta's retaliatory measures against the NEP, the Supreme Court ruled that provincially owned resources directly exported from the province were immune from federal export taxation.[13]

The effect of these rulings was to create some uncertainty about the contours of provincial jurisdiction over natural resources and to provide the industry with a weapon against provincial initiatives even in the absence of federal legislation (Chandler 1986: 111). At minimum, they constrained the provincial governments' choice of instruments. Saskatchewan was able to substitute an income tax for its royalty surcharge to much the same effect. For Alberta to exploit more fully its power to immunize resources against federal export taxation, however, it would have to increase the level of public ownership—in Russell's understated words, it would "have to re-arrange the legal ownership of developed resources in a manner that may be politically and ideologically unattractive" (1985: 167). More importantly, however, these court decisions gave federal and provincial governments (especially the former) useful bargaining resources.

These bargaining resources were brought to bear in the arena of constitutional change. And in that arena questions of the control of energy resources can be treated not only within the context of the control of natural resources in general but also as part of the broader negotiations over the patriation of the constitution, the amending formula, and the charter of rights (Chapter 2). Judicial affirmation of elements of its constitutional jurisdiction over natural resources gave the federal government something to be traded to the western provinces in return for their support of aspects of its constitutional package. Treating oil and gas resources in the context of other natural resources also increased the scope for coalition building across provinces: A 1978 meeting of provincial premiers unanimously declared its support for the principle of strengthened provincial powers in the natural resource field.

In 1979 a set of draft amendments prepared by the Continuing Committee of Ministers on the Constitution (Chapter 2) regarding resource ownership and interprovincial trade was tabled at the Constitutional Conference of First Ministers. Known as the "Best Efforts" draft, this set of proposals confirmed provincial exclusive jurisdiction over exploration, development, primary production, conservation, and management of nonrenewable natural resources, forests, and electricity generation. It gave provinces the authority to use indirect taxation and created concurrent jurisdiction over interprovincial and international trade in primary resource products. Federal legislation was to have paramountcy in the realm of international trade; regarding interprovincial trade, federal paramountcy would be recognized where necessary to serve a "compelling national interest." Provincial legislation could not discriminate across provinces in the exercise of their pricing and taxation powers. In what the federal government saw as a major concession, its power to declare a work to be "for the general advantage of Canada" and thereby under federal jurisdiction would henceforth be subject to the consent of the province within which the work was located (Romanow, Whyte, and Leeson 1984: 25–28).

A number of issues lay unresolved in this draft. Some provinces wished to expand the definition of the resources to which this division of authority would apply, to include *all* natural resources (British Columbia, Alberta, and Quebec) or at least to include water (British Columbia) and off-shore resources (Newfoundland). Alberta wanted a more stringent trigger for federal paramountcy than the test of "compelling national interest." Saskatchewan wished to extend that qualifier to federal paramountcy in international as well as to interprovincial trade.

The federal government tentatively accepted the "Best Efforts" draft on natural resources, and among the provinces only Alberta and Quebec rejected it. As discussed in Chapter 2, however, the 1979 Constitutional Conference, at which these issues among many others were considered, adjourned without reaching agreement. In the ensuing discussions in 1980 and 1981, as in the late 1970s, the federal government was confronted with two underlying dimensions of conflict: the continuing intransigence of Quebec, and the east-west division catalyzed by the issue of oil and gas prices and revenues in the wake of the second oil price shock. The announcement of the NEP in October 1980 exacerbated the latter division. As Romanow, Whyte, and Leeson (1984: 116) put it: "The energy dispute added vigour and new dimensions to the constitutional conflict. The two disputes were inextricably linked, and everyone understood that the resolution of one depended on the other." If it was not to give ground to Quebec on key issues such as language rights and the amending formula, the federal government would have to show some flexibility on resource issues. In this respect the federal powers affirmed in the *CIGOL* and *Central Canada Potash* cases were invaluable: They gave the federal government something to trade away while leaving ample room for insistence on federal paramountcy where it deemed necessary.

In the event, negotiation over these resource issues proved crucial in winning the support of the federal NDP and the western governments for the total constitutional package in 1981. The final outcome was an amendment to the Constitution Act, 1867, section 92A (Reading 6.5). It was similar to the "Best Efforts" draft, except that the concurrency of federal and provincial powers over trade applied only to interprovincial trade, and the federal government was given *unqualified* paramountcy in that field. The federal government retained exclusive jurisdiction over international trade and also retained the unqualified power to establish its jurisdiction over an undertaking by declaring it to be for the general advantage of Canada. Although the provinces (especially Alberta) did not gain all that they wished from the amendment, they viewed it (in a context in which they had made no other jurisdictional gains) as a positive outcome.

One important issue was not resolved in the course of these negotiations, however—the question of the ownership of offshore resources. The courts had previously held that, under the Constitution Act 1867, ownership of offshore mineral resources lay with the federal government.[14] The federal government had chosen, nonetheless, to share authority over these resources through administrative and revenue-sharing arrangements with the provinces.[15] Such a set of arrangements was negotiated between the federal government and New Brunswick, Nova Scotia, and Prince Edward Island in 1977. Newfoundland, however, pressed for constitutional change in this regard—at least with regard to Newfoundland itself. Its campaign was given strong impetus with the discovery of substantial oil reserves in the Hibernia field off the Newfoundland coast in 1979. At the February 1979 conference the federal government appeared to be willing to accede to some of Newfoundland's demands. When the Conservatives took office at the federal level in June 1979, however, they entered into bilateral negotiations with Newfoundland with the purpose of transferring ownership of offshore resources to the province, and the issue was removed from the broader constitutional discussions. With the defeat of the federal Conservatives in February 1980 these bilateral discussions came to an end, and a reinvigorated Liberal government returned to its earlier position that questions involving offshore resources should be treated through federal-provincial agreements, not constitutional change.[16] Despite the support of all of the provinces for Newfoundland's position that there should be no constitutional distinction between offshore and onshore resources, the federal government remained adamantly opposed to *constitutional* change in this respect, and the issue remained at an impasse.

Moving energy issues into the arena of constitutional amendment, then, had enhanced the *incentives* for agreement by expanding the range of issues over which negotiation could occur and the range of actors involved, beyond the polarized set of issues and actors in the oil and gas arena. In another sense, however, it had limited the *scope* of the energy issues involved—to only those provisions that the participants were prepared to entrench in the constitution. The ground for agreement on issues that could be settled "once and for all" (rather than being open to periodic renegotation) was relatively narrow (Dupré 1988: 247–48; Chandler 1986: 124; Romanow, Whyte, and Leeson 1984: 274–75).

Section 92A removed some of the constitutional ambiguity that had characterized the energy field in the past. (Indeed, an attached schedule defining "primary production" is highly unusual in its level of specificity.) Nonetheless, by establishing federal and provincial concurrency over taxation and interprovincial trade, it allowed considerable room for intergovernmental negotiation in the future. In effect, it altered the bargaining resources with which federal and provincial governments would enter such future negotiations.

The Liberal legacy in the energy field was thus one of controversy (surrounding the NEP) and modest compromise (section 92A). Upon assuming office in September 1984, the new Conservative federal government sought almost immediately to abjure the NEP and to extend what might be considered the "spirit" of 92A. In order to manifest its friendly orientation toward the west, industry, and the United States, it could have had no better opportunity than that provided by the NEP. As Toner points out, the NEP ironically benefitted the Conservatives by giving them "*both* an arsenal of power which they could 'give back' to the industry and producing provinces and a hated 'symbol' of the Liberal era, which they could dismantle for significant psychic pay-off" (1986: 120; emphasis in original). Even more ironically, the groundwork for "rolling back" the NEP had been laid under the Liberals, under the aegis of the BCNI, as discussed above. Whether or not the NEP would have suffered the same fate had the Liberals been reelected in 1984 must remain an open question. In the event, the Conservatives quickly moved to reap the political rewards of killing the program.

Soon after assuming office the Conservative federal government entered into multilateral discussions with the western provinces. Although Ontario, the flagbearer of the consumer interest, was not involved in these discussions, it had by this time come to accept the general agenda of price deregulation, and there were few resource rents that it could have urged the federal government to capture. Ontario had, in fact, forfeited its place at the oil price negotiating table with its refusal to agree to price increases in the mid-1970s; and because these discussions did not involve "once and for all" constitutional decisions, there was less rationale to diverge from this pattern.

The Western Accord, signed by the federal government and the governments of Saskatchewan, Alberta, and British Columbia in March 1985, deregulated oil prices and eliminated oil-export charges and a number of taxes, including the Petroleum Compensation Charge. The accord also provided for the phasing out of the PGRT by January 1989 (later brought forward to October 1986) and for the elimination of new PIP grants by March 1986, although it contained grandfathering provisions that eventually extended the program's life into 1989. A subsequent agreement in October 1985 further liberalized controls on natural gas exports, which had been substantially deregulated in 1984, and provided for the deregulation of domestic natural gas prices by November 1986 (Energy, Mines and Resources Canada 1987: 104). Because the transition to the deregulated regime foreseen in this agreement required the compliance of regulatory agencies in consumer provinces, and because those provinces (particularly Ontario and Manitoba) objected that they had not been adequately consulted, the implementation process was a rather rocky one (Toner 1986: 137–40).

Essentially, the Western Accord reestablished the pre-1973 regime for the pricing and marketing of oil and gas. In fiscal terms it took the system back at least to pre-NEP days, and in terms of exports "the Accord provide[d] greater freedom than at any point since the establishment of the National Oil policy in 1961" (ibid.: 127). (The export regime, however, was to be modified by the Free Trade Agreement with the United States, discussed below.) The terms of the accord were, indeed, "remarkably similar to a policy proposed by the Canadian Petroleum Association in 1984" (ibid.: 130). But it did contain some ambiguous clauses to assuage lingering concerns about future market developments and lingering suspicions of the intentions of the industry. One provided that the federal government could, after consultations with the provinces, take "appropriate measures" to protect Canadian interests in the event of sharp price changes in the international market. Another attempted to ensure that all increased industry revenues would be reinvested by providing for increased federal and provincial monitoring of industry investment behaviour.

On the issue of offshore resources the Conservatives followed a similar pattern, negotiating only with "producer" provinces. A Supreme Court

of Canada decision in March 1984 had rejected Newfoundland's arguments regarding its ownership of offshore resources and reaffirmed the
proprietary right of the federal government.[17] While in opposition (in
June 1984), however, Conservative leader Brian Mulroney signed an
agreement-in-principle with the Conservative premier of Newfoundland
regarding resource management and revenue sharing. Having lost the
high constitutional stakes both in the pre-1982 negotiations and in the
courts, the government of Newfoundland was prepared to accept an administrative arrangement. Once the Conservatives had formed the federal
government, the agreement-in-principle became the basis of the Atlantic Accord between the federal and Newfoundland governments, signed
in February 1985. The accord provides for management of offshore resources through a joint management board. In the event of the failure of
the board to reach a consensus, the accord assigned final decision-making
authority to one or the other government, depending on the nature of the
issue. The agreement also provided that Newfoundland could set royalty
rates and receive royalty revenues. An agreement between the federal
government and Nova Scotia in August 1986 extended similar provisions
to that province.

Declining oil prices militated against the development of the Hibernia
field off Newfoundland. Prospects for the highly capital-intensive project
(whose preproduction capital costs were estimated at $3.4 billion in 1987)
dimmed with the collapse of oil prices in 1986. After years of negotiations and pervasive uncertainty regarding future oil prices, an agreement
was signed between the Newfoundland and federal governments in September 1990 to provide financial backing for the Hibernia project. The
rationale for the project, as enunciated by the federal energy minister,
was based at least as much on regional development considerations as on
energy economics (Fagan 1990).

One other Conservative initiative had significant implications for the
energy sector. The Free Trade Agreement with the United States contained provisions for energy trade. The history of energy trade between
the two countries had been marked by various import restrictions by
the United States and export restrictions by Canada as each country
responded to changes in international market conditions and in domestic production and reserves. In the agreement both countries accepted
constraints on their abilities to impose such restrictions, in the interest of secure access for Canadian producers to U.S. markets and secure
access for U.S. consumers to Canadian energy resources. The agree-

ment prohibits export taxes and charges and limits trade restrictions to those allowable under the GATT (essentially temporary emergency restrictions, conservation measures, and measures as part of a government stabilization plan). However, any such restrictions must be proportionate to reductions in domestic supply. They may not, that is, decrease the proportion of energy goods exported (as measured over the previous thirty-six months) in favour of domestic consumption. They may, however, prevent the proportion of exported goods from *increasing*. The two countries are also prohibited from price discrimination through licences, taxes, or minimum price requirements for exported goods. The United States further agreed to allow exports of Alaskan oil to Canada up to a specified limit. Reexports from either country of imports from third countries could be restricted under the agreement.

Despite the general deregulatory thrust of the agreement, these provisions regarding energy amount to a form of "managed trade." There are some potential conflicts between these provisions of the Free Trade Agreement and the more thoroughgoing deregulatory spirit of the Western Accord. Plourde (1988), for example, has speculated that the latter might make it possible for U.S. restrictions on reexports to be circumvented.

Concerns about a threat to Canada's energy security posed by the inability to divert flows of energy goods from exports to domestic consumption were raised vociferously by opponents to the Free Trade Agreement during the rancorous debate that surrounded its adoption (Chapter 5). The fate of these provisions were tied to the fate of the agreement itself. And the decision to adopt them was therefore made well beyond the confines of the energy arena itself, in the grand forum of the 1988 general election.

Consequences

One immediate effect of the NEP was to increase dramatically the federal share of upstream revenues in the oil industry, from 0.4 percent in 1979 to 26.2 percent in 1982. The combined effects of lower oil prices and deregulation in the mid-1980s, however, operated to shrink that share almost as dramatically: In 1986 it stood at 4.6 percent. Given some royalty relief from provincial governments as well, the industry was left in 1986 with a larger share (69.6 percent) than at any time since 1973 (Energy, Mines and Resources Canada 1987: 106).

The NEP foundered not only because of the daring disregard of its framers for the conventions of Canadian policymaking but also because of the unravelling of the economic assumptions upon which it was based. In 1980 the problem with oil prices appeared to be their inexorable escalation. By the beginning of the 1990s—after the oil price collapse of 1986, a period of fluctuation between fifteen and twenty-two dollars (U.S.) a barrel in the late 1980s, a spike after the Iraqi invasion of Kuwait in 1990 during which the price briefly doubled, and a return to prices in the twenty-dollar range in 1991—the problem appeared to be one of price volatility. In such a context the extent to which frontier areas and nonconventional sources will be explored and developed remains in doubt. In June 1987 the federal energy minister issued a statement setting out criteria for federal participation in energy megaprojects, emphasizing that such projects should meet "market tests," including the demonstration that they are backed by "significant private sector equity," that they will be able to produce and market oil and natural gas at a reasonable cost, and that they offer the federal government an acceptable return on its investment (Energy, Mines and Resources Canada 1987: 22). Nonetheless, as noted above, the federal government agreed in 1990 to participate in the Hibernia project offshore Newfoundland, despite uncertainty as to its economic viability (Fagan 1990).

Whether or not Canada remains "self-sufficient" in oil depends very much upon the development of these nonconventional and frontier sources, which in turn depends upon projected developments in the international market. Only at high prices will the development of these sources be economically practical. At lower prices it will be more efficient for Canada to import conventionally produced oil as its own conventional reserves are depleted. In 1983 Canada again became a net exporter of oil, but it has been projected that by the year 2000 it could either become a net importer of oil (of more than 40 percent of total consumption under a "low price" scenario) or remain a net exporter (of the equivalent of more than 10 percent of domestic consumption under a "high price" scenario) (ibid.: 140).

On the demand side Canada's voracious appetite for energy has been little checked—a not surprising result given the subsidization of consumption throughout the period of the oil price shocks and the domestic availability of oil substitutes. A comparison with the United States and Japan is instructive. After the first oil shock, as discussed above, the United States imposed domestic price controls, import quotas, rationing, and conservation measures. After the second shock it moved rapidly to

TABLE 6-1   Energy Consumption in Relation
to Gross Domestic Product (GDP)*

Year	Canada	United States	Japan
1973	100.0	100.0	100.0
1974	93.1	99.8	96.5
1975	93.1	96.0	91.1
1976	91.3	97.6	95.5
1977	91.3	95.0	91.3
1978	90.7	95.8	89.6
1979	91.1	93.0	88.7
1980	93.2	86.8	83.0
1981	89.0	86.2	71.2
1982	86.9	83.9	67.5
1983	83.6	81.3	66.7
1984	80.1	76.5	67.1
1985	79.9	73.8	64.0

Source: Energy, Mines and Resources Canada 1987: 151.
*Calculated as total final demand divided by real domestic production (1980 U.S. dollars), all converted into an index with 1973 = 100.

world prices and to deregulation of oil and gas prices in the early 1980s, relying on market prices to encourage an efficient use of energy sources. Canada maintained domestic price controls and subsidized the consumption of foreign oil from 1973 to early 1985. Japan, however, with its heavy reliance on imported oil, could not rely on the cushion of domestic production. After a brief initial period of confusion after the first price shock, it developed extensive conservation programs. Industrial use of energy was rationalized and coordinated through the Ministry of International Trade and Industry, while industrial federations facilitated innovations in energy-efficient production technology (Pempel 1982: 64–65). The effects of these different approaches are indicated in Table 6-1. Canadian consumption responded to the first oil price shock slightly faster than in United States, and at about the same rate as Japan's. After the second price shock, however, energy consumption as a proportion of GDP declined at a somewhat more rapid rate in the United States than in Canada and declined much more dramatically in Japan. Although Canada was less spurred to energy efficiency than either the United States or Japan, its pattern of consumption did shift somewhat away from oil.[18]

As for ownership in the oil and gas industry, the NEP target of 50 percent Canadian ownership of oil and gas production (measured in terms of upstream revenues) by 1990 had been closely approached by 1986.

Canadians owned about 29 percent of production and controlled just over 20 percent in 1979; by 1986 these proportions had increased to 48 and 49 percent, respectively. (Energy, Mines and Resources Canada 1987: 143). Part of this increase was attributable to an increase in public ownership. Petro-Canada made two major acquisitions of foreign firms in the early 1980s; and with the subsequent acquisition of refining and marketing assets from Gulf Canada, Petro-Canada became the second largest integrated oil company in Canada. The NDP charged that the crown corporation was being "fattened up" for privatization (Toner 1986: 135), and in 1991 the Conservative government began to privatize the corporation with an initial public offering of 20 percent of the shares.

In jurisdictional terms, the de facto concurrency over oil and gas prices and revenues that was developing through intergovernmental competition in the latter part of the 1970s was clarified and made de jure through the section 92A constitutional amendment. Section 92A essentially gave the provinces greater flexibility in their choice of policy instruments: It confirmed a base of authority in addition to ownership and gave the provinces access to indirect taxation. It preserved federal paramountcy, however, in matters of interprovincial and international trade—a major confirmation of authority given the trade flows of these resources. Though it removed some ambiguity, it confirmed federal-provincial concurrency in key matters of energy policy and hence established the context for continual negotiations.

The NEP is widely viewed as an aberration in Canadian public policy. And indeed it was, in both substance and process: in the unequivocal boldness of its initiatives, and in the disregard for consultation and accommodation in its development. It was the product of a particular conjunction of partisan and regional conflict. It was developed and implemented through an alliance of a committed group of senior officials at the centre of the federal government and a group of key cabinet ministers prepared to deal unilaterally with both provincial governments and business interests over their vehement objections. It was also unstable: Its pricing structure proved unworkable; it remained a focus of intense controversy; and the political system strove to reestablish the patterns of elite accommodation that might moderate it. Ultimately, it did not survive the test of partisan change.

But the NEP was also the product of crisis. The reestablishment of patterns of elite accommodation was possible because the crisis of rocketing oil prices itself abated. The constitutional system of concurrency put in place by section 92A had not, by the end of the 1980s, been put to the test of another such crisis. In another oil price crisis, it is unlikely that the conflicts between regional interests would be any less stark than they were in the 1970s and early 1980s. Indeed, the provisions of the Free Trade Agreement constraining export restrictions remove a degree of governmental flexibility and may well add another dimension of conflict in a future crisis. There is no guarantee, moreover, that a mediating interest would emerge in such a situation. A broadly based party at the federal level might attempt to play such a role. But it would still have to deal with provincial governments with clarified authority; and even if it had partisan links with those governments, the lesson of the 1979–80 Conservative government is that regional interest runs thicker than partisanship. The NEP may indeed be the exception that proves the rule in Canadian politics: It was an exception, it failed, and the rules were reasserted. But in another crisis those rules may well be broken again.

READINGS

6-1.   THE GORDON COMMISSION'S VIEW OF FOREIGN INVESTMENT IN CANADIAN OIL *

The Royal Commission on Canada's Economic Prospects, which was appointed by the federal Liberal government in 1955 and reported in 1957, was chaired by Walter Gordon, a federal civil servant who subsequently entered federal politics and became finance minister in the cabinet of Prime Minister Lester Pearson. One of the key themes of the Gordon Commission was concern about the implications of foreign direct investment for the Canadian economy—a concern that Gordon maintained throughout his political career. In these excerpts the commission expresses this concern vis-à-vis the oil industry, which it viewed as one of the most important and promising in the country. (The commission's projections for the growth of the industry proved wide of the mark. Production increased steadily until 1973, when it reached 2.1 million barrels per day, of which

*Royal Commission on Canada's Economic Prospects, *Final Report* (Ottawa: Queen's Printer, 1957), pp. 128–32.

66 percent was exported. It then began to decline, however, to 1.5 million barrels per day in 1980 and 1.3 million barrels per day in 1982, less than 20 percent of which was exported. By 1986 production had recovered to 1.8 million barrels per day, and exports to 45 percent.)

. . . The following 1955 figures may perhaps indicate sufficiently the growing size of the Canadian oil industry: in that year recoverable reserves amounted to 3,000 million barrels, the value of crude oil production was more than $300 million, and the new capital invested in all phases of the industry was more than $450 million.

Those are large figures. But they may seem larger in Toronto or Calgary or Ottawa than they do in New York. The Canadian oil industry provides employment for many Canadians and stimulates activity in many parts of the Canadian economy. But for the most part it is owned and controlled in the United States. If its dimensions and problems are to be seen in perspective, an effort must therefore be made to regard it with binocular vision, to see it as it appears not only to a Canadian but also to the major United States oil companies with interests in many parts of the world. In the board room of such a company the horizons are wider and the pressures different—although not necessarily all less parochial—than they would be in Canada. In that setting, the figures for Canadian production and reserves, while still significant, dwindle a little. Canadian production in 1955 was only approximately one-twentieth of production in the United States and one-sixth of production in Venezuela. It was also far outstripped by production in Kuwait, Saudi Arabia and Iraq. . . .

To the international oil companies with operations in many parts of the world, it may not seem a matter of great urgency or concern whether large new markets are found for Canadian oil. They can supply all these markets from other sources and through other companies with which they are associated. They might even prefer to increase almost indefinitely their reserves of oil in Canada and draw down their reserves elsewhere. Also, as we have suggested, they are under pressure within the United States to do nothing that might disturb domestic prices there. In our opinion, however, it is clearly in the Canadian national interest that new markets be found. Only in this way can there be assurance that a steady and rapid pace of exploration and development in Canada will be maintained. Only in this way can early advantage be taken of this great natural resource and its exploitation not left to the hazards of an uncertain technological future. Above all, it is only in this way that a place can be left within the

Canadian oil industry for the independent Canadian producers, who, unlike the large international companies, must receive some return on their investment in Canada if they are to stay in business and not be forced to sell out to the foreign-owned companies, which already hold such a high proportion of all the acreage now under reservation or lease in Western Canada. It would seem that here is one instance, as is suggested in the discussion of foreign investment in a later chapter, where there might easily be some divergence between the Canadian national interest and the interest of foreign companies operating in Canada. . . .

We have paid special attention to the oil industry in this way because it seems destined to become one of the most important in the country and may show a tenfold growth in output between 1955 and 1980 in response to strong domestic and foreign demand. . . . By 1980 Canadian output may well be about 3 million barrels a day. Of this amount perhaps 1,600,000 barrels would be exported and 1,400,000 barrels consumed in Canada.

There is little doubt that there is plenty of oil in Canada to support production of that order of magnitude. The Western Canada sedimentary basin, stretching from Norman Wells in the Northwest Territories to Red Coulee in southern Alberta and from Fort Saint John at the western end of the Peace River district to Virden in Manitoba, contains approximately 750,000 square miles; and that whole area is considered to be favourable for the discovery of oil. The tempo of new discoveries will no doubt be set at least in part by the rate at which markets open up. But unless the claustrophobia from which the Canadian oil industry is now suffering is to be more prolonged than we anticipate, there would seem nothing unreasonable in the estimate that as much as 25 billion barrels of oil will be found in Western Canada over the next quarter century, and that about half of this amount will still be in place as proved reserves in 1980. In addition, it is always possible that some of the drilling at present being carried out in Eastern Canada will be successful. In any case, there will always be the vast oil reserves known to occur in the bituminous sands of northern Alberta to draw on if our other petroleum resources fall short of our expectations or if the costs of exploration and development rise more rapidly than we are inclined to anticipate.

6-2.   WESTERN CANADIAN RESISTANCE TO THE NATIONAL ENERGY PROGRAM*

In response to the tabling of the federal budget outlining the elements of the National Energy Program, Premier Peter Lougheed of Alberta swiftly announced retaliatory measures to be taken by Alberta, chief among which was a curtailing of oil production in the province. The combative tone of this address reflects the tense relationship between the government of Alberta and the federal government, and the western resentment of the major consuming province, Ontario. The Alberta government's sympathy with the interest of the oil industry is also expressed here.

Fellow Albertans, we face a serious situation in this province as I'm sure you are aware as a result of the federal budget and energy measures announced two days ago. They're an outright attempt to take over the resources of this province, owned by each of you as Albertans. . . . What we're facing here is a situation where more and more decision-making, more and more control will be in the hands of decision-makers in Ottawa and your provincial government will become less and less able to influence your future and to provide for job security and opportunity. . . .

During the '50s and '60s, many young Albertans had to go to other parts of Canada to find jobs. During the course of the '70s, we encouraged activities in many areas, including activity in the oil and gas industry to explore for much-needed supplies for all of Canada.

As a result of that, there was a multiplier effect and jobs developed in many, many areas—in construction, in service industries, in finance [and] throughout the whole province in a multitude of ways.

But Alberta hasn't always been prosperous. We've had our ups and downs, we've had our depressions and we will have good times and bad times—we know that.

What we've done is to develop a strategy to use our oil and gas, if you like, as a lever to improve our standard of living to provide services that are unparalleled. . . .

By ultimatum now we're going to be forced to sell our rapidly depleting oil supplies and oil resources for less than half of value—much, much less than we offered in our proposal of this summer.

*Transcript of television address by Premier Peter Lougheed of Alberta, October 30, 1980, reprinted in the *Edmonton Journal*, October 31, 1980, excerpts.

I don't think it's unfair to say that if the oil was owned by the province of Ontario that we in Alberta, most of us, know that we would in fact—in terms of the history of Canada—be paying world prices for our oil today.

There's a lot of myths about what happens to a barrel of Alberta oil. I'd like to try to clear up those myths by referring . . . to [the price of] a gallon of gasoline [in Toronto] coming from Alberta oil. What happens to it? Twenty-two cents goes to the federal government in tax and almost twenty-two cents goes to the Ontario government in tax.

The industry that has all the cost and takes the risk, [for them] there is thirty-two cents to cover their costs and they get back twenty-four cents approximately by way of risk return and their [sic] reinvesting almost all of it.

And finally we the owner, out of this gallon, in Alberta, that owns the oil, get 18.9 cents a gallon. . . .

[We have] decided to recommend to the legislature that we should reduce the rate in which we're producing our oil to about 85 per cent of its capacity.

We've decided to recommend to the legislature that the capacity be reduced, with adequate notice [of] three months, six and nine months, by a total of 180,000 barrels a day by the end of the nine-month period, but with two very important conditions which I want to emphasize to Albertans.

The first condition is this: If there becomes any shortage problem in Canada, we will suspend such an order. We will not put any Canadian in a position of being concerned with regard to supply.

We Albertans, as Canadians, make this a fundamental condition to this action, and secondly of course we would cancel such an approach if we can get to sit down and negotiate with the federal government a new and fair arrangement.

What other measures, in addition to this, do we intend to take in response to the federal energy ultimatums? Well, with regard to the oil sands, we've decided to hold that matter in abeyance—re-examine our royalty arrangements and assess it.

But with regard to the natural gas export tax, we intend to challenge that legally because we believe we have a reasonable case. And, if we're successful, we can improve the cash flow to our explorers who are out exploring for natural gas—give them the opportunity to get the cash flow.

And, finally, we want to enter into a campaign, in cooperation with all those Canadians who are interested in oil supply and self-sufficiency for the longer-term future of Canada, to convince the federal government that they've made a very serious mistake, that they should readjust their energy policies and encourage supply in Canada.

6-3.   THE FEDERAL DEFENCE OF THE NATIONAL ENERGY
        PROGRAM*

Two years after the adoption of the National Energy Program, and after a number of adjustments had been made to it, the federal government issued this defence of the program. The "decisiveness" and "boldness" of the program were presented as virtues, but in response to criticizms of the NEP as a unilateral and arbitrary action by the federal government, the program was also presented as adaptable.

On October 28, 1980, the Government of Canada announced a set of national decisions about energy. We acted from what we perceived to be a position of national strength—not weakness—in energy.

We knew that with a concerted effort by all Canadians, it was possible to achieve energy security—independence from the world oil market—in this decade.

We knew that Canadians wanted and deserved to own and control more of their oil and gas industry.

We knew there had to be fairness: between governments and to consumers.

We also knew that none of these things was likely to happen unless the Government of Canada took decisive action.

The National Energy Program has been a central topic of debate. Much of the debate has been helpful. More than ever, Canadians are aware that they are part of the solution to a solvable energy problem. More than ever, Canadians recognize how they can grasp the opportunities afforded by Canada's energy strengths. More than ever, Canadians appreciate the balances that must be struck in sharing the burdens and benefits of our energy situation—between producers and consumers, and between regions of the country.

The National Energy Program is not a single document, nor a static set of policies. The National Energy Program is a dynamic and compre-

*Government of Canada, *The National Energy Program: Update 1982* (Ottawa: Minister of Energy, Mines and Resources, 1982), pp. iii, 93–94.

hensive set of evolving responses to a changing world—whether through compromise with provinces, or through necessary mid-course corrections in specific initiatives or the fiscal burden. The National Energy Program has changed, and will continue to do so, as circumstances change and new opportunities emerge. The fundamental strength of the Program is this adaptability around a nationally agreed and unchanging set of objectives:

- Security of oil supply,
- Opportunity for Canadians to participate in their oil and gas industry, and
- Fairness in the distribution of energy benefits and burdens.

Only two and a half years ago Canada's energy situation appeared uncertain and troubling. World oil prices had recently doubled, and the government of the day had been unable to reach agreement with the producing provinces on oil and gas prices. At the 1979 Economic Summit meeting, Canada said that it would need net oil imports of at least 95,000 cubic metres (600,000 barrels) per day in 1985. Oil demand was growing at a rate of 3.5 per cent a year. The oil and gas industry in Canada was dominated by foreign owned oil and gas firms, and the fiscal system reinforced this dominance.

The land regime on the Canada Lands allowed these firms to hold millions of acres for many years, under lenient work requirements, with little prospect for Canadians to participate in these ventures. There was a danger that Petro-Canada, the national oil company, would no longer be an instrument of national policy—rather, it would be "privatized".

The federal government's fiscal situation in respect of this industry was untenable. Oil import compensation alone was costing the Government about $3 billion a year, and yet its share of oil and gas revenues was about one quarter of the provincial share. Canadians, through their taxes, were being asked to bear an unfair share of the burden of running the national economy, because the federal government's share of petroleum revenues was inadequate.

In just a short time, the situation has been fundamentally changed. The National Energy Program, combining initiatives by the Government of Canada, agreements with several provinces, provincial measures, and entrepreneurial initiatives on the part of the private sector, has transformed the situation.

Canadians now have a stable environment guaranteeing made-in-

Canada prices for the next five years. Oil imports will probably never be as high again as they were in 1980. Oil imports in 1985 will be less than half the figure predicted only two and one-half years ago.

Canadian firms are now playing a major role in both the western basin and the Canada Lands, and will own at least half of Canada's oil and gas production by 1990. Canada's national oil company, Petro-Canada, has become the fourth largest oil and gas company in Canada, and operates coast to coast.

The Government of Canada has an agreed and fair share of the revenue from the oil and gas sector, and prospects for continued stability in this respect appear strong.

The National Energy Program represents a bold initiative. Canadians are taking their energy future in their own hands, determined to build on their energy strengths. Much has been accomplished. Much remains to be done. But with the steps now taken, and with continued commitment, the future is clear. We, the Canadian people, will have an energy future which is secure, fair, and belongs to us.

6-4.   THE BUSINESS COMMUNITY AND THE NATIONAL ENERGY PROGRAM *

The hostility of the "dominant coalition" of Canadian business to the National Energy Program and the role of the BCNI as a mediator between business interests and the federal and provincial governments are apparent in these excerpts from the BCNI's submission to the Macdonald Commission, discussed in Chapter 5.

This is not the place to launch into a detailed critique of Canadian energy policy since 1980, but it must be noted that the world has basically failed to unfold in ways congruent with the assumption that underlay both the NEP and the subsequent pricing agreements reached between the federal government and the producing provinces in 1981. Not only have world oil prices not risen at anywhere near the pace anticipated by federal energy policy, but, perhaps equally important, Ottawa's belief that over $50 billion in federal revenue would be obtained over 1981–86

---

*Business Council on National Issues, *National Priorities*, a submission to the Royal Commission on the Economic Union and Development Prospects for Canada (December 12, 1983), pp. 22–26.

thanks to the NEP has been proven wildly inaccurate. In the meantime, the protracted federal-provincial dispute precipitated by the NEP, and the problems and uncertainty which it caused for the petroleum industry, have unquestionably harmed this country's economic interests by undermining energy megaprojects and reducing industry cash flow and exploration initiatives, and generally hurting the climate for investment.

The NEP well illustrates the problems that arise when major policy changes are suddenly introduced without serious consultation with those most affected. Because of huge investments and long lead times, the petroleum industry requires a stable policy environment; this is no less true for Canadian than for foreign-owned companies. Further, because of the division of jurisdictional responsibilities over energy and their legal ownership of natural resources lying within their borders, the producing provinces are by definition key players in the energy industry. The NEP blithely ignored these elemental realities. In view of the unpleasant experience of the NEP, the Business Council strongly urges that future energy policy changes sought by the federal government be thoroughly discussed with the energy industry and provincial governments beforehand. The benefits of such discussion and consultation were evident during a meeting on November 6th and 7th of business leaders with a stake in the development of energy policy. At this meeting, sponsored by the Business Council, and attended by the Premiers of Alberta and Ontario and their respective ministers of energy, along with the federal minister of energy, a process was initiated with the goal of achieving a national consensus on energy policy taking fully into account the views of producers and consumers. Never again should a fundamental change in policy be undertaken by a small circle of federal officials operating in isolation from the outside world (and indeed, even from the views of other federal government departments).

Our second recommendation regarding future Canadian energy policy is that the degree of government regulation that exists in the energy sector be lessened. The NEP established a host of new regulations and administrative bodies, but even before 1980 energy was a highly regulated area in comparison with the rest of the economy. We believe the country's long-term interests would best be served by moving toward a system of market-determined rather than administered prices.

It is widely recognized that, even with the demise of some of the megaprojects, the investments that will be required to tap Canada's energy resources are enormous. We believe that two steps can help to assure that this investment is forthcoming. The first is to move away from discriminatory treatment of foreign-owned petroleum companies, which was, of course, the hallmark of the NEP. In light of both the high cost of exploiting oil and gas reserves in frontier areas and through new recovery techniques, e.g. the oilsands, and the heavy demands which governments will be placing on Canada's capital markets to cover large deficits, it is clear that foreign capital and technology have a role to play in developing Canada's energy potential. . . .

The second step which we believe would assist in the development of our energy potential is for government to move some distance away from the present system of revenue-related taxation towards a profit-based system. The existing tax and royalty regime serves to increase sharply the threshold level which proposed projects must reach before they can be considered economically viable, and this discourages energy development from taking place.

6-5.   FEDERAL AND PROVINCIAL POWERS OVER NATURAL RESOURCES *

These sections of the Canadian constitution, adopted in 1982, revised the federal-provincial division of powers with respect to natural resources. With regard to interprovincial trade and taxation, federal and provincial governments were given concurrent powers, although federal laws were to be paramount in trade matters.

92A. (1) In each province, the legislature may exclusively make laws in relation to

- (*a*) exploration for non-renewable natural resources in the province;
- (*b*) development, conservation and management of non-renewable natural resources and forestry resources in the province, including laws in relation to the rate of primary production therefrom; and
- (*c*) development, conservation and management of sites and facilities in the province for the generation and production of electrical energy.

(2) In each province, the legislature may make laws in relation to the export from the province to another part of Canada of the primary pro-

*Constitution Act, 1867, as amended 1982, Section 92A, and Sixth Schedule.

duction from non-renewable natural resources and forestry resources in the province and the production from facilities in the province for the generation of electrical energy, but such laws may not authorize or provide for discrimination in prices or in supplies exported to another part of Canada.

(3) Nothing in subsection (2) derogates from the authority of Parliament to enact laws in relation to the matters referred to in that subsection and, where such a law of Parliament and a law of a province conflict, the law of Parliament prevails to the extent of the conflict.

(4) In each province, the legislature may make laws in relation to the raising of money by any mode or system of taxation in respect of

(a) non-renewable natural resources and forestry resources in the province and the primary production therefrom, and

(b) sites and facilities in the province for the generation of electrical energy and the production therefrom,

whether or not such production is exported in whole or in part from the province, but such laws may not authorize or provide for taxation that differentiates between production exported to another part of Canada and production not exported from the province.

(5) The expression "primary production" has the meaning assigned by the Sixth Schedule.

(6) Nothing in subsections (1) to (5) derogates from any powers or rights that a legislature or government of a province had immediately before the coming into force of this section.

The Sixth Schedule

Primary Production from Non-Renewable Natural Resources and Forestry Resources

1. For the purposes of section 92A of this Act, (a) production from a non-renewable natural resource is primary production therefrom if

(i) it is in the form in which it exists upon its recovery or severance from its natural state, or

(ii) it is a product resulting from processing or refining the resource, and is not a manufactured product or a product resulting from refining crude oil, refining upgraded heavy crude oil, refining gases or liquids derived from coal or refining a synthetic equivalent or crude oil; and (*b*) production from a forestry resource is primary production therefrom if it consists of sawlogs, poles, lumber, wood chips, sawdust or any other primary wood product, or wood pulp, and is not a product manufactured from wood.

Notes

1. Calculated from Department of Energy, Mines and Resources 1987: 119 and OECD 1988: 109.

2. In 1986, 99.4 percent of Canadian crude oil exports went to the United States, as did 94.8 percent of exported petroleum products and 100 percent of natural gas and electricity exports. Calculated from Energy, Mines and Resources Canada 1987: 120.

3. Important dimensions of Canadian energy policy, such as the significance of government-owned electric utilities at the provincial level, cannot be treated within this brief space. This discussion focuses on those dimensions that presented the greatest challenges for conflict resolution at the national level in the postwar period: that is, oil and gas policies.

4. AGTL was established as a mixed public-private enterprise, whose purpose was to keep the gas-gathering system in the hands of Albertans. The Alberta Gas Trunkline gathered all gas for export in Alberta and distributed it to various gas companies at the provincial border. The Alberta government later gradually reduced its equity participation, and by the early 1980s (as Nova) it was widely held—95 percent in Canada (Canadian Business 1984: 36).

5. The Gordon Commission, which had been established by the former Liberal government and reported in 1957, had a mandate broader than energy policy. It did treat energy policy, however, and indicated a concern absent from the Borden report—that is, a concern with the degree of American ownership in the resource industries.

6. The comparable increase for *ownership* of capital employed was from 43 percent in 1974 to 52 percent in 1978 Statistics Canada 1984: table XI). There is considerable dispute about the appropriate measure of ownership and control in the petroleum industry. Measures based on revenues, used by the framers of the National Energy Program, discussed

below, indicated lower levels of Canadian ownership. For example, the Department of Energy, Mines and Resources (1987: 67) reports that "in 1979, Canadians owned only about 28.5 percent of revenues generated by oil and gas production, and controlled only about 20.5 percent of revenues." A focus on revenues, and hence on production, however, neglects the significant proportion of capital employed in exploration and development activities that have not yet reached the stage of generating revenues on a large scale. For a criticism of revenue-based measures, see Walker 1981: 25–27.

7. See note 6.

8. For competing views of the NEP from policy institutes of the right and left, respectively, see Watkins and Walker 1981 and McDougall 1983.

9. Calculated from International Energy Agency 1981: table 8.2.

10. In 1980 the difference between the price of Canadian and foreign oil was about C$20 per barrel; in 1984 it was less than C$3 and declining.

11. *Canadian Industrial Gas and Oil Ltd. v. Government of Saskatchewan* (1978) 2 S.C.R. 545.

12. *Central Canada Potash Co. Ltd. and Attorney-General for Canada v. Government of Saskatchewan* (1979) 1 S.C.R. 42.

13. *Re Exported Natural Gas Tax* (1982) 1 S.C.R. 1004.

14. *Reference Re the Offshore Mineral Rights of British Columbia* (1967) S.C.R. 792.

15. These arrangements apply to the east coast. There has been a federal moratorium on oil and gas activities off the west coast since 1971.

16. While constitutional discussions were still going on in the fall of 1981, the federal government entered into bilateral discussions with Nova Scotia and Newfoundland with the purpose of coming to administrative agreements on resource management and revenue sharing for offshore resources. These discussions led to an agreement with the government of Nova Scotia in March 1982, but no agreement was reached with Newfoundland.

17. *Reference Re Property in and Legislative Jurisdiction Over the Seabed and Subsoil of the Continental Shelf Offshore Newfoundland* (1984) 1 S.C.R. 86.

18. Oil accounted for 54.2 percent of final energy demand in 1975 and 40.2 percent in 1986. Over the same period the share of natural gas rose from 22.0 to 24.7 percent, coal rose from 9.5 to 13.7 percent, and electricity rose from 10.6 to 16.0 percent (Energy, Mines and Resources Canada 1987: 130).

7 Minority Language Rights

The issue of minority language rights has roots deep in Canadian history. It was the subject of an ambiguous compromise between anglophones and francophones at the time of confederation, flared into conflict in the late nineteenth and early twentieth centuries, and lay smouldering in Canadian policy and politics until the 1960s. Since then, it has been a matter of ongoing conflict in the legislatures and the courts, and occasionally in the streets. In this most recent period of conflict the historic compromise, which has come under increasing pressure as a result of demographic and cultural change, has been revisited and reopened. Attempts to reach a workable alternative compromise have greatly complicated Canadian constitutional politics, as discussed in Chapter 2. Whether such an alternative compromise can be reached is one of the fundamental issues of contemporary Canadian politics.

Issues of minority language rights in Canada entail the same fundamental axes of disagreement that have frustrated constitutional reform: bicultural-multicultural, national-regional, and individual-collective. Is Canada fundamentally a bicultural nation, brought into being by an agreement between its anglophone and francophone "founding peoples," or is it now, whatever its history, primarily a pluralistic and diverse nation comprising a wide variety of cultural groups? Does either of these views imply a consistent nationwide policy approach, a parallelism of treatment for linguistic minorities, or can either tolerate a number of different solutions adopted by provincial governments in response to the linguistic demography of their particular regions? Should individual rights ever be subordinated to the collective interests of cultural communities?

Different visions of Canada incorporate different responses to these questions. Each of these views has an institutional foothold in the structures of the Canadian state. A view of Canada as a bilingual nation, in which the rights of anglophones and francophones are guaranteed by nationwide policies prescribing parallel treatment, is most firmly ensconced at the level of the federal government—the only level with a nationwide mandate. Those who ascribe to this view (most significantly, in the past twenty years, the more "federalist" members of the Quebec francophone political elite) have naturally turned to that level of government with the tools to promote it. The influence of federal politicians from Quebec on this issue in the 1960s and 1970s, especially against the background of the rising tide of separatism in Quebec, was enormous. Under the prime ministership of Pierre Trudeau a massive bilingualism program was implemented in the federal civil service. Given the electoral significance and rising "linguistic consciousness" of Quebec, bilingual fluency became an increasingly important asset for ambitious anglophone federal politicians as well. The careers of both anglophone and francophone politicians and civil servants at the federal level have, since Quebec's "quiet revolution," been bound closely to this view of the nation.

A regional view of the linguistic complexion of the Canadian political community, and of the appropriate policy response, finds its institutional home in provincial governments, especially that of Quebec. According to this view, linguistic policies should be determined at the provincial level and may vary across provinces. This view corresponds more closely to the actual linguistic and cultural demography of the country and hence to the composition of provincial electorates. Only in Quebec and New Brunswick did either an anglophone or a francophone minority constitute more than 6 percent of the population in 1986 (See Table 7-1). Most political and bureaucratic careers in most provinces can in fact be successfully pursued in one language: Even in Quebec (except in a few predominantly anglophone municipalities), it is only at the most senior levels, and only in intergovernmental relations, that politicians and bureaucrats are effectively required to function in English.

These competing views of the political community are complicated by competing views of "individual" and "collective" rights, which are also "built in" to the structures of the state. As we shall see, Quebec legislatures and cabinets have endeavoured strongly to assert concepts of collective rights and other collective values pertaining to both the francophone majority and the anglophone minority, and they have run squarely up against a judicial system (supported by a significant body of

English Canadian public opinion) more committed to an individualistic understanding of linguistic rights.

In other policy arenas the genius of the Canadian system has been to reconcile such tensions by just such an "institutionalization"—by providing competing views with legitimacy within an institutional structure sufficiently ambiguous to allow for informal accommodations among elites. In this arena, however, this institutionalized ambivalence has been least successful in resolving tensions and managing conflict. As in other policy arenas, some of the resultant policies have been characterized by compromise and by informal understandings. But to an even greater extent than in other arenas, minority language policies have been inconsistent; indeed for decades they amounted to *repression* in both the psychological and the political sense. Various governments, for various periods of time, have been "scoff-laws"—ignoring, even in the face of court judgments, fundamental discrepancies between constitutional guarantees, statutory legislation, regulations, and actual practice.

The explanation for the failure of institutionalized ambivalence to manage conflict in this arena lies in the relationship between the structures of the state and the structure of interests. In other arenas it is possible to identify clearly parallel interests—health care providers, labour unions, industries (even resource industries)—across provinces. The existence of the parallel interests provides a basis for elite accommodation: Alliances and coalitions can be built across institutional lines. In the arena of minority language rights, however, the very parallelism of linguistic minorities is a matter of dispute. Hence the mechanisms of diffusion, convergence, or opting for regional diversity, which variously characterize the policy process in other arenas, are disputed *in principle* here.

It is, fundamentally, the unique situation of Quebec that renders this policy arena unlike any other. Francophones are a linguistic minority within Canada, at 25 percent of the population. They also constitute a *declining* proportion of the Canadian population overall, and in all areas outside Quebec (Table 7-1). Within Quebec the proportionate size of the francophone population has held steady over the postwar period, while the anglophone proportion has declined. The proportion of those with mother tongues other than English and French (the so-called "allophones") has increased marginally overall and has nearly doubled in Quebec. As is discussed below, the fear among Quebec francophones that these "allophones" will be assimilated into and hence swell the ranks of the anglophone population in Quebec has been the motivation be-

TABLE 7-1   Language Composition by Mother Tongue, by Province, 1951 and 1986

Province	English 1951	English 1986*	French 1951	French 1986*	Other 1951	Other 1986*
British Columbia	82.7%	82.1%	1.7%	1.6%	15.6%	16.3%
Alberta	69.0	82.3	3.6	2.4	27.4	15.3
Saskatchewan	62.0	81.9	4.4	2.3	33.6	15.7
Manitoba	60.3	73.4	7.0	4.9	32.7	21.8
Ontario	81.7	78.0	7.4	5.3	10.9	16.7
Quebec	13.8	10.4	82.5	82.8	3.7	6.8
New Brunswick	63.1	65.3	35.9	33.5	1.0	1.3
Novia Scotia	91.6	93.8	6.1	4.1	2.3	2.1
Prince Edward Island	90.6	94.1	8.6	4.7	0.8	1.2
Newfoundland	98.9	98.8	0.6	0.5	0.5	0.8
Northwest Territories & Yukon	41.5	65.8	3.5	2.6	55.0	31.5
Canada	59.1	62.1	29.0	25.1	11.9	12.8

Source: Commissioner of Official Languages 1987: 13; Dominion Bureau of Statistics 1951: vol. 1, table 56.

*In 1986, 2.5% of the population gave multiple responses, as allowed for the first time on the questionnaire. These responses were allocated among groups by Statistics Canada in the calculation shown above. This methodology may have slightly overstated the proportion of anglophones, relative to earlier censuses.

hind some particularly controversial policies. The assimilative power of English has been demonstrated elsewhere in Canada: The rise in the proportion of anglophones in the prairie provinces (Table 7-1) is attributable in large part to the assimilation of the descendants of earlier generations of German, Ukrainian, and other immigrants.

However, although it is a declining proportion of the national population, the francophone minority is still sizeable. More significantly, because of its regional concentration in Quebec, it has its "own" provincial government, and it cannot be electorally ignored by any party that hopes to form a majority at the federal level.

The anglophone minority in Quebec is numerically (though not proportionately) the largest linguistic minority in the country. Indeed, Quebec anglophones in 1986 constituted 40.8 percent of the "linguistic minority" population of Canada (English in Quebec, French elsewhere)—a figure that, though substantial, represents a considerable drop from historic levels. Anglophones, too, are regionally concentrated in Quebec, largely in Montreal but also in the "Eastern Townships" between the St. Lawrence River and the U.S. border and along the Ottawa River, the border with Ontario. They have developed an elaborate network of locally based anglophone governmental and paragovernmental institutions (as well, of course, as providing the electoral base for anglophone representatives in the provincial legislature, the National Assembly). Anglophones have historically been represented in the Quebec economic elite out of all proportion to their share of the population (Fournier 1976; Sales 1979), and they share the dominant culture of the North American continent.

The scope of minority language policy in Canada, then, comprehends not only the treatment of francophones by the state at the federal level and in provinces other than Quebec but also, and in a major sense, the treatment of anglophones by the state in Quebec. It also raises questions of the treatment of other linguistic minorities: Germans, Italians, and Ukrainians outnumber francophones in a number of provinces; other linguistic minorities are growing with recent waves of immigration; and aboriginal languages can be said to have claims that predate those of the "founding peoples." In this context it is hardly surprising that conflicting views have arisen regarding the place of anglophones and francophones in the political community, and the appropriate role of the state vis-à-vis linguistic minorities.

In this arena, indeed, we may be testing the limits of the ability of the ambivalent Canadian state to resolve conflict. The traditional mechanisms of ambiguity, informal understandings, and, in this case, repression, have not so far succeeded; and recent experience suggests the increasing use of adversarialism, litigation, and political confrontation.

Context

The British North America Act, 1867 (now known as the Constitution Act, 1867) registered and entrenched a compromise between the two cultural groups that then, as they had throughout the history of European settlement, formed the bulk of the Canadian population: the English (overwhelmingly Protestant) and the French (overwhelmingly Catholic). The constitutional guarantees provided for these groups reflected their concerns at the time—language guarantees related to the legislatures and the courts, denominational guarantees related to education. Section 133 requires that statutes and records of the federal and Quebec legislatures be published in English and French and permits the use of either language in legislative debates and in federal and Quebec courts. Section 93 gives the provinces jurisdiction over education, subject to the proviso that provinces could not abridge denominational education rights and privileges existing at the time of union. In the event of such an abridgement, the constitution provided for an appeal by affected parties to the federal government, which was empowered to provide a remedy by executive or legislative action.

Similar linguistic and educational guarantees were incorporated in the constitution of Manitoba (the Manitoba Act, passed by the federal Parliament and ratified by the British Parliament) at the time it entered confederation in 1870. The Manitoba provisions clearly represented another manifestation of the historic compromise: They were part of the response of the federal government to the French-Metis rebellion under Louis Riel. Provisions for bilingual governmental institutions and for denominational schools were also contained in 1875 federal legislation governing the Northwest Territories (which at that time included what were later to become the provinces of Saskatchewan and Alberta).

The demographic basis for these compromises was not long in changing, however. The history of Canada has been one of increasing regional polarization of French and English communities, beginning with the waves of immigration and the rapid settlement of the west in the late nineteenth and early twentieth centuries.

One of the first policy effects of these changes occurred in Manitoba. Only twenty years after the passage of the Manitoba Act, francophones had lost their status as the majority of the Manitoba population. In 1890 the Manitoba legislature passed the Official Language Act, which flew in the face of the Manitoba Act by declaring English to be the official language of the province. The contradiction between this legislation and the provincial constitution was effectively ignored until 1976.[1] Also in 1890 the Manitoba legislature passed the Schools Acts, replacing the existing denominational school system with a unitary, publicly funded system. The Schools Acts *were* immediately challenged in the courts (which suggests, not surprisingly, that threats to the educational system as a transmitter of culture strike closer to the political nerve than do changes in the official language of governmental institutions). The cases reached the British Privy Council, at that time the highest court of appeal for Canada, which held in two separate cases that the Manitoba legislation, though not unconstitutional, could be appealed to the federal government.

The federal cabinet, in response to an appeal regarding the Manitoba legislation, did issue a remedial order-in-council requiring the restoration of separate schools. Manitoba refused to obey this order, and an attempt by the federal government to secure the passage of remedial legislation broke down in partisan acrimony and strategizing. After a change of government at the federal level, a short-lived compromise was reached. Even this compromise fairly soon broke down, however, and in 1916 the right to instruction in French was rescinded in Manitoba and was not restored until 1970.[2] Federal-provincial negotiation had failed to resolve the contradiction between Manitoba's "bicultural" constitutional obligations and its growing multicultural reality, and successive Manitoba governments were able to tolerate this contradiction simply by repressing it.

Events in Manitoba were bell-wethers of the erosion of francophone rights elsewhere. By the turn of the twentieth century the provision of French language education had been severely curtailed in Ontario, the Maritimes, and the Northwest Territories. In 1905 the provinces of Alberta and Saskatchewan were carved out of the Northwest Territories, and their incorporating acts stated that provisions of the Northwest Territories Act would continue in effect in those provinces until repealed by the respective provincial legislature. The Canadian prime minister, Wilfred Laurier, sought also to insert denominational school rights (which had been removed from the territories legislation) into the legislation establishing Saskatchewan and Alberta, but he was forced to back down in a storm of anglophone political protest. In any event, even the guarantees of bilingual government institutions that were continued in effect as part of the Northwest Territories Act were ignored in Alberta and Saskatchewan until the 1980s.

In Ontario francophone rights per se were never strongly established in other than federal institutions. Provincial government institutions were unilingual; and in the schools, beginning in 1885 and culminating in 1913, a series of regulations progressively established the use of English and restricted the use of French as languages of instruction. The last and most restrictive of these regulatory measures, Regulation 17, was contested unsuccessfully in the courts: The Judicial Committee of the British Privy Council held that constitutional protection was afforded to classes of persons defined by *religious denomination,* not language, and that instruction in French could not be seen as a protected right or privilege for Roman Catholics. Virtually no improvement in the status of French in schools or governmental institutions in Ontario occurred in the next half-century.

Even at the federal level the official status of French in the courts and Parliament did not imply the use of French as a language of service or work in governmental institutions. The proportion of francophones in the federal civil service declined from more than 20 percent in 1918 to just over 12 percent in 1944. In the postwar years this declining trend was reversed, and by the mid-1960s francophone representation in the civil service had returned to 1918 levels—levels that still left them somewhat underrepresented.

Ironically but not surprisingly, the only linguistic minority in Canada that fared well in the first two-thirds of the twentieth century was the anglophone minority in Quebec. Indeed, Quebec in this period came close to exhibiting a form of geographically based *vertzuiling:* Local communities of francophones and anglophones each had their own systems of local government, schools, hospitals, libraries, even universities. This status quo, and indeed the entire system of provisions for linguistic minorities in Canada, was challenged, however, by the "quiet revolution" in Quebec in the 1960s, and by the rise of a new and assertive form of Quebec nationalism, as discussed in Chapters 1 and 2.

Agenda

The "quiet revolution" represented a fundamental shift in the political agenda in Quebec. The profound differences of opinion about the relationship between the French-Canadian "nation" and the Quebec "state" are discussed in Chapter 2. Each of these differing views, of course, had important implications for the treatment of linguistic minorities at federal and provincial levels. Federalists such as Pierre Trudeau held to a vision of a bilingual and bicultural federal nation, a vision that he eloquently propounded in the language of cosmopolitan pluralism (Reading 7-1). Quebec nationalists such as René Lévesque, however, saw French Canadians as forming a "nation" whose "national state" was Quebec. The fact that about one-sixth of the francophone "nation" resided outside Quebec in no way diminished the importance of a strong Quebec state to the survival of that nation. Priority was accordingly to be placed on strengthening the Quebec state, not on securing the rights of francophone minorities in other provinces (Reading 7-2).

The implication of this *indépendantiste* position in the arena of language policy, indeed, was essentially an abandonment of concern for "linguistic minorities"—whether francophones outside Quebec or anglophones in Quebec—and a rejection of bilingualism as a policy option. Anglophones in Quebec were seen, at least amongst the most radical separatists, as "colonizers" from whom the francophone majority needed protection, not vice versa (Reading 7-3); and bilingualism, for

French Canadians, was seen to constitute "a proof of their enslavement" rather than an indication of superior competence (Chaput 1964: 52).

The formulation of the policy agenda with regard to language policy was fraught with tensions between collectivist and individualistic values, between concerns for collective and individual "rights." Though the key protagonists recognized a symbiosis of individual and community, they interpreted that symbiosis in fundamentally different ways. For Trudeau, the vitality of the community depended upon improving the life chances of individuals (see, e.g., Trudeau 1968: 399). For Lévesque, individual development depended on the community: "the nation is almost as vital to [the individual's] growth and balance as the family" (Lévesque 1964: 134).

As mobilization occurred around these various positions, they came to be associated with particular groups. The federal Liberal party, whose leadership Trudeau assumed in 1968, became the main vehicle for the promotion of the "federal bilingual" option in Quebec and across Canada. In Quebec itself the various gradients of opinion found different organizational homes. In the 1960s separatism found violent expression through the Front de libération du Québec and took more legitimate form in a variety of movements and nascent political parties culminating in the establishment of the Parti québécois in 1968. For them, the precariousness of French in North America and the repressive history of anglophone domination required the use of the state to establish an officially unilingual Quebec.

The "established" political parties in Quebec in the 1960s positioned themselves between federalist and *indépendantiste* positions, and somewhat uncomfortably embraced both special status for Quebec and constitutional parallelism for linguistic minorities across Canada. The Liberal Party of Quebec proposed constitutional changes that would recognize Quebec as a "distinctive society" and accord it "special status," but that would also recognize the "community rights of Canadian majorities and minorities." Indeed, for the Quebec Liberal Party, "one advantage of maintaining a federal link would be to make it easier to safeguard and increase basic guarantees regarding French as the language of instruction in schools and of communication in public services throughout Canada" (Quebec Liberal Federation 1968: 375). The Union nationale's position was somewhat more ambiguous. On the one hand, that party emphasized the "binational" character of Canada and the need for parallel treatment and opportunities for linguistic majorities and minorities across Canada

(Reading 7-4). On the other hand, UN leader (and Quebec premier from 1966 to 1968) Daniel Johnson gave a number of indications of separatist leanings, including the orchestrating of the 1968 visit of French president Charles de Gaulle during which de Gaulle fanned separatist sentiments and aroused anglophone anger in his "vive le Québec libre" address.

The fledgling Parti québécois quite clearly saw biculturalism as a "trap" and proposals for the protection of francophone minorities outside Quebec as a "utopian tortoise trudging along after the hare of galloping assimilation" (Lévesque 1968: 84). It vehemently denied the parallelism of linguistic minorities, maintaining that the anglophone minority of Quebec came as "conquerors," while in the rest of Canada "French-speaking minorities arrived poor and timid and have been treated like any other group of foreign immigrants" (ibid.: 85–86). For the PQ, linguistic equality implied more than the rights of individual francophones, and more, indeed, than even the collective rights of the French-Canadian nation as defended by the Liberals and the UN. It implied "political equality," "the essential emancipation of Quebec," although the form that that emancipation might take had not been delineated.

Electoral support for the various provincial parties was consistent with their policy positions: The Liberals received the overwhelming share of nonfrancophone support as well as drawing support from francophones, particularly in managerial ranks, while the PQ drew its support almost entirely from francophones, particularly from those in professional and public sector occupations (Coleman 1983: 22).

Developments in Quebec and at the federal level spurred the mobilization of francophone pressure groups in other provinces. Politically oriented francophone associations had existed in British Columbia, Alberta, Saskatchewan, Ontario, and Prince Edward Island prior to the "quiet revolution" in Quebec, but in the 1960s and 1970s similar groups emerged in Manitoba, Nova Scotia, New Brunswick, Newfoundland, the Yukon, and the Northwest Territories. In 1975 a federal organization, La Fédération des francophones hors Québec (FFHQ), was established as an umbrella organization to foster, encourage, and coordinate provincial groups and to act as a central pressure group vis-à-vis the federal and the Quebec governments (Conseil de la Vie Français en Amérique 1988: 48).[3] The FFHQ receives much of its funding from the federal government.

Anglophone interests both inside and outside Quebec also began to mobilize. Alliance Quebec, a group that has become the major vehicle for the expression of the interests of the anglophone minority in Quebec, was formed in 1981 around the nucleus of an earlier association established in the 1970s. The relationship of Alliance Quebec to francophone associations in other provinces and to the umbrella FFHQ has been somewhat problematic. Alliance Quebec has been a strong supporter of linguistic minority rights across Canada, through lobbying, judicial interventions, and public statements. But as Lise Bissonette reports, "The move was so sudden—Quebec's anglophones had no history of sensitivity to these linguistic minorities before 1976—that it created more suspicion than gratitude, even among leaders of the Canadian francophonie" (Bissonette 1989: F2).

Alliance Quebec could not, of course, draw parallels between the *condition* of Quebec anglophones and that of francophone minorities in other provinces: It acknowledged the anglophones' more privileged position. What it sought to establish, in opposition to legal restrictions on the use of English in Quebec, was a parallelism of minority language *rights*. In this sense it was consistent with discourse in Quebec on these issues throughout the 1970s and 1980s—Quebec's language legislation was, after all, called a *charter*. But as the agenda was cast more and more in terms of rights, the traditional Canadian mechanisms of conflict resolution became less capable of dealing with it. The political system, as we discuss in the next section, strained to deal with issues of minority language through informal accommodation but was increasingly driven into the channels of constitutionalism and litigation.

Process

In the latter third of the nineteenth century and the early years of the twentieth, the policy process in the arena of language rights was, as we have seen, characterized by constitution making, legislative action, and litigation. There followed, however, a remarkable period of dormancy. Governments in the prairie provinces simply ignored constitutional requirements regarding the official status of French as well as English. At the federal level a few significant symbolic changes were made in this period, such as the use of both languages on postage stamps and currency; and a few changes to civil service legislation and regulations were made regarding the language of competitive examinations. Nonetheless, English remained the language of everyday work and service in the federal bureaucracy (Royal Commission on Bilingualism and Biculturalism 1967, vol. III, part 2). In Quebec virtually no legislative action was taken on language in the first century after confederation.[4] As one historian has put it, "the French Canadian majority in Quebec opted for linguistic segregation rather than linguistic confrontation. French Canadians were a majority in the province but in a sense they were still behaving as a beleaguered minority, hoping to be left alone, hoping only to survive" (Neatby 1979: 26).

With the coming of the 1960s, however, the language policy arena sprang to life. The first flurry of activity was at the federal level, with the appointment of the Royal Commission on Bilingualism and Biculturalism in 1963. The mandate of the commission subordinated multiculturalism to biculturalism: It was "to recommend what steps should be taken to develop the Canadian Confederation on the basis of an equal partnership between the two founding races, taking into account the contribution made by other ethnic groups to the cultural enrichment of Canada and the measures that should be taken to safeguard that contribution" (Royal Commission on Bilingualism and Biculturalism 1967, vol. I: 173). Through a process of conducting and commissioning extensive social scientific research, receiving briefs, and holding public hearings, the commission developed important baseline information, largely concerning the anglophone and francophone communities and the use of English and French in the public and the private sector in Canada but also concerning other linguistic and cultural groups. In the process it spurred the political mobilization of a number of linguistic minorities. Some of these groups, moreover, were aided by the Citizenship branch of the federal Department of the Secretary of State in the preparation of briefs for the commission (Pal 1990: 174).

The use of royal commissions to gather information, formulate issues, and build consensus is, as we have seen in other arenas such as health care and economic policy, a conventional part of the policy process in Canada. Through a combination of empirical research, public airing of the views and perspectives of various interests, and informal consultation, they have in many cases laid the groundwork for a process that subsequently edges toward compromise. And, indeed, legislative and administrative change at both federal and provincial levels in the late 1960s and early 1970s suggested this sort of accommodation.

In 1969 the federal Parliament enacted the Official Languages Act, which incorporated a number of the Bilingualism and Biculturalism Commission's recommendations. It declared English and French to be the "official" languages of Canada "for all purposes of the Parliament and

Government of Canada"—the first time that the term "official language" had been used in federal legislation. It essentially elaborated upon and extended the guarantees of section 133 of the British North America Act, 1867—for example, it required the use of English and French in subordinate as well as statutory legislative instruments. The act also provided for the designation of "federal bilingual districts," of which the National Capital Region around Ottawa was to be the prototype. Such a regime represented a compromise between national consistency and regional diversity. Within these districts,⁵ and in other areas where there was "significant demand," federal government services were to be provided in both official languages. Finally, the act established the office of the commissioner of official languages (a language monitor and ombudsman).

The federal government also embarked, in the early 1970s, upon a massive program of bilingualism in the federal public service, the purposes of which were to redress the underrepresentation of francophones, especially at the senior levels, and to establish French as a language not only of service (as provided in the Official Languages Act) but of work. The ability to speak both official languages was defined as an element of "merit" for hiring and promotion (Adie and Thomas 1987: 72–74). Certain positions (including large numbers of managerial and executive positions) were designated as requiring bilingual competence, and extensive language training programs for unilingual public servants were introduced. Two successive Bilingual Districts Advisory Boards attempted to designate bilingual districts for the purposes of the act. But neither set of recommendations survived the controversy they set off in the designated regions (within as well as outside Quebec), and the districts were never created (McRoberts 1989).

Change was also occurring in this period at the provincial level. In 1969 New Brunswick adopted its own Official Languages of New Brunswick Act containing provisions, similar to those in the federal Official Languages Act, regarding the official status and the use of English and French in provincial government institutions, and also providing minority language education guarantees.⁶ The implementation of these provisions has, however, been a slow and periodically contentious process. Ontario took an even more incremental route to legislative and administrative change, amending existing legislation to provide for francophone education in 1968⁷ and for the use of French in designated courts in 1978 (Tetley 1982: 187–90). It refused throughout the 1960s and 1970s, however, to grant "official" status to French.

These conventional processes, however, failed to contain the conflict. The issue had already been formulated as entailing "rights," and as such it moved quickly into the policy channels of constitutional amendment and litigation. At the centre of these developments were two interrelated processes: one involving the passage and subsequent legal challenging of the Charter of the French Language (the so-called bill 101) in Quebec, the other leading to the constitutional entrenchment of language rights in the Canadian Charter of Rights and Freedoms.

The late 1960s marked the reemergence of language rights as a subject of legislation in Quebec after a century of legislative quiescence. The first legislative measures had to do with the language of education and were catalyzed by a dispute between a group of Italian parents and a Montreal-area school board over the replacement of bilingual classes with unilingual French classes. The Union nationale government responded with legislation that would guarantee parents the freedom to choose the language of instruction of their children, while requiring all students to have a working knowledge of French. After one abortive attempt and much vehement and occasionally violent controversy, the legislation was adopted in 1969.

In 1970 the legislative landscape in Quebec was fundamentally altered with the election of the separatist Parti québécois, founded in 1968, as the official opposition to a Liberal government under Robert Bourassa. As noted in Chapter 2, both parties had to be sensitive to the growing if ambivalent current of Quebec nationalism, but they took somewhat different approaches to language issues. The Bourassa government adopted a principle of bilingualism with French preeminence. In 1974 it brought in its major omnibus language legislation, the Official Language Act (note the singular)—more commonly referred to as "bill 22." Its preamble declared French to be the "official language" of Quebec, and its provisions related to the language of instruction and to the use of language in public institutions and in the private sector.

With regard to the language of instruction, bill 22's provisions were directed primarily at stemming the flow of the children of "allophone" immigrants to Quebec (those whose mother tongue was neither English nor French) into English classes, while leaving the educational rights of native English speakers largely intact. The provisions for the use of language in public institutions also allowed the network of anglophone institutions of local government to survive. The use of French was required for official documents and as the language of internal communication and service to the public, but exceptions were made for local government bodies in municipalities with specified proportions of anglophone residents, which were permitted to use English as well as French.

As for the private sector, bill 22 essentially required firms to use French in firm names and advertising, and in communication with their workers, while permitting the accompanying use of English or other languages. In order to be eligible for government subsidies or contracts, firms were required to adopt "francization" programs to increase the use of French in the workplace and the presence of francophones in management. The interpretation and implementation of these provisions, like a number of others in the act, left considerable discretion in the hands of regulatory bodies, notably, the Régie de la Langue Français and the Office de la Langue Français.

Bill 22 proved, in retrospect, to be an unsuccessful attempt at reaching a political compromise in the face of the burgeoning "linguistic consciousness" of Quebec francophones, the presence of an established and economically powerful anglophone minority, and growing allophone immigration into Quebec. Quebec nationalists saw it as conceding much too much to the anglophone minority, and the PQ seized upon the language issue in the period leading up to the 1976 election. Anglophone groups, for their part, saw bill 22 as infringing the "historic rights" of anglophones in Quebec, and the Protestant School Board of Greater Montreal immediately brought a legal challenge to its educational provisions.

The response of the Quebec Superior Court to this challenge was chastening for the anglophone community, in that it found no constitutional basis for linguistic educational rights. Only the educational rights of *denominational*, not linguistic groups, the court held, are protected by section 93 of the British North America Act, and language is not a "right or privilege" of a denominational group. With what may be read as more than a touch of irony, the Quebec Superior Court drew attention to the refusal of past court decisions to grant relief to francophone minorities in other provinces on the basis of section 93 (Reading 7-5). The Protestant School Board appealed this decision, but by the time the Quebec Court of Appeal was to hear the case, it had been overtaken by events. The PQ had won the provincial election of 1976 and had replaced bill 22 with its own language legislation, the Charter of the French Language (colloquially known by *its* initial position on the order paper, as "bill 101").

The Charter of the French Language was "the flagship of the cultural policy of the Parti québécois" (Coleman 1981: 459). Contrary to the "bilingualism with French priority" principle of bill 22, bill 101 was marked by an emphasis on French unilingualism. French was again designated as the "official language" of Quebec. Public institutions were to use French in internal and external communications, and provisions for the use of "other languages" was considerably more restricted. English-language instruction was now guaranteed only to children whose parents or siblings had received English-language instruction in Quebec (under the so-called Quebec clause governing access to minority language education) or who fell under a number of grandfathering provisions.

As for the private sector, bill 101 maintained, tightened, and extended the provisions of bill 22. Francization programs were required for *all* firms with fifty or more employees. Commercial signs were to be in French *only,* except in the cases of very small firms or firms specializing in "ethnic" products. Firm names were to be in French only; a version in "another language" was permitted for use outside Quebec. As in the case of bill 22, considerable discretion in interpreting, elaborating, and implementing these provisions was left to regulatory agencies. As severe as these various provisions might appear in comparison with bill 22, they are considerably milder than those contained in bill 1, the PQ government's first proposed language legislation, which was withdrawn after extensive and heated legislative hearings.[8]

Bill 22 and bill 101 reflect different conceptions within Quebec of the nature of the Quebec political community, and the place of francophones and anglophones therein. The Liberals still saw anglophones and francophones within Quebec as subsets of the two "founding races" of Canada. The PQ, on the other hand, saw Quebec as "a single, predominantly French society" (Coleman 1981: 466) in which Quebec anglophones were to be treated as one linguistic minority among others in "an embryonic nation-state" (ibid.: 462).[9]

Not surprisingly, a number of the provisions of bill 101 were immediately challenged by anglophone groups in the courts. Among the first of the provisions to be challenged were those establishing French as the language of the courts and the legislature, which stood in direct contrast to section 133 of the British North America Act establishing French and English as the language of the courts and legislature in Quebec.

The judicial process again emphasized the *constitutional parallelism* of anglophone and francophone minorities. As Quebec anglophones were challenging the official unilingualism of bill 101, Manitoba francophones were at last roused to challenge the official unilingualism of the eighty-six-year-old Official Language Act of Manitoba, as contrary to Manitoba's constitution. Both the Quebec and the Manitoba cases reached the Supreme Court of Canada at about the same time, and the Court chose to address them in simultaneous judgements issued on December 13, 1979. Both the Manitoba Official Language Act and the provisions of bill 101 relating to the courts and legislatures were struck down as unconstitutional.

The contrast between the relative speed with which the anglophone community of Quebec and the francophone community of Manitoba were able to obtain court judgements against unconstitutional language legislation (three years and eighty-nine years, respectively) was not ignored.[10] Some attributed the discrepancy to the greater mobilization, wealth, and self-confidence of the anglophone minority (Forsey 1980: 22); others, perhaps satirically, attributed it to the accelerating pace of history (Commissioner of Official Languages 1984: 18). In neither case, however, did the Court's judgement mark the end of conflict. In Manitoba, as discussed below, the implications of the decision were highly contentious. And in Quebec challenges to other provisions of bill 101 continued to flow through the courts.

In the meantime the ground on which those challenges could be brought was changing fundamentally. The events in Quebec were drawing a response from the rest of Canada, in the form of a process of constitutional change. That process is discussed in Chapter 2; this chapter deals only with the aspects relating to language rights. The question of extending the limited language rights contained in the Constitution Act, 1867, was of key importance throughout this process, given Prime Minister Trudeau's strong personal commitment to the issue, the perceived need on the part of federal and some provincial politicians to respond to the "French fact" in the face of Quebec separatism, and, of course, the language policies of the Quebec government in the 1970s.

As part of the agenda of constitutional reform, the issue of entrenching language rights was handled primarily through the structures and processes of executive federalism. And therein lies an irony. To the extent that language rights were ultimately entrenched, language policy would be developed under the shadow of judicial challenge, and traditional processes of negotiation and informal understanding would be accordingly constrained. The first ministers, then, in this extremely sensitive area, were negotiating over the issue of constraining the subsequent ability of their governments to negotiate with each other and with affected interests. Most provincial governments indeed had, particularly in the 1960s and 1970s, moved incrementally and more or less informally to improve their provision of education in French. Not surprisingly, of the contentious issues entailed in the formulation and adoption of the Charter of Rights and Freedoms, the issue of minority language rights was one of the thorniest.

Throughout the conferences and committee discussions of the 1970s and early 1980s, tensions between concepts of biculturalism and multiculturalism, between national and regional responses to issues of minority language, and between individual and collective conceptions of rights were painfully apparent. There are a number of ways in which these concepts might be balanced, each with a "tilt" in one direction or another. Virtually all options were canvassed at one time or another. Various proposals differed as to the *scope* of rights to be given constitutional protection—the range of governmental institutions involved, the inclusion of rights to minority language education, and the like—and the extent to which these rights were to be secured at the provincial as well as federal level. Regarding the entrenchment of rights at the provincial level, there were a number of options: entrenched provisions binding in all provinces; or provisions for provinces to "opt out" of or "opt in" to a national rights regime. Consideration was also given to the incorporation of a *principle* of linguistic duality or of multiculturalism, or both, without the explicit granting of rights.

Throughout these discussions, the idea of using a numerical criterion (a minority population of at least 10 percent or the more ambiguous "where numbers warrant") to trigger the operation of a minority language rights regime at the provincial level gained support. As in the case of the federal "bilingual districts," this principle promised a compromise between constitutional parallelism and regional diversity. The criterion would be the same across provinces; the rights regimes in place would vary. This principle found broad support at premiers' conferences in 1977 and 1978, and in fact by 1980 various explicit or implicit numerical "triggers" for the provision of minority language education had been legislated in Alberta, Saskatchewan, Manitoba, Ontario, and New Brunswick (Magnet 1982: 204–5).

The issue of the constitutional *entrenchment* of a "where numbers warrant" provision, however, remained in dispute. Indeed, the constitutional entrenchment of *any* minority language rights provisions binding upon provincial governments was strongly resisted by a number of provinces. These objections were made clear in provincial responses to the federal government's proposals for a constitutionally entrenched Charter of Rights and Freedoms, presented as draft legislation (bill C-60) in the House of Commons in 1978. Bill C-60 set out a model whereby provinces might opt in to a national rights regime. But in this respect, the draft legislation did not treat all provinces equally. It specifically provided for rights to extend to New Brunswick and Ontario, when those provinces chose to opt in; no other provinces were identified by name. The rationale for this approach was that these provinces, in addition to Quebec, had the largest linguistic minorities. But this was also an attempt to put pressure on Ontario to provide a constitutional basis for linguistic rights (most of the rights at issue were already provided in New Brunswick's Official Languages Act).

Ontario, however, while generally supporting the concept of an entrenched Charter of Rights, drew the line at the entrenching of an official status for French in Ontario. While incrementally extending governmental services in French in Ontario, the government feared the electoral reaction to the symbolic effect of declaring Ontario "officially" bilingual. The reaction of other provinces to bill C-60 varied, but most argued for the entrenchment of language rights only at the federal level and insisted that each province have the discretion to determine its own language rights regime (Romanow, Whyte, and Leeson 1984: 43–44). Indeed, Quebec and Manitoba (for different reasons)[11] opposed the principle of entrenchment at any level.

Support for provincial discretion was not limited to provincial governments. In 1979 the Task Force on National Unity, which had been established by the federal Liberal government and cochaired by a prominent federal Liberal from Quebec and a former Ontario Conservative premier, strongly endorsed a position of respect for provincial diversity on language issues, including the policies of the PQ government of Quebec. This unequivocal "provincialism" was surprising—given the genesis and composition of the task force, one might have expected it to produce a more ambiguously phrased document setting forth a compromise—but it is a measure of the strength of the provincialist position in the late 1970s. Nonetheless, the task force report was strongly out of step with the views of the federal Liberal government under Trudeau, which effectively ignored it.[12]

Another fundamental issue in the constitutional discussions over language related to individual as opposed to collective conceptions of rights. Were language rights (to the extent that they were to be recognized at all) to inhere in individuals *as individuals* or *as members of official language minorities*? In the case of education rights, were *all* parents to have freedom of choice as to the language of education of their children, or were only members of official language minorities (somehow defined) to have the right to have their children educated in the minority language? The concrete issue revolved around whether anglophones outside Quebec should have the right to opt for a French education, or francophones (or allophones) in Quebec to opt for an English education.

The principle of parental freedom of choice had underlain Quebec's first language legislation in 1969 and was supported at the federal level by a special Senate-House of Commons committee in 1972. But by the late 1970s this principle had largely been lost. In response to Quebec's bill 101, debate turned rather upon the definition of the rights-bearing group. Bill 101 restricted the right of access to anglophone education to a narrowly defined group: the children and siblings of those educated in English in Quebec. Proposals from the federal government and from other provinces defined minority language groups more broadly, in terms of "mother tongue" or "language primarily spoken."

In the result, the constitutional changes finally agreed to by the first ministers (except the premier of Quebec) in 1981 represented compromises on the parallelism-diversity issue and on the definition of rights-bearing groups. Only one province agreed to "opt in" to an official languages regime—New Brunswick agreed to give constitutional status to provisions essentially similar to its own Official Languages Act. Hence sections 16 to 22 of the Canadian Charter of Rights and Freedoms (Reading 7-5) declare English and French to be the "official languages" of Canada and New Brunswick, and set out a series of guarantees for the use of English and French in institutions of the federal government and the government of New Brunswick.[13]

As for minority language education rights, the Canadian charter responded directly to the contested requirements of Quebec's bill 101. Section 23 of the charter (Reading 7-5) guaranteed access to education in the official minority languages to two overlapping but not identical categories of people: the children of citizens whose mother tongue is that of the francophone or anglophone minority in a province; and the children or siblings of those educated in French or English (as the case may be) *in Canada*. These guarantees included access not just to education but to educational facilities in the minority language, but all were made subject to a "sufficient numbers" proviso. Quebec was exempted from the requirement to provide access to anglophone education on the basis of "mother tongue" until it should choose to opt in to this requirement. But the so-called Canada clause guaranteeing access on the basis of education anywhere in Canada stood in direct conflict with bill 101's "Quebec clause" guaranteeing access on the basis of education *in Quebec*.

Most notably, the "notwithstanding" clause, the clause that allows provincial governments to expressly override certain provisions of the charter for five-year renewable periods (see Chapter 2), does *not* extend to language rights guarantees. Prime Minister Trudeau, who was strongly opposed to the insertion of an override clause at all, was on this issue adamant. Provinces who wished in the future to escape the language rights provisions of the charter would have legal recourse only to section 1 of the charter, which allows the rights declared therein to be subject to "such reasonable limits prescribed by law as can be demonstrably justified in a free and democratic society."

In the wake of the constitutional changes in 1982, then, provincial diversity remained the norm as regards the use of English and French in governmental institutions. A limited degree of constitutional parallelism was brought to the arena of minority language education. But, even apart from the outright conflict between the provisions of the Canadian charter and bill 101, the very phrasing of the constitutional provisions that made agreement possible between the federal government and nine of the provinces contained the seeds of future conflict. What numbers are "sufficient to warrant" the public provision of minority language education or facilities? What is included in the term "facilities"—laboratories, gymnasiums, libraries equivalent to those in the majority language system? What do these rights imply for minority language group participation in or control of school boards? *How much* education must a parent or sibling have had in the minority language to qualify a child for minority language instruction? All of these issues were to be litigated, in a process increasingly dominated by adversarialism. Indeed, this adversarialism is becoming even more institutionalized: The federal government allocated, as of 1988, about $300,000 annually under its Court Challenges program to fund individuals and groups litigating constitutional language rights.

The charter, that is, not only contained the seeds of future conflict over issues of minority language rights but also established the terrain on which that conflict would be waged—that is, in the arena of the courts. Linguistic education "rights" (however ambiguously defined) had for the first time been given constitutional protection. What lay ahead was unfamiliar territory, in which the scope for conventional styles of negotiation and compromise were reduced.

Consequences

The consequences of the legislative, constitutional, and judicial events discussed in the preceding sections were of two kinds: one relating to the life chances of members of linguistic minorities and to changes in "demo-linguistics"; the other relating to levels of political conflict. In neither of these senses could Canadian language policies be considered an unalloyed success. Let us consider first the least successful of these sets of consequences: the continuation of conflict over language.

Throughout the 1980s Canadian governments have sought to escape the either-or, win-lose dynamics implied by charters of rights and court judgements. They attempted for example to have negotiated settlements ratified by the courts, to modify the impact of legislative provisions through discretionary enforcement, to extend services to linguistic minorities incrementally while avoiding the language of "rights," or to escape rights regimes by repealing or overriding legislative or constitutional provisions. But the very fact that the discourse in this arena is dominated by claims of "rights" makes these conventional conflict-resolution strategies now highly contentious in themselves.

One notable example of an attempt to use conventional "elite accommodation" mechanisms to resolve conflict in the wake of a judicial decision occurred in Manitoba. In 1979, as noted earlier, the Supreme Court of Canada upheld a lower court decision that Manitoba's 1890 Official Languages Act was unconstitutional. The ruling itself was a narrow one, relating only to the right to use French in the courts, but its implication was that all laws passed in English only since 1890 (in accordance with the Official Languages Act) were invalid. Indeed, another case challenging two Manitoba statutes on this ground was launched in 1980 by one Roger Bilodeau, supported by the Société Franco-Manitobaine. As the case approached the Supreme Court level, the Manitoba government sought to negotiate a compromise settlement, but its efforts foundered in highly acrimonious partisan conflict between the governing New Democratic Party and the opposition Conservatives. Draft legislation providing for the translation of significant statutes and guaranteeing French language services from a range of provincial government agencies "where numbers warrant" was introduced in the provincial legislature in 1983. This legislation was endorsed (in a very unusual development) by a resolution of the federal House of Commons, supported by all parties, including the federal Conservatives. The Manitoba legislation was ultimately withdrawn and the legislature prorogued in 1984, however, after walkouts and filibusters by the opposition Conservatives had paralysed the legislative process. The federal government then referred to the Supreme Court the question of the constitutionality of *all* laws passed in English only in Manitoba, and asked that the decision be rendered at the same time as the decision in the Bilodeau case.

The Supreme Court rendered its decision in June 1985, declaring all Manitoba laws passed in English only to be invalid. "In the interests of public order and the rule of law," however, the Court provided that such laws would be deemed to have full force and effect until a deadline to be negotiated between the federal and Manitoba attorneys general for their translation. In November 1985 the Supreme Court ratified a settlement between all parties setting translation deadlines. The settlement did not deal with the provision of French language services, but the NDP government proceeded with a policy of the gradual expansion of such services, a policy that was continued after the Conservatives assumed power in 1988.

Meanwhile, somewhat similar developments were occurring in the neighbouring provinces of Saskatchewan and Alberta. When these two provinces were carved out of federally administered territories in 1905, their constitutions carried over the guarantees of bilingual governmental institutions in the federal legislation governing the territories. These guarantees were subsequently ignored. Court challenges to legislation passed in English only were launched in Saskatchewan and Alberta in the early 1980s, on the grounds that such legislation had been passed in contravention of these guarantees. In 1988 the Supreme Court ruled that the guarantees continued in effect but (unlike the Manitoba case) could be repealed by ordinary legislation. Both provinces proceeded to repeal the guarantees. The Saskatchewan government agreed to a language policy "package," negotiated with the federal government and entailing federal financial assistance, to translate selected statutes into French, to aid francophone schools, and to establish a regional language institute to train provincial public servants from Manitoba, Saskatchewan, and Alberta in French and nineteen other minority languages. Saskatchewan also announced a policy of gradual extension of provincial government services in French. Alberta did not agree to translate legislation but passed legislation allowing for some use of French in its legislature and courts.

The Manitoba, Saskatchewan, and Alberta cases just discussed relate to pre-Charter linguistic rights, but the bulk of judicial activity in this arena since 1982 has been taken up with litigation under the Canadian Charter of Rights and Freedoms. The first major conflict in this respect concerned, not surprisingly, the collision of the minority language education rights guarantees in section 23 of the Canadian charter with the provisions of Quebec's bill 101.

In 1982 the educational provisions of bill 101 (the "Quebec clause") were challenged under section 23 of the Canadian charter (the "Canada clause"). The Quebec government attempted to make the ingenious argument that its legislation did not *deny* rights to *individuals,* but rather *limited* the *collective* rights granted to linguistic groups by section 23. These limits, it argued under section 1 of the Canadian charter, were "reasonable" given the threat to the survival of the French language in North America.

The court's reaction to this argument was one of eloquent outrage. It declared itself "amazed, to use a euphemism, to hear this argument from a government which prides itself in maintaining in America the flame of French civilization with its promotion of spiritual values and its traditional respect for liberty," and dismissed Quebec's argument as being "based on a totalitarian conception of society to which the court does not subscribe." "The alleged restriction of a collective right," the court continued, "which would deprive the one hundredth member of [a] group of the rights guaranteed by the Charter constitutes, for this one hundredth member, a real denial of his rights. He cannot simply be counted as an accidental loss in a collective operation: our concept of human beings does not accommodate such a theory." [14]

The Quebec Superior Court thus struck down the educational provisions of bill 101—a decision that was ultimately upheld by the Supreme Court of Canada in 1984. The impact of these decisions was more symbolic than tangible, however. The Quebec government had in fact tolerated a considerable discrepancy between bill 101's provisions and actual practice: At the time of the Supreme Court decision it was estimated that about seven hundred children were attending English schools on "questionable" grounds (Fraser 1984: 2).

Nonetheless, the issue of minority language education rights in Quebec remained before the courts, as the Quebec government attempted to define by regulation the *amount* of English education in Canada anglophones must have had in order for their children to qualify for anglophone education in Quebec, and as each of these attempts was challenged in the courts. Furthermore, the issue of replacing the existing denominational school boards with boards established on a linguistic basis was also the subject of legislation and court challenges.

Although the challenges to bill 101 were the most visible, they were certainly not the only challenges brought under section 23. Cases in virtually all provinces have flowed through the courts under the "sufficient numbers" provisions of section 23. (The courts appear to be taking the position that any particular numerical trigger is too arbitrary, and that case-by-case judgements must be made; see Commissioner of Official Languages 1984: 16; 1985: 14.) Cases have also been brought alleging that francophone facilities are inadequate, and that the right to francophone facilities also implies the right to francophone school boards or francophone school districts. In a highly significant political move the Quebec government intervened before the Supreme Court of Canada in 1989 in a case brought by a group of francophone parents in Alberta who sought the establishment of a francophone school board. Quebec argued that section 23 implied no such right. If it was to be forced to accept parallelism under the charter, the Quebec government sought at least to limit the interpretation of those parallel rights. This position was perceived by both anglophones and francophones outside Quebec as further evidence of the willingness of the Quebec government to sacrifice the interests of francophone minorities outside Quebec in order to preserve its own discretion in dealing with Quebec anglophones. (The court ruling on this case in March 1990 held that official language minorities had the right to manage and control their own schools, although this could be accomplished through specific representation on school boards and did not necessarily require the establishment of independent francophone boards.)

Quebec anglophones, of course, contested not only the educational provisions of bill 101 but also other provisions deemed vulnerable under the charter. Chief among these were the highly contentious "signs" provisions: the requirements that, with few exceptions, commercial signs could be posted in French only. These provisions had twice been exempted from the reach of the charter provisions protecting "fundamental freedoms" (freedom of religion, expression, assembly, and association) and legal and equality rights—first, by Quebec's "blanket" invocation of the notwithstanding clause of the charter in June 1982 (Chapter 2), and again by a routine invocation of the notwithstanding clause when bill 101 was amended in 1984. The "blanket" invocation lapsed in June 1987 and was not renewed by the Liberal government then in power in Quebec, but the 1984 invocation was not due to expire until February 1989.

One of the planks in the Liberal election platform in the 1985 provincial election was a promise to amend bill 101 to allow for bilingual signs. But on assuming office Bourassa announced that in the interests of "social peace" he would await the Supreme Court's decision before making any change. In the meantime, as under the PQ, sporadic enforcement of the contested provisions continued.

In December 1988 the Supreme Court's decision was handed down. It held that bill 101's signs provisions infringed the guarantees of freedom of expression in the Canadian charter, but that they had been shielded from the charter by the use of the notwithstanding clause.[15] Even more important in political terms, however, the Court held that these provisions also infringed Quebec's own Charter of Human Rights.

In response to the Supreme Court decision, the Quebec government moved swiftly to amend the legislation. The majority Liberal government enacted, over the opposition of the PQ, what it presented as a "compromise" amendment to bill 101: only French could be used on signs outside commercial establishments, but in specified cases (notably firms with fewer than fifty employees) other languages could be used on interior signs as long as French was markedly predominant. Regulations amplifying these provisions were to be made by the provincial cabinet (not, as previously, by the Office de la Langue Français). And to preclude further court challenges, the government expressly exempted the legislation (bill 178) from both the Canadian and the Quebec charters.

In the legislative debate on the amending legislation Premier Bourassa made his arguments in terms of the tension between individual and collective rights: "In the end, when it was necessary to arbitrate between individual rights and collective rights, I arbitrated in favour of collective rights, by agreeing to invoke the notwithstanding clause. . . . I am the only head of government in North America who had the moral justification to follow this course. . . . Who can better, and who has more of a duty to defend, protect, and promote the French culture than the Premier of Quebec?" (National Assembly of Quebec, *Debates*, December 20, 1988: 4425; author's translation).

The so-called inside-outside solution and the Quebec government's use of the notwithstanding clause on this highly symbolic issue was extremely contentious.[16] Three of the four anglophone cabinet ministers in Bourassa's government resigned their cabinet positions in protest. Both francophones and anglophones held rallies in protest: francophones protesting any change to bill 101, anglophones protesting the overriding of their court-sanctioned "rights." The headquarters of Alliance Quebec were destroyed by arson. Alliance Quebec itself used the harshest rhetoric in its history to criticize the legislation. It found itself without allies among other linguistic minority groups, however: The FFHQ supported the legislation, seeing Quebec as the bastion for the protection of French in North America (Quebec's intervention in the Alberta school board case had not yet occurred to chill the relationship between the FFHQ and the Quebec government). Representatives of allophone groups in Quebec maintained a careful neutrality.

Political leaders in the rest of Canada expressed varying degrees of outrage at the overriding of anglophone "rights." The federal Conservative caucus, with its large component of Quebec francophones, was riven by dispute. Prime Minister Mulroney indicated that he found the use of the notwithstanding clause "regrettable" but softened his criticism with a statement that Quebec "has no lessons to learn from anyone" in its treatment of its linguistic minority (Parliament of Canada, *Debates*, December 19, 1988: 296). The notwithstanding clause itself came under severe criticism from the premier of Ontario and later from the prime minister—criticism all the more remarkable because it was aimed at a fundamental feature of the 1982 constitutional compromise.

Most significantly, anglophone reaction to Quebec's bill 178 marked the beginning of the end for the set of constitutional amendments known as the Meech Lake Accord. Premier Filmon of Manitoba withdrew the accord from consideration by the Manitoba legislature, arguing that Bourassa's use of the notwithstanding clause presaged further suppression of rights once the distinct-society clause proposed in the Meech Lake Accord entered the constitution (Chapter 2). In fact, the Supreme Court judgement suggested, if anything, that the courts would not likely support such a resort to the distinct-society clause, at least with regard to language rights.[17] The political effect of Filmon's move, however, was to contribute to the polarization of opinion. Anglophone resentment of Bourassa's decision became implicated in the Meech Lake process. And in Quebec francophones were outraged that an English Canadian politician who five years earlier had vehemently opposed the redressing of the Manitoba government's historical neglect of its constitutional obligations to francophones should now presume to "punish" Quebec for its treatment of its linguistic minority.

Adversarialism and confrontation, then, form the dominant motif of language policy in Canada. There are, however, some examples of the persistence of conventional mechanisms of negotiation and incremental legislative change even in this arena. In 1984 Ontario amended its Education Act, going beyond the requirements of section 23 of the Constitution Act, 1982, to guarantee access to francophone education to *all* francophones entitled to it under section 23, without a "sufficient numbers" proviso. Fulfilling these guarantees remains a gradual and ongoing process. In 1986 a section of the Courts of Justice Act was proclaimed, recognizing English and French as official languages of the courts in Ontario. Also in 1986 Ontario enacted the French Language Services Act, which stands as a model of compromise. It stopped short of declaring French as an official language of Ontario governmental institutions generally but did provide the statutory basis for a phased expansion of French-language services.

Despite the modest nature of their provisions, these legislative changes in Ontario became a matter of some controversy. The Association for the Preservation of English in Canada pressed the issue in the 1987 provincial election, and a few small municipalities gratuitously passed by-laws declaring English as their sole official language of administration and service. The issue did not dominate the election; the Liberal government was returned with a majority; and the implementation of the act proceeded. Nonetheless, the conflict continued to simmer and flared up again in the spring of 1990, as a number of larger municipalities adopted English-only resolutions.

At the federal level incremental legislative change also gave rise to some controversy. In 1988 the federal Parliament passed a new Official Languages Act, superseding the 1969 legislation. The language of the new act was more consistent with the 1982 constitutional language regarding official languages—for example, it did not contain references to "bilingual districts" but referred instead to areas where there is "significant demand" for service in either official language. The new act included a fairly lengthy preamble (the 1969 act had had none) that contained, among other things, yet another attempt to reconcile dualist and pluralist views of the nation by sheer juxtaposition: It recognized "the importance of preserving and enhancing the use of languages other than English and French while strengthening the status and use of the official languages." The new act also extended and strengthened a number of the 1969 act's provisions, and it added rights for federal employees regarding the language of work.

The passage of this legislation was not entirely smooth. Although both Alliance Quebec and FFHQ strongly supported it and all three political parties at the federal level endorsed it, anglophone extremist groups attacked the legislation vehemently. A group of self-declared "dinosaurs" among the anglophone members of the Conservative caucus vigorously opposed it in the legislature and in the media. Concerns were also raised by the Quebec government regarding potential conflicts between the provisions of bill 101 and those of the federal legislation regarding the use of English in federal government institutions in Quebec. However, the exercise of caucus discipline and the signing of a letter of understanding between the federal secretary of state and the Quebec justice minister regarding the implementation of the legislation in Quebec removed these obstacles, and the legislation passed by a larger margin than had its predecessor in 1969.

It is worth noting that five days after the House of Commons passed the new Official Languages Act, it passed the Canadian Multiculturalism Act. The preamble to the multiculturalism act juxtaposed commitments to recognize "diversity . . . as a fundamental characteristic of Canadian society" with a recognition of the official status of English and French— a juxtaposition that drew comment from the commissioner of official languages, among others (Reading 7-6). The Canadian Multiculturalism Act established no rights or obligations: It simply gave legislative expression to a number of policy commitments to "promote" and "enhance" cultural diversity and the equitable treatment of "individuals and communities of all origins." [18] Indeed, a program for funding projects and groups for these purposes was already well established under the secretary of state. The act did, however, institutionalize access for ethnic interest groups to the political executive, by giving a legislative base to the existing practice of designating a cabinet minister responsible for multiculturalism.

The passage of the Official Languages Act and the Canadian Multiculturalism Act within five days of each other constitutes yet another example of the by now familiar Canadian pattern of institutionalizing ambivalence and providing for elite-level resolution of conflict. In the minority language policy arena, as we have seen, this pattern has been least successful. The political system, however, still strains to adopt it.

As for the impact of the policies reviewed in this chapter on the linguistic demography of the country, we find something of a paradox. On the one hand, the territorial distribution of anglophones and francophones is becoming more polarized. The proportion of francophones is shrinking nationally (from about 29 percent in 1951 to about 25 percent in 1986) and in virtually all regions except Quebec, northern New Brunswick, and the National Capital Region. The proportion of anglophones in Quebec declined from about 14 percent in 1941 to about 10 percent in 1986 (Commissioner of Official Languages 1987: 12).

On the other hand, more individuals (15.3 percent in 1981 as compared with 12.2 percent in 1961) are reporting themselves to be bilingual in English and French. Moreover, a larger proportion of bilingual individuals (30 percent in 1981 as compared with 24 percent in 1961) are native English speakers. Across Canada a generation of anglophones is being educated in French to a greater extent and in greater proportions than ever before, through "immersion" programs at the primary and secondary level in which some or all subjects are taught to anglophones in French. At the same time, however, concerns have been expressed about the extent and the quality of francophone education for francophone minorities. Enrolment in minority language (not immersion) education declined overall and in six provinces (including Quebec) from 1970–71 to 1986–87 (Commissioner of Official Languages 1986: 216–17). In a survey in which thirteen-year-old students in five countries were tested in mathematics and science, students in francophone schools in Ontario and New Brunswick performed relatively poorly, while Quebec francophone students ranked considerably higher (MacKenzie 1989).

The area in which the clearest francophone gains can be demonstrated is the federal public service. Francophone participation rose from about 22 percent in 1971 to about 28 percent in 1986. Francophone representation in the management category, however, remained lodged at about the 20 percent level from 1981 to 1986 (Commissioner of Official Languages 1984: 60, 1987: 60). There are considerable regional variations in the linguistic "representativeness" of the federal civil service. In particular, francophones remain significantly underrepresented in federal government agencies located in New Brunswick and northern and eastern Ontario, and anglophones are even more sharply underrepresented in Quebec. Furthermore, whereas the representation of francophones in federal offices in New Brunswick and Ontario has been improving slowly over time, the representation of anglophones in federal offices in Quebec has been worsening (Commissioner of Official Languages 1984: 61). As for individual bilingualism within the federal public service, the results have been mixed. The designation of positions as requiring bilingual competence has certainly increased the participation of francophones in those positions.[19] But the reported *use* of French in these positions outside Quebec is limited: In 1983 anglophones in bilingual positions outside Quebec reported using French under 20 percent of the time in internal communications, and even francophones in such positions used French less than half of the time (ibid.: 69).

Finally, we need to consider where these two decades of conflict and policy change have left the state of public opinion in Canada with respect to language policy. In the briefest terms, it leaves a state of sharp divergence between francophones and anglophones. A 1981 national survey, for example, found marked divisions between francophone *québécois* and all others on language issues (Johnston and Blais 1988: S29–33).

A 1987 survey of mass and elite opinion demonstrated that francophones attach much more importance to the principle of official bilingualism at the national level than do anglophones (Sniderman et al. 1989: 264). The same study demonstrated the existence of "double standards" among anglophones, who were more supportive of language rights for anglophone Quebeckers than for francophones outside Quebec. (It should be noted, however, that majorities at both the elite and the mass levels expressed support for francophone rights.) Moreover, francophone elites (particularly members of the PQ) were less likely to support education rights for Quebec anglophones than for francophones outside Quebec (ibid.: 269, 281). In the terms used in this chapter, these "double standards" mean that significant numbers of francophones and anglophones do not see anglophone and francophone minorities as parallel cases.

After two decades of renewed conflict and accommodation, legislative and constitutional provisions relating to francophone and anglophone minorities have been expanded significantly (see Table 7-2). The implementation of these provisions, however, has been incomplete and controversial. Since the 1960s the Canadian political system has striven to reconcile two approaches to the treatment of linguistic minorities, representing different balances of the bicultural-multicultural, national-regional, and individual-collective tensions that pervade this arena. One approach saw Canada as a bilingual nation in which anglophones and francophones are members of "official" language groups with parallel constitutional status and rights throughout the country. The other approach was pluralistic, allowing for policy diversity and different balances across linguistically distinct regions.

The marriage of these two approaches was sought through traditional mechanisms of elite accommodation within an ambiguously designed framework. The 1982 constitutional changes, the product of executive federalism, represented a principle of official bilingualism tempered with pluralism: They established a national linguistic rights regime, but Quebec was indefinitely exempted from one of its provisions, and only New Brunswick fully "opted in" to the regime. The court-ratified negotiated settlement in Manitoba also represented a tempering of official bilingualism with pluralism, as Manitoba received a pragmatic dispensation from the full implications of its constitution. Elsewhere, Alberta and Saskatchewan, once freed by the courts from the ambiguous provisions of their provincial constitutions, chose only to nod in the direction of bilingualism by establishing limited rights for francophones—and Saskatchewan's somewhat more generous package of services was achieved only with substantial federal financial support. Ontario continued to make de facto improvements in rights and services for francophones while resisting official bilingual status. This provincial diversity is, in fact, more consistent with the arrangements in other linguistically divided states than is national bilingualism. Belgium, for example, combines unilingual regions with a bilingual capital; Switzerland has established different linguistic rights regimes in areas of federal and cantonal jurisdiction.

If this were a policy arena like any other in Canada, moreover, this sort of provincial diversity under the umbrella of a national framework would be a recipe for success in accommodating a variety of interests and principles. But this is not an arena like any other. It touches upon one of the founding myths of the country—the parallel treatment of English and French—a myth passionately reasserted and reinterpreted by key members of the political elite since the 1960s. And it brings that myth up sharply against a reality—the lack of parallelism in the situations of the historically privileged anglophone minority of Quebec and the historically disadvantaged francophone minorities of other provinces. This reality makes any policy predicated on parallel treatment of these minorities unstable and frustrates the building of anglophone-francophone coalitions. The growing racial and ethnic diversity of the Canadian population, meanwhile, makes it more difficult to maintain political support for policies privileging two linguistic groups.

The formal and informal accommodations that have occurred in this arena since the 1960s have been made without the participation of the government of Quebec, the only government whose constituency is primarily francophone. Successive governments of Quebec have not as-

TABLE 7-2   Status of Major Official Language Provisions, by Jurisdiction, 1990

	Federal Parliament and Institutions	New-foundland	Nova Scotia	Prince Edward Island	New Brunswick	Quebec
Right to minority language education (S.23 Charter)	*	*	*	*	*	*①
Right to receive federal government services in English and French (*S.20(1) Charter*, Part IV, OLA, 1988)	*	*	*	*	*	*
Right to receive provincial/territorial government services in English or French	N/A				*S.20(2) Charter of Rights* OLA, 1969 Equality of Official Linguistic Communities Act, 1981	Law 142, 1986 (guaranties health and social services in English)
Right to use English or French in debates and proceedings of legislature	*S.133 Constitution Act, 1867*				*S.17(2) Charter of Rights* OLA, 1969	*S.133 Constitution Act, 1867*
Obligation to use English and French in statutes, records, and journals of legislature	*S.133 Constitution Act, 1867*				*S.18(2) Charter of Rights* OLA, 1969	*S.133 Constitution Act, 1867*
Right to use English or French in criminal proceedings	*S.133 Constitution Act, 1867*	④	④ Part XVII Cr.C (for summary conviction offences	④ Part XVII Cr.C (for summary conviction offences)	*S.19(2) Charter of Rights* Part XVII Cr.C OLA, 1969	④ *S.133 Constitution Act, 1867*
Right to use English or French in civil proceedings	*S.133 Constitution Act, 1867*				*S.19(2) Charter of Rights* OLA, 1969	*S.133 Constitution Act, 1867*

Ontario	Manitoba	Saskatchewan	Alberta	British Columbia	Northwest Territories	Yukon
*	*	*	*	*	*	*
*	*	*	*	*	*	*
S.5 French Language Services Act, 1986					② S.15 NWT Official Languages Act, 1984	③ S.6(1) Languages Act, 1988
S.3(1) French Language Services Act, 1986	*S.23 Manitoba Act, 1870*	S.12 Language Act, 1988	S.5(1) Languages Act, 1988		② S.10 NWT Official Languages Act, 1984	③ S.3(1) Languages Act, 1988
S.3(2) French Language Services Act (As of Jan. 1, 1991)	*S.23 Manitoba Act, 1870*				② S.12 NWT Official Languages Act, 1984	S.4 Languages Act 1988 (As of Dec. 31, 1990, and applies only to legislation)
Part XVII Cr.C	Part XVII Cr.C	Part XVII Cr.C	④	④	Part XVII Cr.C	Part XVII Cr.C
Courts of Justice Act, 1984 (Range of French-Language Rights in designated courts)	*S.23 Manitoba Act, 1870*	S.11 Language Act, 1988 (before designated courts)	S.4 Languages Act, 1988 (oral communications before designated courts)		② S.13 NWT Official Languages Act, 1984	③ S.5 Languages Act, 1988

TABLE 7-2   Continued

	Federal Parliament and Institutions	New-foundland	Nova Scotia	Prince Edward Island	New Brunswick	Quebec
CBC TV and radio network: minority language program-ing (Broadcasting Act)	*	*	*	*	*	*
Obligation to use bilingual product labelling (Consumer Packaging and Labelling Act)	*	*	*	*	*	*

Sources: Constitution Act, 1867; Constitution Act, 1982 (Canadian Charter of Rights and Free-doms); Manitoba Act, 1870; Official Languages Act, 1988; Northwest Territories Official Lan-guages Act; Courts of Justice Act, 1984 (Ontario); Criminal Code; An Act to again amend an Act respecting health services and social services (Law 142, Quebec); Languages Act (Yukon); Languages Act (Alberta) An Act respecting the use of the English and French languages in Saskatchewan; French Language Services Act (Ontario); Official Languages Act, 1969 (New Brunswick); An Act recognizing the equality of the two Official Linguistic Communities in New Brunswick (1981). All as summarized in tabular form in Commissioner of Official Languages 1990: 262–63.
*Applies in this jurisdiction. Italics indicate constitutionally entrenched provisions.
Note: Some rights and obligations, such as those relating to Parliament, legislation or the courts, generally have effect as of their date of proclamation. Others such as those relating to services to the

sented to the national framework of parallclism as revised in 1982; and Quebec's attempts to challenge, to override, and to alter that framework have given rise to a level of suspicion and resentment in the rest of Canada that has frustrated attempts at elite accommodation.

Ambivalence, in this arena, is giving way to polarization. Canada's ambivalent constitutional and institutional structures "fit" less and less well with the polarized pattern of interest and opinion. It is possible that a passionate reassertion of a national commitment to bilingualism by a latter-day Trudeau could produce another surge of support for the found-ing myth. But it could not reshape the fundamental structure of interests. What is more likely is the development of a considerably looser associa-tion between Quebec and the rest of Canada, as discussed in Chapter 2. In that case, the pressure for policies of bilingualism in the rest of Canada would be much attenuated. The institutional momentum of the changes at the federal level (and in New Brunswick and possibly Ontario) might

Ontario	Manitoba	Saskatchewan	Alberta	British Columbia	Northwest Territories	Yukon
*	*	*	*	*	*	*
*	*	*	*	*	*	*

public or minority language education rights, may be subject to gradual implementation.

① The so-called "Mother Tongue clause" (Section 23 [1][a]) of the Charter of Rights, whereby "Citizens of Canada whose first language learned and still understood is that of the English or French minority population of the province in which they reside" may have their children educated in the minority language of that province, is not currently applicable to Quebec. The charter, however, grants the provincial legislature the option to declare this provision applicable to Quebec.
② Provisions of this Act came into force on December 31, 1990.
③ Provisions of this Act come into force no later than December 31, 1992.
④ Part XVII Cr.C came automatically into effect Jan. 1, 1990, in those provinces where it was not already in force.

keep them alive in those contexts, but they would remain as monuments to a noble but failed experiment in national bilingualism.

Readings

7-1   TRUDEAU ON LANGUAGE RIGHTS *

Before entering federal politics Pierre Trudeau was a law professor and a regular contributor to Cité Libre, *a progressive intellectual periodi-*

*Pierre-Elliott Trudeau, from *Cité Libre* (April 1962). Reprinted in Frank Scott and Michael Oliver, eds., *Quebec States Her Case* (Toronto: Macmillan 1964), pp. 66–68.

cal in Quebec. The following excerpts from a 1962 issue illustrate the underpinnings of the policies he was later to pursue as prime minister.

The die is cast in Canada: there are two main ethnic and linguistic groups; each is too strong and too deeply rooted in the past, too firmly bound to a mother culture, to be able to engulf the other. But if the two will collaborate at the hub of a truly pluralistic State, Canada could become the envied seat of a form of federalism that belongs to tomorrow's world. Better than the American melting-pot, Canada could offer an example to all those new Asian and African States . . . who must discover how to govern their polyethnic populations with proper regard for justice and liberty. What better reason for cold-shouldering the lure of a Canada annexed to the United States? . . . Canadian federalism is an experiment of major proportions; it could become a brilliant prototype for the molding of tomorrow's civilization.

If English Canadians cannot see it . . . so much the worse for them; they will be subsiding into a backward, short-sighted and despotic nationalism. . . . [I]f, in the face of Anglo-Canadian nationalism, French Canadians retreat into their own nationalistic shell, they will condemn themselves to the same stagnation. [But if, using its powers under the existing Canadian Constitution] Quebec became . . . a shining example, if to live there were to partake of freedom and progress . . . French Canadians would no longer need to do battle for bilingualism; the ability to speak French would become a status symbol, even an open sesame in business and public life. Even in Ottawa, superior competence on the part of our politicians and civil servants would bring spectacular results.

7-2. LÉVESQUE ON FRANCOPHONES OUTSIDE QUEBEC *

René Lévesque made the following comments in an interview with a Montreal journalist while still a Liberal minister in the Quebec cabinet. These views reflect his growing Quebec nationalism, which led him to leave the Quebec Liberals to found the Parti québécois in 1968.

[The French Canadian] nation possesses its national state, Quebec. There are, to be sure, fragments of the nation outside Quebec . . . who

---

*Jean-Marc Léger, "René Lévesque Speaks of Quebec, National State of the French Canadians," *Le Devoir* (Montreal, July 5, 1963). Reprinted in Frank Scott and Michael Oliver, eds., *Quebec States Her Case* (Toronto: Macmillan, 1964), pp. 132–33, 144–45.

numerically amount to, say, a sixth of the nation. They are our French-Canadian "minorities". Their existence in no way lessens the fact that Quebec is our nation state and identifies itself politically with our nation. It is only as Quebec grows stronger in every way . . . that it can be of some assistance to the minorities.

We must take an interest in their lot, but certainly not at the expense of the rights, the prerogatives and the needs of Quebec. If, as some wish, Quebec were to play the pan-Canadian game, forgetting to be wary of the centralizing instincts of the Ottawa government, the whole nation would court suicide. . . .

We must not mislead others into believing, nor end up by convincing ourselves, that "biculturalism" is a basic goal or value. It is infinitely more important to make Quebec progressive, free and strong than to devote the best of our energies to propagating the doubtful advantages of biculturalism.

7-3.   THE MANIFESTO OF QUEBEC'S
        RADICAL NATIONALISTS*

These excerpts are taken from the FLQ manifesto released to Quebec newspapers on April 16, 1963. As McRoberts (1988: 200) notes, the FLQ was "a highly marginal phenomenon, directly involving perhaps no more than 100 people in its various waves of bombings and vandalism during the 1960's." Nonetheless, its activities drew attention to the explosive potential of Quebec nationalism.

Patriots,

Ever since the second world war, the various enslaved peoples of the world have been shattering their bonds to acquire the freedom which is theirs by right. Most of these peoples have overcome their oppressors, and can today live in freedom.

Like so many others before us, the people of Quebec have reached the end of their patience with the arrogant domination of Anglo-Saxon colonialism.

---

*A Message to the Nation by the Front de libération du Québec (FLQ). Translated and reprinted in Frank Scott and Michael Oliver, eds., *Quebec States Her Case* (Toronto: Macmillan, 1964), pp. 83–87.

In Quebec, as in all colonized countries, the oppressor fiercely denies his imperialism and has the support of the so-called national élite which is more interested in protecting its own entrenched economic interests than in serving the vital interests of its nation. This servile group persistently denies obvious facts and raises up endless problems, aimed at distracting the hardpressed population's attention away from the only vital problem: INDEPENDENCE.

Despite all this, the workers' eyes are daily becoming more attuned to reality: Quebec is a colony!

We are a colonized people, politically, socially, and economically. Politically, because we do not have any hold on the political instruments necessary for our survival. Ottawa's colonial government has full powers in the following fields: economic policy, foreign trade, defence, bank credit, immigration, the criminal courts, etc. Moreover, any provincial legislation may be repealed by Ottawa if it so decides. . . .

It is also economically a colony. A single statement will serve to prove it: over 80 per cent of our economy is controlled by foreign interests. We provide the labour, they bank the profits.

Socially, too, Quebec is a colony. We represent 80 per cent of the population, and yet the English language prevails in many fields. French is gradually relegated to the realm of folklore, while English becomes the people's working language. . . .

Quebec is also suffering from the unjust and paradoxical situation which can best be illustrated by a look at two neighbouring communities: Saint-Henri and Westmount. Here, we find the typical poverty and overcrowding of a French district; there, we see an English minority living in shameful luxury. Our progressive economic enslavement, and an ever-fuller foreign control, will not be arrested by provisional, short-sighted solutions. Patriots say NO to COLONIALISM, NO to EXPLOITATION. . . .

Only a full-fledged revolution can build up the necessary power to achieve the vital changes that will be needed in an independent Quebec. A national revolution cannot, of its very nature, tolerate any compromise. There is only one way of overcoming colonialism: to be stronger than it is! Only the most far-fetched idealism may mislead one into thinking otherwise. Our period of slavery has ended.

QUEBEC PATRIOTS, TO ARMS! THE HOUR OF NATIONAL REVOLUTION HAS STRUCK!

INDEPENDENCE OR DEATH!

7-4.   THE UNION NATIONALE GOVERNMENT
        ON THE STATUS OF FRENCH*

*The Confederation of Tomorrow conference, organized at the initiative
of the Conservative government of Ontario under Premier John Robarts,
brought together governmental representatives in an attempt to begin to
forge a common agenda for constitutional change. The following excerpts
are from the statement of the Union nationale government of Quebec under
Premier Daniel Johnson.*

In concluding, it is important to draw very special attention to one of
the major Canadian problems of the day: the status of French in Canada.
We have already touched several times on this question, which we consider basic.

The Québec Government is committed to making French a true
national language in Québec, while respecting the linguistic rights of the
minority. We are currently studying various means of promoting generalized use of French throughout our territory, so that French-Canadian
Quebecers in their home province may live and work in their mother
tongue, just as English-speaking Canadians live and work in their own
language in the other provinces.

But this will not solve the whole problem. Essentially, what French
Canadians want is to be themselves and develop normally like any other
people; in Québec and in other parts of Canada. More particularly, they
want to create in Québec an environment conducive to their own growth.
They also want it to be possible for members of their community settled
in other provinces to develop as English-speaking Canadians can do in
Québec.

In a country like ours, we must begin by ensuring public education
at all levels in Canada's two official languages wherever the English or
French-speaking group is sufficiently large. Obviously, this does not rule
out the necessity of providing the French or English-speaking groups
with means of acquiring good command of the majority language in their
environment. As for other government services such as departments,
courts, administrative bodies, we believe the best way to avoid problems
and render justice to the greatest number of people concerned is to deal
with the question on a regional basis. . . .

*Government of Quebec, "Preliminary Statement" presented to the Confederation of
Tomorrow Conference, Toronto, November 1967, excerpts.

7-5.   THE COURTS ON LINGUISTIC EDUCATION RIGHTS *

Justice Deschênes of the Quebec Superior Court ruled against a challenge of Quebec's language legislation restricting instruction in English. He held, as earlier courts had done, that constitutional guarantees related to denominational but not linguistic education rights. In the following passage he pointedly refers to the inability of francophone minorities to assert constitutional rights to francophone education in the past.

Even if the question is cruel and apt to revive old wounds, the argument of the Protestant School Boards makes it mandatory. When the constitutional text was similar, did anyone think of serving the French culture of the Catholic minority of Manitoba, when the language question was underlying the religious conflict which was jeopardizing its right to denominational schools? And when the constitutional text was identical did anyone think of saving the French culture of the Catholic minority of Ontario, when the language question also jeopardized its system of denominational schools?

At each of these solemn moments in our history the Courts have distinguished between language and faith, between culture and religion; they have recognized constitutional guarantees to the denomination of schools only and never did they interpret the *British North America Act, 1867* as the instrument of the protection of the language or the culture of a particular group.

7-6.   LANGUAGE RIGHTS IN THE CANADIAN
CHARTER OF RIGHTS AND FREEDOMS **

These sections of the Canadian Charter of Rights and Freedoms, adopted in 1982, pertain to language rights. As discussed in the text, there are also other sections of the Canadian and Manitoba constitutions relating to the use of English and French in governmental institutions.

16. (1) English and French are the official languages of Canada and have equality of status and equal rights and privileges as to their use in all institutions of the Parliament and government of Canada.

Protestant School Board of Greater Montreal et al. v. Minister of Education of Quebec et al. (1976), 83 D.L.R. 672.

**The Constitution Act, 1982, sections 16–23.

(2) English and French are the official languages of New Brunswick and have equality of status and equal rights and privileges as to their use in all institutions of the legislature and government of New Brunswick.

(3) Nothing in this Charter limits the authority of Parliament or a legislature to advance the equality of status or use of English and French.

17. (1) Everyone has the right to use English or French in any debates and other proceedings of Parliament.

(2) Everyone has the right to use English or French in any debates and other proceedings of the legislature of New Brunswick.

18. (1) The statutes, records and journals of Parliament shall be printed and published in English and French and both language versions are equally authoritative.

(2) The statutes, records and journals of the legislature of New Brunswick shall be printed and published in English and French and both language versions are equally authoritative.

19. (1) Either English or French may be used by any person in, or in any pleading in or process issuing from, any court established by Parliament.

(2) Either English or French may be used by any person in, or in any pleading in or process issuing from, any court of New Brunswick.

20. (1) Any member of the public in Canada has the right to communicate with, and to receive available services from, any head or central office of an institution of the Parliament or government of Canada in English or French, and has the same right with respect to any other office of any such institution where

(*a*) there is a significant demand for communications with and services from that office in such language; or

(*b*) due to the nature of the office, it is reasonable that communications with and services from that office be available in both English and French.

(2) Any member of the public in New Brunswick has the right to communicate with, and to receive available services from, any office of an institution of the legislature or government of New Brunswick in English or French.

21. Nothing in sections 16 to 20 abrogates or derogates from any right, privilege or obligation with respect to the English and French languages, or either of them, that exists or is continued by virtue of any other provision of the Constitution of Canada.

22. Nothing in sections 16 to 20 abrogates or derogates from any legal or customary right or privilege acquired or enjoyed either before or after the coming into force of this Charter with respect to any language that is not English or French.

23. (1) Citizens of Canada

(*a*) whose first language learned and still understood is that of the English or French linguistic minority population of the province in which they reside, or

(*b*) who have received their primary school instruction in Canada in English or French and reside in a province where the language in which they received that instruction is the language of the English or French linguistic minority population of the province.

have the right to have their children receive primary and secondary school instruction in that language in that province.

(2) Citizens of Canada of whom any child has received or is receiving primary or secondary school instruction in English or French in Canada, have the right to have all their children receive primary and secondary school instruction in the same language.

(3) The right of citizens of Canada under subsections (1) and (2) to have their children receive primary and secondary school instruction in the language of the English or French linguistic minority population of a province

(*a*) applies wherever in the province the number of children of citizens who have such a right is sufficient to warrant the provision to them out of public funds of minority language instruction; and

(*b*) includes, where the number of those children so warrants, the right to have them receive that instruction in minority language educational facilities provided out of public funds.

7-7.   THE COMMISSIONER OF OFFICIAL LANGUAGES ON MULTICULTURALISM*

The tabling of a multiculturalism bill in 1987 (during the same parliamentary session as a revised version of the Official Languages Act) indicated the federal Conservative government's concern to signal to ethnic

---

*Commissioner of Official Languages, *Annual Report, 1987* (Ottawa, 1987), p. 11.

groups of other than British or French extraction that their interests were not being neglected, despite the policy focus on official languages. In these excerpts from his annual report, D'Iberville Fortier, the commissioner of official languages (an ombudsman established under the Official Languages Act), points out the tensions in policies promoting bilingualism and multiculturalism.

The Government has let it be known that it sees the Official Languages Bill, the Multiculturalism Bill and a forthcoming bill on citizenship as a triad of measures which, taken together, can make sweet music of the relationships among Canadians. There is no doubt that they are thematically related in a number of ways or that they must be harmonized among themselves and with other aspects of Canada's vision of itself. The difficulty, of course, is that the national values which are embedded in bilingualism, multiculturalism and citizenship are not identical, so that having set up both positive and negative reverberations in this cultural chord, the policy-makers must be prepared to resolve them.

In producing a Multiculturalism Bill that was richer in policy than in legislative terms, government set aside many of the recommendations of a joint parliamentary committee that had, among other things, recommended a full-fledged Ministry of Multiculturalism and a Commissioner for multicultural matters with ombudsman powers similar to our own. The policy substance of the Bill was perceived by some media observers as simply a legal endorsement of policies and programs that have been in existence for some years and which already have some difficulty meeting their expectations. However, the multicultural associations, while disappointed to varying degrees with the Bill, seem in the end to have appreciated that it represents an important advance for their interests.

The linguistic and cultural make-up of Canada cannot help but evolve. We are trying to strike a healthy balance between our institutional history—our sense of cultural continuity—and the development of a dynamic but cohesive new Canada. In heaven's eyes all languages and cultures are equal, but the laws of nature and of nations are less absolute. The proposition that Canada should evolve, institutionally speaking, as a multicultural but bilingual nation is fraught with ambiguities for the simple reason that languages and cultures are, to some degree, inseparable. We can only repeat that the *national* respect and support which is due to the many languages other than English and French which are spoken in Canada cannot be the same as those given to our official languages.

That could never work, and actively or passively to encourage new Canadians—including, incidentally, those of British or French stock—to believe that their cultural behaviour need suffer no significant adaptation toward Canadian norms is to do them a serious disservice. Many other language groups, beginning with the Native peoples, have contributed much, and should contribute even more, to the special cultural richness in which most Canadians rejoice. It is important that the state recognize that contribution and encourage the diversity that helps to make us the people we are.

The question is not whether an ideal of multiculturalism is fundamental to the Constitution but in what sense and with what practical consequences. Our sincere wish that there be no discrimination among individual Canadians on the basis of their ethno-cultural origins cannot alter the fact that we also aspire to be—even more fundamentally—an English- and French-speaking nation. So, when Bill C-93 says that "WHEREAS the Constitution of Canada and the Official Languages Act provide that English and French are the official languages of Canada . . .", the minister responsible for multiculturalism may "facilitate the acquisition, retention and use of all languages that contribute to the multicultural heritage of Canada", we must be clear what these in some ways "opposed" propositions add up to. They cannot mean that, at the national level at least, those languages are entitled to the same institutional treatment—and promotion—as the official languages. What they should mean is that it is in the national interest that individual Canadians be permitted and enabled to acquire, retain and use those languages to the extent that the fundamental bilingualism of our institutions makes this feasible and affordable. There is, after all, a nationally compelling need first to acquire, retain and use at least one of our two official languages.

Between the so-called "melting pot" approach to ancestral languages and a linguistic free-for-all there are many possible shades of institutional support. Encouragement of "heritage languages" within our public school systems, for instance, whether as bridges to official language education or as second or third language studies that are economically or culturally worthwhile in their own right, seems to us both honourable and productive. This cannot, alas, alter the inescapable economics of student numbers, school programming and affordable educational costs. We share the view that we are still a good way short of doing what Bill C-93 proposes to prohibit ethnic and cultural discrimination and to do so in a positive and workable way. The danger, in this case, may be less one of reconciling this goal with that of bilingualism than simply of reconciling all our many notions of cultural pluralism one with another.

Notes

1. The Official Language Act was challenged in 1909 in the St. Boniface County Court, which ruled it *ultra vires*. However, as Tetley (1982: 180) reports, this decision was "unreported and ignored" until it was finally reported in the course of the legal challenges to the act in the late 1970s.

2. The compromise reflected an early sense of multiculturalism, which contributed to its early demise. It entailed an amendment to the Public Schools Act to require the employment of Roman Catholic teachers where specified enrolments of Roman Catholic students were met, and to require that "[w]hen ten of the pupils in any school speak the French language, *or any language other than English,* as their native language, the teaching of such pupils shall be conducted in French, *or such other language,* and English upon the bi-lingual system" (An Act to Amend the Public Schools Act, chap. 26, section 10, 1897 Man. Stat. 99). As Manzer (1985: 125) reports: "As Manitoba was settled over the next two decades by many immigrants with mother tongues other than English or French, school districts faced growing difficulties in providing adequate schooling in two or three languages besides English."

3. In 1991 the FFHQ changed its name to become the Fédération des communautés francophones et acadiennes du Canada.

4. In 1937 the Quebec government adopted a statute providing that in the case of conflict between the English and French texts of a statute, the French version would prevail. This legislation was, however, repealed in 1938.

5. The act permitted but did not require a region to be designated bilingual if the official language minority (defined in terms of mother tongue) constituted at least 10 percent of the population of the region.

6. Section 12 of the act provides that education in public schools is to be provided in the mother tongue (either English or French) of the student body, with the other official language as a second language of instruction. In schools with both anglophone and francophone pupils "classes

are to be so arranged that the chief language of instruction is the mother tongue of each group with the other official language the second language for those groups." Where this splitting of classes is "not feasible by reason of numbers," the minister of education may make "alternative arrangements to carry out the spirit of this Act" (Tetley 1982: 186).

7. Tetley reports that these amendments "transformed what had been toleration of clandestine French education into full-fledged legal recognition." They essentially provided for instruction to be provided in French to francophones where classes of thirty (at the elementary level) and twenty (at the secondary level) could be assembled. These provisions were later consolidated to provide that such instruction would be provided at both levels where classes of twenty-five could be assembled (Tetley 1982: 189–90).

8. See Coleman (1981, 1983) for comparisons of bill 22, bill 1, and bill 101.

9. Coleman also notes that "the commitment of the [Quebec Liberal Party] to some dualism in Quebec was symbolized by its implicit [sic] references to English in Bill 22. Bill 101 was more classically *pluraliste* using the term 'langue autre que francais' where its predecessor law had used 'anglais'." Of the articles in bill 22, 13.8 percent mentioned the English language at least once, whereas only 5.1 percent of the articles in bill 101 explicitly mentioned English (Coleman 1981: 466).

10. Forsey (1980), in commenting upon this discrepancy, notes that the Court's reasons for judgement in the Manitoba case 1979 were substantially the same as those of the Manitoba judge in the "unreported and ignored" 1909 case declaring the Manitoba Official Language Act unconstitutional.

11. The PQ government of Quebec feared the promotion of bilingualism through the network of federal institutions in Quebec; the Conservative government of Manitoba opposed any entrenchment of rights as an infringement of the principle of "parliamentary sovereignty."

12. The task force report was actually submitted to the federal Conservative government during its brief period in power in 1979, a circumstance that made it easier for the Liberals to ignore the report when they returned to power in 1980.

13. Section 133 of the British North America Act, 1867 (now the Constitution Act, 1867) relating to the use of English and French in the legislatures and courts of the governments of Canada and Quebec, and the parallel section 23 of the Manitoba Act, remain in force.

14. Deschênes, C.J.S.C., in *Quebec Association of Protestant School Boards et al. v. Attorney General of Quebec et al.* (1982), 140 D.L.R. (3d), at 64–65.

15. Indeed, in what may in the long run have been the most significant jurisprudential element of its decision, the Court held the blanket use of the notwithstanding clause to have been constitutional.

16. Although it did not invoke the notwithstanding clause routinely as did its predecessor, the Liberal government did resort to it on occasion. For example, it was invoked in 1986 in legislation regarding grants to young farmers, and regarding retirement ages for men and women under pension plans for public employees.

17. The Quebec government had argued that the Bill 101 signs provisions were compatible with the Quebec Charter of Human Rights and Freedoms, by virtue of section 9.1 of the Quebec Charter, which allows the rights therein to be limited by law in the interest of "democratic values, public order and the general well-being of the citizens of Quebec." The Court rejected this argument. The Court accepted the need to preserve a French "visage linguistique" in Quebec and suggested that requiring French to be in "marked predominance" would be compatible with the Canadian and Quebec charters. The banning of French from commercial signs and firm names, however, was disproportionate to that goal.

18. The act indeed provided even less than had earlier been recommended by a joint parliamentary committee, which had advocated the creation of a ministry of multiculturalism and a commissioner for multicultural matters similar to the commissioner of official languages.

19. Between 1978 and 1983 the percentage of federal bilingual positions occupied by francophones increased from 53.3 to 60.3 in the National Capital Region, from 41.7 to 58.9 in the federal bilingual regions in Ontario, from 90.4 to 91.4 in federal bilingual regions in Quebec, and from 58.7 to 72.7 in New Brunswick (Commissioner of Official Languages 1984: 68).

8 Competence and Crisis: Canada's Ambivalent Institutions

The Canadian tolerance of ambivalence and genuis for moderation were severely tested in the 1970s and 1980s. Conflict erupted along the traditional fault lines of English-French relations (regarding constitutional change and minority language rights), regionalism (regarding oil and gas policy), and Canada-U.S. relations (regarding the Free Trade Agreement). And new tensions emerged. The political system struggled to meld a constitutional charter of rights with the principle of parliamentary supremacy—a combination that, though nobly creative, could only have the effect of raising and at least occasionally frustrating the "rights consciousness" of its citizens. The labour movement struggled to reconcile the preservation of an adversarial model of labour relations with a more collaborative approach to the making of industrial and labour-market policy. The joint emergence and reemergence of these tensions had not an additive but a compounding effect, and the system was placed under an unprecedented level of stress.

Elite Accommodation: The Role of Mediating Interests

All political systems, if they are to respond to policy challenges, require mechanisms for resolving conflict and integrating interests. But different political systems, depending on their institutional configurations, provide different potential for conflict resolution and different mechanisms for the performance of integrative roles. State institutions bring authority to bear upon the resolution of conflict, and their capacity to exercise authority can go a long way toward explaining the potential for conflict resolution in a political system. The actual effect of state institutions, however, will depend upon the way in which they intersect with the organization of social interests.

In Sweden, for example, a highly professionalized state bureaucracy has been matched by the professional bureaucracies serving peak associations of business and labour interests, and a state tradition of administrative boards has provided the vehicle for ongoing tripartite collaboration. In Germany peak associations have not been as comprehensive and cohesive as in Sweden, but institutions bridging state and society and linking different levels of government nonetheless "encompass political opponents in a tight policy network" (Katzenstein 1987: 35) that fosters collaboration and incremental policy change. Some analyses of Japanese policymaking have looked to the elitist central bureaucracy as the key to understanding the policy process (Johnson 1975), but later approaches have insisted that the role of the bureaucracy cannot be understood apart from its relationship to the Liberal Democratic party and its supporting coalition of business and agricultural interests—a relationship that yields a form of "patterned pluralism" (Pempel 1982; Muramatsu and Kraus 1987). In the United States, on the other hand, there is not one key to understanding the policy process; rather, there are many. An exceptional degree of fragmentation in the institutions of the state, and in the organization of social interests, allows for the emergence of different types of politics within different policy arenas. It is no accident that it was an American political scientist, Theodore Lowi, who developed the theory that the different ways in which the coercive authority of the state may be exercised in policies and institutions yield quite different patterns of interaction amongst interests (Lowi 1972, 1985).

In Canada variation also occurs across policy arenas. But all arenas are marked by a distinctive feature that I have termed "institutionalized ambivalence." Traditionally, the Canadian political system has dealt with divergent principles and interests by institutionalizing them—particularly in its federal system, but also in the relationship between the legislatures and the courts. It has provided contending elites with institutional footholds, within a structure ambiguous enough to allow them room to manoeuver in reaching mutual accommodations. The ability of such a system to resolve conflict and to facilitate coherent policy development depends, however, on the structure of the interests represented by elites. More specifically, it requires that there be some form of *mediating* interest. What we must look for in attempting to understand the Canadian policy process are the *opportunities for mediation that are provided by institutional ambiguity and the candidates for the mediator's role*.

The elite groups most likely to play mediating roles are those whose own internal ambivalence renders them open to compromise. That ambivalence may in turn derive from the group's particularly cross-pressured position within the field of interests, or from the fact that it aggregates a number of divergent interests. The possibility of agreement is also enhanced where the range of interests that must be comprehended is relatively narrow. Different policy arenas, then, vary considerably in their capacity to produce mediators, and in the magnitude of the mediator's task.

The cases surveyed in this book illustrate these dimensions of the Canadian system. In the case of health care the medical profession was faced, under universal governmental health insurance, with a trade-off in defending its economic discretion versus its clinical autonomy. Governments were concerned with controlling the costs of the system. Neither of the two models of health care delivery most readily available in the Canadian context—the "statist" approach of the British National Health Service nor the market-oriented U.S. approach—were satisfactory in either professional or governmental eyes. In this case the "mediating interest" was the medical profession itself, particularly that component most concerned with preserving clinical autonomy and arguably the most ambivalent about the respective threats posed by the state and the market—that is, physicians concentrated in the medical schools and the regulatory colleges.

The potential for resolving conflict was also enhanced by the fact that different accommodations could be reached in different provinces. This was possible not simply because health care is constitutionally a matter of exclusive provincial jurisdiction—the federal government had used its "spending power" to become a major actor in the health care arena. Rather, these distinctive provincial accommodations could be reached because interregional spillovers were minimal: Health care providers and consumers in one province were not likely to be greatly helped or harmed by what was done for providers and consumers in another. These provincial accommodations nonetheless occurred around a common national standard. Again, the national standard reflected not only the effect of the federal spending power but also the structure of interests—in this case the *basic* commonality of interest of the medical profession in developing medical technology and encouraging its utilization. Elsewhere in the social policy arena such a mediating interest was not present, and the fiscal interests of governments yielded a limited income-maintenance system heavily weighted to a "default" option relatively free of federal-provincial entanglements—namely, unemployment insurance.

In the labour-relations arena, as in health care, different provincial accommodations were partly facilitated by the extraordinary decentralization of constitutional authority to the provincial level. Interregional spillovers are also limited in this arena: Although labour-relations regimes may be somewhat more likely than health care plans to be used to "bid" for business or for labour, there is little systematic evidence of such bidding. In this arena labour was primarily concerned with preserving the Wagner model of collective bargaining in the face of its erosion in the United States. Business was attempting to develop more "flexible" work rules and compensation arrangements and (in at least some of its segments) to weaken organized labour. Governments sought labour peace and had to reconcile their own roles as guarantors of the Wagner model with their relationships as employers vis-à-vis public-sector unions.

In this case the role of mediator fell to political parties—particularly social democratic parties—at the provincial level. Accommodations among labour, business, and government varied across provinces, the balance depending upon the partisan complexions of their governments. The survival, indeed the reinforcement of the Wagner model in Canada, relative to its weakening in the United States, was due in large part to the influence of social democratic governments either in power or as electoral threats at the provincial level. Their influence in the three largest provinces, Ontario, Quebec, and British Columbia, was particularly crucial. The protection of the Wagner model in these contexts allowed organized labour to maintain its membership base and hence its ability to exercise power at the national as well as the provincial level. The Wagner model remained under pressure, particularly in the public sector, as governments (including social democratic governments) sought to enforce wage restraint in the public sector and to maintain "essential services" in the face of strikes and strike threats by public employees. Nonetheless, the survival of the Wagner model and the growth of union membership in Canada, in a period when both were declining rapidly in the United States, is one of the starkest contrasts between the two nations, and one of the most significant effects of Canadian social democratic parties.

Provincial-level accommodations were possible in arenas such as health policy and labour relations, in which the range of conflict (profession-state; labour-management) could be largely comprehended within provincial boundaries. In policy arenas in which conflicts *between regions* had to be resolved, however, cross-provincial mechanisms of conflict resolution were required, and the role of the mediator was more difficult. In the arenas of labour-market policy and economic adjustment, the chasm between business's concern to protect the autonomy of the individual firm and labour's insistence on full employment strategies was cross-cut by regional fissures and governmental jurisdictional rivalries. Federal political parties attempted to negotiate this rocky terrain as mediators, but they found only the narrowest of common ground: a focus on the protection of those most disadvantaged by economic forces—the poorest regions, the long-term unemployed, workers in need of basic skills, failing or marginally competitive firms. This focus satisfied no one and was the subject of ongoing criticism from business, labour, and governments themselves. In general, however, despite periodic reorganizations of institutions and programs, and despite the rhetoric of increasing competitiveness and flexibility, there was little fundamental change in policy.

The one major policy initiative in the arena of economic adjustment—the signing of the Free Trade Agreement with the United States—was decided outside the regular channels of elite accommodation, through an extraordinary appeal to the mass public in the "referendum" of the 1988 federal election. Even so, this appeal yielded a "resounding maybe," as the electorate returned the party supporting free trade, the Conservatives, with a majority of seats in the House of Commons but cast the majority of votes for the two parties opposing the agreement, the Liberals and the NDP.

A stark case of interregional conflict occurred over oil and gas pricing and rent sharing in the wake of the oil price shocks of the 1970s. Constitutional ambiguity provided each level of government with policy instruments in the oil and gas arena without reconciling potential conflicts between them. Elites were too sharply divided to reach an accommodation—none could play a mediating role. Continental-national, market-state, federal-provincial, producer-consumer, and partisan divisions were distilled in a west-versus-east regional conflict. The governments of the oil-producing western provinces (especially the market-oriented governments of Alberta and British Columbia) supported the industry's demand for world prices and export markets, and also sought to strengthen their own power through access to increased oil and gas revenues. The governments of the eastern consumer provinces placed their highest priority on securing domestic supply at regulated prices. Parties at the federal level were unable to play mediating roles. The governing federal Liberal party supported the interests of its overwhelmingly eastern constituency and also saw the increasing revenues of the western provinces as undermining the fiscal structure of the federation. It also contained a strongly economic nationalist wing. The federal Conservatives were predominantly based in the west, shared the industry's view, and, under a western leader, took a decentralist position. Given the existence of Conservative parties in office in both the producing province of Alberta and the consuming province of Ontario, however, the federal Conservatives might have been able to play a mediating role. But during the brief Conservative tenure in office at the federal level in 1979-80, the fierce regional conflict between Alberta and Ontario overpowered the effects of shared partisanship. The federal Conservatives' attempts at mediation, moreover, were soon overtaken by the second oil price shock.

The federal NDP, with an electoral base in British Columbia and a provincial counterpart in office in Saskatchewan, might have played a mediating role in the crisis over oil and gas policy. However, the closely held process followed by the federal Liberals in developing the National Energy Program in 1980, by abjuring conventional patterns of consultation and accommodation, foreclosed the NDP from such a role. Furthermore, by definitively opting for a nationalist approach and an active state role, the Liberals essentially outflanked the NDP on the left and gave the NDP little room to manoeuver.

Developments with regard to constitutional change in the definition of federal and provincial powers over natural resources, however, followed a different course, leading to a constitutional amendment (section 92A). Because these changes formed part of the wider agenda of constitutional change, the structure of interests was broader and less polarized. The federal Liberal government followed a more traditional pattern of elite accommodation and, on the issue of resource powers, the federal NDP was accordingly able to play a mediating role.

The NEP was an exception that proves the rule. It was a rare instance of an unequivocal nationalist and statist policy initiative, and it resulted from a highly atypical process involving exclusively a small set of key federal politicians and bureaucrats. Furthermore, the process of elite accommodation reasserted itself almost immediately, and the policy did not survive a partisan change in government. The doom of the NEP and the resurrection of elite accommodation in dealing with oil-pricing and revenue-sharing issues were certainly due in part to the NEP's incompatibility with the conventions of the Canadian political system—the contrast between the process surrounding the NEP and that surrounding section 92A makes that clear. But it is also true that subsequent federal-provincial agreements on oil and gas price deregulation and fiscal arrangements were made possible by the abating of the oil price crisis.

The thorniest interregional issue of all is unquestionably that of minority language rights. Indeed, the conflict in this arena is both interregional and "meta-regional"—in addition to regional conflict, there is conflict over whether the issue ought even to be defined in regional terms. The reemergence of this issue in the wake of Quebec's "quiet revolution" in the 1960s threatened the very structure of the Canadian confederation. The gap between the constitutional rights of some francophone minorities outside Quebec and actual governmental policies had effectively been ignored for most of the twentieth century. Meanwhile, the anglophone minority of Quebec had been developing a network of anglophone institutions far more elaborate than that to which it was constitutionally "entitled." In such circumstances the claim of Quebec separatists that only the Quebec "state" could protect the French Canadian "nation"— indeed, that a strengthened Quebec state was essential if the economic and cultural force of anglophone North America was to be resisted—is not surprising. English Canada, for its part, reacted to these claims with various admixtures of shock, offence, and guilt.

The mediating elite that arose in this context was composed of federalist Liberal politicians from Quebec, quintessentially embodied in Pierre Trudeau. Viewing Quebec nationalism as parochial and retrogressive, they pursued a strategy of national bilingualism, based on a principle of constitutional parallelism for English and French, and for francophone and anglophone minorities. They sought, accordingly, to "bilingualize" federal institutions and to enhance the status of francophone minorities outside Quebec, to bring their status closer to that of anglophone Quebeckers. The capstone of this project was the adoption of the Charter of Rights and Freedoms, constitutionally entrenching linguistic as well as democratic and civil rights, in 1982—over the opposition of the Quebec government. An ambivalent Quebec electorate supported both federalist politicians in Ottawa and Quebec nationalist or at least "provincialist" politicians in Quebec City.

Meanwhile, anglophone Quebeckers themselves found their traditional institutions threatened by the policies of successive Quebec governments,

Liberal as well as Parti québécois. In this context linguistic minorities themselves might have made common cause as mediators in defence of constitutional parallelism. The anglophone minority of Quebec could advance its own interests by interceding with governments in English Canada on behalf of francophone minorities, and vice versa. Alliance Quebec, representing Quebec anglophones, did follow such a strategy. But it did not receive the reciprocal support of the Fédération des francophones hors Québec in opposing Quebec policies aimed at restricting the use of English.

Ultimately, the "official myth" of national bilingualism (entrenched as constitutional parallelism) had to confront the reality of a *lack* of parallelism between a traditionally privileged and self-confident anglophone minority in Quebec and traditionally disadvantaged and rapidly assimilating francophone minorities elsewhere. Furthermore, the clear rejection of parallelism by successive Quebec governments fueled anglophone resentment in the rest of Canada. Finally, increasingly mobilized ethnic minorities of other than anglophone or francophone ancestry, including aboriginal groups, perceived themselves to be constitutionally subordinated to the self-described "founding races." In these circumstances, the legitimacy of the myth of constitutional parallelism was progressively eroded. A territorial model, in which language rights regimes could vary across regions, appeared more and more congruent with linguistic demography and with the actual policies of provincial governments.

Trudeau's "national bilingualism," then, became not a mediating policy but increasingly a polar position. It was left for a new set of mediators to attempt to reconcile constitutional parallelism with territorial diversity. With the passing of the era of Trudeau, and of René Lévesque, his principal antagonist in the language policy arena, another segment of the Quebec federalist elite (located in the provincial Liberal party) turned to a legitimating myth with historical resonance in Quebec: the concept of Quebec as a "distinct society." And they found a sympathetic audience for this view in the government of Conservative prime minister Brian Mulroney, the bilingual anglophone Quebecker elected with massive support in Quebec in 1984. The constitutional amendments proposed in the Meech Lake Accord, negotiated in 1987, would have maintained parallel language rights for anglophone and francophone minorities but would have allowed the language rights regime in Quebec (and indeed all constitutional provisions affecting Quebec) to be interpreted in a manner consistent with Quebec's "distinctiveness."

The concept of the distinct society was ambiguous enough to allow for a range of interpretation. It therefore accorded well with Canada's constitutional traditions. As discussed in Chapter 2, the tone of Canadian constitutionalism is one not of ringing declaration but of temperate evenhandedness. Constitutional rights are subject to "reasonable limits." The recognition of Quebec's distinctiveness, as proposed in the Meech Lake constitutional amendments, might thus be considered as justifying certain reasonable limitations on individual rights, including linguistic rights. But it could also be argued (and was so argued by defenders of the Meech Lake Accord in English Canada) that the distinct-society clause merely gave explicit constitutional recognition to a principle that the courts had already recognized in reviewing Quebec's language legislation. Judgements of the courts in these cases, moreover, suggested that there were limits on the extent to which the need to promote francophone culture could justify restrictions on constitutional rights. Despite this artful ambiguity, however, the fate of the Meech Lake Accord suggested that the legitimacy of the distinct-society myth is at least as much in question as that of national bilingualism.

The Meech Lake agreement was reached through the classic processes of executive federalism that had characterized Canadian constitutional politics through the history of the nation. The gamut of ratification the agreement had to run under the amending procedure adopted in 1982, however, was unprecedented. In the new politics of ratification the accord became engulfed in controversy.

As it related to language rights, this controversy entailed three cross-cutting axes of fundamental disagreement. The first had to do with whether Canada is essentially a bicultural or a multicultural nation. The second had to do with whether either biculturalism or multiculturalism should be pursued through national or region-specific policies. And the third had to do with whether the protection of the interests of cultural communities could take precedence over individual rights. The accord itself, despite its nod in the direction of multiculturalism, represented an essentially bicultural and regional view of Canadian diversity—the distribution of anglophones and francophones was enunciated as a fundamental characteristic of Canada, and different regional responses to this characteristic were permissible. The accord also countenanced some limitations on individual rights by requiring the charter to be read together with the distinct-society clause. In opposing the accord, Trudeau and Newfoundland premier Clyde Wells ascribed to a view that was bicultural, national, and individualistic—the existence of the two "founding races" was to be recognized in national institutions and in national guarantees of language rights, and the distinct-society clause was seen as an unwarranted threat to individual rights. In Manitoba, a province whose Ukrainian and German communities far outnumber its francophones, the legislature's view was multicultural, national, and individualist—it wanted Canada's "multicultural communities" and the presence of aboriginal people, as well as the existence of anglophone and francophone communities, to be recognized as fundamental characteristics of the nation and would brook no distinction in the responsibility of all governments to "uphold" these fundamental characteristics. At the same time, however, it insisted that the protection of these characteristics could not justify infringing charter rights. (It should be noted, however, that Manitoba's own record in upholding constitutional protection for francophone rights was abysmal, as discussed in Chapter 7. Given this record, Manitoba's opposition to the Meech Lake Accord was particularly galling to Quebec.) For its part, the Parti québécois, which played the role of wry spectator to the Meech Lake acrimony, held a position that was multicultural, regional, and collective. It held that Quebec was a pluralistic, predominantly francophone society, while the rest of Canada constituted a pluralistic, predominantly anglophone society. Put another way, anglophones in Quebec (and francophones outside Quebec) were simply to be considered as one linguistic minority among a variety of others. Different regional responses to these realities were necessary, and in the case of Quebec the collective interests of Quebec society dictated some compromising of individual rights in order to protect the French language.

The Meech Lake attempt at mediation foundered largely but not entirely on the shoals of these disagreements. Perhaps no constitutional document, no matter how carefully crafted its ambiguity, could meld these competing visions. Canadians, after all, have been able to live with the dissonance of their views of the political community only by not writing them down. What is certain, however, is that the kind of focused executive action necessary to devise and adopt an ambiguous compromise, and then parse out its implications in informal negotiations over time, is more and more controversial in Canadian constitutional politics—a point to which I return below.

Partisanship and Federalism

If mediating interests are crucial to the functioning of Canada's ambivalent institutions, the question arises as to why political parties do not more often play this role. In other federations, notably the Federal Republic of Germany, the party system plays a crucial integrative role, and party strategies at the federal and the state levels are closely aligned. As Chandler reports, "regional party elites are tightly integrated and have an active voice within the federal party organization, a fact which complements and reinforces the formal role of Land governments in the Bundesrat" (1989: 13). Furthermore, political careers are often made by moving from the state to the federal level. As a result, as Katzenstein (1987: 35) found in his study of West Germany, "politics is characterized by an interlocking grid representing territorial interests. Federal politics and policy link up with state and local levels in a West German version of 'cooperative federalism.' "

In the United States the very decentralization of the party system, together with the weak party discipline under the congressional system, means that the parties aggregate distinctive regional interests at the national level and constitute important mechanisms of intrastate federalism (Gibbins 1982). The effect of parties on interstate federalism is small, however—although the coincident timing of state and federal elections may create "coat-tail" or "bandwagon" effects, bringing parties of somewhat similar ideologies to power in state and federal institutions. Furthermore, as in Germany, career moves from state to federal politics are common.

Canada exhibits neither of these sets of characteristics, despite the fact that both major parties at the national level are, like the German Christian Democrats and Social Democrats, and the American Republicans and Democrats, mass brokerage parties. Rather, Canada's party system has tended to exacerbate rather than to mute the combativeness of federal-provincial relations. The difference in the role of parties as integrative mechanisms in these three federations can be traced largely to the intersection of partisanship with institutional factors.

The first institutional factor to be considered in this context is Canada's "jurisdictional" division of powers between federal and provincial levels of government, in contrast with Germany's "functional" division (Chandler 1989). Because the German federation assigns policymaking functions to the Bund level and administrative functions to the Lander, it creates the opportunity, indeed the necessity, for parties to develop integrative strategies. "Parties tend not to distinguish themselves by claiming provincial rights or in terms of resisting the centre but by alternative sets of policy proposals for governing nationally" (ibid.:

12). Canadian "jurisdictional" federalism, on the other hand, in theory assigns each level of government primacy in particular policy arenas. In practice, as we have seen, it has assigned alternative but overlapping sets of policy instruments to the two levels of government. This jurisdictional division of power provides institutional footholds at the provincial level for parties to develop programs of governance that may be quite at odds with those offered by the central government. "Provinces act as if they constitute the partisan opposition to the central government" (ibid.).

Such tendencies are present in all systems of jurisdictional federalism, but in Canada they are compounded by the lack of mechanisms of intra-state federalism. "Regional" representatives in the central government are subject to the constraints of party discipline and the majoritarian-ism of the Westminster model. Provincial governments are accordingly more able to present themselves as the sole defenders of regional interests than are, for example, their American counterparts. Provincial parties commonly run their campaigns "against Ottawa"; and, as discussed in Chapter 1, voters show a marked tendency to split their votes feder-ally and provincially. One dimension of this phenomenon has been the greater strength of social democratic parties at the provincial than at the federal level. More generally, the tendency for parties of different parti-san complexion to be in office federally and provincially builds a certain combativeness into federal-provincial relations. The federal-provincial conflict over the Canada Health Act, for example, was fueled by par-tisan competition. Even where parties of similar partisan stripe are in office federally and provincially, and where there are a number of parti-san siblings at the provincial level, the electoral imperative for provincial governments to distance themselves from Ottawa (and often from each other) as defenders of regional interests provides little scope for partisan mediation. The presence of Conservative governments in Ontario and Alberta did not provide a mechanism of east-west accommodation over oil pricing in the crisis of the late 1970s and early 1980s, even during the brief period in which a Conservative government was also in power at the federal level in 1979–80. The presence of Liberal governments across the spectrum of opinion on the Meech Lake Accord, from Quebec's in-sistence that it be passed without change to Newfoundland's insistence on substantial amendment, could not provide common ground despite the attempts of the Liberal premier of New Brunswick to act as media-tor. On rare occasions an all-party consensus at the federal level leads one of the federal opposition parties to intercede with its counterpart in office provincially, as when the federal NDP leader negotiated with the Saskatchewan NDP government to secure agreement for the 1982 constitutional package. Such consensus, however, is unusual; and even when it occurs, party bonds are not likely to be strong enough to allow for mediation. For example, the federal Conservatives, while in opposition in 1984, could not dissuade their counterparts in Manitoba from thwarting the passage of legislation extending services to francophones, which all federal parties had endorsed.

The Need for Institutional Change

The general inability of parties to play the role of interregional mediators has a number of consequences for the Canadian system. In the first place, it has meant that the system has performed best in balancing interests when the need for interregional mediation can be obviated— when decision making can be decentralized. The decentralist thrust of the Meech Lake Accord was essentially a recognition of this fundamental fact of Canadian political life. But there are limits to decentralization. Interregional transfers, including the diffusion of basic national standards in social programs, are part of the national bargain. And decentralization is further constrained by a nationalist sentiment that sees Canada as more than the sum of its provinces—a sentiment to which Pierre Trudeau appealed eloquently in his critique of the Meech Lake Accord. These limits to decentralization were sharply apparent in the broader opposition to the accord.

Second, the absence of partisan ties among federal and provincial politicians has allowed (or indeed required) other ties to be forged. The small-group dynamics of executive federalism have fostered relationships in which informal and ad hoc accommodations can be reached. While never resolving interregional tensions, these accommodations have rendered them politically tolerable. But at the beginning of the 1990s this mechanism of living with interregional tensions was under severe pressure. The tensions themselves were increasing, particularly those between Quebec and the rest of Canada. Moreover, the legitimacy of traditional mechanisms of elite accommodation was in question, particularly in the arena of constitutional politics that was so central to the management of interregional tensions. Institutional change was increasingly being pressed forward on the political agenda. And these pressures were occurring along two dimensions: one pertaining to the structures of government, the other pertaining to the relationships of societal interests to the state.

Along each of these dimensions the challenge was to shift power balances while preserving the capacity of the system to allow opportunities for mediating interests to act and to generate delicate accommodations.

The Dilemmas of Executive Federalism

The process of constitutional change is perhaps the best example of the strengths and the weaknesses of executive federalism. Canadians lived for more than fifty years with the constitutional fiction that only Britain could amend the Canadian constitution, because federal and provincial governments could not agree on a Canadian amending formula and relied by default on ad hoc agreements as the need for constitutional amendments arose. The resulting delay allowed a broader agenda of constitutional reform, including proposals for a charter of rights, to evolve.

From the mid-1960s through the 1980s the political system wrestled with these issues through conventional structures of executive federalism. However, whereas political executives essentially defined the *content* of the resulting constitutional changes, the *legitimacy* of the changes was enhanced by two mechanisms of public participation outside the channels linking federal and provincial executives. The first of these mechanisms was the Quebec referendum of 1980, which denied the PQ government of Quebec a mandate to insist upon its model of "sovereignty-association" and effectively provided the federal government with a mandate to proceed with constitutional change even in the face of the continuing opposition of the Quebec government. The second participatory mechanism was the "eleventh hour" involvement of interest groups in parliamentary hearings on the package of proposals negotiated by the federal and provincial governments. The changes made in 1982, moreover, did not (with the exception of natural resources) address the fundamental issues of the federal-provincial division of powers or the structure of federal institutions. They rather offered a framework within which future governments might "agree to disagree," by allowing up to three provinces (representing less than 50 percent of the population) to opt out of future constitutional amendments affecting provincial rights and powers. The federal-provincial balance remained unresolved, to be effectively renegotiated in particular arenas with each new policy issue.

This agreement to disagree might have been viable, had it included the government of Quebec. But Quebec dissented, and the 1982 constitution thus did not resolve the major issue of Canadian constitutional policy and politics—the relationship of Quebec to the rest of Canada.

Ultimately no mediation was possible between the Quebec nationalism of the PQ government of Quebec under Premier René Lévesque and the strongly centralist position (and disdain for Quebec nationalism) of Prime Minister Pierre Trudeau.

With the passing of the Trudeau and Lévesque eras, and with changes of government at both federal and Quebec provincial levels, it was possible, as noted earlier, for a mediating elite of Quebec federalists open to some form of "special status" for Quebec to play a stronger role. Premier Robert Bourassa typified the ambivalence toward Canada of this segment of the Quebec political elite: He strongly considered leaving the Quebec Liberal Party with René Lévesque to found the PQ in 1968 but remained a "pragmatic federalist," persuaded that Quebec was better off within Canadian confederation than outside it. He signed the Victoria Charter of 1971 and then quickly withdrew his endorsement. Bourassa's "ambivalence, prudence and canny refusal to come down on either side of the fence" has been a matter of much journalistic commentary (see, e.g., McKenzie 1990).

The Bourassa government was hence able to present a relatively modest list of Quebec's "minimum demands." With a decentralist prime minister from Quebec, Brian Mulroney, in office, this list could become the basis of the Meech Lake Accord in 1987. The concerns addressed by the accord were so sensitive, however, that the role of the mediating elite could be played only (or so the participants themselves believed) within the compressed scope of the "club" of first ministers, and only by recourse to very ambiguous language. But the agreement of federal and provincial executives alone was even less sufficient to legitimate constitutional change in 1987 than it had been in 1982. Despite the fact that the accord, unlike the 1982 changes, enjoyed the unanimous support of federal and provincial executives at the time at which it was negotiated, it almost immediately aroused a storm of controversy focused not only on its content but on the process by which it was reached.

More than the 1982 changes, the Meech Lake Accord attempted to grapple with issues of the federal-provincial division of power and the processes of federal-provincial relations. In recognition of the ambiguity that has traditionally surrounded these relationships, and to preserve the discretion of federal and provincial governments, the provisions of the accord were themselves equivocally phrased. Ironically, the constitutional inscription of such requirements, however ambiguous, would have broadened the shadow of judicial interpretation under which federal-provincial negotiations—in key areas such as the exercise of the federal spending power—would henceforth occur.

In seeking to legitimate executive federalism through constitutional recognition, then, federal and provincial governments could not help but circumscribe it. With the death of the Meech Lake Accord, this dilemma must still be faced. If Quebec is to be accommodated within the Canadian federation, federal-provincial relations must be somehow redefined. Any definition is likely to be an ambiguous compromise that will, in Canada's new constitutional politics, be publicly scrutinized and challenged. It will inevitably be contested in and interpreted by the courts—an arena that allows less scope for elite mediation and accommodation than does the federal-provincial executive club.

It is possible that some form of intrastate federalism, such as a reformed Senate, could be developed as an alternative to the structures of executive federalism for the resolution of interregional conflicts. Indeed, Senate reform was being strongly pressed forward on the agenda by the premiers of the western provinces at the end of the 1980s, and the beginning of the 1990s, and a commitment to Senate reform was part of the ill-fated "companion resolution" proposed to save the Meech Lake Accord. Although some observers of the current debate have recalled the comment of the French-Canadian nationalist Henri Bourassa in 1926 that Senate reform is "that famous question . . . which comes periodically, like other forms of epidemics and current fevers" (Fraser 1990), it may well be that pressures for institutional change in the 1990s cannot be resolved without the reform of the Senate or its replacement by another body representing regional interests. As the decade began, however, questions of the appropriate powers of such a body, and the balance of representation between more- and less-populous provinces, were far from resolved.

Even if, on the other hand, Quebec "independence" were to be recognized, it is likely that some sort of "supranational" structure relating Quebec and Canada would be put in place, and the role of the remaining Canadian provinces as well as the federal government within that structure would have to be defined. Quebec Premier Robert Bourassa and a number of his advisers have mused publicly about the salience of the model of the European Community as a reference point and an inspiration to those attempting to define Quebec-Canada relations.

Ironically, traditional Canadian processes of executive federalism and elite accommodation might be better preserved under supranational arrangements linking Canada to an independent Quebec than under any possible domestic reconstitution of the Canadian federation. Those traditional processes, indeed, have been described as akin to "diplomacy" among sovereign states in the international arena (Simeon 1972). Major international agreements are not immune from public scrutiny and debate and political mobilization, as the experience with the Canada-U.S. Free Trade Agreement makes clear. Nor would a Canada-Quebec supranational system remove the role of the courts as arbiters of the relationship: Any such structure would involve a judicial mechanism, perhaps on the model of the European Court of Justice. But on an ongoing basis, moving Canada-Quebec dealings into the realm of "international" relations would likely accord political executives the greater discretion that is generally associated with that arena.

Even if the reconstitution of the Canadian federation does not entail the according of independence to Quebec, reliance upon elite accommodation as the normal mode of policymaking and conflict resolution is not likely to be abandoned. The thrust of this book has been to argue that policymaking in the context of the ambivalences and tensions that characterize the Canadian political system has been possible only because of the flexibility and latitude accorded by institutional ambiguity, and the potential for negotiation afforded by the closed circles of elites in particular policy arenas. These facts of Canadian political life have not changed, despite challenges to the legitimacy of elite accommodation (and particularly to executive federalism in the constitutional arena), and they will continue to shape the policy process.

As Quebec looks toward European models, and the European Community continues to deepen its institutions, it may indeed be that Canada and the European Community will converge on roughly similar models of federalism. There is, in the European Community, no counterpart to the Canadian federal cabinet. But the Commission of the European Community, as an executive whose members have functional portfolios but regional political bases, bears a slight resemblance. The parallels between the Council of Ministers and Canadian federal-provincial conferences of functional ministers are somewhat closer. Finally, the parallel between the European Council (the "summit" of heads of government and foreign ministers) and the Canadian First Ministers' Conferences is closest—both are characterized by informal accommodations, and both play a central role in policymaking. If Canada and Europe build their future institutions on these models, these similarities may increase.

Indeed, some of the problems with which the European Community is wrestling in the 1990s are very familiar to participants in intergovernmental processes in Canada. Tensions are growing between the closed processes of the Commission and the Council of Ministers and demands for "democratic" participation. On constitutional matters, there is ongoing debate as to which categories of issues must require unanimous agreement and which can be dealt with through more flexible arrangements (Lodge 1989). More generally, there is the fundamental problem of developing a multinational political community, and the contested role of social and regional development spending by the community in building loyalty to the centre.

Finally, economic interests are so far relatively weakly organized at the Community level in Europe (Nugent 1989: 194–206; Teague and Grahl 1990), a fact that, as in Canada, means that there are few nongovernmental mechanisms for mediating interregional conflicts. The future shape of both systems depends heavily upon the extent to which societal interests capable of interregional mediation do in fact evolve. In Europe there are at least some precedents at the national level for strong intersectoral organizations of business and labour, and for the participation of these organizations in the "interlocking grid representing territorial interests" to provide a mechanism of regional accommodation. In Canada, as is discussed in the next section, such intersectoral collaboration, even at the provincial level, is much less well developed. But the development of such mechanisms may be as important as is change in the institutions of government in determining the capacity of the political system to overcome interregional conflicts in responding to policy challenges.

The State and Economic Interests

In Canada there have been some indications of change in the mechanisms through which business and labour interests relate to each other and to the state, particularly in the development of policies of economic adjustment. These changes have been driven in part by the failure of elites within traditional structures to mediate interregional conflicts and hence to find more than the lowest common denominator amongst contending interests. The resulting limited focus on the poorest regions, the long-term unemployed, and, in an ad hoc manner, failing firms has satisfied neither business nor labour interests and has been continually criticized by spokesmen for those interests and by commissions of inquiry appointed by governments themselves.

Business and labour interests are accordingly experimenting with bipartite (business and labour) and tripartite (business, labour, and government) mechanisms of collaboration at the sectoral, provincial, and central levels with regard to industrial and labour-market policy, and occupational health and safety. These mechanisms are more formalized and more comprehensive than traditional processes of ad hoc bilateral consultation between governmental and nongovernmental interests, but they are very much in an experimental phase. They also represent attempts to build a collaborative superstructure upon a base of adversarial workplace relations. They are therefore unlikely ever to approximate Swedish or German models, which combine central and sectoral collaboration with workplace codetermination. Britain and Australia provide closer approximations, although even in those two nations central labour federations wield more authority than is the case in Canada.

In Canada the development of these mechanisms will depend upon the ability of business and labour organizations to play mediating roles. There are no peak associations to comprehensively *aggregate* business and labour interests, respectively. But it is possible that organizations such as the BCNI and the CLC at the central level, or individual trade associations and labour unions at the sectoral level, or provincial labour federations and business associations at the provincial level, can be *mediators*. In their internal ambivalence about European-style "social partnership" and collaboration, on the one hand, and North American "hard bargaining" and adversarialism, on the other, these associations may find the incentives and the ability to act as catalysts for new arrangements. Such a scenario—in which ambivalent interests perform mediating roles within loosely defined hybrid authority structures—is entirely consistent with Canadian experience. And it illustrates the possibility of a model alternative to either comprehensive corporatism (in its state or societal variations) or competitive pressure-group pluralism.

It must be emphasized that at the beginning of the 1990s there were only intimations of such a Canadian model, in the form of such bodies as the Canadian Labour Market Productivity Centre and the Labour Force Development Board at the federal level, the Commission de la santé et de la sécurité du travail in Quebec, and the Workplace Health and Safety Agency in Ontario. There were, moreover, substantial obstacles to the evolution of this model. Whether business and labour groups can be any better interregional mediators than political parties have been in the Canadian context remains to be seen. The involvement of these groups in formal policymaking structures may provide a counterbalance to the interests of governments "as governments" in defending their respective regions. But the business community and the labour movement are also fraught with regional tensions. And, at least in the case of the labour movement, its decentralized structure also provides some incentive for local executives to oppose central collaboration in defence of their own raison d'être.

Where interregional conflicts can be obviated through provincial-level collaboration or strategies allowing for local discretion (such as those of the federal Industrial Adjustment Service), these mechanisms may be more successful. Even at the provincial level different provincial political traditions—for example, the statism of Quebec, the incrementalism of Ontario, the populism and polarization of British Columbia—provide different degrees and kinds of support for the development of new institutional arrangements. Furthermore, the effects of the accelerated adjustment pressure resulting from the Free Trade Agreement with the United States are difficult to predict. On the one hand, this pressure may increase the urgency to develop facilitative industrial, labour-market and labour-relations policies, and hence may increase incentives to develop collaborative mechanisms. On the other hand, it may strengthen a current of opinion within the business community, despite the evidence of nations such as Germany and Japan, that international competitiveness demands that business operate free of institutional constraints. On balance, a period of tentative and uneven experimentation with collaborative models can be expected. Their success, especially at the federal level, will depend upon whether the effect of global economic pressures is to forge more cohesive business and labour associations that are capable of acting as interregional mediators, or to further fracture the organization of economic interests in Canada.

Summary

All western industrial nations must deal, to some degree, with ambivalence about the role of the state and the nature of the political community. But few experience that ambivalence to the degree encountered in Canada, where tensions between English and French "founding races," and between a British institutional legacy and an American environment, are exacerbated by a continental range of regional diversity. Canadians have learned to live with ambivalence by institutionalizing it in ambiguously and equivocally defined state structures. The inability to agree upon a federal-provincial division of powers, in particular, has meant that this balance must be continually renegotiated in different policy arenas. And these negotiations have also entailed a continual rebalancing of the roles of the market and the state, of the appropriate level of unity within the political community, and of the priority of individual and collective values, as espoused by federal and provincial governments.

Within these institutions elites have reached accommodations, usually through the mediation of groups whose own ambivalence leads them to seek compromise. These structures and processes are under severe pressure in the late twentieth century to reconcile widely divergent interests while allowing for a broader base of participation. Institutional changes are inevitable in such circumstances: Indeed, several were underway in constitutional and labour-management arenas in the 1980s. These changes may open the Canadian policymaking process to a wider range of elite groups (including the leadership of organized labour). They may also make informal accommodations among elites more difficult to achieve and to maintain by providing more opportunities for public debate and for judicial challenges of policy decisions. But change will be shaped by Canada's institutional legacy and by the challenges of governing a diverse nation. Given that legacy, and in that context, accommodation among elites is likely to continue to be the dominant motif of the Canadian policymaking process.

References

Introduction (Chapter 1)

Adams, Michael. 1988. "Poll says Canadians Want to Renegotiate, Not Rip Up Trade Deal." *Globe and Mail* (Toronto), November 11, pp. A1, A14.

Adie, Robert, and Paul Thomas. 1987. *Canadian Public Administration: Problematical Perspectives*, 2d ed. Toronto: Methuen.

Atkinson, Michael, and William Coleman. 1989. *The State, Business and Industrial Change in Canada*. Toronto: University of Toronto Press.

Banting, Keith. 1986. "The State and Economic Interests: An Introduction." In Keith Banting, ed., *The State and Economic Interests*, vol. 32 of the Research Studies for the Royal Commission on the Economic Union and Development Prospects for Canada, pp. 1–33. Toronto: University of Toronto Press.

Black, Edwin R., and Alan C. Cairns. 1966. "A Different Perspective on Canadian Federalism." *Canadian Public Administration* 9 (March): 27–44.

Blake, Donald. 1985. *Two Political Worlds: Parties and Voting in British Columbia*. Vancouver: University of British Columbia Press.

Breton, Raymond. 1981. "Regionalism in Canada." In David Cameron, ed., *Regionalism and Supranationalism: Challenges and Alternatives to the Nation State in Canada and Europe*, pp. 57–80. Montreal: Institute for Research on Public Policy.

Cairns, Alan C. 1968. "The Electoral System and the Party System in Canada, 1921–1965." *Canadian Journal of Political Science* 1 (March): 55–80.

———. 1977. "The Government and Societies of Canadian Federalism." *Canadian Journal of Political Science* 10 (December): 495–525.

Cameron, David. 1978. "The Expansion of the Public Economy: A Comparative Analysis." *American Political Science Review* 72 (December): 1243–61.

———. 1984. "Social Democracy, Corporatism, Labour Quiescence and the Representation of Economic Interest in Advanced Capitalist Society." In John H. Goldthorpe, ed., *Order and Conflict in Contemporary Capitalism*, pp. 143–78. New York: Oxford University Press.

367

Cameron, David M., and J. Stephan Dupré. 1983. "The Financial Framework of Income Distribution and Social Services." In Stanley M. Beck and Ivan Bernier, eds., *Canada and the New Constitution: The Unfinished Agenda*, pp. 333–99. Montreal: Institute for Research on Public Policy.

Campbell, Colin. 1983. *Governments under Stress: Political Executives and Key Bureaucrats in Washington, London and Ottawa*. Toronto: University of Toronto Press.

Canadian Business. 1984. *The Top 500 Companies*, Special Issue (June).

Canadian Institute of Public Opinion. June 7, 1980; September 24, 1980; January 30, 1986; August 7, 1986; December 18, 1986. *The Gallup Report*. Toronto: Canadian Institute of Public Opinion.

Cheffins, R. I., and P. A. Johnson. 1986. *The Revised Canadian Constitution: Politics as Law*. Toronto: McGraw-Hill Ryerson.

Clarke, Harold, et al. 1979. *Political Choice in Canada*. Toronto: McGraw-Hill Ryerson.

Coleman, William D. 1988. *Business and Politics: A Study of Collective Action*. Montreal: McGill-Queen's University Press.

Coleman, William D., and Henry Jacek. 1983. "The Roles and Activities of Business Interest Associations in Canada." *Canadian Journal of Political Science* 16 (June): 257–80.

Dufour, Christian. 1989. *Le défi québécois*. Montreal: l'Hexagone.

———. 1990. *A Canadian Challenge/ Le défi québécois*. Vancouver: Oolichan.

Dupré, J. Stephan. 1988. "Reflections on the Workability of Executive Federalism." In R. D. Olling and M. W. Westmacott, *Perspectives on Canadian Federalism*, pp. 233–56. Scarborough, Ont.: Prentice Hall.

Elazar, Daniel J. 1972. *American Federalism: A View from the States*. 2d ed. New York: Crowell.

Elkins, David J. 1980. "The Sense of Place." In David J. Elkins and Richard Simeon, eds., *Small Worlds: Provinces and Parties in Canadian Political Life*, pp. 1–30. Toronto: Methuen.

———. 1985. "British Columbia as a State of Mind." In Donald Blake, *Two Political Worlds: Parties and Voting in British Columbia*, pp. 49–73. Vancouver: University of British Columbia Press.

———. 1989. "Facing Our Destiny: Rights and Canadian Distinctiveness." *Canadian Journal of Political Science* 22 (December): 699–716.

Esser, Josef, Wolfgang Fach, and Kenneth Dyson. 1984. " 'Social Market' and Modernization Policy." In Kenneth Dyson and Stephen Wilks, eds., *Industrial Crisis: A Comparative Study of the State and Industry*, pp. 102–27. New York: St. Martin's.

Forbes, H. D. 1987. "Hartz-Horowitz at Twenty: Nationalism, Toryism and Socialism in Canada and the United States." *Canadian Journal of Political Science* 20 (June): 287–316.

Gallup Canada. January 4, 1990. *The Gallup Report*. Toronto: Gallup Canada.

Gibbins, Roger. 1982. *Regionalism: Territorial Politics in Canada and the United States*. Toronto: Butterworths.

Goar, Carol. 1988. "Quebec: Ruling Rekindles Fires of Nationalism." *Toronto Star*, December 24, pp. D1, D4.

Gourevitch, Peter, et al. 1984. *Unions and Economic Crisis: Britain, West Germany and Sweden*. London: George Allen and Unwin.

Green, Christopher. 1980. *Canadian Industrial Organization and Policy*. Toronto: McGraw-Hill Ryerson.

Hartz, Louis. 1955. *The Liberal Tradition in America*. Toronto: Longman.

Heclo, Hugh, and Hendrik Madsen. 1987. *Policy and Politics in Sweden: Principled Pragmatism*. Philadelphia: Temple University Press.

Heidenheimer, Arnold, Hugh Heclo, and Carolyn Teich Adams. 1990. *Comparative Public Policy: The Politics of Social Choice in Europe and America*, 3d ed. New York: St. Martin's.

Hogg, Peter. 1985. *Constitutional Law of Canada*. Toronto: Carswell.

Horowitz, Gad. 1966. "Conservatism, Liberalism and Socialism in Canada." *Canadian Journal of Political Science* 42 (May): 143–71.

Irvine, William P. 1979. *Does Canada Need a New Electoral System?* Kingston, Ont.: Queen's University Institute of Intergovernmental Relations.

Jenkin, Michael. 1983. *The Challenge of Diversity: Industrial Policy in the Canadian Federation*. Ottawa: Minister of Supply and Services.

Katzenstein, Peter. 1987. *Politics and Policy in West Germany: Growth in a Semisovereign State*. Philadelphia: Temple University Press.

Kumar, Pradeep, Mary Lou Coates, and David Arrowsmith. 1986. *The Current Industrial Relations Scene in Canada, 1986*. Kingston, Ont.: Queen's University Industrial Relations Centre.

———. 1987. *The Current Industrial Relations Scene in Canada, 1987*. Kingston, Ont.: Queen's University Industrial Relations Centre.

Lambert, Ronald D., et al. 1986. "In Search of Left/Right Beliefs in the Canadian Electorate." *Canadian Journal of Political Science* 19 (September): 541–64.

Laponce, Jean. 1978. "Measuring Party Preference: The Problem of Ambivalence." *Canadian Journal of Political Science* 11 (March): 139–52.

L'Écuyer, Gilbert. 1978. *La cour suprême du Canada et le partage des compétences 1949–1978*. Québec: Gouvernement du Québec, Ministère des Affaires Intergouvernmentales.

LeDuc, Lawrence. 1985. "Partisan Change and Dealignment in Canada, Great Britain and the United States." *Comparative Politics* 17 (July): 379–98.

Lévesque, René. 1964. Interview with Jean-Marc Léger. *Le Devoir* (Montreal), July 5, 1963. Translated and reprinted in Frank Scott and Michael Oliver, eds., *Quebec States Her Case*, pp. 132–45. Toronto: Macmillan.

Lipset, Seymour Martin. 1968. *Agrarian Socialism: The Cooperative Common-wealth Federation in Saskatchewan*. New York: Anchor.

Lipsey, Richard G., and Murray G. Smith. 1985. *Taking the Initiative: Canada's Trade Options in a Turbulent World*. Montreal: C. D. Howe Institute.

Lithwick, N. Harvey. 1986. "Federal Government Regional Economic Development Policies: An Evaluative Survey." In Kenneth Norrie, ed., *Disparities and Inter-regional Adjustment*, vol. 64 of the Research Studies for the Royal Commission on the Economic Union and Development Prospects for Canada, pp. 109–58. Toronto: University of Toronto Press.

McNaught, Kenneth. 1982. *The Pelican History of Canada*. Harmondsworth: Penguin.

Macpherson, C. B. 1953. *Democracy in Alberta: The Theory and Practice of a Quasi-Party System*. Toronto: University of Toronto Press.

McRae, Kenneth. 1964. "The Structure of Canadian History." In Louis Hartz, ed., *The Founding of New Societies*, pp. 219–74. Toronto: Longmans.

McWhinney, Edward. 1983. "The Canadian Charter of Rights and Freedoms: The Lessons of Comparative Jurisprudence." *Canadian Bar Review* 61 (March): 55–66.

Mallory, J. R. 1977. "Confederation: The Ambiguous Bargain." *Journal of Canadian Studies* 12 (July): 18–23.

Mansell, Robert L., and Lawrence Copithorne. 1986. "Canadian Regional Economic Disparities: A Survey." In Kenneth Norrie, ed., *Disparities and Inter-regional Adjustment*, vol. 64 of the Research Studies for the Royal Commission on the Economic Union and Development Prospects for Canada, pp. 1–52. Toronto: University of Toronto Press.

Morton, F. L., et al. 1989. "Judicial Nullification of Statues under the Charter of Rights and Freedoms, 1982–1988." Paper presented at the joint session of the annual meetings of the Canadian Political Science Association and the Canadian Law and Society Association, Quebec City, June 3.

Organization for Economic Cooperation and Development (OECD). 1988. *OECD Economic Surveys: Canada*. Paris: OECD.

Ornstein, Michael, H. Michael Stevenson, and A. Paul Williams. 1980. "Region, Class and Political Culture in Canada." *Canadian Journal of Political Science* 13 (June): 227–71.

Pauly, Louis. 1988. *Opening Financial Markets: Banking Politics on the Pacific Rim*. Ithaca, N.Y.: Cornell University Press.

Pempel, T. J. 1982. *Policy and Politics in Japan: Creative Conservatism*. Philadelphia: Temple University Press.

Rose, Richard. 1989. *Ordinary People in Public Policy*. London: Sage.

Russell, Peter. 1983. "The Political Purposes of the Canadian Charter of Rights and Freedoms." *Canadian Bar Review* 61 (March): 30–54.

———. 1985. "The Supreme Court and Federal-Provincial Relations: The Political Use of Legal Resources." *Canadian Public Policy* 11 (June): 161–70.

————. 1987. *The Judiciary in Canada: The Third Branch of Government*. Toronto: McGraw-Hill Ryerson.

Sabetti, Filipp. 1984. "The Historical Context of Constitutional Change in Canada." In Paul Davenport and Richard Leach, eds., *Reshaping Confederation: The 1982 Reform of the Canadian Constitution*, pp. 11–32. Durham, N.C.: Duke University Press.

Schultz, Richard J. 1980. *Federalism, Bureaucracy and Public Policy*. Montreal: McGill-Queen's University Press.

Simeon, Richard. 1972. *Federal-Provincial Diplomacy: The Making of Public Policy in Canada*. Toronto: University of Toronto Press.

Simeon, Richard, and Donald E. Blake. 1980. "Regional Preferences: Citizens' Views of Public Policy." In David J. Elkins and Richard Simeon, eds., *Small Worlds: Provinces and Parties in Canadian Political Life*, pp. 77–105. Toronto: Methuen.

Smiley, D. V. 1987. *The Federal Condition in Canada*. Toronto: University of Toronto Press.

Smith, Peter. 1987. "The Ideological Origins of Canadian Confederation." *Canadian Journal of Political Science* 20 (March): 3–30.

Sniderman, Paul M., et al. 1989. "Political Culture and the Problem of Double Standards: Mass and Elite Attitudes toward Language Rights in the Canadian Charter of Rights and Freedoms." *Canadian Journal of Political Science* 22 (June): 259–84.

Statistics Canada. 1973. *Canada Year Book, 1973*. Ottawa: Information Canada.

————. 1986a. *Canadian Income and Expenditure Accounts: Description of Revisions*. Ottawa: Minister of Supply and Services, July (Cat. no. 13-0001).

————. 1986b. *Income after Tax, 1986*. Ottawa: Minister of Supply and Services (Cat. no. 13-210).

————. 1987. *Canada Year Book, 1988*. Ottawa: Ministry of Supply and Services.

————. 1988. *Quarterly Estimates of the Canadian International Balance of Payments, June 1987*. Ottawa: Ministry of Supply and Services (Cat. no. 67-001P).

Sutherland, Sharon, and G. Bruce Doern. 1985. *Bureaucracy in Canada: Control and Reform*, vol. 43 of the Research Studies for the Royal Commission on the Economic Union and Development Prospects for Canada. Toronto: University of Toronto Press.

Swinton, Katherine. 1988. "Competing Visions of Constitutionalism: Of Federalism and Rights." In Katherine E. Swinton and Carol J. Rogerson, eds., *Competing Constitutional Visions: The Meech Lake Accord*, pp. 279–94. Toronto: Carswell.

Task Force on Canadian Unity. 1979. *A Future Together*. Ottawa: Minister of Supply and Services.

Taylor, Charles. 1990. "A Free, Independent Quebec in a Strong, United

Canada." *Compass* 8 (May): 46–48.

Van Loon, Richard, and Michael Whittington. 1976. *The Canadian Political System: Environment, Structure, and Process*, 2d ed. Toronto: McGraw-Hill Ryerson.

Vipond, Robert. 1991. *Liberty and Community: Canadian Federalism and the Failure of Constitutional Vision*. Albany: State University of New York Press.

Wheare, K. C. 1964. *Federal Government*, 4th ed. New York: Oxford University Press.

Young, R. A., Phillippe Faucher, and André Blais. 1984. "The Concept of Province-Building: A Critique." *Canadian Journal of Political Science* 17 (December): 783–818.

Zussman, David. 1987. "Walking the Tightrope: The Mulroney Government and the Public Service." In Michael J. Prince, ed., *How Ottawa Spends, 1986–87: Tracking the Tories*, pp. 250–87. Toronto: Methuen.

Constitutional Change (Chapter 2)

Adams, Michael, and Donna Dasko. 1990. "English Canadians Want a New Deal." *Toronto Star*, May 16, p. A1.

Dellinger, Walter. 1984. "The Amending Process in Canada and the United States: A Comparative Perspective." In Paul Davenport and Richard H. Leach, eds., *The 1982 Reform of the Canadian Constitution*, pp. 283–302. Durham, N.C.: Duke University Press.

Gallup Canada. June 18, 1987; January 16, 1989; May 3, 1990. *The Gallup Report*. Toronto: Gallup Canada Inc.

Gibbins, Roger. 1982. *Regionalism: Territorial Politics in Canada and the United States*. Toronto: Butterworths.

Gusfield, Joseph R. 1963. *Symbolic Crusade*. Urbana: University of Illinois Press.

Kornberg, Allan, and Keith Archer. 1984. "A Note on Quebec Attitudes toward Constitutional Options." In Paul Davenport and Richard H. Leach, eds., *The 1982 Reform of the Canadian Constitution*, pp. 71–87. Durham, N.C.: Duke University Press.

Lévesque, René. 1968. *An Option for Quebec*. Toronto: McClelland and Stewart.

McRoberts, Kenneth. 1988. *Quebec: Social Change and Political Crisis*, 3d ed. Toronto: McClelland and Stewart.

McWhinney, Edward. 1982. *Canada and the Constitution, 1979–1982: Patriation and the Charter of Rights*. Toronto: University of Toronto Press.

Mallory, J. R. 1977. "Confederation: The Ambiguous Bargain." *Journal of Canadian Studies* 12 (July): 18–23.

Morin, Claude. 1976. *Quebec versus Ottawa: The Struggle for Self-government, 1960–1972*. Toronto: University of Toronto Press.

Organization for Economic Cooperation and Development (OECD). 1988. *OECD Economic Surveys: Canada*. Paris: OECD.

Pinard, Maurice. 1975. "La dualité des loyautés et les options constitutionelles des Québécois francophones." In *La nationalisme québécois à la croisée des chemins*. Québec: Centre québécois des rélations internationales.

Posgate, Dale, and Kenneth McRoberts. 1976. *Quebec: Social Change and Political Crisis*. Toronto: McClelland and Stewart.

Quebec, Government of. 1968. "Preliminary Statement," presented to the Confederation of Tomorrow Conference, Toronto, November 1967. Reprinted as "What Does Quebec Want?" In J. Peter Meekison, ed., *Canadian Confederation: Myth or Reality?*, pp. 354–67. Toronto: Methuen.

Quebec Liberal Federation. 1968. "Report by the Constitution Committee of the Quebec Liberal Federation Policy Commission," presented to the annual convention of the Quebec Liberal Federation 1967. Reprinted in J. Peter Meekison, ed., *Canadian Confederation: Myth or Reality?*, pp. 367–78. Toronto: Methuen.

Romanow, Roy, John Whyte, and Howard Leeson. 1984. *Canada . . . Notwithstanding: The Making of the Constitution, 1976–82*. Toronto: Carswell Methuen.

Russell, Peter. 1987. *The Judiciary in Canada: The Third Branch of Government*. Toronto: McGraw-Hill Ryerson.

———. 1988. "The Politics of Frustration: The Pursuit of Formal Constitutional Change in Australia and Canada." *Australian-Canadian Studies* 6 (March): 3–32.

Simeon, Richard, and Donald E. Blake. 1980. "Regional Preferences: Citizens' Views of Public Policy." In David J. Elkins and Richard Simeon, eds., *Small Worlds: Provinces and Parties in Canadian Political Life*, pp. 77–105. Toronto: Methuen.

Southam News. 1990. "55% Say Meech Deal Should Be Ratified." *Toronto Star*, June 13.

Winsor, Hugh. 1991. "Quebeckers Face Future in Uncertainty: Many Committed to Sovereignty Still Hold Pro-Canada Sentiments." *Globe and Mail* (Toronto), April 22, pp. A1, A6, A7.

Health Care Delivery (Chapter 3)

Aldrich, Jonathan. 1982. "The Earnings Replacement Rate of Old-Age Benefits in 12 Countries, 1969–80." *Social Security Bulletin* 45 (November): 3–11.

Altenstetter, Christina. 1989. "Health Policy: Federal Republic of Germany." In Jack Paul DeSario, ed., *International Public Policy Sourcebook, Volume 1: Health and Social Welfare*, pp. 33–62. Westport, Conn.: Greenwood.

Banting, Keith. 1987. *The Welfare State and Canadian Federalism*, 2d ed. Montreal: McGill-Queen's.

Barer, Morris, and Robert G. Evans. 1986. "Riding North on a South-bound Horse: Expenditures, Prices, Utilization and Incomes in the Canadian Health

Care System." In Robert G. Evans and Greg L. Stoddart, eds., *Medicare at Maturity*, pp. 53–164. Calgary: University of Calgary Press.

Bird, Richard. 1981. "The Public Finance of Health Care: Reflections on the Hall Report." In *Commentaries on the Hall Report*. Toronto: Ontario Economic Council.

Bjorkman, James W. 1985. "Who Governs the Health Sector?" *Comparative Politics* 17 (July): 399–420.

Blendon, Robert J. 1989. "Three Systems: A Comparative Survey." *Health Management Quarterly* 11, no. 1: 2–10.

Boase, Joan Price. 1986. "Public Policy and the Regulation of the Health Disciplines." Ph.D. dissertation, York University, Toronto, Ont.

Brown, Lawrence. 1990. "Influences from the United States." In S. Mathwin Davis, ed., *Healthy Populace/Healthy Policy: Medicare toward the Year 2000*, pp. 161–70. Kingston, Ont.: Queen's University School of Policy Studies.

Canada, Government of. 1983. *Preserving Universal Medicare*. Ottawa: Minister of National Health and Welfare.

Contandriopoulos, Andre-Pierre, Claudine Laurier, and Louise-Helene Trottier. 1986. "Toward an Improved Work Organization in the Health Services Sector." In Robert G. Evans and Greg L. Stoddart, eds., *Medicare at Maturity*, pp. 287–324. Calgary: University of Calgary Press.

Crichton, Anne. 1984. "Health Policies in Canada, 1984: Stability and Change." University of British Columbia, Department of Health Care and Epidemiology, mimeo.

Desrosiers, Georges. 1986. "The Quebec Health Care System." *Journal of Health Policy, Politics and Law* 11 (Summer): 211–17.

Detsky, Allan S., Sidney Stacey, and Claire Bombardier. 1983. "The Effectiveness of a Regulatory Strategy in Containing Hospital Costs." *New England Journal of Medicine* 309 (July 21): 151–59.

Dixon, Maureen. 1981. "The Organization of Health Councils in Ontario." Ph.D. dissertation, Brunel University, London.

Evans, Robert G. 1984. *Strained Mercy: The Economics of Canadian Health Care*. Toronto: Butterworths.

Evans, Robert G., et al. 1989. "Controlling Expenditures—the Canadian Reality." *New England Journal of Medicine* 320, (March 2): 571–77.

Falcone, David J., and William Mishler. 1989. "Health Policy: Canada." In Jack Paul DeSario, ed., *International Public Policy Sourcebook, Volume 1: Health and Social Welfare*, pp. 9–32. Westport, Conn.: Greenwood.

Fraser, Graham. 1989. *Playing for Keeps: The Making of the Prime Minister, 1988*. Toronto: McClelland and Stewart.

Fuchs, Victor R. 1983. "The Battle for the Control of Health Care." *Health Affairs* 1 (Summer): 5–13.

Gosselin, Roger. 1984. "Decentralization/Regionalization in Health Care: The

Quebec Experience." *Health Care Management Review* 9 (Winter): 7–23.

Griffith, Frederick H. 1990. "Consideration of Alternative Approaches." In S. Mathwin Davis, ed., *Healthy Populace/Healthy Policy: Medicare toward the Year 2000*, pp. 103–10. Kingston, Ont.: Queen's University School of Policy Studies.

Heiber, S., and R. Deber. 1987. "Banning Extra-Billing in Canada." *Canadian Public Policy* 13, no. 1: 62–74.

Heidenheimer, Arnold, Hugh Heclo, and Carolyn Teich Adams. 1983. *Comparative Public Policy*, 2d ed. New York: St. Martin's.

Hollingsworth, J. Rogers, Jerald Hage, and Robert A. Hanneman. 1990. *State Intervention in Medical Care*. Ithaca, N.Y.: Cornell University Press.

Katzenstein, Peter. 1987. *Policy and Politics in West Germany: The Growth of a Semisovereign State*. Philadelphia: Temple University Press.

Kirkman-Liff, Bradford L. 1990. "Physician Payment and Cost-Containment Strategies in West Germany." *Journal of Health Politics, Policy and Law* 15 (Spring): 69–100.

Lewin, Lawrence S., Robert A. Derzon, and Rhea Marguilies. 1981. "Investor-owneds and Nonprofits Differ in Economic Performance." *Hospitals* 55 (July 1): 52–58.

Lomas, Jonathan, and Morris L. Barer. 1986. "And Who Shall Represent the Public Interest? The Legacy of Canadian Health Manpower Policy." In Robert G. Evans and Greg L. Stoddart, eds., *Medicare at Maturity*, pp. 221–86. Calgary: University of Calgary Press.

Lomas, Jonathan, et al. 1989. "Paying Physicians in Canada." *Health Affairs* 8 (Spring): 81–102.

Luft, Howard. 1981. *Health Maintenance Organizations: Dimensions of Performance*. New York: Wiley.

McAdam, W. Murray. 1983. "Incentives Recommended for Health Care System." *Ontario Medical Review* 51 (July): 342–43.

Marcoux, Gérard. 1987. "La régionalisation/décentralisation." In George Desrosiers, ed., *Le Système de Santé de l'Ontario*, pp. 63–66. Montréal: Les éditions administration de la santé.

Morone, James A. 1990. "American Political Culture and the Search for Lessons from Abroad." *Journal of Health Politics, Policy and Law* 15 (Spring): 129–44.

Myles, John. 1988. "Postwar Capitalism and the Extension of Social Security into a Retirement Wage." In Margaret Weir, Ann Shola Orloff, and Theda Skocpol, eds., *The Politics of Social Policy in the United States*, pp. 265–84. Princeton, N.J.: Princeton University Press.

Naylor, C. David. 1986. *Private Practice, Public Payment: Canadian Medicine and the Politics of Health Insurance, 1911–1966*. Montreal: McGill-Queen's University Press.

Organization for Economic Cooperation and Development (OECD). 1987. *Financing and Delivering Health Care: A Comparative Analysis of OECD Countries*. Paris: OECD.

————. 1989. *OECD in Figures*, supplement to *The OECD Observer* 158 (June/July).

Parliamentary Task Force on Federal-Provincial Arrangements. 1981. *Fiscal Federalism in Canada*. Ottawa: Minister of Supply and Services.

Pattison, Robert V., and Hallie M. Katz. 1983. "Investor-owned and Not-for-profit Hospitals: A Comparison Based on California Data." *New England Journal of Medicine* 309 (August 11): 347–53.

Rachlis, Michael, and Catherine Fooks. 1988. "Utilization Analysis: Current Initiatives across Canada." Paper presented at the Centre for Health Economics and Policy Analysis annual conference on Reviewing Utilization, Hamilton, Ontario, May 27.

Rachlis, Michael, and Carol Kushner. 1989. *Second Opinion*. Toronto: Collins.

Relman, Arnold. 1989. "American Medicine at the Crossroads: Signs from Canada." *New England Journal of Medicine* 320, (March 2): 590–91.

Schieber, George J. 1985. "Health Spending: Its Growth and Control." *OECD Observer* 137 (November): 13–17.

———— and Jean-Pierre Poullier. 1987. "Recent Trends in International Health Care Spending." *Health Affairs* 6 (Fall): 105–12.

————. 1988. "International Health Spending and Utilization Trends." *Health Affairs* 7 (Fall): 105–12.

Schwartz, William B., and Henry J. Aaron. 1984. "Rationing Hospital Care: Lessons from Britain." *New England Journal of Medicine* 310 (January 5): 52–56.

Smeeding, Timothy, Barbara Torrey, and Martin Rein. 1988. "Patterns of Income and Poverty, The Economic Status of Children and the Elderly in Eight Countries." In Isabel Palmer, Timothy Smeeding, and Barbara Torrey, eds., *The Vulnerable*, pp. 89–119. Washington, D.C.: The Urban Institute.

Starr, Paul. 1982. *The Social Transformation of American Medicine*. New York: Basic Books.

Stevenson, H. Michael, Eugene Vayda, and A. Paul Williams. 1987. "Medical Politics after the Canada Health Act: Preliminary Results of the 1986 Physicians' Survey." Paper delivered at the annual meeting of the Canadian Political Science Association, McMaster University, Hamilton, Ont.

Stevenson, H. Michael, and A. Paul Williams. 1985. "Physicians and Medicare: Professional Ideology and Canadian Health Care Policy." *Canadian Public Policy* 11 (September): 504–21.

Stoddart, Greg L. 1985. "Rationalizing the Health Care System." In D. Conklin, G. Cook, and T. Courchene, eds., *Ottawa and the Provinces: The Distribution of Money and Power*. Toronto: Ontario Economic Council.

Stone, Deborah L. 1977. "Professionalism and Accountability: Controlling Health Services in the United States and West Germany." *Journal of Health Politics, Policy and Law* 2 (Spring): 32–47.

Taylor, Malcolm G. 1973. "The Canadian Health Insurance Program." *Public Administration Review* 33 (January/February): 31–39.

———. 1978. *Health Insurance and Canadian Public Policy*. Montreal: McGill-Queen's University Press.

Tuohy, Carolyn J. 1982a. "Smoke and Mirrors: Professional Ideology and Symbolism in Health Policy." *Proceedings of the Conference on Health in the '80's and '90's*, pp. 185–203. Toronto: Council of Ontario Universities.

———. 1982b. "Does a Claims Monitoring System Influence High-volume Medical Practitioners?" *Inquiry* 19 (Spring): 18–33.

———. 1986. "Conflict and Accommodation in the Canadian Health System." In Robert G. Evans and Greg L. Stoddart, eds., *Medicare at Maturity*, pp. 393–434. Calgary: University of Calgary Press.

———. 1988. "Medicine and the State in Canada: The Extra-billing Issue in Perspective." *Canadian Journal of Political Science* 21 (June): 268–96.

———. 1989. "Federalism and Canadian Health Care Policy." In William M. Chandler and Christian W. Zollner, eds., *Challenges to Federalism: Policy-Making in Canada and the Federal Republic of Germany*, pp. 141–60. Kingston, Ont.: Queen's University Institute for Intergovernmental Relations.

Tuohy, Carolyn J., and Robert G. Evans. 1984. "Pushing on a String: The Decentralization of Health Planning in Ontario." In Robert T. Golembiewski and Aaron Wildavsky, eds., *The Costs of Federalism*, pp. 89–116. New Brunswick, N.J.: Transaction.

Wilson, P. R., D. Chappell, and R. Lincoln. 1986. "Policing Physician Abuse in British Columbia." *Canadian Public Policy* 12 (March): 236–44.

Wolfson, Alan D., and Carolyn J. Tuohy. 1980. *Opting Out of Medicare*. Toronto: Ontario Economic Council.

Industrial Relations and Labour-Market Policy (Chapter 4)

Adams, Roy J. 1988. *North American Industrial Relations: Divergent Trends in Canada and the United States*, Working Paper no. 307. Hamilton, Ont.: McMaster University Faculty of Business.

Advisory Council on Adjustment. 1989. *Adjusting to Win*. Ottawa: Minister of Supply and Services, March.

Ashford, Nicholas. 1976. *Crisis in the Workplace*. Cambridge, Mass.: MIT Press.

Auditor General for Canada. 1987. *Report of the Auditor General*. Ottawa: Minister of Supply and Services.

Bruce, Peter G. 1989. "Political Parties and Labour Legislation in Canada and the U.S." *Industrial Relations* 28 (Spring): 115–41.

Cameron, David. 1984. "Social Democracy, Corporatism, Labour Quiescence and the Representation of Economic Interest in Advanced Capitalist Society." In John H. Goldthorpe, ed., *Order and Conflict in Contemporary Capitalism*, pp. 143–78. New York: Oxford University Press.

Coleman, William D. 1988. *Business and Politics: A Study of Collective Action.* Montreal: McGill-Queen's University Press.

Davies, Robert J. 1986. "The Structure of Collective Bargaining in Canada." In W. Craig Riddell, ed., *Canadian Labour Relations*, vol. 16 of the Research Studies for the Royal Commission on the Economic Union and Development Prospects for Canada, pp. 211–56. Toronto: University of Toronto Press.

Employment and Immigration Canada. 1981. *Labour Market Development in the 1980's.* Ottawa: Ministry of Supply and Services.

———. 1985. *Canadian Jobs Strategy.* Ottawa: Ministry of Supply and Services.

Ergas, Henry, and Jeffrey Shafer. 1987–88. "Cutting Unemployment through Labour-Market Flexibility." *OECD Observer* 149 (December/January): 19–22.

Fournier, Pierre. 1986. "Consensus Building in Canada: Case Studies and Prospects." In Keith Banting, ed., *The State and Economic Interests*, pp. 291–336. Toronto: University of Toronto Press.

Goldthorpe, John H. 1984. "The End of Convergence: Corporatist and Dualist Tendencies in Modern Western Societies." In John H. Goldthorpe, ed., *Order and Conflict in Contemporary Capitalism*, pp. 315–43. New York: Oxford University Press.

Katzenstein, Peter. 1985. *Small States in World Markets.* Ithaca, N.Y.: Cornell University Press.

Kochan, T. A., H. C. Katz, and N. Mower. 1984. *Worker Participation and American Unions: Threat or Opportunity?* Kalamazoo: Upjohn Institute for Employment Research.

Kumar, Pradeep. 1986. "Union Growth in Canada: Retrospect and Prospect." In W. Craig Riddell, ed., *Canadian Labour Relations*, vol. 16 of the Research Studies for the Royal Commission on the Economic Union and Development Prospects for Canada, pp. 95–160. Toronto: University of Toronto Press.

Kumar, Pradeep, Mary Lou Coates, and David Arrowsmith. 1986. *The Current Industrial Relations Scene in Canada, 1986.* Kingston, Ont.: Queen's University Industrial Relations Centre.

———. 1987. *The Current Industrial Relations Scene in Canada, 1987.* Kingston, Ont.: Queen's University Industrial Relations Centre.

Lipsig-Mummé, Carla. 1984. "The Web of Dependence: Quebec Unions in Politics before 1976." In Alain G. Gagnon, ed., *Quebec: State and Society*, pp. 286–313. Toronto: Methuen.

Martin, Andrew. 1986. "The Politics of Employment and Welfare." In Keith Banting, ed., *The State and Economic Interests*, pp. 157–241. Toronto: University of Toronto Press.

Meltz, Noah M. 1985. "Labour Movements in Canada and the United States." In T. A. Kochan, ed., *Challenges and Choices Facing American Labour* pp. 315–34. Cambridge, Mass: MIT Press.

Muszynski, Leon. 1986. "The Politics of Labour Market Policy." In G. Bruce Doern, ed., *The Politics of Economic Policy*, vol. 40 of the Research Studies for the Royal Commission on the Economic Union and Development Prospects for Canada, pp. 251–305. Toronto: University of Toronto Press.

Muszynski, Leon, and D. A. Wolfe. 1989. "New Technology and Training: Lessons from Abroad." *Canadian Public Policy* 15 (September): 245–64.

Organization for Economic Cooperation and Development (OECD). 1985. "Job Growth, Flexibility and Security." *OECD Observer* 136 (September): 3–8.

———. 1986. "Country Problems and Strategies: Canada." *OECD Observer* 138 (January): 22–23.

———. 1988. *Employment Outlook*. Paris: OECD, September.

Pal, Leslie A. 1985. "Revision and Retreat: Canadian Unemployment Insurance, 1971–1981." In Jacqueline S. Ismael, ed., *Canadian Social Welfare Policy*, pp. 75–104. Montreal: McGill-Queen's University Press.

Panitch, Leo, and Donald Swartz. 1984. "Towards Permanent Exceptionalism: Coercion and Consent in Canadian Industrial Relations." *Labour/Le Travail* 13 (Spring): 133–57.

Pempel, T. J. 1982. *Policy and Politics in Japan*. Philadelphia: Temple University Press.

Premier's Council. 1989. *Competing in the Global Economy*, vol. 3. Toronto: Queen's Printer for Ontario.

Riddell, W. Craig. 1986a. "Canadian Labour Relations: An Overview." In W. Craig Riddell, ed., *Canadian Labour Relations*, vol. 16 of the Research Studies for the Royal Commission on the Economic Union and Development Prospects for Canada, pp. 1–94. Toronto: University of Toronto Press.

———. 1986b. "Labour-Management Cooperation in Canada: An Overview." In W. Craig Riddell, ed., *Labour Management Cooperation in Canada*, vol. 15 of the Research Studies for the Royal Commission on the Economic Union and Development Prospects for Canada, pp. 1–56. Toronto: University of Toronto Press.

Rose, Joseph B. 1983. "Some Notes on the Building Trades–Canada Labour Congress Dispute." *Industrial Relations* 22 (Winter): 87–93.

Rose, Joseph B., and G. N. Chaison. 1985. "The State of the Unions: United States and Canada." *Journal of Labour Research* (Winter).

Schmidt, Manfred G. 1982. "Does Corporatism Matter? Economic Crisis, Politics and Rates of Unemployment in Capitalist Democracies in the 1970's." In Gerhard Lehmbruch and Phillippe Schmitter, eds., *Patterns of Corporatist Policy-making*, pp. 237–58. Beverley Hills, Calif.: Sage.

Shaw, R. P. 1985. "The Burden of Unemployment in Canada." *Canadian Public Policy* 11 (June): 143–60.

Statistics Canada. 1984. *Unemployment Insurance 1984*. Ottawa: Minister of Supply and Services.

———. 1986. *Canadian Income and Expenditure Accounts: Description of Revisions*. Ottawa: Minister of Supply and Services, July 18 (Cat. no. 13-001).

Tuohy, Carolyn. 1990. "Institutions and Interests in the Occupational Health Arena: The Case of Quebec." In William Coleman and Grace Skogstad, eds., *Policy Communities and Public Policy in Canada*, pp. 238–65. Toronto: Copp Clark Pittman.

Waldie, K. G. 1986. "The Evolution of Labour-Government Consultation on Economic Policy." In W. Craig Riddell, ed., *Labour Management Cooperation in Canada*, vol. 15 of the Research Studies for the Royal Commission on the Economic Union and Development Prospects for Canada, pp. 151–201. Toronto: University of Toronto Press.

Weiler, Joseph. 1985. "The Role of Law in Labour Relations." In Ivan Bernier and Andree Lajoie, eds., *Labour Law and Urban Law in Canada*, vol. 51 of the Research Studies for the Royal Commission on the Economic Union and Development Prospects for Canada, pp. 1–65. Toronto: University of Toronto Press.

Weiler, Paul. 1980. *Reconcilable Differences*. Toronto: Carswell.

———. 1983. "Promises to Keep: Securing Workers' Rights to Self-organization under the NLRA." *Harvard Law Review* 96 (June): 1769–1829.

———. 1984. "Striking a New Balance: Freedom of Contract and the Prospect for Union Representation." *Harvard Law Review* 98 (December): 351–420.

———. 1990. "The Charter at Work: Reflections on the Constitutionalizing of Labour and Employment Law," *University of Toronto Law Journal* 40 (Spring): 117–190.

Economic Development and Adjustment (Chapter 5)

Adams, Michael. 1988. "Poll Says Canadians Want to Renegotiate, Not Rip Up Trade Deal." *Globe and Mail* (Toronto), November 11, pp. A1, A14.

Advisory Council on Adjustment. 1989. *Adjusting to Win*. Ottawa: Minister of Supply and Services, March.

Atkinson, Michael, and William Coleman. 1989. *The State, Business and Industrial Change in Canada*. Toronto: University of Toronto Press.

Baker, Samuel R. 1985. "From FIRA to Investment Canada." In Earl Fry and Lee H. Radebaugh, eds., *Canada-US Economic Relations in the "Conservative" Era of Mulroney and Reagan*. Provo, Utah: Brigham Young University.

Bakvis, Herman. 1989. "Regional Politics and Policy in the Mulroney Cabinet, 1984–88." *Canadian Public Policy* 15 (June): 121–34.

Bernier, Ivan. 1988. "L'Accord de libre-échange Canada-États-Unis et la Constitution." In Marc Gold and David Leyton-Brown, eds., *Trade-offs on Free*

Trade: The Canada-US Free Trade Agreement, pp. 100–106. Toronto: Carswell.

Blais, André. 1986a. "Industrial Policy in Advanced Capitalist Economies." In André Blais, ed., *Industrial Policy*, vol. 44 of the Research Studies for the Royal Commission on the Economic Union and Development Prospects for Canada, pp. 1–54. Toronto: University of Toronto Press.

———. 1986b. "The Debate on Canadian Industrial Policy." In André Blais, ed., *Industrial Policy*, vol. 44 of the Research Studies for the Royal Commission on the Economic Union and Development Prospects for Canada, pp. 55–82. Toronto: University of Toronto Press.

Brooks, Stephen, and A. Brian Tanguay. 1985. "Quebec's Caisse de dépôt et placement: Tool of Nationalism?" *Canadian Public Administration* 28 (Spring): 99–119.

Canadian Labour Congress. 1976. *Labour's Manifesto for Canada*. Ottawa: Canadian Labour Congress.

———. 1985. "Surrendering National Sovereignty." In Duncan Cameron, ed., *The Free Trade Papers*, pp. 135–42. Toronto: Lorimer.

Canadian Manufacturers' Association. 1983. *Future Making: The Era of Himan Resources*, Submission by the Canadian Manufacturers' Association to the Royal Commission on the Economic Union and Development Prospects for Canada, Vancouver, B.C., September 6.

Carmichael, Edward A. 1986. *New Stresses on Confederation: Diverging Regional Economies*. Toronto: C. D. Howe Institute.

Carmichael, Edward A., Katie Macmillan, and Robert C. York. 1989. *Ottawa's Next Agenda*. Toronto: C. D. Howe Institute.

Chandler, M. A. 1986. "The State and Industrial Decline: A Survey." In André Blais, ed., *Industrial Policy*, vol. 44 of the Research Studies for the Royal Commission on the Economic Union and Development Prospects for Canada, pp. 171–218. Toronto: University of Toronto Press.

Doern, G. Bruce. 1986. "The Tories, Free Trade and Industrial Adjustment Policy." In Michael J. Prince, ed., *How Ottawa Spends, 1987–87: Tracking the Tories*, pp. 61–94. Toronto: Methuen.

Doern, G. Bruce, and Richard Phidd. 1983. *Canadian Public Policy: Ideas, Structure, Process*. Toronto: Methuen.

Drache, Daniel, and Duncan Cameron, eds. 1985. *The Other Macdonald Report*. Toronto: Lorimer.

Employment and Immigration Canada. 1989. *Success in the Works: A Profile of Canada's Emerging Workforce*. Ottawa: Minister of Supply and Services.

Esser, Josef, Wolfgang Fach, and Kenneth Dyson. 1984. " 'Social Market' and Modernization Policy: West Germany." In Kenneth Dyson and Stephen Wilks, eds., *Industrial Crisis: A Comparative Study of the State and Industry*, pp. 102–27. New York: St. Martin's Press.

Fairley, H. Scott. 1988. "Jurisdictional Limits on National Purpose: Ottawa, The Provinces and Free Trade with the United States." In Marc Gold and David Leyton-Brown, eds., *Trade-offs on Free Trade: The Canada-US Free Trade Agreement*, pp. 107–16. Toronto: Carswell.

Le Fonds de Solidarité. 1988. *Rapport annuel, 1986–1987*. Montreal: Fédération des travaillers et travailleuses du Québec, February.

General Agreement on Tariffs and Trade (GATT). 1987. *International Trade, 1986–87*. Geneva: GATT.

Gerschenkron, Alexander. 1962. *Economic Backwardness in Historical Perspective*. Cambridge, Mass.: Harvard University Press.

Gibson, Dale. 1988. "The Free Trade Agreement and the Provinces." In Marc Gold and David Leyton-Brown, eds., *Trade-offs on Free Trade: The Canada-US Free Trade Agreement*, pp. 117–30. Toronto: Carswell.

Gold, Marc, and David Leyton-Brown, eds. 1988. *Trade-offs on Free Trade: The Canada-US Free Trade Agreement*. Toronto: Carswell.

Grant, Wyn, and Stephen Wilks. 1983. "British Industrial Policy: Structural Change, Policy Inertia." *Journal of Public Policy* 3 (February): 15–28.

Green, Diana. 1981. "Promoting the Industries of the Future: The Search for Industrial Strategy in Britain and France." *Journal of Public Policy* 1 (August): 333–51.

Hawes, Michael. 1988. "The National Economy." In R. B. Byers, ed., *The Canadian Annual Review, 1985*. pp. 103–153. Toronto: University of Toronto Press.

Heclo, Hugh, and Hendrik Madsen. 1987. *Policy and Politics in Sweden: Principled Pragmatism*. Philadelphia: Temple University Press.

Jenkin, Michael. 1983. *The Challenge of Diversity: Industrial Policy in Canadian Federalism*, Background Study no. 50 for the Science Council of Canada. Ottawa: Minister of Supply and Services.

Johnston, Richard, and André Blais. 1988. "A Resounding Maybe." *Globe and Mail* (Toronto), December 19, p. A7.

Katzenstein, Peter J. 1985. *Small States in World Markets: Industrial Policy in Europe*. Ithaca, N.Y.: Cornell University Press.

———. 1987. *Policy and Politics in West Germany: Growth in a Semi-sovereign State*. Philadelphia: Temple University Press.

Lithwick, N. Harvey. 1986. "Federal Government Regional Economic Development Policies: An Evaluative Survey." In Kenneth Norrie, ed., *Disparities and Inter-regional Adjustment*, vol. 64 of the Research Studies for the Royal Commission on the Economic Union and Development Prospects for Canada, pp. 109–58. Toronto: University of Toronto Press.

McCorquodale, Susan. 1988. "Fisheries and Oceans: 1977–87." In Katherine Graham, ed., *How Ottawa Spends, 1988/89*, pp. 139–64. Ottawa: Carleton University Press, 1988.

Manzer, Ronald. 1985. *Public Policies and Political Development in Canada*. Toronto: University of Toronto Press.

Organization for Economic Cooperation and Development (OECD). 1986a. "Country Problems and Strategies: Canada." *OECD Observer* 138 (January): 22–23.

———. 1986b. "Science and Technology Indicators." *OECD Observer* 138 (January): 15–20.

———. 1988. *OECD Economic Surveys: Canada.* Paris: OECD.

Pempel, T. J. 1982. *Policy and Politics in Japan: Creative Conservatism.* Philadelphia: Temple University Press.

Pilkington, Marilyn. 1988. "Free Trade and Constitutional Jurisdiction." In Marc Gold and David Leyton-Brown, eds., *Trade-offs on Free Trade: The Canada-US Free Trade Agreement*, pp. 92–99. Toronto: Carswell.

Premier's Council. 1989. *Competing in the Global Economy*, vol. 3. Toronto: Queen's Printer.

Savoie, Donald. 1986. *Regional Economic Development: Canada's Search for Solutions.* Toronto: University of Toronto Press.

Science Council of Canada. 1979. *Forging the Links: A Technology Policy for Canada.* Ottawa: Science Council of Canada.

Takefield, Tayce A. 1988. "The Canada-US Free Trade Agreement and the Canadian Auto Industry." In Marc Gold and David Leyton-Brown, eds., *Trade-offs on Free Trade: The Canada-US Free Trade Agreement*, pp. 283–87. Toronto: Carswell.

Trebilcock, Michael, et al. 1985. *The Political Economy of Business Bailouts.* Toronto: Ontario Economic Council.

Tuohy, Carolyn J. 1988. "Implications of the Canada-US Free Trade Agreement for the Health Services Sector in Canada." In Marc Gold and David Leyton-Brown, eds., *Trade-offs on Free Trade*, pp. 310–19. Toronto: Carswell.

Tupper, Allan. 1986. "Federalism and the Politics of Industrial Policy." In André Blais, ed., *Industrial Policy*, vol. 44 of the Research Studies for the Royal Commission on the Economic Union and Development Prospects for Canada, pp. 347–78. Toronto: University of Toronto Press.

Waldie, K. G. 1986. "The Evolution of Labour-Government Consultation on Economic Policy." In W. Craig Riddell, ed., *Labour Management Cooperation in Canada*, vol. 16 of the Research Studies for the Royal Commission on the Economic Union and Development Prospects for Canada, pp. 151–201. Toronto: University of Toronto Press.

Wonnacutt, Paul. 1988. "Autos and the Free Trade Agreement." In Marc Gold and David Leyton-Brown, eds., *Trade-offs on Free Trade: The Canada-US Free Trade Agreement* pp. 269–75. Toronto: Carswell.

Oil and Gas Policy (Chapter 6)

Canada. 1980. *The National Energy Program.* Ottawa: Minister of Supply and Services.

Canadian Business. 1984. *The Top 500 Companies*, special issue (June).

Carmichael, Edward, and J. Stewart. 1983. *Lessons from the National Energy Program*. Toronto: C. D. Howe Institute.

Chandler, Marsha A. 1986. "Constitutional Change and Public Policy: The Impact of the Resource Amendment (Section 92A)." *Canadian Journal of Political Science* 19 (March): 103–26.

Clarkson, Stephen. 1982. *Canada and the Reagan Challenge*. Toronto: Lorimer.

Coleman, William D. 1988. *Business and Politics: A Study of Collective Action*. Montreal: McGill-Queen's University Press.

Doern, G. Bruce, and Richard Phidd. 1983. *Canadian Public Policy: Ideas, Structure, Process*. Toronto: Methuen.

Doern, G. Bruce, and Glen Toner. 1985. *The Politics of Energy*. Toronto: Methuen.

Dupré, J. Stephan. 1988. "Reflections on the Workability of Executive Federalism." In R. D. Olling and M. W. Westmacott, *Perspectives on Canadian Federalism*, pp. 233–56. Scarborough, Ont.: Prentice Hall.

Economic Council of Canada. 1982. *Financing Confederation: Today and Tomorrow*. Ottawa: Minister of Supply and Services.

Energy, Mines and Resources Canada. 1987. *Energy in Canada: A Background Paper*. Ottawa: Minister of Supply and Services.

Fagan, Drew. 1990. "Jury's Out on Hibernia." *Globe and Mail* (Toronto), September 15, pp. B1–2.

International Energy Agency. 1981. *Energy Prices and Taxes, First Quarter 1981*. Paris: Organization for Economic Cooperation and Development.

McDougall, I. A. 1983. *Marketing Canada's Energy: A Strategy for Security in Oil and Gas*, Canadian Institute for Economic Policy series. Toronto: James Lorimer.

Organization for Economic Cooperation and Development (OECD). 1988. *OECD Economic Surveys: Canada*. Paris: OECD.

Pempel, T. J. 1982. *Policy and Politics in Japan: Creative Conservatism*. Philadelphia: Temple University Press.

Plourde, André. 1988. "Oil Import Charges and the Canada-US Free Trade Agreement." In Marc Gold and David Leyton-Brown, eds., *Trade-offs on Free Trade: The Canada-US Free Trade Agreement*, pp. 233–40. Toronto: Carswell.

Richards, John, and Larry Pratt. 1979. *Prairie Capitalism: Power and Influence in the New West*. Toronto: McClelland and Stewart.

Romanow, Roy, John Whyte, and Howard Leeson. 1984. *Canada . . . Notwithstanding: The Making of the Constitution, 1976–82*. Toronto: Carswell Methuen.

Russell, Peter. 1985. "The Supreme Court and Federal-Provincial Relations: The Political Use of Legal Resources." *Canadian Public Policy* 11 (June): 161–70.

Statistics Canada. 1984. *Canada's International Investment Position, 1979 and*

1980. Ottawa: Minister of Supply and Services (Cat. no. 67–202).
———. 1985. *Canada Year Book, 1985*. Ottawa: Minister of Supply and Services.
Toner, Glen. 1986. "Stardust: The Tory Energy Program." In Michael J. Prince, ed., *How Ottawa Spends, 1986–87: Tracking the Tories*, pp. 119–48. Toronto: Methuen.
Toner, Glen, and Francois Bregha. 1984. "The Political Economy of Energy." In M. S. Whittington and Glen Williams, eds., *Canadian Politics in the 1980's*, 2d ed. Toronto: Methuen.
Walker, Michael. 1981. "The National Energy Program: An Overview of Its Impact and Objectives." In G. C. Watkins and M. A. Walker, eds., *Reaction: The National Energy Program*. Vancouver: Fraser Institute.
Watkins, G. C., and M. A. Walker, eds. 1981. *Reaction: The National Energy Program*. Vancouver: Fraser Institute.

Minority Language Rights (Chapter 7)

Adie, Robert, and Paul Thomas. 1987. *Canadian Public Administration: Problematical Perspectives*, 2d ed. Toronto: Methuen.
Bissonette, Lise. 1989. "Support for Orr, But Not for His Cause." *Globe and Mail* (Toronto), January 28, p. F2.
Chaput, Marcel. 1964. "Pourquoi je suis un séparatiste," trans. C. Ryerson. In Frank Scott and Michael Oliver, eds., *Quebec States Her Case*, pp. 48–53. Toronto: Macmillan.
Coleman, William. 1981. "From Bill 22 to Bill 101: The Politics of Language under the Parti Québécois." *Canadian Journal of Political Science* 14 (September): 459–85.
———. 1983. "A Comparative Study of Language Policy in Quebec." In Michael M. Atkinson and Marsha A. Chandler, eds., *The Politics of Canadian Public Policy*, pp. 21–42. Toronto: University of Toronto Press.
Commissioner of Official Languages. 1984, 1985, 1986, 1987, 1988, 1989, 1990. *Annual Reports* Ottawa: Minister of Supply and Services.
Conseil de la Vie Française en Amérique. 1988. *Le répertoire de la vie française en Amérique*. Quebec: Conseil de la Vie Française en Amérique.
Dominion Bureau of Statistics. 1953. *Census of Canada, 1951*. Ottawa: Minister of Industry, Trade and Commerce.
Forsey, Eugene. 1980. "Languages and the Law." *Language and Society* 2 (Summer): 19–27.
Fournier, Pierre. 1976. *The Quebec Establishment*. Montreal: Black Rose Books.
Fraser, Graham. 1984. "Ruling Takes Away Control of Schools, Minister Contends." *Globe and Mail* (Toronto), July 27, pp. 1–2.
Johnston, Richard, and André Blais. 1988. "Meech Lake and Mass Politics: The

'Distinct Society' Clause." *Canadian Public Policy* 14, supplement (September): S25–42.

Lévesque, René. 1964. Interview with Jean-Marc Léger. *Le Devoir* (Montreal), July 5, 1963. Reprinted in Frank Scott and Michael Oliver, eds., *Quebec States Her Case*, pp. 132–45. Toronto: Macmillan.

————. 1968. *An Option for Quebec*. Toronto: McClelland and Stewart.

MacKenzie, Colin. 1989. "B.C. Students Excel in International Survey." *Globe and Mail* (Toronto), February 1, p. A8.

McRoberts, Kenneth. 1988. *Quebec: Social Change and Political Crisis*, 3d ed. Toronto: McClelland and Stewart.

————. 1989. "Making Canada Bilingual: Illusions and Delusions of Federal Language Policy." In David P. Shugarman and Reg Whitaker, eds., *Federalism and Political Community: Essays in Honour of Donald Smiley*, pp. 141–71. Toronto: Broadview Press.

Magnet, Joseph. 1982. "The Charter's Official Languages Provisions: The Implications of Entrenched Bilingualism." *Supreme Court Law Review* 4: 163–93.

Manzer, Ronald. 1985. *Public Policies and Political Development in Canada*. Toronto: University of Toronto Press.

Neatby, Blair. 1979. "A Tale of Two Languages." *Language and Society* 1 (Autumn): 24–26.

Pal, Leslie A. 1990. "Official Language Minorities and the State." In William Coleman and Grace Skogstad, eds., *Policy Communities and Public Policy in Canada*, pp. 170–90. Toronto: Copp Clark Pitman.

Quebec Liberal Federation. 1968. "Report by the Constitution Committee." Presented to the annual convention of the Quebec Liberal Federation, October 1967. Reprinted in J. Peter Meekison, ed. *Canadian Federalism: Myth of Reality*, pp. 367–78. Toronto: Methuen.

Romanow, Roy, John Whyte, and Howard Leeson. 1984. *Canada . . . Notwithstanding: The Making of the Constitution, 1976–82*. Toronto: Carswell Methuen.

Royal Commission on Bilingualism and Biculturalism. 1967. *Report*. Ottawa: Queen's Printer.

Sales, Arnaud. 1979. *La bourgeoisie industrielle au Québec*. Montreal: Presses de l'Université de Montréal.

Sniderman, Paul M., et al. 1989. "Political Culture and the Problem of Double Standards: Mass and Elite Attitudes toward Language Rights in the Canadian Charter of Rights and Freedoms." *Canadian Journal of Political Science* 22 (June): 259–84.

Tetley, William. 1982. "Language and Education Rights in Quebec and Canada (A Legislative History and Personal Political Diary)." *Law and Contemporary Problems* 44 (Autumn): 177–219.

Trudeau, Pierre. 1968. "De la vérité et de la liberté en politique: Les Canadi-

ens francais et le défi fédéral." Speech delivered April 2, 1968, in Montreal
to the members of the Richelieu Club. Reprinted in J. Peter Meekison, ed.,
Canadian Federalism: Myth or Reality, pp. 386–96. Toronto: Methuen.

Competence and Crisis (Chapter 8)

Chandler, William. 1989. "Challenges to Federalism: Comparative Themes."
In William Chandler and Christian Zollner, eds., *Challenges to Federalism:
Policymaking in Canada and the Federal Republic of Germany*, pp. 3–22.
Kingston: Queen's University Institute of Intergovernmental Relations.

Gibbins, Roger. 1982. *Regionalism: Territorial Politics in Canada and the United
States*. Toronto: Butterworths.

Fraser, Graham. 1990. "Senate Reform Proposals Only Latest 'Epidemic' to
Sweep the Nation." *Globe and Mail* (Toronto), May 30, p. A3.

Johnson, Chalmers. 1975. "Japan: Who Governs? An Essay on Official Bureaucracy." *Journal of Japanese Studies* 2 (Autumn): 1–28.

Katzenstein, Peter. 1987. *Politics and Policy in Canada: Growth in a Semisovereign State*. Philadelphia: Temple University Press.

Lodge, Juliet. 1989. "EC Policymaking: Institutional Considerations." In Juliet
Lodge, ed., *The European Community and the Challenge of the Future*, pp.
26–57. New York: St. Martin's.

Lowi, Theodore. 1972. "Four Systems of Policy, Politics and Choice." *Public
Administration Review* 32 (July/August): 298–310.

———. 1985. "The State in Politics: The Relation between Policy and Administration." In Roger Noll, ed., *Regulatory Policy and the Social Sciences*, pp.
67–105. Berkeley: University of California Press.

McKenzie, Robert. 1990. "Ambiguous Bourassa Unlikely to Bend." *Toronto
Star*, May 15, p. A21.

Muramatsu, Michio, and Ellis S. Krauss. 1987. "The Conservative Policy Line
and the Development of Patterned Pluralism." In K. Yamamura and Y. Yasuba,
eds., *The Political Economy of Japan: Volume 1, The Domestic Transformation*,
pp. 516–54. Stanford: Stanford University Press.

Nugent, Neil. 1989. *The Government and Politics of the European Community*.
Durham, N.C.: Duke University Press.

Pempel, T. J. 1982. *Policy and Politics in Japan: Creative Conservatism*. Philadelphia: Temple University Press.

Simeon, Richard. 1972. *Federal-Provincial Diplomacy: The Making of Public
Policy in Canada*. Toronto: University of Toronto Press.

Teague, Paul, and John Grahl. 1990. "1992 and the Emergence of a European Industrial Relations Area." *Journal of European Integration* 13 (Winter/
Spring): 167–83.

Index

389